MEDICAL LIBRARY
ASSOCIATION *Guide*

D1124400

THE MEDICAL LIBRARY ASSOCIATION
Guide to
HEALTH LITERACY

Edited by

Marge Kars, Lynda M. Baker,
and Feleta L. Wilson

Neal-Schuman Publishers, Inc.
New York   *London*

Published by Neal-Schuman Publishers, Inc.
100 William St., Suite 2004
New York, NY 10038

Printed and bound in the United States of America.

The paper used in this publication meets the minimum requirements of American National Standard for Information Sciences-Permanence of Paper for Printed Library Materials, ANSI Z39.48-1992.

Library of Congress Cataloging-in-Publication Data

The Medical Library Association guide to health literacy / Marge Kars, Lynda M. Baker, Feleta L. Wilson, editors.
        p. cm.
    Includes bibliographical references and index.
    ISBN 978-1-55570-625-8 (alk. paper)
    1. Medical librarianship—United States—Handbooks, manuals, etc. 2. Health education—United States—Handbooks, manuals, etc. 3. Patient education—United States—Handbooks, manuals, etc. 4. Literacy—United States—Health aspects. 5. Social medicine—United States. 6. Medical libraries—Reference services—United States. 7. Libraries and illiterate persons. 8. Libraries and people with social disabilities. 9. Libraries and community. 10. Communication in medicine. I. Kars, Marge, 1947- II. Baker, Lynda. III. Wilson, Feleta, 1945-

Z675.M4M497 2008
026'.610973—dc22

                                                                        2008023323

Contents

Part II. Health Literacy Issues in Special Populations: The Influence of Culture, Ethnicity, Special Needs, and Age on Health

Part III. Health Literacy Issues in Public and Hospital Libraries: Providing Programs and Services to Help Consumers Understand Their Healthcare

List of Figures, Tables, and Appendices

Preface

Health literacy is a vital component of consumer health. The publication of the Institute of Medicine's report *Health Literacy: A Prescription to End Confusion* (2004), coupled with the 2003 *National Assessment of Adult Literacy* (NAAL), brought national attention to a serious problem: people with low literacy skills often cannot read or understand information about their diagnosis, medications, or appointments with their physician. They may be unable to understand the directions for preparing for a medical test, or use written information about staying healthy. These same individuals have a higher incidence of disease, risk higher use of the emergency room, have longer hospital stays with higher hospital admission rates, and suffer medication errors because they cannot read or understand a prescription label. Librarians in all types of libraries can play a major role in health literacy, helping consumers to access and better understand health information.

The idea for *The Medical Library Association Guide to Health Literacy* evolved from my own experience working in a hospital-based consumer health library providing health information to consumers, and from discussions with colleagues who work with customers, in all types of libraries, looking for understandable health information.

The Medical Library Association, the world's preeminent educational organization for health information professionals, recognizing the important role that librarians play in providing health information, has partnered with other library organizations, on the state and national levels, to increase awareness of the seriousness of this issue and collaborate to create solutions for healthcare consumers.

In 2006, I invited two colleagues from Wayne State University, Detroit, Michigan—Lynda M. Baker (Library and Information Science Program) and Feleta L. Wilson (College of Nursing)—to work with me on this book about health literacy. Lynda and Feleta were the first to publish in LIS journals studies of the literacy levels of consumer health materials. Because the importance of health literacy transcends any particular library boundary, we decided the book should be a forum for LIS professionals involved in the health literacy movement. To provide a comprehensive overview, we recruited practitioners from all types of libraries, as well as researchers in academia, to write about health literacy from their unique perspectives. After reading this guide, librarians should be better able to understand the issues that comprise health literacy, learning how to help others become health literate and how to become change agents within their organizations.

As editors, we have tried to ensure the use of gender-neutral language throughout the book. Because we find "he/she" to be clunky, we have chosen to use either "she" or "he" as equally as possible. This book is not meant to be read from cover to cover; rather, we believe readers will select chapters relevant to their situations and interests. Therefore, instead of having one definition of health literacy located in the Preface, we have allowed authors to define health literacy as it relates to and forms the basis of their work.

The Medical Library Association Guide to Health Literacy features 16 chapters, divided into four parts. The four parts:

- cover the essential issues surrounding health literacy;
- identify often overlooked implications of the influence of culture, ethnicity, special needs, and age in health;
- highlight the nation's best practices for public and hospital library consumer health programs and services; and,
- suggest proven ways libraries can initiate their own and partner with other organizations' health literacy programs.

In Chapter 1 the editors provide an introduction to the issues of health literacy. The different types of health literacy are defined in Chapter 2, along with a discussion on causes, effects, and solutions. A comprehensive list of readability formulae and literacy tests used in the healthcare setting is included with this chapter.

Chapter 3 looks at the role social bias plays in health encounters and how it affects health literacy. The author discusses theories of language and their contribution to health literacy, the health encounter as a literacy event, and social biases in relation to health literacy and their effects on provider and patient behavior and institutional practices. Health literacy within the context of culture, as well as the importance of cultural competency of librarians in relation to a client's health literacy skills is the subject of Chapter 4. An outline and sequence of activities for a course titled "Cultural Competence for Health Information Professionals," developed by the author, is presented in this chapter.

Chapter 5 covers the impact of low literacy on the patient and the family from a nursing perspective. The author discusses characteristics of patients with low literacy, the association between low literacy and health disparities, and the need for partnership between nurses and librarians. This disturbing divide is further explored in Chapter 6, which summarizes the literature on the relationship between low literacy levels and the effects on patient care and health outcomes. The authors also discuss the role librarians can take in helping to narrow the health literacy gap.

Raising awareness of the complexities of health literacy for people with disabilities is the focus of Chapter 7. The author addresses how librarians can partner with people with disabilities and the community. She includes some personal perspectives of people with various types of disabilities about health literacy and ways libraries and librarians can help them find information.

Chapter 8 posits a new model of health literacy. The author looks at health literacy within the context of senior citizens, provides some examples of health literacy interventions both inside and outside the library. Chapter 9 describes the authors' efforts to build a foundation of health literacy among adolescents in Philadelphia. Useful information on what worked and what does not work in their collaboration with the teens is also presented.

The health reference interview is part of the individual's ability to obtain or access health information. This initial step in the health literacy process is the focus of Chapter 10.

Public libraries should be the major provider of consumer health information. Chapter 11 features a particularly successful collaboration between a public library and a hospital library. The author also provides a list of sources of non-English language materials for a library's collection.

Some of the health literacy initiatives by Canadian librarians and the difficulties in finding information on the activities of librarians in the area of health literacy are addressed in Chapter 12.

The results of a study on consumer health services provided by hospital librarians are provided in Chapter 13; this chapter also highlights what other hospital libraries have done to address health literacy. The partnering of hospital librarians with other hospital departments to provide consumer health services is described in Chapter 14, where the author also offers an in-depth look some of the health literacy initiatives that are taking place at one teaching hospital.

The numerous intervention programs for professionals engaged in health literacy efforts are presented in Chapter 15.

Examples of health literacy collaborations are provided in Chapter 16, including examples from New York City. The authors also discuss how to find funding support for health literacy initiatives.

I would like to thank my co-editors, Lynda and Feleta, and each of the authors who agreed to contribute to *The Medical Library Association Guide to Health Literacy*. We hope this guide will both inform and inspire our colleagues in all types of libraries to help their communities live longer and healthier lives.

Marge Kars

REFERENCES

Nielsen-Bohlman, Lynn, Allison M. Panzer, and David A. Kindig (eds.). 2004. *Health Literacy: A Prescription to End Confusion*. Committee on Health Literacy, Institute of Medicine. Washington, DC: National Academies.

Kutner, Mark, Elizabeth Greenberg, Ying Jin, and Christine Paulsen. 2006. *The Health Literacy of America's Adults: Results from the 2003 National Assessment of Adult Literacy* (NCES 2006-483). U.S. Department of Education. Washington, DC: National Center for Education Statistics.

Part I

Health Literacy: Understanding the Issues

Chapter 1

Introduction to Health Literacy

Lynda M. Baker, Marge Kars,
and Feleta L. Wilson

What is health literacy? According to the American Medical Association (1999: 553), health literacy requires a number of skills including the ability to perform "basic reading and numerical tasks required to function in the health care environment." In addition, people who have adequate health literacy skills can "read, understand, and act on health care information." Librarians who work with customers seeking health information know that this definition is missing a key element—the recognition of a need for information. The Medical Library Association (MLA) (2007) rectified this omission by incorporating that element into its definition, along with the ability to identify relevant sources of information, use them to find the necessary information, assess the quality and appropriateness of the information, and finally to analyze, comprehend, and use the retrieved information to make an informed healthcare decision. Although people with low literacy skills may identify a need for information, they would not be able to complete the remaining steps in order to make an informed decision.

A factor that has not received much attention in the health literacy literature, but that may affect one's ability to perform these health literacy tasks, is whether the individual actually wants information about her (or his or a family member's) health condition. During times of stress, which is an integral part of any illness, people cope in different ways. Miller (1987) studied people who were facing uncontrollable stress and noted that some people (monitors) sought information to cope with the stress, while others (blunters) turned away from it because information increased their anxiety level. In her study of women with multiple sclerosis, Baker (1995) found that while monitors wanted more information than did blunters, the latter eventually wanted information after they had coped with the disease for a number of years. Therefore, more research is needed to determine whether individual coping skills and time factors in the illness trajectory affect one's recognition of and desire for health information.

The first national survey, *National Adult Literacy Survey*, raised awareness of how vast the problem of low literacy was in the United States (Kirsch et al., 1993). While health literacy was not addressed in this survey, it did receive attention in the 2003 survey, *National Assessment of Adult Literacy* (NAAL). Similar to elements of the 1993 survey, this literacy assessment used 28 health literacy tasks that were "mapped" on the domains of prose, quantitative, and document literacy and each domain was scored as *below basic* (indicates no more than the most basic literacy skills), *basic* (indicates skills necessary to perform everyday tasks), *intermediate* (indicates skills necessary to perform moderately challenging activities) or *proficient* (indicates the ability to perform "more complex and challenging" activities) (Kutner et al., 2006: 3). "Of the health literacy tasks: 3 represented *clinical*, 14 represented *prevention*, and 11 represented *navigation of the health care system*" (3). An example of a *clinical* task was "filling out a patient form for an office visit"; a task from the *prevention* domain included "following guidelines for age-appropriate preventive health services" and from the navigation of the healthcare system was "understanding what a health insurance plan will and will not pay for" (3).

Of the 19,000 participants in this study, 65 percent were found to have *intermediate* or *proficient* health literacy skills, while 36 percent had *basic* or *below basic* health literacy skills (10). While these results can inform librarians and other healthcare professionals who are responsible for educating consumers, they must be interpreted with caution because there are no comparable national data. In addition, the study participants may not have been in a health-related situation wherein they needed the information. In other words, reading, interpreting, and responding to the study in a nonstressful situation may have affected their scores, a fact noted by The Joint Commission (2007), who stated that even people with high literacy skills "may be compromised in the understanding of health care information when they are challenged by sickness and feelings of vulnerability" (4).

Kutner et al. (2006) discussed sources of health information. The results revealed that although all participants reported getting health information from newspapers, magazines, books or the Internet, a higher percentage of people with *below basic* health literacy skills reported not getting health information from them than did people with *basic, intermediate,* or *proficient* health literacy skills (19). Conversely, radio and television were more popular sources of health information for both participants with basic or below basic health literacy skills. Unfortunately, libraries were not mentioned in this study as potential sources of health information.

In his article on health education as a social service activity, Simonds (1974: 9) coined the phrase "health literacy." He saw health education as a "social responsibility" and stated that healthcare, education, and mass communication should share the responsibility for making and implementing policies to ensure a healthier population. According to Simonds, a healthier population is one that "takes a greater responsibility for protecting and maintaining its own health, that utilizes the health care system as effectively as possible, and that takes an active role in shaping the health care system of the future."

To date, there is a plethora of literature on health literacy. The National Library of Medicine has compiled two bibliographies on this topic (Selden et al., 2000; Zorn, Allen, and Horowitz, 2004). The Institute of Medicine issued a report, *Health Literacy: A Prescription to End Confusion*, highlighting the fact that millions of adults in the United States are unable to read and understand information about their health, and outlined the issues that result from their inability to read (Nielsen-Bohlman, Panzer, and Kindig, 2004). Compounding the problems of health literacy is the current American healthcare system that requires individuals to take more responsibility for their health and to understand health information in order to make more informed healthcare choices and decisions.

Librarians have been involved in the provision of consumer health information to patients or their families for many years (Gann, 1987; 1991). In 1981, the Medical Library Association established the Ad Hoc Committee on Consumer Health Information, which issued its report in 1983 acknowledging that health sciences librarians have a role in the provision of consumer health material (Gartenfield et al., 1983). One of the first public libraries to respond to its community's need for health information was the Tulsa City-County Library, which received a Library Services and Construction Grant in 1974 (Flaherty et al., 1995).

As the consumer health information movement progressed, it became clear that information was being provided at a reading level that was difficult for most people to read and understand. For example, in 1996, Baker and Wilson published an article on the reading levels of consumer health resources commonly found in public and academic libraries. The following year, Baker, Wilson, and Kars (1997) collaborated on a project that examined the readability of medical and health information on a popular resource for health information (Info-Trac). In both studies, the authors found that the reading level of all the material was equal to or above the 10th grade level, making this information inaccessible to many people with low literacy skills. In a more recent study, Baker and Gollop (2004) found that even well-educated people (that is, graduate students in two library and information science programs) were unable to understand some of the terminology in medical textbooks that are often found in consumer health libraries.

Given library and information scientists' (LIS) expertise, what role or roles can librarians and researchers play in the health literacy movement? The possibilities seem endless. Librarians are specialists in managing information resources and locating information appropriate to a specific audience. They can work with other healthcare professionals and provide current bibliographies, culled from various disciplines, on health literacy. They can start a health literacy program in their hospitals or healthcare organizations to ensure that all patient-related forms are written at the fifth-grade level. Librarians can collect consumer health material in various formats so that people with low literacy skills can access the information they need to make healthcare decisions. In addition, LIS researchers can bring a unique perspective to the body of research literature on health literacy. For example, they can study how people with low literacy skills cope in today's information-rich environment, as well as address the role of information in their lives and especially in their ability to make healthcare decisions. With a lot of work by many people, the problem of low literacy/health literacy can be eradicated. LIS professionals can be part of the solution!

REFERENCES

American Medical Association. Ad Hoc Committee on Health Literacy for the Council on Scientific Affairs. 1999. "Health Literacy. Report of the Council on Scientific Affairs." *JAMA* 281, no.6 (February 10): 552–557.

Baker, Lynda M. 1995. "A New Methods for Studying Patient Information Needs and Information-seeking Patterns." *Topics in Health Information Management* 16, no.2 (November): 19–28.

Baker, Lynda M., and Claudia J. Gollop. 2004. "Medical Textbooks: Can Lay People Read and Understand Them?" *Library Trends* 53, no.2 (Fall): 336–347.

Baker, Lynda M., and Feleta L. Wilson. 1996. "Consumer Health Materials Recommended for Public Libraries. Too Tough to Read?" *Public Libraries* 35, no.2 (March/April): 124–130.

Baker, Lynda M., Feleta L. Wilson, and Marge Kars. 1997. "The Readability of Medical Information on InfoTrac: Does it Meet the Needs of People with Low Literacy Skills?" *Reference and User Services Quarterly* 37, no.2 (Winter): 155–160.

Flaherty, Kelly, Kate Gillette, Karen Jordan, and Julie Virgo. 1995. *Consumer Healthcare Information Services: A National Model*. Chicago: Public Library Association.

Gann, Robert. 1987. "The People Their Own Physicians: 2000 Years of Patient Information." *Health Libraries Review* 4, no.3 (September): 151–155.

Gann, Robert. 1991. "Consumer Health Information: The Growth of an Information Specialism." *Journal of Documentation* 47, no.3: 284–308.

Gartenfield, Ellen, Jennifer E. Angier, Eleanor Goodchild, Eleanor McNutt, Alan Rees, and Ruth Wender. 1983. *Report to the Medical Library Association Board of Directors from the Ad Hoc Committee on Consumer Health*. Chicago: Medical Library Association.

The Joint Commission. 2007. "'*What Did the Doctor Say?' Improving Health Literacy to Protect Patient Safety.*" Oakbrook, IL: The Joint Commission. (January 2008) Available: www.jointcommission.org

Kirsch, Irwin S., Ann Jungeblut, Lynn Jenkins, and Andrew Kolstad. 1993. *Adult Literacy in America: A First Look at the Findings of the National Adult Literacy Survey.* Washington, DC: National Center for Education Statistics.

Kutner, Mark, Elizabeth Greenberg, Ying Jin, and Christine Paulsen. 2006. *The Health Literacy of America's Adults: Results from the 2003 National Assessment of Adult Literacy* (NCES 2006–483). U.S. Department of Education. Washington, DC: National Center for Education Statistics.

Medical Library Association. 2007. "Health Information Literacy Fact Sheet." Chicago: Medical Library Association. (September 2007) Available: www.mlanet.org/resources/healthlit/healthliteracy.html

Miller, Suzanne M. 1987. "Monitoring and Blunting; Validation of a Questionnaire to Assess Styles of Information Seeking Under Threat." *Journal of Personality and Social Psychology* 52, no.2 (February): 345–353.

Nielsen-Bohlman, Lynn, Allison M. Panzer, and David A. Kindig. (eds.). 2004. *Health Literacy: A Prescription to End Confusion.* Committee on Health Literacy, Institute of Medicine. Washington, DC: National Academies.

Selden, Catherine, Marcia Zorn, Scott C. Ratzan, and Ruth M. Parker (compilers). 2000. "Health Literacy." (Current Bibliographies in Medicine, no. 2000–1). Bethesda, MD: National Library of Medicine. (September 2007) Available: www.nlm.nih.gov/archive//20061214/pubs/ cbm/hliteracy.html

Simonds, Scott K. 1974. "Health Education as Social Policy." Health Education Monograph 2: 1–10.

Zorn, Marcia, Marin P. Allen, and Alice M. Horowitz (compilers). 2004. "Understanding Health Literacy and its Barriers." Bethesda, MD: National Library of Medicine. (September 2007) Available: www.nlm .nih.gov/pubs/cbm.healthliteracybarriers.html

Chapter 2

Review of the Literature

Nancy Schaefer

The vast amount of research and reports on health literacy attests to the importance of this issue to healthcare professionals. The National Library of Medicine has compiled two bibliographies on this topic that together contain 1,130 citations from January 1990 to November 2003 (Selden et al., 2000; Zorn, Allen, and Horowitz, 2004). This chapter provides an overview and some definitions of health literacy, insight into the various aspects of health literacy, and a comparison of the readability and literacy assessment tools used in the healthcare environment. It also outlines some possible solutions as discussed in the literature on health literacy.

DEFINITIONS OF HEALTH LITERACY

To comprehend the term "health literacy," it helps to review the meaning of "literacy." Today, the term "literacy" stands for functional literacy, which includes reading comprehension and inference-making skills that enable a person to understand the front page of a newspaper (written at 7th–8th grade reading level in the United States) and graphical representations like charts and tables, plus the skills to correctly fill out forms and perform basic arithmetic calculations needed for everyday life (Cook, 1977; Doak, Doak, and Root, 1996; Rogers, Ratzan, and Payne, 2001). The National Literacy Act of 1991 defines literacy as the ability to execute reading and numeracy tasks at "levels of proficiency necessary to function on the job and in society" (P.L. 102–73 102nd Congress, 1st session, H.R. 751).

In 1992, the National Adult Literacy Survey tested reading and writing in prose and document formats as well as quantitative skills, such as locating specific information in a written text, using writing to complete survey forms, and doing math problems related to a bank account (Institute of Medicine, 2002: 345). Approximately 25 percent of American adults tested at or below the 3rd grade reading g level on general interest material. Adding those with marginal literacy (scoring in the second of five levels of literacy, as measured by the 1992 NALS), the percentage of poor readers rises to 33 percent or nearly 90 million people. The 1992 NALS contained a few items related to health. This was expanded to 36 health-related questions in the 2003 NALS (Mika et al., 2005).

According to Evensen (2003: 13–14), the Joint Committee on National Health Education Standards has defined health literacy as "the capacity of an individual to obtain, interpret, and understand basic health information and services and the competence to use such information and services in ways which are health-enhancing."

In 1999, the American Medical Association's Ad Hoc Committee on Health Literacy defined health literacy as a "constellation of skills, including the ability to perform basic reading and numerical tasks required to function in the healthcare environment" (552–557). The U.S. Department of Health and Human Services' Healthy People 2010 (2000) Objective 11–2 explicitly includes decision-making in its definition of health literacy: "the degree to which individuals have the capacity to obtain, process, and understand basic health information and services needed to make appropriate health decisions" (11–20).

The World Health Organization's definition broadens the meaning still further to include motivation as well as skill: "the achievement of the cognitive and social skills that determine the motivation and ability of individuals to gain access to, understand and use information in ways that promote and maintain good health" (Levin-Zamir and Peterburg, 2001: 88).

Health literacy researchers Parker, Ratzan, and Lurie (2003) described "health literate" or "informed" patients as capable of understanding new health information in the appropriate context; feeling more comfortable asking questions when they do not understand; tending to come to the same conclusions as healthcare professionals, based on somewhat similar knowledge backgrounds; and seeking care earlier because they recognize warning signs.

Nutbeam (2000) divides health literacy into three levels listed below. Included are examples from the Centre for Literacy of Quebec (2001: 6):

- Functional—understanding and communicating facts about diseases, health risks or services; knowing how to access health information
- Interactive—making inferences; extracting information from different forms of communication; applying information to changing circumstances.
- Critical—analyzing information; using information to advocate for personal or community well-being.

COMPONENTS OF HEALTH LITERACY

Numeracy

In addition to reading ability, health literacy encompasses numeracy—"the degree to which individuals have the capacity to access, process, interpret, communicate and act on numerical, quantitative, graphical, biostatistical, and probabilistic health information needed to make effective health decisions" (Golbeck et al., 2005: 375). Numeracy skills such as reading blood glucose levels, taking body temperature, and understanding the correct timing and dosage of medication can be critical to health maintenance. As with reading ability, health numeracy has been divided into four categories of skills useful for/crucial to independent functioning within today's healthcare system. These are listed below with examples adapted from Golbeck et al. (2005:375–376).

- Basic—identify the number of pills from a prescription label or the date and time of a doctor's appointment.
- Computational—determine fees based on sliding scale or net carbohydrates from a nutrition label.
- Analytical—determine whether cholesterol levels are within normal range; compare benefits from various insurance programs.
- Statistical—determine treatment efficacy and side effects; compare information presented on different scales (proportion, percent, probability.)

Patients need to compute risks and probabilities in therapy decisions and especially in genetic counseling situations (Braithwaite et al., 2004; Christensen et al., 2003; Croyle and Lerman, 1999; Marteau and Croyle, 1998; Michie et al., 2005; Walter and Emery, 2005; Walter et al., 2004).

Computer/Information Literacy

Pew's 2000 "Online Health Revolution" study estimated that more than 1 million U.S. residents had searched for health information online in the year prior to the study. More than 70 percent of those using the Internet claimed that health information they had found online influenced a treatment decision (Fox and Rainie, 2000). While computers offer 24/7 availability, audio-assisted and animated video, and anonymity/privacy, they share with print the problems of mismatched reading skill vs. demand and credulity vs. credibility (Berland et al., 2001; Birru et al., 2004; D'Alessandro, Kingsley, and Johnson-West, 2001; Friedman and Hoffman-Goetz, 2006; Gray et al., 2005; Smalley and Scourfield, 2004). In addition, computers pose unique challenges: ignorance/underuse of navigation tools (Baur, 2005; Sutherland et al., 2001); inefficient search strategies and poorly indexed Web pages (Berland et al., 2001; Gray et al., 2005); inadequate bandwidth (Smalley and Scourfield, 2004); special visual and physical difficulties, especially for the disabled (Baur, 2005; Feys et al., 2001; Smeltzer et al., 2004); and lack of specifically local information, such as a nearby self-help group (Hansen et al., 2003). Systematic remedies for computer illiteracy and widespread use of computers to remedy health literacy may have to wait until experts arrive at a clearer consensus of what it means to be computer literate (Bernhardt and Cameron, 2003).

Navigating the Healthcare System

Very little seems to have been written on this aspect of health literacy despite widespread acknowledgment that the U.S. healthcare system is "increasingly fragmented, complex, specialized and technologically sophisticated" (McCray, 2005: 155) and "intricate, disjointed and specialized" (Mika et al., 2005: 351). Every patient needs to know how to access affordable preventive, primary, and emergency care; act on payment-for-care instructions and forms; and appeal decisions orally and in writing (Singleton, 2003).

SPECIAL HEALTH LITERACY

In addition to general health literacy, researchers have begun to examine mental health literacy, oral health literacy, nutritional literacy and public health literacy. A few examples of this literature are provided in the following section.

Mental Health Literacy

Jorm and his colleagues introduced the term "mental health literacy" in 1997, defining it as "knowledge and beliefs about mental disorders which aid their recognition, management or prevention" (182). Mental health literacy includes the ability to recognize specific disorders or types of psychological distress, knowledge and beliefs about risk factors and causes, self-help interventions, and how to seek professional help. Research on mental health literacy in the past ten years has focused on depression and schizophrenia, with relatively little on Alzheimer's disease or substance dependency, despite the aging of populations and the prevalence of alcohol and drug problems (Werner, 2005). According to Kitchener and Jorm (2006), mental health illiteracy may result in treatment noncompliance, and inappropriate service use might be ameliorated by information campaigns and improved media coverage.

Oral Health Literacy

The American public in general seems unaware that most oral disease can be prevented or controlled, and that chronic oral infection may be associated with heart and lung diseases, diabetes, stroke, and pre-term low birth weight (Rudd and Horowitz, 2005; U.S. Department of Health and Human Services, 2000). Increasing legal and ethical concern about informed consent and equal access to care has focused attention on this issue of oral health literacy. The National Institute of Dental and Craniofacial Research (2005) has suggested directions for research and the Academy of General Dentistry Foundation has secured significant funding (Diogo, 2002).

Nutritional Literacy

Macario et al. (1998) examined factors that influence nutritional education for patients with low literacy. In addition to difficulty reading medical terms, illegible physician handwriting, cultural knowledge (e.g., knowing how to recognize/prepare healthy ingredients), and traditions (overweight as symbol of affluence) complicate nutrition information communications. Diamond (2007) recently unveiled the Nutritional Literacy Scale—28 modified Cloze items with acceptable internal consistency (0.84 Cronbach's alpha) and construct validity demonstrated by a Pearson correlation with the S-TOFLA test of 0.61.

Public Health Literacy

Public health workers may not always effectively meet their professional obligation to communicate important health messages and to educate the public in distinguishing between crucial and less critical public health messages (Gazmararian et al., 2005). In recent years, threats of bioterrorism and outbreaks of bovine spongiform encephalitis (mad cow disease), brucellosis, SARS, and avian flu have increased public health literacy and improved control of these infectious diseases (Pappas et al., 2007). Yet, efforts at increasing public health literacy in other, non-infection public health areas, such as social determinants of health and occupational health, seem to have only just begun (Bouchard, 2007; Kickbusch, 2001).

CHARACTERISTICS CORRELATING TO LOW HEALTH LITERACY

Low health literacy is a worldwide problem affecting people of all races, socioeconomic status, and ages. Researchers have found some correlation between low health literacy and the following variables:

- Age (Baker et al., 2000; Baker et al., 2002; Gazmararian, Parker, and Baker, 1999; Greene, Hibbard, and Tusler, 2005; Howard, Sentell, and Gazmararian, 2006; Murray et al., 2004; Rogers, Ratzan, and Payne, 2001; Sudore et al., 2006; Weiss, Reed, and Kligman, 1995; Wolf, Gazmararian, and Baker, 2005; Wolf, Gazmararian, and Baker, 2007)
- Education (Davis et al., 1990; Shea et al., 2004; Yen and Moss, 1999)
- Race/ethnicity (Shea et al., 2004; Wilson et al., 2003)
- Rural residence (Wood, 2005)

- Long-term chronic illness (Greenberg, 2001; Kirsch et al., 1993)
- Socioeconomic status (Williams et al., 1995)
- Non-English native language (California Health Literacy Initiative, 2003; Carter-Pokras et al., 2004; Elder et al., 2000; Flores et al., 2002).

In general, those with low health literacy tend to be older, of lower socio-economic status, of a minority, and more recently immigrated to the country (Parikh et al., 1996; Weiss and Coyne, 1997). The majority of patients who have scored low on health literacy tests have been native-born American English speakers over the age of 65, even after excluding those with significant visual, aural or cognitive deficits (Weiss, 2005). Perhaps because low literacy is prevalent among core patient groups in internal medicine (the elderly and others with chronic diseases), many of the most active researchers in health literacy are internal medicine specialists and/or have published in internal medicine specialty journals (Mika et al., 2005; Wilson, 2003).

REASONS FOR CONCERN

Low literacy/health literacy/numeracy has been associated with poor health outcomes, high healthcare costs, inefficient use of health services, poor patient satisfaction, legal infractions (especially informed consent for research), and disparities in healthcare. A few examples are provided below.

Health Outcomes

Researchers analyzing statistics from the U.S. Department of Health and Human Services' *Health, USA 2002* attributed about half the deaths in the United States to *largely preventable* [this author's emphasis] behaviors and exposures (poor diet/ physical inactivity, substance abuse, sexual behavior, firearms, motor vehicles, and toxic agents such as pollutants). These conditions are also associated with reduced productivity, high rates of disability, and decreased quality of life (Mokdad et al., 2004). Patients with low literacy were generally 1.5–3 times more likely to experience a given poor outcome, displaying less knowledge of disease and intermediate disease markers, lower general health status, higher measures of morbidity, and less efficient use of health resources (Berkman et al., 2004; DeWalt et al., 2004; Gazmararian et al., 2003; Williams et al., 1998). Health literacy may also impact outcomes of research (Perrin et al., 2006) if low literate patients do not comply with or follow protocol, so that researchers conclude the problem rests in the intervention rather than its implementation.

Use of Services

Studies over the past decade have associated higher reading ability with increased use of screening services and lower rates of hospitalization (Baker et al.,

1997; Baker et al., 2002; DeWalt et al., 2004; Fortenberry et al., 2001; Lindau, Basu, and Leitsch, 2006; Scott et al., 2002). The study by Scott et al. (2002) of nearly 2,300 Medicare enrollees (mean age 71) found inadequate health literacy to be independently associated with lower use of four preventive services: influenza and pneumococcal vaccinations, Papanicolaou smears, and mammograms. In the study of 800 15–85-year-olds, Fortenberry et al. (2001) found that those who read above the 9th grade level had a 10 percent higher probability of having undergone a gonorrhoea test in the past year than those with reading levels below 9th grade. Lindau, Basu, and Leitsch (2006) found that physician subjective assessment of patient reading skills more significantly predicted follow-up of abnormal Pap test results than an objective reading test, patient's educational level or physician's prediction of follow-up. Three studies of between 600 and 1,500 patients by Baker and colleagues (1997; 1998; 2002) found that those who tested in the "inadequate" range on a health literacy test (Test of Functional Health Literacy in Adults or TOFHLA) consistently had a 6–10 percent greater probability of having been hospitalized one or more times during the one to two years surrounding the study periods.

Patient Satisfaction

Lower health literacy has been associated with dissatisfaction with asthma disease status and less positive assessment of treatment results. As one socioeconomic variable that can be improved in the healthcare setting, health literacy may hold a key to stopping the cycle of dissatisfaction leading to decreased compliance, which then leads to poor outcomes. Thus, it holds promise for both improved health for both the individual and improved outcomes for the healthcare system (Mancuso and Rincon, 2006; Shea et al., 2007).

Disparities

Healthcare providers are often perceived to have biases or preconceptions about certain groups of patients (California Health Literacy Initiative, 2003; Institute of Medicine, 2002). Disparities have been associated with cardiovascular disease, diabetes, and cancer, as well as with access and possible interventions—translator services, health literacy improvements and diversity in healthcare professionals (Mullins et al., 2005). Studies indicate physicians may deliver less information and engage in less participatory decision-making with ethnic minorities (Cooper, Beach, and Clever, 2005).

Identification of Patients with Low Health Literacy

Identifying patients with low health literacy may help healthcare providers tailor messages efficiently. Some common coping methods suggesting possible literacy problems are: complaints of tiredness, poor eyesight, leaving glasses at home or not liking to read; slowly, incompletely, or incorrectly filling out forms; not appearing to notice if materials are handed out upside down; identifying medications by their appearance rather than by name; requesting return of old prescription bottles (marked by rubber bands, numbers, symbols, etc.); failing to follow written instructions regarding the treatment regimen; performing poorly on assessment tools; regularly bringing a friend/family member or asking to consult family before making a decision (Erlen, 2004; Gershenson, 2004; Hardin, 2005; Parker, 2000; Powell, 2004). Of the 86 patients (aged 18–88, mean age of 41.4) with low scores on a health literacy test, 67.4 percent admitted to researchers that they have trouble reading, and 19 percent claimed they had never told anyone—even those providing their healthcare (Parikh et al., 1996: 36).

Without a literacy assessment or an admission of low literacy from a patient, a healthcare provider might judge such a patient to be cognitively impaired (Blacksher, 2002) but at the least has to estimate the amount of information the patient needs/can handle. Misjudgment could result in the provider skipping details he assumes the patient already knows or omitting specific instructions he believes the patient incapable of comprehending and executing. Both residents and healthcare professionals' estimations of patients' literacy abilities have differed significantly from the patients' health literacy test scores (Bass et al., 2002; Praska et al., 2005; Wittich et al., 2007).

Chew, Bradley, and Boyko (2004) suggested three criteria to identify patients with limited literacy: (1) how frequently they ask others for help reading hospital materials, (2) how often they have problems learning about medical conditions because of difficulty understanding written information, and (3) how confident they are in filling out forms independently. According to Wallace et al. (2006), a person's confidence in completing forms independently might be sufficient to identify limited and marginal health literacy.

Innumeracy appears even harder to identify than illiteracy. Even those who consider themselves good with numbers and who have had at least some college education have scored low on numeracy questions (Lipkus, Samsa, and Rimer, 2001; Sheridan, Pignone, and Lewis, 2003). Scores on a test of asthma numeracy were associated somewhat with educational achievement but varied widely even among those who scored highest on the S-TOFHLA health literacy and numeracy test (Apter et al., 2006). Thus, providers may need to assess patients' understanding of numeracy concepts as well as their literacy skills.

Even health professionals and medical students have scored low on some numeracy measures. In one study, 82.5 percent of 45 medical personnel (physicians, nurses, doctorate faculty, and medical students) missed two or more questions of a six-item questionnaire designed to assess health numeracy (Estrada et al., 1999: 527). In a U.K. study, many of the nurses and general practitioners who were tested "failed to understand the risk information" in six scenarios of five-year coronary risk (Bryan et al., 2005: 378).

The National Asthma Education and Prevention Program (1997) guidelines provide an example of why numeracy matters. They recommend that patients with moderate or severe persistent asthma be able to arithmetically compute dosages, use percentages to understand results of peak flow meter use, and perform more complex tasks such as estimation, probability, risk assessment, and problem solving. Gigerenzer and Edwards (2003) provide a nice explanation of statistics used in medical probability and risk situations.

Informed Consent

Medical malpractice litigation seems to have prompted increased use of informed consent forms whereby the patient agrees in writing with the treatment plan (Office of the General Counsel, 2007: 1; Wu et al., 2005). The legality of a signed consent form rests on the competence of the patient to make a reasoned decision based on his/her understanding of specific informational components: the diagnosis/real nature of the condition, probability of success and specific nature of proposed treatment, and the risks and benefits of all reasonable possible treatment alternatives (Mazur, 2001; Quallich, 2004).

Informed consent involves both the message and the receiver: the nature of the information and its delivery on the one hand, and the competency of the patient on the other. The Joint Commission—the main body responsible for accreditation of American hospitals—mandates health providers receiving federal funding to give patients information they can understand (Faguy, 2004; Lee, Arozullah, and Cho, 2004). Yet studies of informed consent forms consistently showed reading grade levels between 11 and 22 (PhD), while patient reading levels ranged from 5.5 and 6.5 (Erlen, 2004; Jackson et al., 1991; Jubelirer, 1991).

Those whose native language differs from that of the consent form or who have sensory or cognitive impairments also present challenging ethical situations. In 1974, the signature of a native Spanish-speaking 7th-grade graduate on a consent form written in English was declared invalid because the signer did not understand what she was signing (Faguy, 2004). The ability to understand medical information sufficiently to make informed decisions has become known as "competency to consent." This competency may vary over time or within a given situation due to reduced alertness or emotional stress from medication or physical trauma (Grisso and Appelbaum, 1998). It also figures largely in patients with more chronic cognitive decline and mental disorders. The lower scores of a group of people with schizophrenia on a recall/recognition test of consent in one study calls into question the legality and ethics of using consent forms with such patients (Stiles et al., 2001). Others have found that careful and repeated (if necessary) explanations can effectively improve the "decisional capacity" of many psychotic patients (Carpenter et al., 2000; Wirshing et al., 1998), and repetitions of the consent process have improved the ability of patients without mental disorders but who had literacy and language barriers (Sudore et al., 2006). The outcome of a 1994 Louisiana case involving a hearing-impaired patient implies that a healthcare provider's oral prompt "do you have any questions"—without an assessment of patient understanding—may not satisfy the Joint Commission's requirement of providing comprehensible information (Faguy, 2004; McEntee, 1995).

Translation

Executive Order 13166 of August 11, 2000, requires recipients of federal financial assistance to provide "meaningful access" to services for people with limited English proficiency (Clinton, 2000). However, in their study of emergency room situations, Baker et al. (1996) found a lack of training in and underutilization of medical translation. Ebden et al. (1988) found 23–50 percent of physician questions mistranslated or not translated at all. Flores' (2000) systematic review of the impact of medical interpreter service on healthcare quality revealed:

1. better preventive screening rates when interpreters were used;
2. more office visits and filled prescriptions when trained interpreters were used;
3. more medical tests, higher test costs, and higher risk of hospitalization in patients with limited English proficiency who had no interpreter or used ad hoc interpreters (friends, family, medical personnel without formal training in translation/interpretation); and
4. a need for additional studies with rigorous methodology, especially formal cost analyses and comparisons of types of interpreting services (phone, ad hoc vs. trained on-site interpreters, etc.) and studies of the influence of cultural beliefs of healthcare providers and patients of various ethnicities on acceptance of these services.

Less than half of the non-native English speakers interviewed for the 2001 Commonwealth Fund Healthcare Quality Survey who claimed to need a translator said that they were always or usually provided with one (Collins et al., 2002). Materials originally written in English then translated sometimes "lose their original meaning," though careful production of translated materials will include back-translation into the original language to check for such errors (Mika et al., 2005: 355). Due to different accents and word usage among dialects of a language, communication can break down even with a healthcare provider who claims to speak the patient's language. This can result in a loss of trust in the doctor (California Health Literacy Initiative, 2003).

CONSEQUENCES OF LOW HEALTH LITERACY

Direct Costs

Adults with low literacy seem to have higher use of healthcare services, including more hospital visits (Baker et al., 2002), longer stays per visit, and use of more hospital resources, incurring greater costs (Friedland, 1998; Hibbard, Greene, and Tusler, 2005; Howard, Gazmararian, and Parker, 2005; Institute of Medicine, 2004; Weiss and Palmer, 2004). Parker, Ratzan, and Lurie (2003) hypothesize that lack of insurance or lack of recognition of early symptoms may cause patients to delay seeking care until the disease becomes more severe, costing more to treat. Depending on the inclusion of the marginally literate to the inadequately literate and assuming equal proportions of health literacy to general literacy as measured by the 1996 NALS, the estimated national costs of low literacy range $30 billion to $73 billion/year in 1998 dollars (Bar-Yam, 2002: 21; Center for Healthcare Strategies, n.d.: 1–2; Friedland, 1998: 6–10; Howard, Gazmararian, and Parker, 2005: 372; Mantone, 2005: 30; Parker, Ratzan, and Lurie, 2003: 150). As much as 64 percent of these additional costs may be paid by public programs (National Academy on an Aging Society, 1998; Parker, Ratzan, and Lurie, 2003: 150).

The Alliance for Excellent Education (2006) estimated that every high school student who graduates rather than dropping out would save an average of $13,706 in Medicaid/uninsured care costs in 2005 dollars, varying from $7,026 per graduate in Mississippi to $15,143 in most New England states.

As more of the burden of healthcare costs is shifted to consumers, they increasingly seek information about charges, treatment options, insurance coverage, and so on to ensure the best value for their healthcare dollar (Oliva, 2005; Seidman, 2005). Unfortunately, while the "consumer-driven health plan" has freed consumers of administrative controls over many of their options, it does not protect them from basing their choices on poor quality information (Ginsburg, 2001: 17).

Absenteeism and Lost Productivity

Patients with inadequate health literacy may not recognize symptoms or sufficiently comprehend self-management instructions to ward off ill health. Untreated symptoms may in turn affect their productivity and attendance at work or school for long periods of time before these people seek the medical attention that can help return them to their full productive capacity. Some studies of patients with manageable diseases—oral disease (Gift, Reisine, and Larach, 1992), rheumatoid arthritis (Puolakka et al., 2005) and depression (Berndt et al., 2000)—indicate that patients with low educational attainment have significantly greater absenteeism and reduced productivity compared with patients with the same diseases who have greater educational achievement. Two studies by Schillinger et al. (2002; 2003) seem to indicate that health literacy can affect knowledge of chronic disease (diabetes), its management, and health outcomes. This connection is, admittedly, tenuous—Schillinger's studies did not calculate increased productivity or reduced absenteeism in patients provided additional self-management nor did the productivity/absenteeism studies measure health literacy.

Noncompliance

When patients do not understand the treatment regimen and cannot read instructions, they may not follow the regimen and/or return for follow-up care (Mayeaux et al., 1996; Paasche-Orlow et al., 2006; Park and Jones, 1997; Wolf et al., 2007). The result is likely though not necessarily increased morbidity/mortality rates (Erlen, 2004). Ethicists and healthcare professionals debate which should be the greater priority: a patient exercising his/her right to autonomy in choosing whether to follow a planned treatment regimen or healthcare professionals dutifully protecting the patient from his/her own decisions that appear likely to lead to a poor health outcome. The possibility of conflict between provider duty and patient right should be resolved more frequently and compliance should improve when the patient has knowledge and understanding (Beauchamp and Childress, 1994).

Patient Satisfaction

Patients with lower health literacy in Mancuso and Rincon's (2006) study reported more dissatisfaction with their disease status and treatment outcomes than did patients with higher health literacy. Noting that those with low health literacy often have difficulty obtaining information on their own, Riley, Cloonan, and Norton (2006) notes that critical care facilities often do not meet patients'/families' great need for information, despite the impact of provision of information on patient satisfaction.

PROPOSED SOLUTIONS

Healthcare providers, educators, people in the media, policymakers, researchers, and librarians all occupy positions that enable them to investigate and implement possible remedies for poor health literacy. Some solutions suggested to date are outlined below.

Readability

While the 1992 NALS results showed one in four adults in America reading at or below the 3rd grade reading level, studies have estimated the readability of health promotion/educational materials at 9th grade or higher, medical textbooks at a minimum of 12th grade, and Direct to Consumer text materials ranging from grades 10.5 through 14 (college sophomore) (Baker and Gollop, 2004; Berland et al., 2001; Emmer, 2003; Hoffmann et al., 2004; Kang et al., 2005; Kaphingst et al.,

2004). Readability tests generally sample some portion of a text and apply a formula to calculate the level of reading required for comprehension. The formulae vary but often include number of syllables per word and number of words per sentence. Some of the most common readability formulae are the Flesch Reading Ease, Flesch-Kincaid, Gunning-Fog, SMOG (Simple Measure of Gobbledygook), and Dale-Chall (see Appendix 2-1 for more detailed information on each test).

Researchers have also investigated the readability of Web sites (D'Alessandro, Kingsley, and Johnson-West, 2001; Friedman, Hoffman-Goetz, and Arocha, 2006). In a study of 54 Web sites by Berland et al. (2001), all 40 English Web sites required at least a 10th grade reading level; over half were written at college reading level. One of the 14 Spanish-language Web sites was at the elementary school reading level, though all others required at least a 9th grade reading level. Removing medical terms reduced these grade levels only by 0.3 grade levels on average. Kellerman and Weiss (1999) noted that handouts from the *JAMA* Patient Page published in 1998–1999 tested at 10th–12th grade reading levels via the Flesch Reading Ease, Flesch-Kincaid, and SMOG formulae.

Simplifying Written Health Information

Several strategies facilitate written communication in print and online. Plain Language is active, simple, natural writing rather than jargon-laden, complex, formal writing. Plain Language advocate Joe Kimble provided guidelines in The *Michigan Bar Journal* in October, 2002. The Suitability of Assessment Materials instrument, CDC's *Scientific and Technical Information Simply Put*, and other sources also provide suggestions for other ways to facilitate reading: typography, layout, illustrations, word choice, lists, organization of information and cultural/ age appropriateness (Doak, Doak, and Root, 1996; Griffin, McKenna, and Tooth, 2003; Office of Communication, 1999).

Microsoft Office's Tools-Spelling&Grammar-Options-"Show readability statistics" will calculate the readability level of a document based on the Flesch Reading Ease and Flesch Kincaid formulae. Grammatik, a readability software program that is often bundled with WordPerfect, incorporates the Fog and Flesch-Kincaid methods (Murphy et al., 2001).

Literacy Assessment Measures

Assessing patient literacy may enable healthcare providers to adjust their communication strategies. Davis et al. (1998) suggest such assessments be carried out as aggregate rather than individual assessments and then only for specific purposes, such as tailoring messages. Perhaps because it could be considered violating patients' privacy rights and potentially imperil employment or job security (Davis et al., 1998), only one study in the present literature review specifically mentioned attaching the results of individual literacy assessments to the patient files. That study by Seligman et al. (2005) found physicians more likely to use recommended communication strategies when the results of such an assessment was attached to patient files. However, the physicians also reported feeling less satisfied and less effective, and no short-term improvement in patient self-efficacy was observed. Davis et al. (1998) cautioned that patient physical health and emotional state, time available for testing, aspects of location in which test is administered, and training required for ease of administration and scoring can all affect scores. Weiss, Reed, and Kligman (1995) also caution that testing reading may not be valid for a given population if that population uses some other mechanism to obtain information.

Healthcare providers have used some general reading tests and created others that fall roughly into two categories: word recognition and comprehension tests. Word recognition tests assess a reader's ability to correctly pronounce words arranged in a list or series of lists in order of increasing length and conceptual complexity. These tests, which can be administered and scored quickly with minimal training for the administrators, are considered indicative of readers' ability to comprehend full sentences and passages. However, Feifer (2003) claims that word recognition tests cannot truly assess a reader's ability to comprehend full sentences/passages because a poor reader's time and effort at decoding individual words may reduce his/her ability to connect the words, make inferences, and glean the overall significance of an entire string of words. This position is supported by Lundquist's (2004) research on the effect of processing time on reading comprehension; Swanson, Howard, and Sáez's study (2006) of the interaction between working memory and reading comprehension; Stanovich's review (1982) of research on the effect of context on reading performance; and deJong and van der Leij's study (2002: 74) indicating that at least for children learning to read, word recognition (decoding) and reading comprehension are distinct processes with "at least partly different cognitive determinants."

Comprehension tests consist of complete sentences or passages of one or more paragraphs with questions. Many tests present these questions in multiple-choice format, tapping the reader's recognition of concepts within the material. Another common comprehension test format is Cloze, in which every fifth to seventh word is intentionally deleted (Taylor, 1953). In many such tests, the reader must recognize which of four possible choices would logically fill the blank; in some, the reader must generate the completing word on his/her own.

According to Andrus and Roth (2002), healthcare systems have used the Peabody, Slosson, and REALM word recognition tests and the WRAT and TOFHLA comprehension tests. Because they were designed for use in medical settings, the REALM and TOFHLA include medical concepts and terminology. TOFHLA also includes a section on numeracy and is available in a Spanish version (TOFHLA-S) and a shortened version (S-TOFHLA). See Appendix 2-2 for a more detailed description of literacy tests.

Golbeck et al. (2005) and others (Parker, Ratzan, and Lurie, 2003; Peterson, Cooper, and Laird, 2001) advocate the establishment of a universally recognized set of health literacy and health numeracy competencies needed by individuals to function in health situations.

Multimedia Patient Education

Health providers increasingly employ nonprint media in patient education. Audiotapes of consultations and presentations have been associated with improvements in patients' understanding and/or recall of information (Bernhardt and Cameron, 2003; Butt, 1977; Santo, Laizner, and Shohet, 2005). Video has proven effective in informing low literate women about cervical and breast cancer screening (Davis et al., 1998; Yancey et al., 1995). Photo novella or photo essays have been used for colon and breast cancer screening and diabetes education (Rogers, Ratzan, and Payne, 2001). Patient-produced self-portraits and films about their experiences of such chronic diseases as cystic fibrosis or spina bifida can reveal gaps in provider-patient communication that have resulted in inappropriate use of medication (Rich, 2004). Pictures of medications that are accurate in color and size have benefited HIV patients with low literacy (Kalichman, Cherry, and Cain, 2005) and anatomy flash cards stored on handheld devices have facilitated discussions with patients (Johnson, 2006).

Computers

With consumers paying an increasing share of their own healthcare costs, loss of trust in healthcare institutions, and physician visits lasting only an average of 15 minutes, consumers are increasingly turning to the Internet for disease and treatment information and data on provider quality (Blumenthal et al., 1999). Pew surveys in 2002 and 2005 showed an increase of 2 percent or 6 million adults using online resources to help someone with a major illness (Madden and Fox, 2006). According to these authors, specific uses included finding the advice or support from other people and professional or expert services, and comparing options. Only 6 percent reported getting bad information or advice that made their experience more difficult. Only 38 percent said the most important source was one found offline; 58 percent said the most important source of information they used was something they had found on the Internet.

Stand-alone computer programs running on single computers or through chat rooms can aid in patient education and data collection. Two examples are touchscreen data entry forms and talking touchscreen self-reports of health outcomes (Hahn et al., 2004; Sutherland et al., 2001). Web-based programs and assignments have reportedly increased knowledge of diabetes and nutrition as well as heightening awareness of evaluative criteria for health information (Bell, Patel, and Malasanos, 2006; Donovan 2005; Smalley and Scourfield, 2004).

Reviewing nearly 22,000 Web pages, 30 English and four English-Spanish board-eligible or board-certified physicians found irrelevant information, promotional material/ads, and contradictory, incomplete, or inaccurate material on both English and Spanish search engine results pages (Berland et al., 2001). Researchers noted that consumers who were comfortable with computers seemed to assume greater quality than these medical professionals found.

Miscellaneous Non-print Solutions

Several nonprint solutions have been proposed. Hixon (2004) advocates referrals between health and educational services and recommends that staff physically check their building for potential improvements to aid low literate patients. O'Connor et al. (2003) reviewed practical techniques for facilitating decision support services and practices, while other researchers investigated the possible effect of improving language services by certified professional interpreters and telephone interpreting services (Carter-Pokras et al., 2004; Flores 2005). Several authors focused on the use of technology including computer kiosks for history-taking (Hahn et al., 2004; Sutherland et al., 2001), patient video creation for health education (Rich, 2004), and interoperable two-way, secure systems for delivering customized patient education (Seidman, 2005).

Health Education in Classroom Settings

Matthews and Sewell (2002) recommended educational institutions collaborate more with healthcare organizations. Golbeck (2005) and Tout and Schmitt (2002) advocate the incorporation of health information/skills in regular K-12 and Adult Basic Education curricula, such as dosage calculations with a math lesson. The 2004 Institute of Medicine report (Nielsen-Bohlman, Panzer, and Kindig, 2004) discusses obstacles and strategies for each of these suggestions.

Outside the traditional classroom, No Child Left Behind community centers could actively promote extracurricular activities that strengthen reading and other "prevention skills" (Lee, 2003: 14) and teachers could refer students with specific serious concerns to a professional health educator (Greenberg, 2001; Russett, 2002). Preprofessional education requirements for classroom teachers could include service learning and an introduction to evidence-based medicine and evaluation sources of reliable health information (Peterson, Cooper, and Laird, 2001; Tappe and Galer-Unti, 2001).

The 1995 Joint Commission on National Health Education Standards focus health educators' efforts on core concepts and self-management skills, including accessing and evaluating health information, decision-making, goal-setting, interpersonal communication, and advocacy. However, the effectiveness of these standards and their implementation is still unclear, perhaps because students drop out of the educational system at multiple levels (McCray, 2005; Mika et al., 2005).

Health literacy programs in workplace, correctional facilities, job-training, family literacy, and English as a Second Language settings offer the potential to catch those outside the formal educational structure (Gazmararian et al., 2005). However, if longitudinal cohort studies indicate that health illiteracy among the elderly stems primarily from cognitive decline, such classroom-based interventions may be insufficient to prevent it (Parker, Ratzan, and Lurie, 2003).

Libraries

Libraries can represent more neutral ground than formal classrooms or clinical settings. They offer private interaction between the user and the information, with current collections and few time limits. Material in libraries is also collected in multiple formats and languages, and at various readability levels. People can use library computers to access health information. Finally, librarians provide training in online searching and critical evaluation of sources (Burnham and Peterson, 2005; Grant, 2002; Logan, 2007; Stephenson et al., 2004). Research on the differences in information needs for those just diagnosed as opposed to those with chronic conditions could help streamline reference transactions. Librarians can also enhance mini-med school programs in their communities by presenting consumer resources to community members participating in the mini-med school programs (Van Moorsel, 2001).

Healthcare Professional Communication

Researchers have suggested many ways physicians and other healthcare professionals can improve their communication effectiveness. Here are a few examples:

- Listen to patients more intently (Beckman and Frankel, 1984; Langewitz et al., 2002).
- Note and follow up on patient moods and concerns (Baker, O'Connell, and Platt, 2005; Baron, 2004; Starfield et al., 1981).
- Allow adequate time for questions (Vastag, 2004; Mayeaux et al., 1996).
- Do not use medical or abstract language (Bourhis, Roth, and MacQueen, 1989; Mayeaux et al., 1996; Williams, 2002).
- Frame the message within the patient's experiences or lifestyle (Powell, 2004).
- Use visuals (Powell, 2004; Williams, 2002).
- Assess patient baseline understanding of at least one piece of information during the visit (Braddock et al., 1997; Kripalani and Scudder, 2004; Michie et al., 2005).
- Use teach-back/show-me methods that require patients to repeat or demonstrate message just imparted (Falvo, 2004; Powell, 2004; Schillinger et al., 2003; Wilson, 2003; Mayeaux et al., 1996).

- Ask open-ended rather than yes-no questions (Rogers, Ratzan, and Payne, 2001).
- Avoid "elastic" terminology subject to multiple interpretations (Edwards, 2004; Edwards, Elwyn, and Mulley, 2002).
- Provide honest and balanced explanations without minimizing less desirable information or uncertainties (Edwards, 2004).
- Allow patients time to perform the mental arithmetic before explicitly stating the conclusion—especially when discussing tradeoffs (Waters et al., 2006).
- Help patients consider time in treatment decisions—the possible costs of acting before getting more information/new research vs. the costs of waiting (Mazur, 2001).
- Become aware of their own conversational patterns, especially in terms of eliciting patient opinions (Makoul, Arntson, and Schofield, 1995).

When discussing risks, physicians should use graphic displays like bar charts and natural frequencies (such as 1 in 10), especially when presenting information on which patients must make treatment decisions (Edwards, Elwyn, and Mulley, 2002), compare the medical risk with an everyday risk (Edwards, Elwyn, and Mulley, 2002; Paling, 2003; 2006), and give lifetime risks (Edwards, Elwyn, and Mulley, 2002).

Young healthcare providers can receive training in communication skills. In fact the Accreditation Council for Graduate Medical Education now requires evaluation of communication skills (Duggan, 2006). The University of Virginia's School of Medicine in Charlottesville integrates health literacy into regular classes with demonstrations, role-playing exercises, and feedback on videotaped interactions with patients (Kripalani and Weiss, 2006; Vastag, 2004). Medical educators could also systematically train their students in the use of natural frequencies and in how to translate probabilities into natural frequencies (Hoffrage et al., 2000) to facilitate understanding of medical risk by those with low numeracy.

Pharmacists are another group of healthcare providers who could receive training (Sicat and Hill, 2005). They should be encouraged to become more proactive in identifying and counseling patients with limited literacy (Praska et al., 2005; Sicat and Hill, 2005; Youmans and Schillinger, 2003).

Finally, healthcare providers or their staff can refer patients to literacy programs or have literacy materials in their offices. For example, through the national Reach Out and Read program, primary care physician office staff give a book to children on visits and have volunteers reading in waiting rooms (Mika et al., 2005).

Patient Communication

An estimated 60–80 percent of diagnostic information derives from patient speech, but patients may not know what information is relevant and necessary, how to verbalize accurately, or how to sequence the information (California Health

Literacy Initiative, 2003; Roter, Rudd, and Comings, 1998; Williams et al., 2002). The Partners for Clear Health Communication coalition (www.askme3.org) urges patients to employ the Ask Me 3 strategy to focus communication on three questions: (1) What is my main problem? (2) What do I need to do about it? (3) Why is it important for me to do this? (Anonymous, 2004; Vastag, 2004; Wilson, 2003).

Patients could also benefit by improving their skills in negotiating, posing questions, and seeking information—particularly when interacting with healthcare providers or healthcare system representatives from insurance agencies or health management organizations. Communicative skills such as those above can temporarily disappear or decline under conditions of emotional stress or physical pain and when the patient feels intimidated by the power or assertive communicative style of the health system representative (Barton, 1997; Bernhardt and Cameron, 2003; Duggan, 2006; Kickbusch, 2001).

Patients' ability to listen to what they are being told by healthcare providers can also create problems. Unfortunately, according to one health literacy expert, no established test exists, as yet, that measures comprehension of spoken health-related information (Baker, 2006).

The Media

Journalists and others who communicate with the public can receive training in statistics and other health literacy issues (Payne and Schulte, 2003). Training could include responsible use of statistics for health issues (DeSilva, Muskavitch, and Roche, 2004; Rivers, 2003; 2006), pulling together fragmented medical facts for the public (Ginman et al., 2003), and socialization into the profession via organizations such as the National Association of Science Writers, Coalition for Health Communication, the Association of Healthcare Journalists, and the American Medical Writers Association's (Willis, 1997). One possible model for this training is the University of Minnesota School of Public Health and School of Journalism and Mass Communication's Master of Arts in health journalism (Johnson, 2006).

Classroom teachers could incorporate health into media literacy lesson plans. One assignment required students to analyze health infomercials for the persuasive techniques used and specific health/social/emotional benefits mentioned/implied (Hill and Lindsay, 2003).

Finally, the media can help in the fight against health illiteracy through their ability to entertain and promote health awareness at the same time. One example was the increase in inquiries about immunization following a soap opera discussion on the issue (Ratzan, 2001).

Political Solutions

Funding and mandates can effect behavioral changes that are resistant to other efforts. Health literacy could become part of preventive services. Government agencies could mandate standards for health literacy learning at all educational levels and for health information systems aimed at consumers. They could also mandate stricter certification requirements and enforcement for interpreters, classroom teachers, and health educators. Interagency communication—particularly between public health workers and mass media—could be made more efficient. To effect these changes may require that federal/state/local policymakers learn of the effect of education on health and the effect of health literacy on their constituents and budgets (Ad Hoc Committee on Health Literacy for the Council on Scientific Affairs, 1999; Monsen, 2007; Parker, Ratzan, and Lurie, 2003; Payne and Schulte, 2003; Rogers, Ratzan, and Payne, 2001; Seidman, 2005).

Partnerships

The complexity of the problem of health literacy has spawned new organizations, special committees and task forces in existing ones, and new partnerships. Among these are Partnership for Clear Health Communication (a coalition that includes AMA and other health and educational agencies/organizations/institutions), National Work Group on Literacy and Health of the National Cancer Institute, the Ad Hoc Committee on Health Literacy for the Council on Scientific Affairs of the American Medical Association, California Health Literacy Initiative, Centre for Literacy of Quebec's Health Literacy Project, and the people who contributed information to the Virginia Adult Education Health Literacy Tool Kit. Private organizations such as Pfizer Foundation and Robert Wood Johnson Foundation have provided significant funding for these partnerships.

Thus, health literacy constitutes a complex set of skills useful in or even necessary for functioning in today's healthcare environment: literacy, numeracy, oral communication and listening comprehension skills, decision-making ability, and media/technology literacy. Multiple segments of the population can aid in improving the health literacy of our population: healthcare system representatives, educators, librarians, government policymakers and the media. The growing body of research investigating root causes, complications and effective interventions and valid assessment instruments for the latter holds promise.

REFERENCES

Ad Hoc Committee on Health Literacy for the Council on Scientific Affairs, American Medical Association. 1999. "Health Literacy: Report of the Council on Scientific Affairs." *JAMA* 281, no.6 (February): 552–557.

Alliance for Excellent Education. 2006. *Healthier and Wealthier: Decreasing Healthcare Costs by Increasing Educational Attainment.* Washington, DC: Alliance for Excellent Education. (December 2006) Available: www .all4ed.org/publications/HandW.pdf

Andrus, Miranda R., and Mary T. Roth. 2002. "Health Literacy: A Review." *Pharmacotherapy* 22, no.3 (March): 282–302.

Anonymous. 2004. "Program Targets Clear Communication Between Healthcare Provider and Patient: Ask Me 3 Aimed at Patients with Low Health Literacy to Improve Outcomes." *Patient Education Management* 11, no.2 (February): 13–15.

Apter, Andrea J., Jing Cheng, Dylan Small, Ian M. Bennett, Claire Albert, Daniel G. Fein, Maureen George, and Simone Van Horne. 2006. "Asthma Numeracy Skill and Health Literacy." *Journal of Asthma* 43, no.9 (November): 705–710.

Baker, David W. 2006. "The Meaning and the Measure of Health Literacy." *Journal of General Internal Medicine* 21, no. 8(August): 878–883.

Baker, David W., Julie A. Gazmararian, Joseph Sudano, and Marian Patterson. 2000. "The Association Between Age and Health Literacy Among Elderly Persons." *Journal of Gerontology. Series B, Psychological Sciences and Social Sciences* 55, no.6 (November): S368–374.

Baker, David W., Julie A. Gazmararian, Joseph Sudano, Marian Patterson, Ruth M. Parker, and Mark V. Williams. 2002. "Health Literacy and Performance on the Mini-Mental State Examination." *Aging & Mental Health* 6, no.1 (February): 22–29.

Baker, David W., Julie A. Gazmararian, Mark V. Williams, Tracy Scott, Ruth M. Parker, Diane Green, Junling Ren, and Jennifer Peel. 2002. "Functional Health Literacy and the Risk of Hospital Admission Among Medicare Managed Care Enrollees." *American Journal of Public Health* 92, no.8 (August): 1278–1283.

Baker, David W., Ruth M. Parker, Mark V. Williams, and W. Scott Clark. 1998. "Health Literacy and the Risk of Hospital Admission." *Journal of General Internal Medicine* 13, no.12: 791–798.

Baker, David W., Ruth M. Parker, Mark V. Williams, W. Scott Clark, and Joanne Nurss. 1997. "The Relationship of Patient Reading Ability to Self-Reported Health and Use of Health Services." *American Journal of Public Health* 87, no.6 (June): 1027–1030.

Baker, David W., Ruth M. Parker, Mark V. Williams, Wendy C. Coates, and Kathryn Pitkin. 1996. "Use and Effectiveness of Interpreters in an Emergency Department." *JAMA* 275, no.10 (March): 783–788.

Baker, Laurence H., Daniel O'Connell, and Frederic W. Platt. 2005. "'What else?' Setting the Agenda for the Clinical Interview." *Annals of Internal Medicine* 143, no.10 (November): 766–770.

Baker, Lynda M., and Claudia J. Gollop. 2004. "Medical Textbooks: Can Lay People Read and Understand Them?" *Library Trends* 53, no.2 (Fall): 336–347.

Baron, Jeremy H. 2004. "If I Were Dean: A Challenge to New Medical Students." *The Mount Sinai Journal of Medicine, New York* 71, no.2 (March): 134–138.

Barton, Ellen L. 1997. "Literacy in (Inter)Action." *College English* 59, no.4 (April): 408–437.

Bar-Yam, Naomi B. 2002. "Low Health Literacy: A Problem for All in the Healthcare Circle." *International Journal of Childbirth Education* 17, no.3 (September): 21–23.

Bass, Pat F., 3rd, John F. Wilson, Charles H. Griffith, and Don R. Barnett. 2002. "Residents' Ability to Identify Patients with Poor Literacy Skills." *Academic Medicine* 77, no.10 (October): 1039–1041.

Baur, Cynthia E. 2005. "Using the Internet to Move beyond the Brochure and Improve Health Literacy." In *Understanding Health Literacy: Implications for Medicine and Public Health*, edited by J. C. Schwartzberg, J. B. VanGeest and C. C. Wang. Chicago: American Medical Association.

Beauchamp, Tom L., and James F. Childress. 1994. *Principles of Biomedical Ethics*. 4th ed. New York: Oxford University Press.

Beckman, Howard B., and Richard M. Frankel. 1984. "The Effect of Physician Behavior on the Collection of Data." *Annals of Internal Medicine* 101, no.5 (November): 692–696.

Bell, Julie A., Bhavin Patel, and Toree Malasanos. 2006. "Knowledge Improvement with Web-Based Diabetes Education Program: Brainfood." *Diabetes Technology & Therapeutics* 8, no.4 (August): 444–448.

Berkman, Nancy D., Darren A. DeWalt, Michael P. Pignone, Stacey L. Sheridan, Kathleen N. Lohr, Linda Lux, Sonya F. Sutton, Tammeka Swinson, and Arthur J. Bonito. 2004. "Literacy and Health Outcomes." *Evidence Report/Technology Assessment (Summary)* (87), no.87 (January): 1–8.

Berland, Gretchen K., Marc N. Elliott, Leo S. Morales, Jeffrey I. Algazy, Richard L. Kravitz, Michael S. Broder, David E. Kanouse, Jorge A. Munoz, Juan-Antonio Puyol, Marielena Lara, Katherine E. Watkins, Hannah Yang, and Elizabeth A. McGlynn. 2001. "Health Information on the Internet: Accessibility, Quality, and Readability in English and Spanish." *JAMA* 285, no.20 (May): 2612–2621.

Berndt, Ernst R., Lorrin M. Koran, Stan N. Finkelstein, Alan J. Gelenberg, Susan G. Kornstein, Ivan M. Miller, Michael E. Thase, George A. Trapp, and Martin B. Keller. 2000. "Lost Human Capital from Early-Onset Chronic Depression." *American Journal of Psychiatry* 157, no.6 (June): 940–947.

Bernhardt, Jay M., and Kenzie A. Cameron. 2003. "Accessing, Understanding, and Applying Health Communication Messages: The Challenge of Health Literacy." In *Handbook of Health Communication*, edited by Teresa L. Thompson, Alicia M. Dorsey, Katherine I. Miller, and Roxanne Parrott. Mahwah, NJ: Lawrence Erlbaum.

Birru, Mehret S., Valerie M. Monaco, Charles Lonelyss, Drew Hadiya, Valerie Njie, Timothy Bierria, Ellen Detlefsen, and Richard A. Steinman. 2004. "Internet Usage by Low-Literacy Adults Seeking Health Information: An Observational Analysis." *Journal of Medical Internet Research* 6, no.3 (September): e25.

Blacksher, Erika. 2002. "On Being Poor and Feeling Poor: Low Socioeconomic Status and the Moral Self." *Theoretical Medicine and Bioethics* 23, no.6 (November): 455–470.

Blumenthal, David, Nancyanne Causino, YuChiang Chang, Larry Culpepper, William Marder, Dehmet Saglam, Randall Stafford, and Barbara Starfield. 1999. "The Duration of Ambulatory Visits to Physicians." *Journal of Family Practice* 48, no.4 (April): 264–271.

Bouchard, Christine. 2007. "Literacy and Hazard Communication: Ensuring Workers Understand the Information They Receive." *AAOHN* 55, no.1 (January): 18–25.

Bourhis, Rirchard Y., Sharon Roth, and Glenda MacQueen. 1989. "Communication in the Hospital Setting: A Survey of Medical and Everyday Language Use amongst Patients, Nurses and Doctors." *Social Science & Medicine (1989)* 28, no. 4: 339–346.

Braddock, Clarence H., 3rd, Stephan D. Fihn, Wendy Levinson, Albert R. Jonsen, and Robert A. Pearlman. 1997. "How Doctors and Patients Discuss Routine Clinical Decisions. Informed Decision Making in the Outpatient Setting." *Journal of General Internal Medicine* 12, no.6 (June): 339–345.

Braithwaite, Dejana, Jon Emery, Fiona Walter, A. Toby Prevost, and Stephen Sutton. 2004. "Psychological Impact of Genetic Counseling for Familial Cancer: A Systematic Review and Meta-Analysis." *Journal of the National Cancer Institute* 96, no.2 (January): 122–133.

Bryan, S., P. Gill, S. Greenfield, K. Gutridge, Tom Marshall, and Birmingham Patient Preferences Group. 2005. "Clinicians' Preferences for Treatments to Prevent Coronary Heart Disease: A Postal Survey." *Heart* 91, no.3 (March): 377–378.

Burnham, Erica, and Eileen Beany Peterson. 2005. "Health Information Literacy: A Library Case Study." *Library Trends* 53, no.3 (Winter): 422–433.

Butt, Hugh R. 1977. "A Method for Better Physician-Patient Communication." *Annals of Internal Medicine* 86, no.4 (April): 478–480.

California Health Literacy Initiative. 2003. *Low Literacy, High Risk: The Hidden Challenge of Facing Healthcare in California.* Oakland, CA: California Literacy.

Carpenter, William T., Jr., James M. Gold, Adrienne C. Lahti, Caleb A. Queern, Robert R. Conley, John J. Bartko, Jeffrey Kovnick, and Paul S. Appelbaum. 2000. "Decisional Capacity for Informed Consent in Schizophrenia Research." *Archives of General Psychiatry* 57, no.6 (June): 533–538.

Carter-Pokras, Olivia, Marla J. O'Neill, Vasana Cheanvechai, Mikhail Menis, Tao Fan, and Angelo Solera. 2004. "Providing Linguistically Appropriate Services to Persons with Limited English Proficiency: A Needs and Resources Investigation." *American Journal of Managed Care* 10 Spec No, SP29–36.

Center for Healthcare Strategies, Inc. n.d. *Impact of Low Health Literacy Skills on Annual Healthcare Expenditures.* Fact Sheet 3. (August 2007) Available: www.chcs.org/usr doc/Health Literacy Fact Sheets. pdf

Centre for Literacy of Quebec. 2001. *Needs Assessment of the Health Education and Information Needs of Hard-to-Reach Patients.* Vol. Health Literacy Project, Phase 1, Part 1. Montreal, Quebec: Author.

Chew, Lisa D., Katharine A. Bradley, and Edward J. Boyko. 2004. "Brief Questions to Identify Patients with Inadequate Health Literacy." *Family Medicine* 36, no.8 (September): 588–594.

Christensen, Palle M., Kim Brosen, Kim Brixen, Morten Andersen, and Ivar Sonbo Kristiansen. 2003. "A Randomized Trial of Laypersons' Perception of the Benefit of Osteoporosis Therapy: Number Needed to Treat Versus Postponement of Hip Fracture." *Clinical Therapeutics* 25, no.10 (October): 2575–2585.

Clinton, William J. 2000. "Executive Order #13166 - Improving Access to Services for Persons With Limited English Proficiency - Enforcement of Title VI of the Civil Rights Act of 1964-National Origin Discrimination against Persons with Limited English Proficiency." *Federal Register* 65, no.159 (August): 50120–50125.

Collins, Karen S., Dora L. Hughes, Michelle M. Doty, Brett L. Ives, Jennifer N. Edwards, and Katie Tenney. 2002. *Diverse Communities, Common Concerns: Assessing Healthcare Quality for Minority Americans.* New York: The Commonwealth Fund.

Cook, Wanda D. 1977. *Adult Literacy Education in the United States.* Newark, DE: International Reading Association.

Cooper, Lisa A., Mary C. Beach, and Sarah L. Clever. 2005. "Participatory Decision-making in the Medical Encounter and its Relationship to Patient Literacy." In *Understanding Health Literacy: Implications for Medicine and Public Health,* edited by J. C. Schwartzberg, J. B. VanGeest and C. C. Wang. Chicago: American Medical Association.

Croyle, Robert T., and Caryn Lerman. 1999. "Risk Communication in Genetic Testing for Cancer Susceptibility." *Journal of the National Cancer Institute. Monographs,* no.25 (January): 59–66.

D'Alessandro, Donna M., Peggy Kingsley, and Jill Johnson-West. 2001. "The Readability of Pediatric Patient Education Materials on the World Wide Web." *Archives of Pediatrics & Adolescent Medicine* 155, no.7 (July): 807–812.

Davis, Terry C., Hans J. Berkel, Connie L. Arnold, Indrani Nandy, Robert H. Jackson, and Peggy W. Murphy. 1998. "Intervention to Increase Mammography Utilization in a Public Hospital." *Journal of General Internal Medicine* 13, no.4 (March): 230–233.

Davis, Terry C., Michael A. Crouch, Georgia Wills, Sarah Miller, David M. Abdehou. 1990. "The Gap Between Patient Reading Comprehension and the Readability of Patient Education Materials." *Journal of Family Practice* 31, no.5 (November): 533–538.

Davis, Terry C., Robert Michielutte, Eunice N. Askov, Mark V. Williams, and Barry D. Weiss. 1998. "Practical Assessment of Adult Literacy in Healthcare." *Health Education & Behavior* 25, no.5 (October): 613–624.

de Jong, Peter F., and Aryan van der Leij. 2002. "Effects of Phonological Abilities and Linguistic Comprehension on the Development of Reading." *Scientific Studies of Reading* 6, no.1 (January): 51–77.

DeSilva, Malini, Marc A. T. Muskavitch, and John P. Roche. 2004. "Print Media Coverage of Antibiotic Resistance." *Science Communication* 26, no.1 (September): 31–43.

DeWalt, Darren A., Nancy D. Berkman, Stacey Sheridan, Kathleen N. Lohr, and Michael P. Pignone. 2004. "Literacy and Health Outcomes: A Systematic Review of the Literature." *Journal of General Internal Medicine* 19, no.12 (December): 1228–1239.

Diamond, James J. 2007. "Development of a Reliable and Construct Valid Measure of Nutritional Literacy in Adults." *Nutrition Journal* 6 (February): 5.

Diogo, Steven J. 2002. "Academy Backs Amalgam, Oral Health Literacy." *General Dentistry* 50, no.5 (September-October): 394–396.

Doak, Cecilia C., Leonard G. Doak, and Jane H. Root. 1996. *Teaching Patients with Low Literacy Skills.* 2nd ed. Philadelphia: J.B. Lippincott.

Donovan, Owen M. 2005. "The Carbohydrate Quandary: Achieving Health Literacy through an Interdisciplinary WebQuest." *Journal of School Health* 75, no.9 (November): 359–362.

Duggan, Ashley. 2006. "Understanding Interpersonal Communication Processes Across Health Contexts: Advances in the Last Decade and Challenges for the Next Decade." *Journal of Health Communication* 11, no.1 (January-February): 93–108.

Ebden, Philip, Oliver J. Carey, Arvind Bhatt, and Brian Harrison. 1988. "The Bilingual Consultation." *Lancet* 1, no.8581 (February): 347.

Edwards, Adrian. 2004. "Flexible Rather than Standardised Approaches to Communicating Risks in Healthcare." *Quality & Safety in Healthcare* 13, no.3 (June): 169–170.

Edwards, Adrian, Glyn Elwyn, and Al Mulley. 2002. "Explaining Risks: Turning Numerical Data into Meaningful Pictures." *BMJ (Clinical Research Ed.)* 324, no.7341 (April): 827–830.

Elder, John P., Jeanette I. Candelaria, Susan I. Woodruff, Michael H. Criqui, Gregory A. Talavera, and Joan W. Rupp. 2000. "Results of Language for Health: Cardiovascular Disease Nutrition Education for Latino English-as-a-Second-Language Students." *Health Education & Behavior* 27, no.1 (February): 50–63.

Emmer, Casey. 2003. "Oral Health Literacy Annotated Bibliography." Harvard School of Public Health. (October 2006) Available: www.hsph.Harvard .edu/healthliteracy/literature/lit oral.html

Erlen, Judith A. 2004. "Functional Health Illiteracy. Ethical Concerns." *Orthopaedic Nursing* 23, no.2 (March-April): 150–153.

Estrada, Carlos, Vetta Barnes, Cathy Collins, and J. C. Byrd. 1999. "Health Literacy and Numeracy." *JAMA* 282, no.6 (August): 527.

Evensen, Sonja. 2003. "Teaching the Standards: Decision Making Skills Enhance Student Health." *Pacific Educator* 2, no.1 (February): 13–14.

Faguy, Katie. 2004. "Health Literacy." *Radiologic Technology* 76, no.2 (November–December): 139–149.

Falvo, Donna R. 2004. "Illiteracy in Patient Education and Patient Compliance." In *Effective Patient Education: A Guide to Increasing Compliance*, by Donna R. Falvo. 3rd ed. Sudbury, MA: Jones and Bartlett.

Feifer, Richard. 2003. "How a Few Simple Words Improve Patients' Health." *Managed Care Quarterly* 11, no.2 (Spring): 29–31.

Feys, Peter, Anders Romberg, Juhani Ruutiainen, Angela Davies-Smith, Rosemary Jones, Carlo Alberto Avizzano, Massimo Bergamasco, and Pierre Ketelaer. 2001. "Assistive Technology to Improve PC Interaction for People with Intention Tremor." *Journal of Rehabilitation Research and Development* 38, no.2 (March-April): 235–243.

Flores, Glenn. 2000. "Culture and the Patient-Physician Relationship: Achieving Cultural Competency in Healthcare." *Journal of Pediatrics* 136, no.1 (January): 14–23.

Flores, Glenn. 2005. "The Impact of Medical Interpreter Services on the Quality of Healthcare: A Systematic Review." *Medical Care Research and Review* 62, no.3 (June): 255–299.

Flores, Glenn, Elena Fuentes-Afflick, Oxiris Barbot, Olivia Carter-Pokras, Luz Claudio, Marielena Lara, Jennie A. McLaurin, Lee Pachter, Francisco J. Ramos-Gomez, Fernando Mendoza, R. Burciaga Valdez, Antonia M. Villarruel, Ruth E. Zambrana, Robert Greenberg, and Michael Weitzman. 2002. "The Health of Latino Children: Urgent Priorities, Unanswered Questions, and a Research Agenda." *JAMA* 288, no.1 (July): 82–90.

Fortenberry, J. Dennis, M. M. McFarlane, M. Hennessy, S. S. Bull, D. M. Grimley, J. St. Lawrence, B. P. Stoner, and N. VanDevanter. 2001. "Relation of Health Literacy to Gonorrhoea-Related Care." *Sexually Transmitted Infections* 77, no.3 (June): 206–211.

Fox, Susannah, and Lee Rainie. 2000. *The Online Health Revolution: How the Web Helps Americans Take Better Care of Themselves.* Washington, DC: Online Health, Pew Internet and American Life Project. (April 2007) Available: www.pewinternet.org/pdfs/PIP Health Report.pdf

Friedland, Robert B. 1998. *Understanding Health Literacy: New Estimates of the Costs of Inadequate Health Literacy*, edited by National Academy on an Aging Society. Washington, DC: Pfizer.

Friedman, Daniela B., Laurie Hoffman-Goetz, and José F. Arocha. 2006. "Health Literacy and the World Wide Web: Comparing the Readability of Leading Incident Cancers on the Internet." *Medical Informatics and the Internet in Medicine* 31, no.1 (March): 67–87.

Friedman, Daniela B., and Laurie Hoffman-Goetz. 2006. "A Systematic Review of Readability and Comprehension Instruments Used for Print and Web-Based Cancer Information." *Health Education & Behavior* 33, no.3 (June): 352–373.

Gazmararian, Julie A., James W. Curran, Ruth M. Parker, Jay M. Bernhardt, and Barbara A. DeBuono. 2005. "Public Health Literacy in America: An Ethical Imperative." *American Journal of Preventive Medicine* 28, no.3 (April): 317–322.

Gazmararian, Julie A., Ruth M. Parker, and David W. Baker. 1999. "Reading Skills and Family Planning Knowledge and Practices in a Low-Income Managed-Care Population." *Obstetrics and Gynecology* 93, no.2 (February): 239–244.

Gazmararian, Julie A., Mark V. Williams, Jennifer Peel, and David W. Baker. 2003. "Health Literacy and Knowledge of Chronic Disease." *Patient Education and Counseling* 51, no.3 (November): 267–275.

Gershenson, Terri A. 2004. "Language of Health Literacy." *Nursing Spectrum:New York & New Jersey Edition* 16, no.8 (April): 17.

Gift, Helen C., Susan T. Reisine, and Dina C. Larach. 1992. "The Social Impact of Dental Problems and Visits." *American Journal of Public Health* 82, no.12 (December): 1663–1668.

Gigerenzer, Gerd, and Adrian Edwards. 2003. "Simple Tools for Understanding Risks: From Innumeracy to Insight." *BMJ (Clinical Research Ed.)* 327, no.7417 (September): 741–744.

Ginman, Mariam, Kristina Eriksson-Backa, Stefan Ek, Margit Mustonen, Sinikka Torkkola, Kimmo Tuominen, and Marianne Wikgren. 2003. "Health Communication and Knowledge Construction." *Health Informatics Journal* 9, no.4 (December): 301–313.

Ginsburg, Paul B. 2001. *Rough Seas Ahead for Purchasers and Consumers.* 2001 Annual Report—President's Message. Washington, DC: Center for Studying Health System Change. (October 2006) Available http:// hschange.org/CONTENT/452/essay.html

Golbeck, Amanda L., Carolyn R. Ahlers-Schmidt, Angelina M. Paschal, and S. E. Dismuke. 2005. "A Definition and Operational Framework for Health Numeracy." *American Journal of Preventive Medicine* 29, no 4 (November): 375–376.

Grant, Sharon. 2002. *Information Literacy and Consumer Health.* Washington, DC: U.S. National Commission on Libraries and Information Science.

Gray, Nicola J., Jonathan D. Klein, Peter R. Noyce, Tracy S. Sesselberg, and Judith A. Cantrill. 2005. "The Internet: A Window on Adolescent Health Literacy." *Journal of Adolescent Health* 37, no.3 (September): 243.

Greenberg, Daphne. 2001. "A Critical Look at Health Literacy." *Adult Basic Education* 11, no.2 (Summer): 67–79.

Greene, Jessica, Judith Hibbard, and Martin Tusler. 2005. *How Much Do Health Literacy and Patient Activation Contribute to Older Adults' Ability to Manage Their Health?* Vol. 2005–05. Washington, DC: AARP.

Griffin, Janelle, Kryss McKenna, and Leigh Tooth. 2003. "Written Health Education Materials: Making Them More Effective." *Australian Occupational Therapy Journal* 50, no.3 (September): 170–177.

Grisso, Thomas, and Paul S. Appelbaum. 1998. "Abilites Related to Competence." In *Assessing Competence to Consent to Treatment: A Guide for Physicians and Other Health Professionals.* New York: Oxford University Press.

Hahn, Elizabeth A., David Cella, Deborah Dobrez, Gail Shiomoto, Elizabeth Marcus, Samuel G. Taylor, Mala Vohra, Chih-Hung Chang, Benjamin D. Wright, John M. Linacre, Barry D. Weiss, Veronica Valenzuela, Hsaio-Lin Chiang, and Kimberly Webster. 2004. "The Talking Touchscreen: A New Approach to Outcomes Assessment in Low Literacy." *Psycho-Oncology* 13, no.2 (February): 86–95.

Hansen, Derek L., Holly A. Derry, Paul J. Resnick, and Caroline R. Richardson. 2003. "Adolescents Searching for Health Information on the Internet: An Observational Study." *Journal of Medical Internet Research* 5, no.4 (October–December): e25.

Hardin, Laurie R. 2005. "Counseling Patients with Low Health Literacy." *American Journal of Health-System Pharmacy* 62, no.4 (February): 364–365.

Hibbard, Judith, Jessica Greene, and Martin Tusler. 2005. *Identifying Medicare Beneficiaries with Poor Health Literacy Skills: Is a Short Screening Index Feasible?* Vol. 2005. Washington, DC: AARP Policy Institute.

Hill, Susan C., and Gordon B. Lindsay. 2003. "Using Health Infomercials to Develop Media Literacy Skills." *Journal of School Health* 73, no.6 (August): 239–241.

Hixon, Allen L. 2004. "Functional Health Literacy: Improving Health Outcomes." *American Family Physician* 69, no.9 (May): 2077–2078.

Hoffmann, Tammy, Kryss McKenna, Linda Worrall, and Stephen J. Read. 2004. "Evaluating Current Practice in the Provision of Written Information to Stroke Patients and Their Carers . . . including Commentary by O'Connell B, Sullivan K." *International Journal of Therapy & Rehabilitation* 11, no.7 (July): 303–310.

Hoffrage, Ulrich, Samuel Lindsey, Ralph Hertwig, and Gerd Gigerenzer. 2000. "Medicine. Communicating Statistical Information." *Science* 290, no.5500 (December): 2261–2262.

Howard, David H., Julie A. Gazmararian, and Ruth M. Parker. 2005. "The Impact of Low Health Literacy on the Medical Costs of Medicare Managed Care Enrollees." *American Journal of Medicine* 118, no.4 (April): 371–377.

Howard, David H., Tetine Sentell, and Julie A. Gazmararian. 2006. "Impact of Health Literacy on Socioeconomic and Racial Differences in Health in an Elderly Population." *Journal of General Internal Medicine* 21, no.8 (August): 857–861.

Institute of Medicine. 2002. "Assessing Potential Sources of Racial or Ethnic Disparities in Care: The Clinical Encounter." In *Unequal Treatment: Confronting Racial and Ethnic Disparities in Healthcare*, edited by Brian D. Smedley, Adrienne Y. Stith and Alan R. Nelson. Washington, DC: The National Academies Press.

Jackson, Robert H., Terry C. Davis, Lee E.Bairnsfather, Ronald B. George, Michael A. Crouch, and Helena Gault. 1991. "Patient Reading Ability: An Overlooked Problem in Healthcare." *Southern Medical Journal* 84, no.10 (October): 1172–1175.

Johnson, M. L. 2006. "More Medical Schools Requiring PDAs." *Washington Post* 4/22/06.

Jorm, Anthony F., Ailsa E. Korten, Patricia A. Jacomb, Helen Christensen, Bryan Rodgers, and Penelope Pollitt. 1997. " 'Mental Health Literacy': A Survey of the Public's Ability to Recognise Mental Disorders and Their Beliefs about the Effectiveness of Treatment." *Medical Journal of Australia* 166, no.4 (February): 182–186.

Jubelirer, Steven J. 1991. "Level of Reading Difficulty in Educational Pamphlets and Informed Consent Documents for Cancer Patients." *The West Virginia Medical Journal* 87, no.12 (December): 554–557.

Kalichman, Seth C., Jacqueline Cherry, and Demetria Cain. 2005. "Nurse-Delivered Antiretroviral Treatment Adherence Intervention for People with Low Literacy Skills and Living with HIV/AIDS." *Journal of the Association of Nurses in AIDS Care* 16, no.5 (September-October): 3–15.

Kang, Edith, Henry W. Fields, Sandy Cornett, and F. M. Beck. 2005. "An Evaluation of Pediatric Dental Patient Education Materials Using Contemporary Health Literacy Measures." *Pediatric Dentistry* 27, no.5 (September-October): 409–413.

Kaphingst, Kimberly A., Rima E. Rudd, William DeJong, and Lawren H. Daltroy. 2004. "Literacy Demands of Product Information Intended to Supplement Television Direct-to-Consumer Prescription Drug Advertisements." *Patient Education and Counseling* 55, no. 2 (November): 293–300.

Kellerman, Rick, and Barry D. Weiss. 1999. "Health Literacy and the JAMA Patient Page." *JAMA* 282, no.6 (August): 525–527.

Kickbusch, Ilona S. 2001. "Health Literacy: Addressing the Health and Education Divide." *Health Promotion International* 16, no.3 (September): 289–297.

Kimble, Joe. 2002. "The Elements of Plain Language." *Michigan Bar Journal* 81, no.10 (October): 44–45.

Kirsch, Irwin, Ann Jungeblut, Lynn Jenkins, and Andrew Kolstad. 1993. *Adult Literacy in America: A First Look at the Results of the National Adult Literacy Survey*. Washington, DC: National Center for Education Statistics.

Kitchener, Betty A., and Anthony F. Jorm. 2006. "Mental Health First Aid Training: Review of Evaluation Studies." *The Australian and New Zealand Journal of Psychiatry* 40, no.1 (January): 6–8.

Kripalani, Sunil, and Laurie Scudder. 2004. "Ask the Expert: Common Questions about Health Literacy." *National Women's Health Report* 26, no.5 (October): 7.

Kripalani, Sunil, and Barry D. Weiss. 2006. "Teaching about Health Literacy and Clear Communication." *Journal of General Internal Medicine* 21, no.8 (August): 888–890.

Langewitz, Wolf, Martin Denz, Anne Keller, Alexander Kiss, Sigmund Ruttimann, and Brigitta Wossmer. 2002. "Spontaneous Talking Time at Start of Consultation in Out-patient Clinic: Cohort Study." *BMJ (Clinical Research Ed.)* 325, no.7366 (September): 682–683.

Lee, Harvey. 2003. "Supporting Health Literacy: NCLB Funds Community Learning Centers." *Pacific Educator* 2, no.1 (February): 14. (August 2007) Available: www.eric .ed.gov/ERICDocs/data/ericdocs2sql/content_storage_01/0000019b/80/1a/cd/0a.pdf

Lee, Shoou-Yih D., Ahsan M. Arozullah, and Young I. Cho. 2004. "Health Literacy, Social Support, and Health: A Research Agenda." *Social Science & Medicine (1982)* 58, no.7 (April): 1309–1321.

Levin-Zamir, Diane, and Yitzhak Peterburg. 2001. "Health Literacy in Health Systems: Perspectives on Patient Self-Management in Israel." *Health Promotion International* 16, no.1 (March): 87–94.

Lindau, Stacy T., Anirban Basu, and Sara A. Leitsch. 2006. "Health Literacy as a Predictor of Follow-up after an Abnormal Pap Smear: A Prospective Study." *Journal of General Internal Medicine* 21, no.8 (August): 829–834.

Lipkus, Isaac M., Greg Samsa, and Barbara K. Rimer. 2001. "General Performance on a Numeracy Scale Among Highly Educated Samples." *Medical Decision Making* 21, no.1 (January-February): 37–44.

Logan, Robert A. 2007. "Clinical, Classroom, or Personal Education: Attitudes about Health Literacy." *Journal of the Medical Library Association* 95, no.2 (April): 127–137, e48.

Lundquist, Eric N. 2004. Phonological Complexity, Decoding, and Text Comprehension. Ph.D. diss., ProQuest Information & Learning.

Macario, Everly, Karen M. Emmons, Glorian Sorensen, Mary Kay Hunt, and Rima E. Rudd. 1998. "Factors Influencing Nutrition Education for Patients with Low Literacy Skills." *Journal of the American Dietetic Association* 98, no.5 (May): 559–564.

Madden, Mary, and Susannah Fox. 2006. *Finding Answers Online in Sickness and in Health.* Washington, DC: Pew Internet & American Life Project. (April 2007) Available www.pewinternet.org/pdfs/PIP Health Decisions 2006.pdf .

Makoul, Gregory, Paul Arntson, and Theo Schofield. 1995. "Health Promotion in Primary Care: Physician-Patient Communication and Decision Making about Prescription Medications." *Social Science & Medicine (1982)* 41, no.9 (November): 1241–1254.

Mancuso, Carol A., and Melina Rincon. 2006. "Asthma Patients' Assessments of Healthcare and Medical Decision Making: The Role of Health Literacy." *The Journal of Asthma* 43, no.1 (January-February): 41–44.

Mantone, Joseph. 2005. "Reading, Writing and Relating. Providers—Rural and Urban—Urged to Pay More Attention to Health Literacy." *Modern Healthcare* 35, no.32 (August): 30–31.

Marteau, Theresa M., and Robert T. Croyle. 1998. "The New Genetics. Psychological Responses to Genetic Testing." *BMJ (Clinical Research Ed.)* 316, no.7132 (February): 693–696.

Matthews, T. L., and J. C. Sewell. 2002. *State Official's Guide to Health Literacy.* Lexington, KY: The Council of State Governments.

Mayeaux, Edward J., Jr., Peggy W. Murphy, Connie L. Arnold, Terry C. Davis, Robert H. Jackson, and Tetine Sentell. 1996. "Improving Patient Education for Patients with Low Literacy Skills." *American Family Physician* 53, no.1 (January): 205–211.

Mazur, Dennis J. 2001. Introduction to Research on Shared Decision Making: Understanding its Range of Content and Complexity." In *Shared Decision Making in the Patient-Physician Relationship.* Tampa, FL: American College of Physician Executives.

Mazur, Dennis J. 2001. "What Goes on in Patient/Physician Discussions? What Does the Research Show? In *Shared Decision Making in the Patient-Physician Relationship: Challenges Facing Patients, Physicians, and Medical Institutions.* Tampa, FL: American College of Physician Executives.

McCray, Alexa T. 2005. "Promoting Health Literacy." *Journal of the American Medical Informatics Association* 12, no.2 (March-April): 152–163.

McEntee, Maureen K. 1995. "Deaf and Hard-of-Hearing Clients: Some Legal Implications." *Social Work* 40, no.2 (March): 183–187.

Michie, Susan, Kathryn Lester, Julia Pinto, and Theresa M. Marteau. 2005. "Communicating Risk Information in Genetic Counseling: An Observational Study." *Health Education & Behavior* 32, no.5 (October): 589–598.

Mika, Virginia S., Patricia J. Kelly, Michelle A. Price, Maria Franquiz, and Roberto Villarreal. 2005. "The ABCs of Health Literacy." *Family & Community Health* 28, no.4 (October-December): 351–357.

Mokdad, Ali H., James S. Marks, Donna F. Stroup, and Julie L. Gerberding. 2004. "Actual Causes of Death in the United States, 2000." *JAMA* 291, no.10 (March): 1238–1245.

Monsen, Rita B. 2007. "Child Health Literacy." *Journal of Pediatric Nursing* 22, no.1 (February): 69–70.

Mullins, C. Daniel, Lisa Blatt, Confidence M. Gbarayor, Hui-Wen Keri Yang, and Claudia Baquet. 2005. "Health Disparities: A Barrier to High-Quality Care." *American Journal of Health-System Pharmacy* 62, no.18 (September): 1873–1882.

Murphy, Peggy W., Andrew L. Chesson, Stephen A. Berman, Connie L. Arnold, and Gloria Galloway. 2001. "Neurology Patient Education Materials: Do Our Educational Aids Fit Our Patients' Needs?" *Journal of Neuroscience Nursing* 33, no.2 (April): 99–104.

Murray, Michael D., Daniel G. Morrow, Michael Weiner, Daniel O. Clark, Wanzhu Tu, Melissa M. Deer, D. Craig Brater, and Morris Weinberger. 2004. "A Conceptual Framework to Study Medication Adherence in Older Adults." *American Journal of Geriatric Pharmacotherapy* 2, no.1 (March): 36–43.

National Academy on an Aging Society. 1998. *Low Health Literacy Skills Contribute to Higher Utilization of Healthcare Services.* Washington, DC: Author. (April 2007) Available: www.agingsociety.org/agingsociety/publications/fact/fact low.html

National Asthma Education and Prevention Program. 1997. *Guidelines for the Diagnosis and Management of Asthma.* Expert Panel Report 2. Bethesda, MD: National Institutes of Health-National Heart, Lung and Blood Institute.

National Institute of Dental and Craniofacial Research, National Institute of Health, U.S. Public Health Service, Department of Health and Human Services. 2005. "The Invisible Barrier: Literacy and its Relationship with Oral Health. A Report of a Workgroup Sponsored by the National Institute of Dental and Craniofacial Research, National Institute of Health, U.S. Public Health Service, Department of Health and Human Services." *Journal of Public Health Dentistry* 65, no.3 (Summer): 174v182.

Nielsen-Bohlman, Lynn, Allison M. Panzer, and David A. Kindig. (eds.). 2004. *Health Literacy: A Prescription to End Confusion.* Washington, DC: National Academies Press.

Nutbeam, Don. 2000. "Health Literacy as a Public Health Goal: A Challenge for Contemporary Health Education and Communication Strategies into the 21st Century." *Health Promotion International* 15, no.3 (September): 259–267.

O'Connor, Annette M., France Legare, and Dawn Stacey. 2003. "Risk Communication in Practice: The Contribution of Decision Aids." *BMJ (Clinical Research Ed.)* 327, no.7417 (September): 736–740.

Office of Communication. 1999. *Scientific and Technical Information Simply Put.* 2nd ed. Atlanta, GA: Centers for Disease Control and Prevention.

Office of the General Counsel. "Informed Consent." In American Medical Association [database online]. Chicago, 2007. (August 2007) Available: www.ama-assn.org/ama/pub/category/4608.html

Oliva, J. 2005. "Consumer Directed Healthcare: Zeroing in on Physician Practices." *Physician Executive* 31, no.3 (May-June): 66–68.

Paasche-Orlow, Michael K., Debbie M. Cheng, Anita Palepu, Seville Meli, Vincent Faber, and Jeffrey H. Samet. 2006. "Health Literacy, Antiretroviral Adherence, and HIV-RNA Suppression: A Longitudinal Perspective." *Journal of General Internal Medicine* 21, no.8 (August): 835–840.

Paling, John. 2003. "Strategies to Help Patients Understand Risks." *BMJ (Clinical Research Ed.)* 327, no.7417 (September): 745–748.

Paling, John. 2006. *Helping Patients Understand Risks: 7 Simple Strategies for Successful Communication.* Gainesville, FL: The Risk Communication Institute.

Pappas, Georgios, Vasiliki Siozopoulou, Kaiti Saplaoura, Artemis Vasiliou, Leonidas Christou, Nikolaos Akritidis, and Epameinondas V.Tsianos. 2007. "Health Literacy in the Field of Infectious Diseases: The Paradigm of Brucellosis." *Journal of Infection* 54, no. 1 (January): 40–45.

Parikh, Nina S., Ruth M. Parker, Joanne R. Nurss, David W. Baker, and Mark V. Williams. 1996. "Shame and Health Literacy: The Unspoken Connection." *Patient Education and Counseling* 27, no.1 (January): 33–39.

Park, Denise C., and Timothy R. Jones. 1997. "Medication Adherence and Aging." In *Handbook of Human Factors and the Older Adult,* edited by Arthur D. Fisk and Wendy A. Rogers. San Diego: Academic Press.

Parker, Ruth. 2000. "Health Literacy: A Challenge for American Patients and Their Healthcare Providers." *Health Promotion International* 15, no.4 (December): 277–283.

Parker, Ruth M., Scott C. Ratzan, and Nicole Lurie. 2003. "Health Literacy: A Policy Challenge for Advancing High-Quality Healthcare." *Health Affairs (Project Hope)* 22, no.4 (July/August): 147–153.

Payne, J. G., and Skye K. Schulte. 2003. "Mass Media, Public Health, and Achieving Health Literacy." *Journal of Health Communication* 8 Suppl. 1 (June): 124–125.

Perrin, Karen M., Somer Goad Burke, Danielle O'Connor, Gary Walby, Claire Shippey, Seraphine Pitt Barnes, Rorbert J. McDermott, and Melinda S. Forthofer. 2006. "Factors Contributing to Intervention Fidelity in a Multi-Site Chronic Disease Self-Management Program." *Implementation Science* 1 (October): 26. Available: www.implementation-science.com/ content/1/1/26

Peterson, Fred L., Randy J. Cooper, and Justin M. Laird. 2001. "Enhancing Teacher Health Literacy in School Health Promotion: A Vision for the New Millennium." *Journal of School Health* 71, no.4 (April): 138-144.

Powell, Suzanne K. 2004. "Health Literacy: A Concern for Case Managers." *Lippincott's Case Management : Managing the Process of Patient Care* 9, no.4: 161–162.

Praska, Jessica L., Sunil Kripalani, Antoinette L. Seright, and Terry A. Jacobson. 2005. "Identifying and Assisting Low-Literacy Patients with Medication Use: A Survey of Community Pharmacies." *Annals of Pharmacotherapy* 39, no.9 (September): 1441–1445.

Puolakka, K., T. Mottonen, P. Hannonen, M.Hakala, M. Korpela, K. Ilva, U. Yli-Kerttula, H. Piirainen, M. Leirisalo-Repo, and FIN-RACo Trial Group. 2005. "Predictors of Productivity Loss in Early Rheumatoid Arthritis: A 5 Year Follow Up Study." *Annals of the Rheumatic Diseases* 64, no.1 (January): 130–133.

Quallich, Susanne A. 2004. "The Practice of Informed Consent." *Urologic Nursing* 24, no.6 (December): 513–515.

Ratzan, Scott C. 2001. "Health Literacy: Communication for the Public Good." *Health Promotion International* 16, no.2 (June): 207–214.

Rich, Michael. 2004. "Health Literacy via Media Literacy: Video Intervention/Prevention Assessment." *American Behavioral Scientist* 48, no.2 (October): 165–188.

Riley, Joan B., Patricia Cloonan, and Colleen Norton. 2006. "Low Health Literacy: A Challenge to Critical Care." *Critical Care Nursing Quarterly* 29, no.2 (April-June): 174–178.

Rivers, David S. 2003. "Communicating Risk: Journalists Take Note." *BMJ (Clinical Research Ed.)* 327, no.7428 (December): 1403–1404.

Rogers, Everett M., Scott C. Ratzan, and J. G. Payne. 2001. "Health Literacy: A Nonissue in the 2000 Presidential Election." *American Behavioral Scientist* 44, no. 12 (August): 2172–2195.

Roter, Debra L., Rima E. Rudd, and John Comings. 1998. "Patient Literacy. A Barrier to Quality of Care." *Journal of General Internal Medicine* 13, no.12 (December): 850–851.

Rudd, Rima E., and Alice M. Horowitz. 2005. "The Role of Health Literacy in Achieving Oral Health for Elders." *Journal of Dental Education* 69, no. 9 (September): 1018–1021.

Russett, Beth. 2002. "The Elizabeth West Project: A Health Professional Joins a Literacy Program in Downeast Maine." *Focus on Basics: Connecting Research & Practice* 5, no. C (February): 30–33. (December 2006) Available: www.ncsall.net/?id=241

Santo, Anelise, Andrea M. Laizner, and Linda Shohet. 2005. "Exploring the Value of Audiotapes for Health Literacy: A Systematic Review." *Patient Education and Counseling* 58, no.3 (September): 235–243.

Schillinger, Dean, Kevin Grumbach, John Piette, Frances F. Wang, Dennis Osmond, Carolyn Daher, Jorge L. Palacios, Gabriela Diaz Sullivan, and Andrew B. Bindman. 2002. "Association of Health Literacy with Diabetes Outcomes." *JAMA* 288, no.4 (July): 475–482.

Schillinger, Dean, John D. Piette, Kevin Grumbach, Frances F. Wang, Clifford C. Wilson, Carolyn Daher, Krishelle Leong-Grotz, Cesar Castro, and Andrew B. Bindman. 2003. "Closing the Loop: Physician Communication with Diabetic Patients Who Have Low Health Literacy." *Archives of Internal Medicine* 163, no.1 (January): 83–90.

Scott, Tracy L., Julie A. Gazmararian, Mark V. Williams, and David W. Baker. 2002. "Health Literacy and Preventive Healthcare Use Among Medicare Enrollees in a Managed Care Organization." *Medical Care* 40, no.5 (May): 395–404.

Seidman, Joshua. 2005. *Lost in Translation: Consumer Health Information in an "Interoperable" World.* Oakland, CA: California HealthCare Foundation.

Selden, Catherine, Marcia Zorn, Scott C. Ratzan, and Ruth M. Parker (compilers). 2000. "Health literacy" (Current bibliographies in medicine; no. 2000-1). Bethesda, MD: National Library of Medicine. Available: www.nlm.nih.gov/archive//20061214/pubs/cbm/hliteracy.html

Seligman, Hilary K., Frances F. Wang, Jorge L. Palacios, Clifford C. Wilson, Carolyn Daher, John D. Piette, and Dean Schillinger. 2005. "Physician Notification of Their Diabetes Patients' Limited Health Literacy. A Randomized, Controlled Trial." *Journal of General Internal Medicine* 20, no.11 (November): 1001–1007.

Shea, Judy A., Benjamin B. Beers, Vanessa J. McDonald, D. Alex Quistberg, Karima L. Ravenell, and David A. Asch. 2004. "Assessing Health Literacy in African American and Caucasian Adults: Disparities in Rapid Estimate of Adult Literacy in Medicine (REALM) Scores." *Family Medicine* 36, no.8 (September): 575–581.

Shea, Judy A., Carmen E. Guerra, Karima L. Ravenell, Vanessa J. McDonald, Camille A. Henry, and David A. Asch. 2007. "Health Literacy Weakly but Consistently Predicts Primary Care Patient Dissatisfaction." *International Journal for Quality in Healthcare* 19, no.1 (February): 45–49.

Sheridan, Stacey L., Michael P. Pignone, and Carmen L. Lewis. 2003. "A Randomized Comparison of Patients' Understanding of Number Needed to Treat and Other Common Risk Reduction Formats." *Journal of General Internal Medicine* 18, no.11 (November): 884–892.

Sicat, Brigitte L., and Lilian H. Hill. 2005. "Enhancing Student Knowledge about the Prevalence and Consequences of Low Health Literacy." *American Journal of Pharmaceutical Education* 69, no.4 (August): 460–466.

Singleton, Kate. Virginia Adult Education Health Literacy Toolkit. (2003). Richmond, VA: Virginia Adult Learning Resource Center. (April 2006) Available: www.aelweb.vcu .edu/publications/healthlit/index.shtml .

Smalley, Nina, and Jonathan Scourfield. 2004. "The Potential of Research Project Websites." *British Journal of Social Work* 34, no.4 (June): 591–598.

Smeltzer, Suzanne C., Vanessa Zimmerman, Marita Frain, Lynore DeSilets, and Janice Duffin. 2004. "Accessible Online Health Promotion Information for Persons with Disabilities." *Online Journal of Issues in Nursing* 9, no.1 (January): 61–75.

Stanovich, Keith E. 1982. "Individual Differences in the Cognitive Processes of Reading: II. Text-Level Processes." *Journal of Learning Disabilities* 15, no.9 (November): 549–554.

Starfield, Barbara, Christine Wray, Kelliann Hess, Richard Gross, Peter S. Birk, and Burton C. D'Lugoff. 1981. "The Influence of Patient-Practitioner Agreement on Outcome of Care." *American Journal of Public Health* 71, no.2 (February): 127–131.

Stephenson, Priscilla L., Brenda F. Green, Richard L. Wallace, Martha F. Earl, Jan T. Orick, and Mary Virginia Taylor. 2004. "Community Partnerships for Health Information Training: Medical Librarians Working with Health-Care Professionals and Consumers in Tennessee." *Health Information and Libraries Journal* 21 Suppl. 1 (June): 20–26.

Stiles, Paul G., Norman G. Poythress, Alicia Hall, Diana Falkenbach, and Robyn Williams. 2001. "Improving Understanding of Research Consent Disclosures Among Persons with Mental Illness." *Psychiatric Services* 52, no.6 (June): 780–785.

Sudore, Rebecca L., C. Seth Landefeld, Brie A. Williams, Deborah E. Barnes, Karla Lindquist, and Dean Schillinger. 2006. "Use of a Modified Informed Consent Process Among Vulnerable Patients: A Descriptive Study." *Journal of General Internal Medicine* 21, no.8 (August): 867–873.

Sudore, Rebecca L., Kala M. Mehta, Eleanor M. Simonsick, Tamara B. Harris, Anne B. Newman, Suzanne Satterfield, Caterina Rosano, Ronica N. Rooks, Susan M. Rubin, Hilsa N. Ayonayon, and Kristine Yaffe. 2006. "Limited Literacy in Older People and Disparities in Health and Healthcare Access." *Journal of the American Geriatrics Society* 54, no.5 (May): 770–776.

Sutherland, Lisa A., Marci Campbell, Katherine Ornstein, Barbara Wildemuth, and David Lobach. 2001. "Development of an Adaptive Multimedia Program to Collect Patient Health Data." *American Journal of Preventive Medicine* 21, no.4 (November): 320–324.

Swanson, H. L., Crystal B. Howard, and Leilani Sáez. 2006. "Do Different Components of Working Memory Underlie Different Subgroups of Reading Disabilities?" *Journal of Learning Disabilities* 39, no.3 (May-June): 252–269.

Tappe, Marlene K., and Regina A. Galer-Unti. 2001. "Health Educators' Role in Promoting Health Literacy and Advocacy for the 21st Century." *Journal of School Health* 71, no.10 (December): 477–482.

Taylor, Wilson L. 1953. "'Cloze Procedure': A New Tool for Measuring Readability." *Journalism Quarterly* 30 (Fall): 415–433.

ZZZZ

Tout, Dave, and Mary J. Schmitt. 2002. The Inclusion of Numeracy in Adult Basic Education. *Review of Adult Learning and Literacy* vol. 3. Boston, MA: National Center for the Study of Adult Learning and Literacy. (April 2006) Available: www.ncsall.net/?id=573

U.S. Department of Health and Human Services. 2000. "Objective 11: Health communication - Terminology." In *Healthy People 2010.* Washington, DC: U.S. Dept. of Health and Human Services.

U.S. Department of Health and Human Services. 2000. *Oral Health in America: A Report of the Surgeon General.* Rockville, MD: U.S. Department of Health and Human Services, National Institute of Dental and Craniofacial Research, National Institutes of Health. (January, 2007) Available: www.surgeongeneral.gov/library/oralhealth/

Van Moorsel, Guillaume. 2001. "Do You Mini-Med School? Leveraging Library Resources to Improve Internet Consumer Health Information Literacy." *Medical Reference Services Quarterly* 20, no.4 (Winter): 27–37.

Vastag, Brian. 2004. "Low Health Literacy Called a Major Problem." *JAMA* 291, no.18 (May): 2181–2182.

Wallace, Lorraine S., Edwin S. Rogers, Steven E. Roskos, David B. Holiday, and Barry D. Weiss. 2006. "Brief Report: Screening Items to Identify Patients with Limited Health Literacy Skills." *Journal of General Internal Medicine* 21, no.8 (August): 874–877.

Walter, Fiona M., and Jon Emery. 2005. "'Coming Down the Line'— Patients' Understanding of Their Family History of Common Chronic Disease." *Annals of Family Medicine* 3, no.5 (September–October): 405–414.

Walter, Fiona M., Jon Emery, Dejana Braithwaite, and Theresa M. Marteau. 2004. Lay "Understanding of Familial Risk of Common Chronic Diseases: A Systematic Review and Synthesis of Qualitative Research." *Annals of Family Medicine* 2, no.6 (November/December): 583–594.

Waters, Erika A., Neil D. Weinstein, Graham A. Colditz, and Karen Emmons. 2006. "Formats for Improving Risk Communication in Medical Tradeoff Decisions." *Journal of Health Communication* 11, no.2 (March): 167–182.

Weiss, Barry D. 2005. "Epidemiology of Low Health Literacy." In *Understanding Health Literacy: Implications for Medicine and Public Health,* edited by Joanne G. Schwartzberg, Jonathan B. VanGeest and Claire C. Wang. Chicago: American Medical Association Press.

Weiss, Barry D., and Cathy Coyne. 1997. "Communicating with Patients Who Cannot Read." *New England Journal of Medicine* 337, no.4 (July): 272–274.

Weiss, Barry D., and Raymond Palmer. 2004. "Relationship Between Healthcare Costs and Very Low Literacy Skills in a Medically Needy and Indigent Medicaid Population." *Journal of the American Board of Family Practice* 17, no.1 (January): 44–47.

Weiss, Barry D., Richard L. Reed, and Evan W. Kligman. 1995. "Literacy Skills and Communication Methods of Low-Income Older Persons." *Patient Education and Counseling* 25, no.2 (May): 109–119.

Werner, Perla. 2005. "Lay Perceptions about Mental Health: Where is Age and Where is Alzheimer's Disease?" *International Psychogeriatrics / IPA* 17, no.3 (September): 371–382.

Williams, Mark V. 2002. "Recognizing and Overcoming Inadequate Health Literacy, a Barrier to Care." *Cleveland Clinic Journal of Medicine* 69, no.5 (May): 415–418.

Williams, Mark V., David W. Baker, Ruth M. Parker, and Joanne R. Nurss. 1998. "Relationship of Functional Health Literacy to Patients' Knowledge of Their Chronic Disease. A Study of Patients with Hypertension and Diabetes." *Archives of Internal Medicine* 158, no.2 (January): 166–172.

Williams, Mark V., Terry C. Davis, Ruth M. Parker, and Barry D. Weiss. 2002. "The Role of Health Literacy in Patient-Physician Communication." *Family Medicine* 34, no.5 (May): 383–389.

Williams, Mark V., Ruth M. Parker, David W. Baker, Nina S. Parikh, Kathryn Pitkin, Wendy C. Coates, and Joanne R. Nurss.1995. "Inadequate Functional Health Literacy Among Patients at Two Public Hospitals." *JAMA* 274, no. 21 (December): 1677–1682.

Willis, William J. 1997. *Reporting on Risks: The Practice and Ethics of Health and Safety Communication.* Westport, CT: Praeger.

Wilson, Feleta L., Eric Racine, Virginia Tekieli, and Barbara Williams. 2003. "Literacy, Readability and Cultural Barriers: Critical Factors to Consider When Educating Older African Americans about Anticoagulation Therapy." *Journal of Clinical Nursing* 12, no. 2 (March): 275–282.

Wilson, Jennifer F. 2003. "The Crucial Link Between Literacy and Health." *Annals of Internal Medicine* 139, no.10 (November): 875–878.

Wirshing, Donna A., William C. Wirshing, Stephen R. Marder, Robert P. Liberman, and Jim Mintz. 1998. "Informed Consent: Assessment of Comprehension. *American Journal of Psychiatry* 155, no.11 (November): 1508–1511.

Wittich, Angelina R., Joan Mangan, Roni Grad, Wenquan Wang, and Lynn B. Gerald. 2007. "Pediatric Asthma: Caregiver Health Literacy and the Clinician's Perception." *Journal of Asthma* 44, no.1 (January–February): 51–55.

Wolf, Michael S., Terry C. Davis, Chandra Y. Osborn, Silvia Skripkauskas, Charles L. Bennett, and Gregory Makoul. 2007. "Literacy, Self-Efficacy, and HIV Medication Adherence." *Patient Education and Counseling* 65, no.2 (February): 253–260.

Wolf, Michael S., Julie A. Gazmararian, and David W. Baker. 2007. "Health Literacy and Health Risk Behaviors Among Older Adults." *American Journal of Preventive Medicine* 32, no.1 (January): 19–24.

Wolf, Michael S., Julie A. Gazmararian, and David W. Baker. 2005. "Health Literacy and Functional Health Status Among Older Adults." *Archives of Internal Medicine* 165, no.17 (September): 1946–1952.

Wood, Felecia G. 2005. "Health Literacy in a Rural Clinic." *Online Journal of Rural Nursing & Healthcare* 5, no.1 (Spring): 9–18.

Wu, Helen W., Robyn Y. Nishimi, Christine M. Page-Lopez, and Kenneth W. Kizer. 2005. *Improving Patient Safety through Informed Consent of Patients with Limited Health Literacy: An Implementation Report.* Washington, DC: National Quality Forum. (August, 2007) Available: www.qualityforum .org/pdf/reports/informed consent.pdf

Yancey, Antronette K., Sora Park Tanjasiri, Mary Klein, and Janice Tunder. 1995. "Increased Cancer Screening Behavior in Women of Color by Culturally Sensitive Video Exposure." *Preventive Medicine* 24, no.2 (March): 142–148.

Yen, Irene H., and Nancy Moss. 1999. "Unbundling Education: A Critical Discussion of What Education Confers and How It Lowers Risk for Disease and Death." *Annals of the New York Academy of Sciences* 896 (December): 350–351.

Youmans, Sharon L., and Dean Schillinger. 2003. "Functional Health Literacy and Medication Use: The Pharmacist's Role." *Annals of Pharmacotherapy* 37, no.11 (November): 1726–1729.

Zorn, Marcia, Marin P. Allen, and Alice M. Horowitz (compilers). 2004. "Understanding Health Literacy and its Barriers." Bethesda, MD: National Library of Medicine. Available: www.nlm.nih.gov/pubs/cbm/ healthliteracybarriers.html

Appendix 2-1. Readability Formulae

Formula Name	Sample	Formula	Score relationship to grade level
Fry (Iowa Department of Health, n.d.; Klare 1975)	100 words	The following counts are plotted on the Fry graph (Iowa Department of Health, n.d.) Horizontal axis = average # of sentences Vertical axis = average # of syllables	Resulting point falls in section of graph marked with corresponding grade level
Gunning-Fog (Gunning, 1969; Klare, 1975)	Samples (usually 3) of 100 words	0.4 x (ASL + %age of polysyllabic words	Grade level equivalent
Flesch Reading Ease (Farr, Jenkins, and Paterson, 1951; Flesch, 1948; Institute of Education Sciences, University of Memphis, n.d.)	206.835 – (1.015 x ASL) – (84.6 x ASW)		90–100 = 5th grade 60–70 = 8th–9th grade 0–30 = college graduate
Flesch-Kincaid (Institute of Education Sciences, University of Memphis, n.d.; Klare, 1975)	(0.39 x ASL) + (11.8 x ASW) – 15.59		Grade level equivalent (Used in Word & Word Perfect)
SMOG (Department of Society, Human Development and Health, Harvard School of Public Health, Harvard University, n.d.; McLaughlin, 1969)	10 consecutive sentences from each: beginning, middle, and end of text	Nearest [square root] to # of polysyllabic words	Grade level equivalent
Dale-Chall (Dale and Chall, 1948a; Dale and Chall, 1948b)	100-word sample throughout a book (every 10 pages)	(0.1579 x # of words not on Dale list of 3,000 known by 4th grade children) + (.0496 x ASL) + 3.6365	"4.9 = grade 4 and below 5.0–5.9 = grades 5–6 6.0–6.9 = grades 7–8 7.0–7.9 = grades 9–10 8.0–8.9 = grades 11–12 9.0–9.9 = grades 13–15 (college) "10.0 = grades 16+ (college graduate)

ASL = average sentence length = # of words per sentence = # words ÷ # sentences
ASW = average word length = # of syllables per word = # syllables ÷ # words
Polysyllabic words = words of 3 or more syllables

References
Dale, Edgar, and Jeanne S. Chall. 1948a. "A Formula for Predicting Readability." *Educational Research Bulletin* 27, no.1 (January): 11–20.
Dale, Edgar, and Jeanne S. Chall. 1948b. "A Formula for Predicting Readability: Instructions." *Educational Research Bulletin* 27, no.1 (January): 38–54.
Department of Society, Human Development and Health, Harvard School of Public Health, Harvard University. n.d. *How to Test for Readability*. Appendix B. (April 2007) Available: www.hsph.harvard.edu/healthliteracy/how_to/smog_2.pdf
Farr, James N., James J. Jenkins, and Donald G. Paterson. 1951. "Simplification of Flesch Reading Ease Formula." *Journal of Applied Psychology* 35, no.5 (October): 333–337.
Flesch, Rudolph. 1948. "A New Readability Yardstick." Journal of Applied Psychology 32, no.3 (June): 221–233.
Gunning, Robert. 1969. "The Fog Index after Twenty Years." *Journal of Business Communication* 6, no.2 (Winter): 3–13.
Institute of Education Sciences, The University of Memphis. n.d. *Readabilty Formulas* (August, 2007) Available: http://cohmetrix.memphis.edu/cohmetrixpr/readability.html
Iowa Department of Health. n.d. *To Accurately Calculate Readability with Fry's Readability Graph*. (August 2007) Available: www.idph.state.ia.us/health_literacy/common/pdf/tools/fry.pdf
Klare, George R. 1975. "Assessing Readability." *Reading Research Quarterly* 10, no.1: 62–102.
McLaughlin, G. H. 1969. "SMOG Grading: A New Readability Formula." *Journal of Reading* 12, no.8 (May): 639–646.

Appendix 2-2. Literacy Tests Used in Healthcare Settings

Reading tests

Test Name	Test type	Admin mode	# items	Item type	Admin Train Time	Admin time (minutes)	Score range
HALS		W	191?	WC		30–40 for Locator test; 60 for Full test	0–500
IDL	RC	W & O			Silent reading of text from particular grade level then oral M/C literal and inferential?s	No limit for reading or answering questions (Lee et al., 2006, 1392–1412)	
MART (Hanson-Divers, 1997, 56–69) as identified in (Andrus and Roth, 2002, 282–302)	WR	O		Pronun-ciation			3–5
NVS (Weiss et al., 2005, 514–522)	Sce-narios	RC, #	Originally 21 questions on 5 scenarios, shortened to 1 scenario with 6 questions			For short version, average = 3.4, range = 1.5–6.2	
PIAT-R (Benes, 1992, 647–654; Cross and Fager, 2004)	WR, RC, #, Writing		100 WR, 82 RC, 100 Math*	Mostly 4-choice MC; RC = read sentence and match picture that best represents its meaning	(computer program ASSIST)	60 for text	Grades K–12 or ages 5–19, national percentile rank, standard

(Columns Continued)

Appendix 2-2. Literacy Tests Used in Healthcare Settings *(Continued)*

Reading tests *(Columns Continued)*

Reliability	Validity	Consistency, Internal	Consistency, External	Applicable Age	Advantages	Limits
					Assesses systems navigation, understanding of health maintenance	Length of time to administer. Possibly expense and control over time between test and results
				All	English and Spanish versions (Pawlak, 2005, 173–180, 147) RC—not just WR	Should have private room for actual reading task
	Grade equivalent		WRAT 0.98	High school	Quick; specific to medical terms. Terms on prescription bottle labels so replicates actual reading task. nonthreatening (Pawliak, 2005, 173–180, 147)	Small print Glossy glare No RC
	Criterion $r = 0.59$, $P < .001$	Good Cronbach $\alpha = 0.76$ for English version, 0.69 for Spanish version	Correlation with TOFHLA $r = 0.49$, $P < .001$		Spanish version checked via back translation. May be more sensitive to marginal health literacy than TOFLA. Admin in under 3 minutes Incl. #	May overestimate percentage of patients with limited literacy
Most subtests' interrater reliability 0.94 for both grade and age	2–4 wk test-retest = most subtests above 0.90, some below 0.80	Varied by subtest from 0.46 for age 12s on general info subtest to 0.97 for age 14s on total test	Kaufman Test of Educational Achievement K-TEA; Woodcock Reading Mastery Tests Revised (WRMT-T)	All	LEP individuals not included in normative testing, so may not be appropriate for Hispanics and other populations	Scores have become more variable in years since original (1970) test

(Table Continued)

Appendix 2-2. Literacy Tests Used in Healthcare Settings *(Continued)*

Reading tests *(Table Continued)*

Test Name	Test type	Admin mode	# items	Item type	Admin Train Time	Admin time (minutes)	Score range
REALM (Bass, Wilson, and Griffith, 2003, 1036–1038; Davis et al., 1991, 433–435; Davis et al., 1993, 391–395; Safeer and Keenan, 2005, 463–468)	WR	O	Original 125, shortened to 66, then 22, then 8 (last-REALM-R tested in 2001 on 50 patients (Bass footnote 15 in Shea et al., 2004, 575–581)	Pronunciation		2–7 (1–3 in (Baker et al., 1999, 33–42)	Raw score converted to approx grade range: 3rd and below; 4th–6th; 7th–8th; 9th+ for word recognition test
SAHLSA (Lee et al., 2006, 1392–1412)	WR & RC		50	MC	Minimal	Approxi-mately 3–6	<37 = inadequate literacy (obtained by plotting SAHLSA scores vs. educational achievement and TOFHLA scores
SORT-R (Cohen and Cohen, 1985, 623–626; Shaw and Swerdlik, 1995, 958–960)	WR	O	10 lists of 20 items	Pronunciation	"a few minutes"	3–5 for test;	1–2 minutes for scoring
S-TOFHLA (Baker et al., 1999, 33–42)	RC, #	W & O	2 prose passages (upper GI & Medicaid Applic) with 36 Close questions; 4 #	Written, then oral questions	7–12	Should be substan-tially less than 10 minutes for most groups (Aguirre, Ebrahim, and Shea, 2005, 332–339)	Inadequate 0–16, Marginal 17–22, Adequate 23–36

(Columns Continued)

Appendix 2-2. Literacy Tests Used in Healthcare Settings *(Continued)*

Reading tests *(Columns Continued)*

Reliability	Validity	Consistency, Internal	Consistency, External	Applicable Age	Advantages	Limits
Overall score below 6 implies Grade 6 level (Friedman and Hoffman-Goetz, 2006, 352–373)	Content: words taken from patient education materials and forms	Criterion: compared with SORT, PIAT, and WRAT—strong evidence (DeWalt et al., 2004, 1228–1239)	WRAT 0,88, SORT-R 0.96, PIAT-R 9.97, TOFHLA 0.84	Adults only	Easy and quick to administer. Uses medical terms. Highly correlated with other reading tests (DeWalt et al., 2004, 1228–1239) Adolescent version validated (Davis et al., 2006, 3/16/07)	Available in Spanish; not intimidating (Friedman and Hoffman-Goetz 2006, 352–373)
Good internal reliability (Cronbach's alpha = 0.92) and test-retest (Pearson's r = 0.86)	Positively associated with physical health status of Spanish-speaking subjects (p < .05)	Correlated with TOFHLA r = 0.65		Adults only	High cut-off point for adequate health literacy, so particularly useful in IDing Spanish speakers with low health literacy	May not be generalizable for Spanish speakers from various regions/countries where different idiomatic expressions are used. May not discriminate well for patients scoring above 37
Grade and age equivalents (preschool to 12th grade or ages 4+)	0.99 1 wk test-retest (better with young kids)	0.96 w/Grays Standardized Oral Readings	SORT-R 0.83, PIAT 0.68; Slosson Intellivence Test 0.87	4 years and older	Quick sensitive measure of outcome for individuals in reading programs. Valid Reliable	
Reliability, validity within age groups not reported. Tends to over-estimate reading level (no RC)	Cronbach's a: # = 0.68, RC = 0.97, Correlation between RC & # = 0.60 (Baker et al., 1999, 33–42)	Realm 0.80 total (0.61 #, 0.81 RC) though significant differences in midrange of test scores	(Aguirre, Ebrahim, and Shea 2005, 332–339)		Tests RC & # Independent predictor of patient knowledge of chronic disease/self-management skills, health status, and use of healthcare services	Longer to administer than REALM (Baker et al., 1999, 33–42) No numeracy items (Aguirre, Ebrahim, and Shea, 2005, 332–339) Inapplicable content (Friedman and Hoffman-Goetz, 2006, 352–373)

(Table Continued)

Appendix 2-2. Literacy Tests Used in Healthcare Settings *(Continued)*

Reading tests *(Table Continued)*

Test Name	Test type	Admin mode	# items	Item type	Admin Train Time	Admin time (minutes)	Score range
TOFHLA (Parker et al., 1995, 537-541)	RC, #	W & O	50 4-choice M/C Cloze on upper GI series, Medicaid application, informed consent form; 17 # on Rx labels, blood glucose values, appt. slips	Written, then oral questions		22	Inadequate 0-59, Marginal 60-74, Adequate 75-100 (Wallace and North American Primary Care Research Group 2006, 85-86)
WRAT-R (Reinehr, 1984, 758-761)	WR, spelling, #	O	42 words			5-10	Raw score 1-57 converted to age and grade equivalents (Pawlak, 2005, 173-180, 147) Score Grade 7 implies good reader (Friedman and Hoffman-Goetz, 2006, 352-373)

(Columns Continued)

Appendix 2-2. Literacy Tests Used in Healthcare Settings *(Continued)*

Reading tests *(Columns Continued)*

Reliability	Validity	Consistency, Internal	Consistency, External	Applicable Age	Advantages	Limits
	Good face validity Content validity good (used actual hospital medical instructions)	REALM 0.80 (Spearman's correlation coefficient from Baker 2006, 878–883; Williams et al., 1995, 1677–1682) Adults only Available in Spanish and English		Adults only	Available in Spanish and English. Tests RC & # Independent predictor of patient knowledge of chronic disease/self-management skills, health status, and use of healthcare services (Baker et al., 1999, 33–42)	Longer to administer than REALM, S-TOFHLA (Baker et al., 1999, 33–42) Spanish and English versions demonstrated consistency in 1 test, but Spanish version not examined as thoroughly as English version (Aguirre, Ebrahim, and Shea, 2005, 332–339) Inapplicable content (Friedman and Hoffman-Goetz, 2206, 352–373)
Test-retest "Adequate" "Adequate" WRAT validity: Content: Compared to vocabulary taught in K–12th grades	Construct/criterion validity; age, cognitive ability, WRAT-R, Rasch model, standardized achievement tests, discriminate analysis—strong evidence (DeWalt et al., 2004, (1228–1239) Low face validity (Friedman and Hoffman-Goetz, 2006, 352–373)	Subtests highly correlated with each other	PIAT-R; 0.83–0.90	5–74 years Quick; 2 levels 5–11 yo, 12–75 yo	Well validated and studied—standard by which other reading ability tests are compared (DeWalt et al., 2004, 1228–1239)	Not specific to medicine (Aguirre, Ebrahim, and Shea, 2005, 332–339) Small print Scoring manual confusing, potentially misleading; RC excluded; content too limited to allow generalization esp. in reading, math; words not chosen from healthcare context; not available in Spanish (DeWalt et al., 2004, 1228–1239)

(Table notes follow)

Appendix 2-2. Literacy Tests Used in Healthcare Settings *(Continued)*

Reading tests *(Notes)*

Notes: Statistics derived from *Test Critiques*, Volume VIII, 1991, p. 557 of which explains difference in item numbers from those reported by Andrus and Roth (Andrus and Roth, 2002).

PIAT-R psychometric data derived from *Mental Measurements Yearbook* (14th ed.) and *Test Critiques* (Vol. VIII, 1991)

SORT-R psychometric data derived from Mental Measurements Yearbook (12th ed.) and *Test Critiques* (Vol. IV, 1985)

WRAT-R psychometric data derived from Test Critiques (Vol. I. 1984)

* All ages except on SAHLSA from Pawlak (Pawlak, 2005).

Test Name Abbreviations

HALS = Health Activities Literacy Tests. Educational Testing Services. (May 2007). Available: www.ets.org/portal/site/es/menuitem/c988ba0e5dd572bada20bc47c3921509/?vgnextoid=248eaf5e44df4010VgnVCM10000022f95190RCRD&vgnextchannel=6332e3b5f64f4010VgnVCM10000022f95190RCRD

IDL = Instrument for the Diagnosis of Reading

MART = Medical Terminology Achievement Reading Test

NVS = Newest Vital Sign

PIAT-R = Peabody Individual Achievement Test–Revised (psychometric data derived from *Test Critiques*, Volume VIII)

REALM = Rapid Estimate of Adult Literacy in Medicine

SAHLSA = Short Assessment of Health Literacy for Spanish-Speaking Adults

SORT-R = Slosson Oral Reading Test–Revised (psychometric data from *Test Critiques*, Volume IV)

S-TOFHLA = (Short form) Test of Functional Health Literacy in Adults

TOFHLA = Test of Functional Health Literacy in Adults

WRAT-R = Wide Range Achievement Test–Revised

Other Abbreviations

WR = word recognition (oral pronunciation of words, naming of letters)

RC = reading comprehension

= numeracy

O = oral

W = written

M/C = multiple choice

? = question

GI = gastrointestinal

Rx = prescriptions

References

Aguirre, Abigail C., Nadia Ebrahim, and Judy A. Shea. 2005. "Performance of the English and Spanish S-TOFHLA Among Publicly Insured Medicaid and Medicare Patients." *Patient Education and Counseling* 56, no.3 (March): 332–339.

Andrus, Miranda R., and Mary T. Roth. 2002. "Health Literacy: A Review." *Pharmacotherapy* 22, no.3 (March): 282–302.

Baker, David W. 2006. "The Meaning and the Measure of Health Literacy." *Journal of General Internal Medicine* 21, no.8 (August): 878–883.

Baker, David W., Mark V. Williams, Ruth M. Parker, Julie A. Gazmararian, and Joanne Nurss. 1999. "Development of a Brief Test to Measure Functional Health Literacy." *Patient Education and Counseling* 38, no.1 (September): 33–42.

Bass, Pat F.,3rd, John F. Wilson, and Charles H. Griffith. 2003. "A Shortened Instrument for Literacy Screening." *Journal of General Internal Medicine* 18, no.12 (December): 1036–1038.

Benes, Kathryn M. 1992. "Peabody Individual Achievement Test-Revised." In *Mental Measurements Yearbook*, edited by Jack J. Kramer and Jane Close Conoley. Lincoln, NE: Buros Institute of Mental Measurements.

Cohen, Stanley H., and M. Judith Cohen. 1985. "Slosson Oral Reading Test." In *Test Critiques*, edited by Daniel J. Keyser and Richard C. Sweetland. Kansas City, MO: Test Corporation of America.

Cross, Laurence H., and Jennifer J. Fager. 2004. "Peabody Individual Achievement Test–Revised 1998 Normative Update." In *Mental Measurements Yearbook*, 14th ed., edited by Barbara S. Plake and James C. Impara. Lincoln, NE: Buros Institute of Mental Measurements.

Davis, Terry C., Michael A. Crouch, Sandra W. Long, Robert H. Jackson, Ronald B. George, and Lee E. Bairnsfather. 1991. "Rapid Assessment of Literacy Levels of Adult Primary Care Patients." *Family Medicine* 23, no.6 (June): 433–435.

Davis, Terry C., Sandra W. Long, Robert H. Jackson, Edward J. Mayeaux, Ronald B. George, Peggy W. Murphy, and Michael A. Crouch. 1993. "Rapid Estimate of Adult Literacy in Medicine: A Shortened Screening Instrument." *Family Medicine* 25, no.6 (June): 391–395.

Davis, Terry C., Michael S. Wolf, Connie L. Arnold, Robert S. Byrd, Sandra W. Long, Thomas Springer, Estela Kennen, and Joseph A. Bocchini. 2006. "Development and Validation of the Rapid Estimate of Adolescent Literacy in Medicine (REALM-Teen): A Tool to Screen Adolescents for Below-Grade Reading in Health Care Settings." *Pediatrics* 118, no.6: E1707–1714. (April 2007) Available: http://pediatrics.aappublications .org/cgi/content/abstract/118/6/e1707

DeWalt, Darren A., Nancy D. Berkman, Stacey Sheridan, Kathleen N. Lohr, and Michael P. Pignone. 2004. "Literacy and Health Outcomes: A Systematic Review of the Literature." *Journal of General Internal Medicine* 19, no.12 (December): 1228–1239.

Friedman, Daniela B., and Laurie Hoffman-Goetz. 2006. "A Systematic Review of Readability and Comprehension Instruments Used for Print and Web-Based Cancer Information." *Health Education & Behavior* 33, no.3 (June): 352–373.

Hanson-Divers, E. Christine. 1997. "Developing a Medical Achievement Reading Test to Evaluate Patient Literacy Skills: A Preliminary Study." *Journal of Health Care for the Poor and Underserved* 8, no.1 (February): 56–69.

Lee, Shoou-Yih D., Deborah E. Bender, Rafael E. Ruiz, and Young I. Cho. 2006. "Development of an Easy-to-Use Spanish Health Literacy Test." *Health Services Research* 41, no. 4, Pt. 1 (August): 1392–1412.

Parker, Ruth M., David W. Baker, Mark V. Williams, and Joanne R. Nurss. 1995. "The Test of Functional Health Literacy in Adults: A New Instrument for Measuring Patients' Literacy Skills." *Journal of General Internal Medicine* 10, no.10 (October): 537–541.

Pawlak, Roberta. 2005. "Economic Considerations of Health Literacy." *Nursing Economic$* 23, no.4 (July–August): 173–180.

Reinehr, Robert C. 1984. "Wide Range Achievement Test-Revised." In *Test Critiques*, edited by Daniel J. Keyser and Richard C. Sweetland. Kansas City, MO: Test Corporation of America.

Safeer, Richard S., and Jann Keenan. 2005. "Health Literacy: The Gap between Physicians and Patients." *American Family Physician* 72, no.3 (August): 463–468.

Shaw, Steven R., and Mark E. Swerdlik. 1995. "Slosson Oral Reading Test [Revised]." In *Mental Measurements Yearbook*, edited by Jane C. Conoley and James C. Impara. Lincoln, NE: Buros Institute of Mental Measurements.

Shea, Judy A., Benjamin B. Beers, Vanessa J. McDonald, D. Alex Quistberg, Karima L. Ravenell, and David A. Asch. 2004. "Assessing Health Literacy in African American and Caucasian Adults: Disparities in Rapid Estimate of Adult Literacy in Medicine (REALM) Scores." *Family Medicine* 36, no.8 (September): 575–581.

Wallace, Lorraine, and North American Primary Care Research Group. 2006. "Patients' Health Literacy Skills: The Missing Demographic Variable in Primary Care Research." *Annals of Family Medicine* 4, no.1 (January–February): 85–86.

Weiss, Barry D., Mary Z. Mays, William Martz, Kelley Merriam Castro, Darren A. DeWalt, Michael P. Pignone, Joy Mockbee, and Frank A. Hale. 2005. "Quick Assessment of Literacy in Primary Care: The Newest Vital Sign." *Annals of Family Medicine* 3, no.6 (November–December): 514–522.

Williams, Mark V., Ruth M. Parker, David W. Baker, Nina S. Parikh, Kathryn Pitkin, Wendy C. Coates, and Joanne R. Nurss. 1995. "Inadequate Functional Health Literacy Among Patients at Two Public Hospitals." *JAMA* 274, no.21 (December): 1677–1682.

Chapter 3

Social Practices in Talk as Components of Health Literacy

Charlene Pope

INTRODUCTION

Whose problem is low health literacy? What happens during health encounters where providers fail to perceive their patients do not understand health information and patients do not or cannot identify their lack of understanding? A focus on reading and written texts (American Medical Association, 1999) cannot account for how social biases and particular social practices influence provider and patient interactions in health encounters affected by low health literacy. Most health communication research concentrates on information exchange and relationship building (Street, 2003), but omits the subtleties of social bias, the social practices in talk that involve multiple forms of literacy, and the provider's role in the health literacy event, a more recent concern in communication studies (Ellis, 1999) and in medicine (Schwartzberg, VanGeest, and Wang 2005).

The traditional definitions and identification of health literacy concentrate more on a patient's interaction with text rather than talk or demonstrated understanding. The focus on reading, writing, and numeracy as the basis for health literacy as presented by the National Assessment of Adult Literacy (Kutner et al., 2003) follows the tradition of measuring adult overall literacy in the form of prose, document, and quantitative tasks, a functional approach (Kirsh et al., 2002). Earlier recommendations (Kirsch and Guthrie, 1977) set this definition for functional literacy as tasks involving reading, writing, and calculation tasks as well as affective attributions that could be shared with employers. Later, critics charged this approach ignored or denied the contribution of social contexts, resource needs or inequalities, and other forms of literacy practices that contribute to a person's understanding (de Castell, Luke and MacClennan, 1981; Levine, 1982; Liddicoat, 2004). Most text-based approaches derived from these restrictive functional literacy capacities screen for health literacy associated with word recognition, pronunciation, and reading comprehension of health-related words (DeWalt et al., 2004), rather than practices that reflect how understanding is co-constructed with providers during the literacy event, what people understand, and how specific literacy practices contribute to competent decision-making in healthcare.

Dewalt and his colleagues (2004) suggest that there may be mediating structural and interpersonal process of care factors, beyond the patient's reading ability, that affect health literacy and healthcare. As a result, a functional text-based literacy approach often cannot find consistent relationships between patient outcomes and health literacy. For example, in analysis of health literacy and medication adherence, Gazmararian and colleagues (2006) did not find low health literacy a significant predictor in multivariate analysis despite its association with less adherence, but found an independent relationship between adherence and race within a managed care plan with equal access.

Since multiple confounding factors may affect provider-patient communication during the health encounter and mediate health literacy, microanalysis of communication as a process can identify where social practices in communication create these differences (Heritage and Maynard, 2006). This chapter will examine the need for an expanded definition of health literacy and for additional attention to the social biases and social practices that affect health literacy events during health encounters. The idea of social practices refers to the actions during speaking that invoke roles, identities, status, stereotypes, bias, rank, deference, recognition, differing contexts, disrespect, and relationships (van Dijk, 1997). Such social practices affect speaker and listener ability to attend to, listen, perceive, process, validate, and understand one another.

THE EXPANDING DEFINITION

Systematic review of interventions to improve health outcomes for patients with low literacy found only five well-designed studies and observed that the few available studies had mixed results (Pignone et al., 2005), a deficit that requires not only more research but an expanded definition of health literacy. *Healthy People 2010* has defined health literacy "... *as the degree to which individuals have the capacity to obtain, process, and understand basic health information and services needed to make appropriate health decisions*" (USDHHS, 2000, 11–21), a definition that goes beyond functional text-based literacy. Yet that definition still locates health literacy as a static property or problem of the patient. Although the *Healthy People 2010* health literacy recommendations include a goal to increase the proportion of persons who report that their healthcare providers have satisfactory communication skills, the roles of the health provider and provider-patient participation during health literacy events in health encounters remain unarticulated. Subsequent action plans developed to encourage more effective implementation of the health communication portion of *Healthy People 2010* expand the scope of health literacy and open the discussion to include health professional skills and institutional bureaucratic processes in the improvement of health literacy (Rudd, 2003).

The Institute of Medicine (IOM) report, *Health Literacy, a Prescription to End Confusion* (Nielsen-Bohlman, Panzer, and Kindig, 2004), expands the conceptual framework for health literacy by suggesting that health literacy is a co-construction with other sectors beyond the patient, including the cultural competency of providers, health systems, educational systems, and other societal factors. Additionally, the IOM report proposes that the skills included in health literacy are multiple, including reading, writing, numeracy, speaking, listening, participating in health encounters, using technology, networking, navigating the health system, interpreting health information accurately, advocating for oneself, the expressive or rhetorical ability to argue, and the ability to complain and consent. The list captures a broader view of health literacy as a larger set of delineated skills still located in the patient, while the health literacy skills of providers necessary to provider-patient communication for successful health literacy are portrayed as more general and vague. Without either examples or explanation, the IOM *Health Literacy* report refers to undefined communication failures, a need to tailor education materials, and admonitions to consider cultural contexts. Though communication in doctor-patient interactions has emerged as a major area of interest in medical interaction research (Candlin and Candlin, 2003), less attention is paid to the specific social practices that contribute to health literacy during the social interaction between the patient and provider as the site of health literacy events. From health communication research, Roter (2005) provides a framework that integrates Freire's (1992) elements of critical consciousness (disclosure and reflection, dialogue, and social action) with specific elements from the study of patient-physician communication (participation in medical discussion, patient activation through engagement, question-asking, information appraising, and negotiation; and, taking control and responsibility for health actions) that can be used to identify where provider-patient relations shift when health literacy differs.

Outside of healthcare, from the focus on literacy studies in sociolinguistics, Cook-Gumperz (2006) advises that literacy not be seen as merely a set of skills, but also as ways of accessing and using knowledge, as a set of beliefs or ideology affected by historical, material, and social resources, and as joint communicative practices placed in a particular context, such as healthcare encounters. Building on this vision, Nutbeam (2000) proposed for the World Health Organization (WHO) that health literacy should include functional literacy (as defined earlier), communicative or interactive literacy, and critical literacy (the combination of social and cognitive skills that people use in decision-making and control over their health and lives). Without this more multidimensional vision of health literacy, social biases and social practices remain invisible and unidentified in the construction of health literacy. Without these key concepts, plans for effective interventions are less than successful, as seen in how few rigorously constructed studies of health literacy interventions can be said to affect health outcomes (Berkman et al., 2004). At the same time, differences in health literacy affect the quality of provider-patient communication, as Schillinger and colleagues (2004) demonstrate with English- and Spanish-speaking diabetics.

THEORIES OF LANGUAGE AND THEIR CONTRIBUTION TO HEALTH LITERACY

Differing approaches to health literacy begin with differing theories of language. Where language is envisioned as a universal structure with standard grammar, fixed human capacities, and a standardized way of knowing (Chomsky, 1978), transmission models of communication in healthcare offer predominantly functional views of health communication or tasks related to a dominant medical agenda, and situate the problem of health literacy as residing in the patient. Where language use is framed for specific purposes, the role of unintentional or less than conscious behavior that informs social bias would be excluded. Where language is seen as both a system of meaningful signs and ways of making meaning (de Saussure, 1968), then health literacy would attend to the patient as a listener and their decoding of messages as interpretations as well. Whether this theory of language contributes to a deficit model of the patient portrayed as poor, illiterate and a less than competent decoder would depend on whether ways of making meaning are seen as social practices mobilized in social interaction (Thibault, 1996). Alternatively, language use can be seen as a set of acquired and shared practices that contribute to learning and literacy (Vygotsky, 1978). The tools of language may be written and spoken text, but language in use serves also as a nonmaterial tool to accomplish social goals while interacting (Duranti, 1997). In language use approaches to literacy, social positions and their consequences in society dictate differing access and opportunities for acquisition, so that how one uses language with others serves as an indicator of social class and access to social resources as well as a source of evidence of social stratification (Bernstein, 2000), contributing to the potential for literacy and what literacies are available or possible.

SOCIAL PRACTICE IN THE NEW FORMS
OF HEALTH LITERACY

Increasingly, adult literacy studies employ language use as a social practice perspective (Papen, 2005), similar to social ecological theories in public health (Jamner and Stokols, 2001) in their complexity and intent to address multiple dimensions. Moving beyond reading scales as the measure of literacy, Papen (2005) employs more inclusive definitions of health literacy and encourages the use of more ethnographic methods to understand the health literacy event and the environment in which it occurs. Consideration of the literacy event and the literacy environment in which patients find themselves provides social, cultural, and linguistic contexts excluded previously for the patient whose REALM score was low. The Rapid Estimate of Adult Literacy in Medicine or REALM test is a validated instrument based on recognition of words often used in health information texts (Davis et al., 1993). In contrast, Anderson, Teale, and Estrada (1997) first articulated the idea of a literacy event and literacy environments in the study of literacy with small children. Rather than an exclusive focus on message transmission and text deconstruction in considering literacy, Anderson and associates use the theoretical approach of the educator Vygotsky (1978) from language use and activity theories originally developed for early literacy acquisition, an approach that could benefit those in healthcare who see the provider-patient encounter as a literacy event requiring closer description.

In terms of child learning originally but applicable to adult health literacy, Vygotsky (1978) proposed the zone of proximal development (ZPD) as the space in which children could learn and problem solve on their own and in collaboration with adults or peers through social practices and interaction. For adult health literacy, the health literacy event during a health encounter becomes a specifically situated ZPD where particular patient and provider social practices involve, extend, and validate what is known, understood, and in need of clarification or discovery, a form of sense making found in education (Wertsch and Minnick, 1990) that can be applied to health communication. The systematic comparison of health encounters of patients with higher and lower health literacy could identify the communication practices in health literacy events that contribute to disparities in health outcomes. Most current approaches to health literacy investigation compare health literacy scores based on skills, such as word recognition on the REALM, to knowledge of a disease or lab outcomes, such as glycemic control (Powell, Hill, and Clancy, 2007), leaving the actual talk between providers and patients outside of analysis.

Moving away from health literacy skill lists, Zarcadoolas, Pleasant, and Greer (2006) propose multiple forms of health literacy that can be addressed in intervention designs. Rather than a static definition, health literacy in this framework evolves and changes across the lifespan, involves a wide range of ways of finding and interpreting health information, and uses this understanding to negotiate health decisions within health encounters and navigate health and human service institutions, and participate in the life of the community and society. This multidimensional model of health literacy includes:

- functional or fundamental health literacy (reading, writing, speaking, numeracy skills)
- science and technology literacy (familiarity or assistance with science and technology that lets patients understand what they are offered, how change influences their choices, and the role of uncertainty in decisions)
- civic literacy (the capacity to actively participate in health decisions on an individual and community level, to negotiate institutional and governmental agencies and processes, and be aware of how their individual status contributes to public health)
- cultural literacy (the ability to identify and use their social identity, world view and cultural beliefs as a resource to interpret and act on health information with health providers)

An addition to the model would require:

- language access (the availability of fluency or assistance from qualified interpreters for use in health institutions for those who are limited in English proficiency)

Each level of this model includes attention to social practice, the potential to examine communication, and the possibility of social biases as sources of barriers.

SOCIAL BIASES AND THEIR ROLE IN SOCIAL PRACTICE AND HEALTH LITERACY

Since patterns of racial/ethnic disparities persist in health services (Smedley, Stith, and Nelson, 2003) and especially where second languages and differing literacy play a role (Bazarian et al., 2003), how the patient and provider use language to achieve health literacy requires closer investigation. The burden of health literacy carries a weight of bias that acts both independently and as a contributing factor in racial and ethnic disparities. Patients with less education are more likely to report being treated with less respect (Johnson et al., 2004), and to feeling shamed (Parikh et al., 1996), and more likely to be admitted to the hospital (Baker et al., 2002). As a proxy for low literacy, patients with less education are less likely to be active participants in health encounters (Street et al., 2005). They receive less preventive care even in systems with equal access (Scott et al., 2002). Yet, regardless of their level of experience, physicians who receive little training in health literacy tend to overestimate the literacy of their patients (Kelly and Haidet, 2007; Bass et al., 2002). Kelly and Haidet (2007) found that overestimation of the patient's health literacy occurred significantly more often with African Americans than with non-Hispanic white patients. In this case, race serves as a priming mechanism, though patients from other groups may also have low health literacy. Priming is the less than conscious activation of social bias as a taken for granted way of believing or social cognition (Bargh, 2006). Though little research has examined how physicians perceive patients with low literacy, one study found that physicians tended to perceive African Americans and patients of lower socioeconomic status more negatively, as being less intelligent, with fewer feelings of affiliation, and less likely to follow advice (van Ryn and Burke, 2000), tendencies that would feed priming for patients with low literacy.

Though specific social practices have not been studied in low literacy health encounters, a number of social practices in communication have been associated with disparities and could provide units of analysis for investigation, such as poor use of interpreters (Flores et al., 2003), less patient-centered focus (Rivadeneyra et al., 2000), dispreferences or communication practices suggesting a physician preference for particular types of questions (Frankel, 1990) or patients (Ashton et al., 2003), and inaccuracy in information delivered to one type of patient when compared with another (Ritchey et al., 1995). In other types of communication, social and cultural differences are associated with less control (Itakura, 2001), misunderstanding (Ulichny, 1997), failed narratives (Slobin, 1996), missed cues (Stubbe, 1998), and interruptions (Li, 2001). Particular social practices in talk are thought to position people cueing "who they are," to allow them to build or resist identities, and to signal what roles they are taking (de Fina, Schiffrin, and Bamberg, 2006). Though often dismissed as the sign of an attentive patient and less identified with health literacy, silence as a social practice can serve as a powerful tool and a compelling sign that a problem exists if providers fail to notice that people have withdrawn from a conversation and participation (Jaworski, 2005) or may not understand what the provider is saying. Whether conscious or less than conscious, health providers make a decision whether they will attend to or dismiss a patient's silence. If, as the sociologist Derber (2000) proposes, attention in a health encounter is a nonmaterial commodity for which the participants negotiate, then literacy serves as an additional marker of social stratification or worth, which is likely to prime attention or less attention from health providers.

BRIDGES TO A MORE MULTIDIMENSIONAL
HEALTH LITERACY SOLUTION

The transmission, construction, and use of knowledge during a health literacy event requires communication competence, defined as the knowledge a speaker must have to participate as a member of a social group or within a particular context (Morgan, 2004), such as a health service visit. In the context of a health encounter as a health literacy event, both the patient and the provider need communication competence. How each speech partner uses language with one another works as a mediator in the development of health literacy (Baque-dano-López, 2004), through practices such as clarification, validation, attending to cues, asking open-ended questions that permit fuller disclosure, responding to cues with prompting and elaboration, and the use of re-wording until the goal is reached. As an example of this approach, a study of consent forms used with patients having limited literacy used a teach-to-goal strategy in which appropriate language and linguistically congruent health workers used an iterative approach to reviewing and clarifying information in successive passes until understanding was reached (Sudore et al., 2006). Unfortunately, an observational study of 38 physicians and 74 patients with diabetes who had low literacy found that physicians rarely checked patients recall or understanding of new concepts (Schillinger et al., 2003). Low literacy diabetics whose physicians did check their understanding by having them "teach back" had better glycemic control. As social practices, the teach-back technique as well as strategies for clear communication are now advocated to improve health outcomes for those with low literacy (Kripalani and Weiss, 2006), but included rarely in a medical or nursing school curriculum. Until provider-patient encounters reflect on social practices of communication that include mutual understanding as a clinical goal, health literacy will remain a serious threat to health outcomes.

The technical functional literacy skills needed to work with patients with low literacy are well-known (Doak, Doak, and Root, 1996) and have been adapted to print materials in healthcare (National Cancer Institute, 1994). In a randomized controlled trial, Seligman et al. (2005) investigated whether screening patients for literacy skills and notifying physicians of the results improved their care. Physicians who were told of low literacy status were more likely to try strategies to improve visits and patients thought such screening useful. Yet physicians who received the training felt less satisfied and effective in the intervention for low literacy and patients did not feel their self-efficacy had improved. This mutual dissatisfaction suggests that the intervention left other requirements for health literacy unaddressed. Of greater need, the social practices related to communication competence that contribute to health literacy for such physicians and patients require a patient-centered care model and institutional changes that reward attention to the quality of care for vulnerable patients (Paasche-Orlow et al., 2006). The three principles that Paasche-Orlow and colleagues propose to meet the challenge of health literacy include:

1. Promote productive interactions
2. Address the organization of healthcare
3. Embrace a community-level ecological perspective

Among the institutional changes necessary, the Office of Minority Health (2001) proposed 14 *National Standards for Culturally and Linguistically Appropriate Services* (CLAS Standards) that provide the basis for a social ecological model for culturally diverse patients that would improve health literacy but are rarely integrated into health services. Only four of the 14 CLAS Standards are required by law, those dealing with language access for patients with limited English proficiency (U.S. Department of Justice, 2002), but even these are rarely enforced though part of Title VI of the U.S. Civil Rights law. Patient navigators have also been demonstrated as promising for Latino patients with low health literacy (Sarfaty et al., 2005). The Institute of Medicine report *Unequal Treatment* (Smedley, Stith, and Nelson, 2003) called for the development of continuing education for health professionals to increase awareness of disparities and improve patient-provider communication, an approach that could be tailored to include clear communication for health literacy, the potential for social biases, and the need for more reflection on the social practice dimension of provider-patient interaction. Not only do health providers need to employ teach back with patients, institutions need a feedback loop to clinicians so that they receive continuing evidence of their efficacy with patients of low literacy.

SOLUTIONS

So what must be considered as next steps in the development of interventions to improve care for those with limited health literacy? The Agency for Healthcare Research and Quality (AHRQ) reports that low health literacy contributes to poor health outcomes, including less health knowledge, increased chronic disease, less use of preventive health services, and poorer markers of health status, whether by self-report or clinical indicators such as those found in glycemic control (Berkman et al., 2004). The Institute of Medicine report, *Health Literacy, a Prescription to End Confusion*, provides an evidence-based diagnosis of the elements of provider-patient communication that would improve care for those with low health literacy (Nielsen-Bohlman, Panzer, and Kindig, 2004). Yet effective interventions that apply these observations to activate patients and health providers and identify when social biases affect care remain to be implemented and tested. Until health providers and health service investigators involve persons with limited literacy in the construction of interventions sensitive to social practices in talk, advice for change will remain partial and insufficient.

As an example of community-based intervention using community participatory action research, the *Colonias* Project on the Texas-Mexico border (Olney et al., 2007) applies the National Library of Medicine *Strategic Plan for Addressing Health Disparities* recommendations to involve communities with language and literacy barriers in problem solution. The partnership of *promotoras*, or community outreach workers, with health science librarians provides examples of outreach strategies with promise to increase confidence, capacity, and health literacy at the community level. At the level of provider-patient communication, Kokanovic and Manderson (2007) provide an inside look when immigrants to Australia are told they are diabetics in a small sample, based on patient perceptions from in-depth interviews. Responses highlight what it is like to be told a life-changing diagnosis in a visit filled with complex information, difficult even when there are not literacy and language barriers. The dominant description of provider style was described as hierarchical and nonparticipatory with little attention to literacy needs, yet without recordings of visits the picture remains unclear.

The pursuit of health literacy interventions would benefit from more multidisciplinary perspectives that health science librarians could facilitate for clinical and health service investigators. This facilitation could enable practitioners to understand how social practices in talk contribute to health literacy. For example, the qualitative method called ethnography of communication (Erickson and Shultz, 1982) provides a 360-degree perspective of provider-patient interactions. This qualitative method records the actual interaction, then later plays the encounter for participants as the investigator asks them to listen to the playback and explain what was going on from their perspective and recall what they were thinking, as Frankel and Beckman (1982) described over two decades ago. The comparison of the actual social practices within a health encounter with participant accounts and interpretations could explain how health literacy affects attitudes and behaviors as well as knowledge. Despite its respected place in qualitative research (Katz and Mishler, 2003), ethnography of communication is rarely used in the study of health disparities; its use, as well as other approaches dealing with social practices in talk, could contribute vital information to the development of health literacy interventions that involve both patients and providers.

REFERENCES

American Medical Association. 1999. "Health Literacy: Report of the Council on Scientific Affairs." *JAMA* 281, no.6 (February): 552–557.

Anderson, Alonzo, William Teale, and Elette Estrada. 1997. "Low-income Children's Literacy Experiences: Some Naturalistic Observations." In *Mind, Culture and Activity: Seminal Papers from the Laboratory of Comparative Human Cognition*, edited by Michael Cole, Yrjö Engeström, and Olga Vasquez. Cambridge, UK: Cambridge University Press.

Ashton, Carol M., Paul Haidet, Debora A. C. Paterniti, Tracie E. Collins, Howard S. Gordon, Kimberly O'Malley, Laura A. Petersen, Barbara F. Sharf, Maria E. Suarez-Almazor, Nelda P. Wray and Richard L. Street, Jr. 2003. "Racial and Ethnic Disparities in the Use of Health Services: Bias, Preferences, or Poor Communication?" *Journal of General Internal Medicine* 18, no.2 (February): 146–152.

Baker, David W., Julie A. Gazmararian, Mark V. Williams, Tracy Scott, Ruth M. Parker, Diane Green, Junling Ren, and Jennifer Peel. 2002. "Functional Health Literacy and the Risk of Hospital Admission among Medicare Managed Care Enrollees." *American Journal of Public Health* 9, no.8 (August): 1278–1283.

Baquedano-López, Patricia. 2004. "Literacy Practices across Learning Contexts." In *A Companion to Linguistic Anthropology*, edited by Alessandro Duranti. Malden, MA: Blackwell.

Bargh, John A. 2006. "What Have We Been Priming all these Years? On the Development, Mechanisms, and Ecology of Nonconscious Social Behavior." *European Journal of Social Psychology* 36, no.2 (March-April): 147–168.

Bass, Pat F., John F. Wilson, Charles H. Griffith, and Don R. Barnett. 2002. "Residents' Ability to Identify Patients with Poor Literacy Skills." *Academic Medicine* 77, no.10 (October): 1039–1041.

Bazarian, Jeffery J., Charlene A. Pope, Jason McClung, Yen Ting Cheng, and William Flesher. 2003. "Ethnic and Racial Disparities in Emergency Department Care for Mild Traumatic Brain Injury." *Academic Emergency Medicine* 10, no.11 (November): 1209–1217.

Berkman, Nancy D., Darren A. DeWalt, Michael P. Pignone, Stacey L. Sheridan, Kathleen N. Lohr, Linda Lux, Sonya F. Sutton, Tammeka Swinson, and Arthur J. Bunito. 2004. *Literacy and Health Outcomes*. Evidence Report/Technology Assessment No. 87. AHRQ Publication No. 04-E007-2. Rockville, MD: Agency for Healthcare Research and Quality.

Bernstein, Basil. 2000. *Pedagogy, Symbolic Control and Identity: Theory, Research, Critique*. Revised ed. London, UK: Taylor & Francis.

Candlin, Christopher C., and Sally Candlin. 2003. "Health Care Communication: A Problematic Site for Applied Linguistics Research." *Annual Review of Applied Linguistics* 23 (April): 134–154.

Chomsky, Noam. 1978. *Rules and Representations*. New York: Columbia University Press.

Cook-Gumperz, Jenny (Ed.). 2006. *The Social Construction of Literacy*. 2nd ed. New York: Cambridge University Press.

Davis, Terry C., Sandra W. Long, Robert H. Jackson, Edward J. Mayeaux, Jr., Ronald B. George, Peter W. Murphy, and Michael A. Crouch. 1993. "Rapid Estimate of Adult Literacy in Medicine: A Shortened Screening Instrument." *Family Medicine*, 25, no.6 (June): 391–395.

de Castell, Suzanne, Allan Luke, and David MacLennan, D. 1981. "On Defining Literacy." *Canadian Journal of Education, Revue Canadienne de l'Éducation* 6, no.3: 7–18.

de Fina, Anna, Deborah Schiffrin, and Michael Bamberg (Eds.). 2006. Discourse and Identity. Cambridge, UK: Cambridge University Press.

de Saussure, Ferdinand. 1968. *Course in General Linguistics*. New York: McGraw-Hill.

DeWalt, Darren A., Nancy D. Berkman, Stacey Sheridan, Kathleen N. Lohr, and Michael P. Pignone, 2004. "Literacy and Health Outcomes: A Systematic Review of the Literature." *Journal of General Internal Medicine* 19, no.12 (December): 1228–1239.

Derber, Charles. 2000. *The Pursuit of Attention: Power and Ego in Everyday Life.* 2nd ed. Oxford, UK: Oxford University Press.

Doak, Cecilia C., Leonard G. Doak, and Jane H. Root. 1996. *Teaching Patients with Low Literacy Skills.* 2nd ed. Philadelphia, PA: J. B. Lippincott.

Duranti, Alessandro. 1997. *Linguistic Anthropology.* Cambridge, UK: Cambridge University Press.

Ellis, Donald. 1999. *Crafting Society. Ethnicity, Class, and Communication Theory.* Mahwah, NJ: Lawrence Erlbaum.

Erickson, Frederick, and Jeffrey Shultz. 1982. *The Counselor as Gatekeeper. Social Interaction in Interviews.* New York: Academic Press.

Flores, Glenn, M. Barton Laws, Sandra J. Mayo, Barry Zuckerman, Milagros Abreu, Leonardo Medina, and Eric J. Hardt. 2003. "Errors in Medical Interpretation and Their Potential Clinical Consequences in Pediatric Encounters." *Pediatrics* 111, no.1 (January): 6–14.

Frankel, Richard. 1990. "Talking in Interviews: A Dispreference for Patient-initiated Questions in Physician-patient Encounters." In *Interaction Competence*, edited by George Pathas. Washington, DC: University Press of America.

Frankel, Richard, and Howard Beckman. 1982. "Impact: An Interaction-based Method for Preserving and Analyzing Clinical Transactions." In *Straight Talk: Explorations in Provider and Patient Interaction*, edited by L. Pettigrew. Louisville, KY: Humana Press.

Freire, Paulo. 1992. *Education for Critical Consciousness.* English language edition prepared with the Center for the Study of Development and Social Change, Cambridge, Massachusetts. New York: Continuum Publishing.

Gazmararian, Julie, Sunil Kripalani, Michael J. Miller, Katharina V. Echt, Junling Ren, and Kimberly Rask. 2006. "Factors Associated with Medication Refill Adherence in Cardiovascular-related Diseases: A Focus on Health Literacy." *Journal of General Internal Medicine* 21, no.12 (December): 1215–1221.

Heritage, John, and Douglas Maynard. 2006. "Introduction: Analyzing Interaction between Primary Care Doctors and Patients in Primary Care Encounters." In *Communication in Medical Care: Interaction Between Primary Care Physicians and Patients*, edited by John Heritage and Douglas Maynard. New York: Cambridge University Press.

Itakura, Hiroko. 2001. "Describing Conversational Dominance." *Journal of Pragmatics* 33, no.12 (December): 1859–1880.

Jamner, Margaret S., and Daniel Stokols (Eds.). 2001. *Promoting Human Wellness. New Frontiers for Research, Practice, and Policy.* Berkeley, CA: University of California Press.

Jaworksi, Adam. 2005. *The Power of Silence: Social and Pragmatic Perspectives.* Thousand Oaks, CA: Sage.

Johnson, Rachel L., Somnath Saha, Jose J. Arbelaez, Mary Catherine Beach, and Lisa A. Cooper. 2004. "Racial and Ethnic Differences in Patient Perceptions of Bias and Cultural Competence in Health Care." *Journal of General Internal Medicine* 19, no.2 (February): 101–110.

Katz, Arlene, and Eliot G. Mishler. 2003. "Close Encounters: Exemplars of Process-oriented Qualitative Research in Health Care." *Qualitative Research* 3, no.1 (April): 35–56.

Kelly, P. Adam, and Paul Hiadet. 2007. "Physician Overestimation of Patient Literacy: A Potential Source of Health Care Disparities." *Patient Education and Counseling* 66, no.1 (April): 119–122.

Kirsch, Irwin, and John T. Guthrie. 1977. "The Concept and Measurement of Functional Literacy." *Reading Research Quarterly* 13, no.4, 485–507.

Kirsch, Irwin S., Ann Jungeblut, Lynn Jenkins, and Andrew Kolstad. 2002. *Adult Literacy in America. A First Look at the Findings of the National Adult Literacy Survey.* 3rd ed. Washington, DC: National Center for Education Statistics (NCES 1993-275)/U.S. Department of Education.

Kokanovic, Renata, and Lenore Manderson. 2007. "Exploring Doctor-patient Communication in Immigrant Australians with Type 2 Diabetes: A Qualitative Study." *Journal of General Internal Medicine* 22, no.4 (April): 459–463.

Kripalani, Sunil, and Barry D. Weiss. 2006. "Teaching about Health Literacy and Clear Communication." *Journal of General Internal Medicine* 21, no.8 (August): 888–890.

Kutner, Mark, Elizabeth Greenberg, Ying Jin, and Christine Paulsen. 2006. *The Health Literacy of America's Adults: Results from the 2003 National Assessment of Adult Literacy* (NCES 2006-483). U.S. Department of Education. Washington, DC: National Center for Education Statistics.

Levine, Kenneth. 1982. "Functional Literacy: Fond Illusions and False Economies." *Harvard Educational Review* 52, no.3 (August): 249–266.

Li, Han Z. 2001. "Cooperative and Intrusive Interruptions in Inter- and Intracultural Dyadic Discourse." *Journal of Language & Social Psychology* 20, no.3 (April): 259–284.

Liddicoat, Anthony J. 2004. "Language Planning for Literacy: Issues and Implications." *Current Issues in Language Planning* 5, no.1 (January): 1–17.

Morgan, Marcyliena. 2004. "Speech Community." In *A Companion to Linguistic Anthropology*, edited by Alessandro Duranti. Malden, MA: Blackwell Publishing.

National Cancer Institute/NIH. 1994. *Clear & Simple. Developing Effective Print Materials for Low-literate Readers.* NIH Pub. No. 95-3594. Rockville, MD: NCI/NIH/USDHHS.

Nielsen-Bohlman, Lynn, Allison M. Panzer, and David A. Kindig (Eds.). 2004. *Health Literacy: A Prescription to End Confusion.* Committee on Health Literacy, Institute of Medicine. Washington, DC: National Academies Press.

Nutbeam, Don. 2000. "Health Literacy as a Public Health Goal: A Challenge for Contemporary Health Education and Communication Strategies in the 21st Century." *Health Promotion International* 15, no.3 (September): 259–267.

Office of Minority Health. "National Standards on Culturally and Linguistically Appropriate Services (CLAS)." 2001. Washington, DC: USDHHS. Available: www.omhrc.gov/templates/browse.aspx?lvl+2&lvl1ID=15

Olney, Cynthia A., Debra G. Warner, Greysi Reyna, Fred B. Wood, and Elliot R. Siegal. 2007. "MedlinePlus and the Challenge of Low Health Literacy: Findings from the *Colonias* Project." *Journal of the Medical Library Association* 95, no.1 (January): 31–39.

Paasche-Orlow, Michael K., Dean Schillinger, Sarah M. Greene, and Edward H. Wagner. 2006. "How Health Care Systems Can Begin to Address the Challenge of Limited Literacy." *Journal of General Internal Medicine* 21, no.8 (August): 884–887.

Papen, Uta. 2005. *Adult Literacy as Social Practice.* New York: Routledge.

Parikh, Nina S., Ruth M. Parker, Joanne R. Nurss, David W. Baker, and Mark V. Williams. 1996. "Shame and Health Literacy: The Unspoken Connection." *Patient Education and Counseling* 27, no.1 (January): 33–39.

Pignone, Michael, Darren A. DeWalt, Stacey Sheridan, Nancy Berkman, and Kathleen N. Lohr. 2005. "Interventions to Improve Health Outcomes for Patients with Low Literacy." *Journal of General Internal Medicine* 20, no.2 (February): 185–192.

Powell, Caroline K., Elizabeth G. Hill, and Dawn E. Clancy. 2007. "The Relationship between Health Literacy and Diabetes Knowledge and Readiness to Take Health Actions." *The Diabetes Educator* 33, no.1 (January/February): 144–151.

Ritchey, Ferris J., William C. Yoels, Jeffrey M. Clair, and Richard M. Allman. 1995. "Competing Medical and Social Ideologies and Communication Accuracy in Medical Encounters." *Research in the Sociology of Health Care* 12, no.1 (January): 189–211.

Rivadeneyra, Rocio, Virginia Elderkin-Thompson, Roxane Cohen Silver, and Howard Waitzkin. 2000. "Patient Centeredness in Medical Encounters Requiring an Interpreter." *American Journal of Medicine* 108, no.6 (April): 470–474.

Roter, Debra. 2005. "Health Literacy and the Patient-provider Relationship." In *Understanding Health Literacy: Implications for Medicine and Public Health*, edited by Joanne G. Schwartzberg, Jonathan B. VanGeest, and Claire Wang. Chicago: AMA Press.

Rudd, Rima. 2003. "Improvement of Health Literacy in Communicating Health: Priorities and Strategies for Progress. Objective 11-2." In *Communicating Health: Priorities and Strategies for Progress. Action Plans to Achieve the Health Communication Objectives for Healthy People 2010*, edited by Cynthia Baur and Mary Jo Deering. Washington DC: USDHHS, Office of Disease Prevention and Health Promotion. Available: http://odphp.osophs.dhhs.gov/projects/HealthComm/

Sarfaty, Mona, Christine Hurley Turner, and Elizabeth Damotta. 2005. "Use of a Patient Assistant to Facilitate Medical Visits for Latino Patients with Low Health Literacy." *Journal of Community Health* 30, no.4 (August): 299–307.

Schillinger, Dean, John Piette, Kevin Grumbach, Frances Wang, Clifford Wilson, Carolyn Daher, Krishelle Leong-Grotz, Cesar Castro, and Andrew B. Bindman. 2003. "Closing the Loop: Physician Communication with Diabetic Patients who Have Low Health Literacy." *Archives of Internal Medicine* 13, no.1 (January): 83–90.

Schwartzberg, Joanne G., Jonathan B. VanGeest, and Claire C. Wang (Eds.). 2005. *Understanding Health Literacy: Implications for Medicine and Public Health*. Chicago: AMA Press.

Scott, Tracy L., Julie Gazmararian, Mark V. Williams, and David W. Baker. 2002. "Health Literacy and Preventive Health Care Use among Medicare Enrollees in a Managed Care Organization." *Medical Care* 40, no.5 (May): 395–404.

Seligman, Hillary K., Frances F. Wang, Jorge L. Palacios, Clifford C. Wilson, Carolyn Daher, John D. Piette, and Dean Schillinger. 2005. "Physician Notification of their Diabetes Patients' Limited Health Literacy. A Randomized Controlled Trial." *Journal of General Internal Medicine* 20, no.11 (November): 1001–1007.

Slobin, Dan I. 1996. "From 'Thought and Language' to 'Thinking for Speaking.'" In *Rethinking Linguistic Relativity*, edited by John J. Gumperz and Stephen C. Levinson. Cambridge, UK: Cambridge University Press.

Smedley, Brian D., Adrienne Y. Stith, and Alan R. Nelson (Eds.). 2003. *Unequal Treatment. Confronting Racial and Ethnic Disparities in Health Care*. Institute of Medicine/Committee on Understanding and Eliminating Racial and Ethnic Disparities in Health Care. Washington, DC: National Academies Press.

Street, Richard L. Jr. 2003. "Interpersonal Communication Skills in Health Care Contexts." In *Handbook of Communication and Social Interaction Skills*, edited by Brant R. Burleson and John O. Greene. Mahwah, NJ: Lawrence Erlbaum.

Street, Richard L. Jr., Howard S. Gordon, Michael M. Ward, Edward Krupat, and Richard L. Kravitz. 2005. "Patient Participation in Medical Consultations: Why Some Patients Are More Involved than Others." *Medical Care* 43, no.10 (October): 960–969.

Stubbe, Maria. 1998. "Are You Listening? Cultural Influences on the Use of Supportive Verbal Feedback in Conversation." *Journal of Pragmatics* 29, no.3 (March): 257–289.

Sudore, Rebecca L., C. Seth Landefeld, Brie A. Williams, Deborah E. Barnes, Karla Lindquist, and Dean Schillinger. 2006. "Use of a Modified Consent Process among Vulnerable Patients." *Journal of General Internal Medicine* 21, no.8 (August): 867–873.

Thibault, Paul J. 1996. *Re-reading Saussure: The Dynamics of Signs in Social Life*. London: Routledge.

Ulichny, Polly. 1997. "The Mismanagement of Misunderstandings in Cross-cultural Interactions." *Journal of Pragmatics* 27, no.2 (February): 233–246.

U.S. Department of Health and Human Services (USDHHS). 2000. *Healthy People 2010. 2nd ed. With Understanding and Improving Health and Objectives for Improving Health.* 2 vols. Washington, DC: U.S. Government Printing Office. (November 2000) Available: www.healthypeople.gov/document/tableofcontents.htm#uih (Volume 1. Chapter 11. Health Communication/pdf)

U.S. Department of Justice. 2002. Guidance to Federal Financial Assistance Recipients Regarding Title VI Prohibition Against National Origin Discrimination Affecting Limited English Proficient Persons. Policy Guidance Document. *Federal Register* (June, 18, 2002), 67 (117), 41455–41472. Available: www.usdoj.gov/crt/cor/lep/DOJFinLEPFR-Jun182002.htm

van Dijk, Teun (ed.). 1997. *Discourse as Social Interaction. From Discourse Studies: A Multidisciplinary Introduction*, Volume 2. London: Sage.

van Ryn, Michelle, and Jane Burke. 2000. "The Effect of Patient Race and Socioeconomic Status on Physicians' Perceptions of Patients." *Social Science and Medicine* 50, no.6 (March): 813–829.

Vygotsky, Lev. 1978. *Mind in Society: The Development of Higher Psychological Processes*. Cambridge, MA: Harvard University Press.

Wertsch, James V., and Norris Minnick. 1990. "Negotiating Sense in the Zone of Proximal Development." In *Promoting Cognitive Growth Across the Lifespan*, edited by Milton Schwebel, Charles A. Maher, and Nancy S. Fagley. Hillsdale, NJ: Lawrence Erlbaum.

Zarcadoolas, Christina, Andrew F. Pleasant, and David S. Greer. 2006. *Advancing Health Literacy: A Framework for Understanding and Action*. San Francisco, CA: Jossey-Bass.

Part II

Health Literacy Issues in Special Populations: The Influence of Culture, Ethnicity, Special Needs, and Age on Health

Chapter 4

Cultural Competence and Health Literacy

Misa Mi

INTRODUCTION

Racial/ethnic disparities in health and health care in the United States have been well documented in medical and nursing literature, and cultural competence has emerged as a strategy to address these disparities. Today, cultural competence has become a priority for healthcare providers to improve health status and health outcomes of vulnerable and underserved populations and to break down barriers to health and health care (Betancourt et al., 2003; Anderson et al., 2003; Wolf, Gazmararian, and Baker, 2005; Taylor, 2005). Librarians in academic health sciences and hospital libraries interact with a wide range of individuals from culturally, linguistically, and ethnically diverse backgrounds. In response to the multicultural trends in the society and to the challenges presented to libraries in the ever-changing healthcare environment, librarians need to develop cultural competence and to provide services and health information resources to enhance the provision of culturally effective healthcare and promote health literacy.

This chapter addresses cultural issues related to health and illness, the concept of cultural competence, and some barriers to cultural competence in healthcare. Models developed to integrate cultural competence into different areas of healthcare practice and education are introduced to explore the applications for librarians in many areas of library services such as health literacy promotion. Coverage also includes an outline for a proposed training course that could be used to teach librarians cultural competence. With the understanding of health literacy in the context of culture and language, the chapter reviews how

librarians could partner with community-based organizations or agencies to provide programs to improve the health literacy level of culturally and ethnically
diverse populations. Finally, the chapter presents challenges and opportunities
for librarians to apply and incorporate the approach of cultural competence into
the health literacy promotion and education of health professionals.

CULTURE AND HEALTH

As discussed below, each profession, organization, community, and country has
its own culture. Culture has a powerful influence on what we believe and value,
how we think, behave, live, or communicate with others, even if we are not conscious of it. Usually, we do not become aware of our own culture unless we are
exposed to and learn about other cultures.

Culture is the shared ideas, meanings, and values that are acquired by individuals as members of a society (The Institute of Medicine, 2002). It is the pat-
tern of learned behavior, knowledge, and beliefs transmitted from generation to
generation by members of a particular society (Salzmann, 1993). Culture can be
also defined as the totality of socially transmitted behavioral patterns, arts,
beliefs, values, customs, lifestyles, and all other products of human work and
thought characteristics of a population of people that guide their worldview,
decision-making (Purnell and Paulanka, 2003), and communications and relationships with others. Culture is socially learned or transmitted within and
through the family and is shared by most members of the same community. It is
not static for individuals or for societies (Nielsen-Bohlman, Panzer, and Kindig,
2004) but changes and continually evolves in response to global phenomena.

Culture can shape our thinking and behavior. Similarly, culture affects
responses to illness and treatment outcomes (Amodeo and Jones, 1997). From
an anthropological point of view, people's cultural setting fundamentally shapes
their perception and experience of sickness. As individuals grow up in society,
they are taught how to label their sickness experiences; they learn the cultural
explanations of these conditions, the standard treatments, and the appropriate
responses to others with the same conditions. It is the patient's experiences and
life goals that define the distinction of normal and abnormal functions (Hahn,
1995). People from diverse cultural and ethnic backgrounds have differing systems of beliefs about health and illness. Their health beliefs and perceptions of
illness shape how they think and feel about their health and health problems,
when and from whom they seek healthcare, and how they respond to recommendations for lifestyle change, healthcare interventions and treatment adherence (Culture and Society, 2004). For example, Asian medical beliefs and
practices differ significantly from standard Western approaches (Ngo-Metzger et
al., 2003). Chinese or Japanese people do not typically seek professional help for

mental illness in order to avoid bringing shame to the family. For the Chinese, the family may shield the patient from bad medical news in the belief that disclosing the news may make the patient's condition worse. The patient's family automatically expects healthcare providers not to tell the patient the diagnosis (e.g., cancer). For Muslim patients, medical decision-making typically involves the patient's immediate family even when the patient is conscious and competent. The family may deliver bad news gradually to the patient or may even choose to conceal information (Pennachio, 2005). In light of the cultural influences on interpersonal communications, health beliefs, perceptions of illness, and treatment outcomes, it is important to develop cultural competence when dealing with culturally and ethnically diverse patients.

CULTURAL COMPETENCE FOR HEALTHCARE PROVIDERS

The 2002 report by the Institute of Medicine documented racial/ethnic disparities existing in the diagnosis and treatment of various conditions, even when analyses controlled for socioeconomic status, insurance status, site of care, stage of disease, co-morbidity, and age, among other potential confounders (Smedley, Stith, and Nelson, 2002). For instance, African American patients are more likely to receive less aggressive treatment for heart disease. The prevalence of diabetes is higher among Hispanics, and they have higher mortality rates compared with their white counterparts. Among many causes of disparities that have been explored and discussed, variations in patients' health belief systems, practices, values, preferences, behaviors, and level of health literacy are thought to influence patient and physician decision-making, relationship, and interactions, thus contributing to health disparities. These variations include patient recognition of symptoms; access to healthcare services; thresholds for seeking care and social services; the ability to communicate symptoms and needs to a provider who understands them; the ability to understand the prescribed management strategy; expectations of care; and adherence to preventive measures and medications (Carrillo, Green, and Betancourt, 1999; Eisenberg, 1979; Kleinman, Eisenberg, and Good, 1978; Ngo-Metzger et al., 2003; van Ryn and Burke, 2000). The lack of sensitivity and responsiveness to the linguistic needs and health beliefs of different cultures can impact quality of care, safety, patient satisfaction, and the course of treatment (Anderson et al., 2003; Ngo-Metzger et al., 2003; Aplin, 2007).

People with diverse cultural and ethnic backgrounds need culturally sensitive and competent healthcare. Given the racial/ethnic disparities in health in the United States, it is essential to provide culturally competent healthcare services that are respectful, appropriate, and responsive to an individual's language, culture, health beliefs, and practices. To that end, healthcare professionals and healthcare organizations need to develop cultural and linguistic competence—

an ability to understand and respond to the cultural and linguistic needs brought by patients to the healthcare encounter.

The Office of Minority Health (2005) defines cultural and linguistic competence in health as "a set of congruent behaviors, attitudes, and policies that come together in a system, agency, or among professionals that enables effective work in cross-cultural situations" (para.1). Based on their review of relevant literature on racial/ethnic disparities in quality of care, Betancourt and his colleagues (2003) concluded that cultural competence includes understanding the importance of social and cultural influences on patients' health beliefs and behaviors; considering the interaction of these factors at multiple levels of the healthcare delivery system; and providing interventions that take these factors into account to assure quality healthcare delivery to diverse patient populations. Cultural competence also entails that healthcare professionals be aware of and sensitive to their own values, biases, and power differences with their clients as well as skills in verbal and nonverbal communications (Yan and Wong, 2005). The ultimate goal of culturally competent care is to assure the provision of appropriate health services and reduce the incidence of medical errors resulting from misunderstandings caused by differences in language or culture (Anderson et al., 2003).

As cultural competence has potential for improving the efficiency of care through reduction of unnecessary diagnostic testing or inappropriate use of services (Anderson et al., 2003), it is now recognized by health policymakers, managed care administrators, healthcare providers, social services workers, and consumers as one strategy to address racial/ethnic disparities in health and healthcare. Various government institutes and professional organizations have taken initiatives to promote cultural competence. For example, the American Medical Association (1999) has developed an initiative to establish cultural competence as the "Fifth Physician Competence" and has produced an extensive collection of resources for physicians to advance this effort called the Cultural Competence Compendium. The National Conference of State Legislatures, Resources for Cross Cultural Health Care, and the Henry J. Kaiser Family Foundation (2005) sponsored a Web site—Diversity Rx. The site was designed to promote "language and cultural competence to improve the quality of health care for minority, immigrant, and ethnically diverse communities" (para. 1).

BARRIERS TO CULTURAL COMPETENCE

Although the need for cultural competence in healthcare settings is well established, the integration of cultural competence into healthcare is not yet a reality (Goode and Sockalingam, 2000). Healthcare providers still face a variety of barriers to the practice of cultural competence that can affect patient-physician relationship and interaction, patient interventions, and patient outcomes. In her article addressing barriers to cultural competence, Taylor (2005) pointed out that nurses lack the awareness, knowledge, skills, and organizational support to be effective providers of culturally competent healthcare, and that ethnocentrism and prejudice exist among healthcare providers that prevent them from addressing differences effectively. Other barriers nurses face include the lack of time to handle different issues in cross-cultural interactions, as well as a lack of educational preparation and practical experiences with diverse clients.

Betancourt and his colleagues (2003) identified sociocultural barriers to care at three major levels: organizational (leadership/workforce), structural (process of care), and clinical (provider-patient encounter). Examples of barriers to care at the organizational level include lack of diversity in the leadership and workforce of healthcare organizations and racial discordance between patient and physician. Structural barriers arise when patients are faced with the challenge of obtaining healthcare from systems that are complex, inadequate, bureaucratic, or outdated in design. These barriers include lack of interpreter services or culturally/linguistically appropriate health education material, limited clinical hours of service that are compatible with community work patterns, bureaucratic intake processes, long waiting times to schedule routine appointments or to see the physician at the time of the visit (Ngo-Metzger et al., 2003; Flores et al., 1998). Clinical barriers have to do with interaction and level of trust between the healthcare provider and the patient or family. Clinical barriers occur when healthcare providers fail to take into account socioculturally based health beliefs and practices or the perception of and attitudes toward medical care (Betancourt et al., 2003).

MODELS FOR CULTURAL COMPETENCE

Several models for cultural competence have been proposed to reduce these barriers to cultural competence and to develop and implement cultural competence within areas of practice, education, and research. Campinha-Bacote (2002) proposed a model of cultural competence in the delivery of healthcare services. According to the model, cultural competence is defined as "the ongoing process in which the health care provider continuously strives to achieve the ability to effectively work within the cultural context of the client (individual, family, community)" (203). This ongoing process involves the integration of five dimensions—cultural awareness, cultural knowledge, cultural skill, cultural encounters, and cultural desire. The key point of the model is its recognition of cultural competence as a process instead of an event or destination and as an essential component in rendering effective and culturally responsive services to culturally and ethnically diverse clients. Another concept embraced in the model is that there is more variation within ethnic groups than across ethnic groups (intra-ethnic variation). Campinha-Bacote contended that the model is applicable to all areas of practice, including culturally sensitive research, psychiatric and mental health services, rehabilitation nursing, case management, community services, healthcare professional education, policy development, and management and administration. As noted above, Betancourt et al. (2003) identified sociocultural barriers to care at the organizational, structural, and clinical levels that contribute to racial/ethnic disparities in health and healthcare. To address the disparities, they developed a framework for cultural competence that entails three key components: understanding the social and cultural influences on patients' health beliefs and practices, considering interaction of factors at the three levels of the healthcare delivery system, and providing interventions responsive to various factors facing diverse patient populations.

In the nursing literature, several models of cultural development have been developed to assist nurses and other healthcare professionals in conducting cultural assessment and incorporating cultural data into nursing care plans. Drawing upon these models, Wells (2000) presents a cultural development model that consists of six stages along a continuum. According to the model, change occurs as healthcare professionals and their institutions progress along the continuum from the cognitive through the affective phase. The cognitive phase is characterized by a transition through three stages from cultural incompetence (lack of knowledge), to cultural knowledge, and then cultural awareness. This phase emphasizes learning and acquiring knowledge about culture and its manifestations. The affective phase also includes three stages: cultural sensitivity, cultural competence, and cultural proficiency. During the affective phase, the goal is to achieve attitudinal and behavioral change through the application of the cultural knowledge acquired in the cognitive phase. Progression through the stages of the affective phase requires actual experience working with members of culturally and ethnically diverse groups.

Clearly, the cultural competence models are applicable in many areas of library operations such as services, information access and provision, library management, and professional development.

CULTURAL COMPETENCE FOR LIBRARIANS

In facilities and settings where cross-cultural encounters occur between clients and staff, cultural competence has been highlighted as a required characteristic or competence in interactions with culturally and ethnically diverse populations, such as interactions between physician and patient, teacher and student, social worker and care recipient (Suh, 2004), therapist and client (Imber-Black, 1997), and lawyer and client (Bryant, 2001). Issues of cultural competence have been well documented in healthcare settings and providing cultural competent care has been recognized as an important strategy to reduce racial/ethnic disparities. Many libraries, however, have been slow to respond to the changing ethnic demographic needs of their communities (Gomez, 2000). In addition, there is a dearth of literature on issues of cultural competence in relation to medical libraries and librarians.

The library in the healthcare environment is positioned to play a key role in the parent institution. It serves as the primary department responsible for developing systems and services to meet the knowledge-based information (KBI) needs of the organization (Gluck et al., 2002). The Medical Library Association has developed "Standards for Hospital Libraries" as a guide for hospital administrators, librarians, and accrediting bodies to ensure that hospitals have the resources and services to meet their KBI needs effectively. Given that librarians provide information services to clients whose languages, customs, values, lifestyles, beliefs, and behaviors may differ from their own, it is essential for librarians to understand their cultural surround and recognize the importance of being culturally competent in meeting these needs. With their crucial role in improving health literacy and supporting healthcare providers in delivering effective, evidence-based patient care (Holst, 2000), librarians must be aware of the driving forces which have brought policy and practice changes to the healthcare environment. With understanding and awareness, librarians can position themselves as being "responsive members of the healthcare team" (Foster and Warden, 2000: 20).

Developing cultural competence skills can help librarians interact effectively with healthcare providers and consumers from ethnically and culturally diverse backgrounds and provide effective information services that are responsive and relevant to their informational needs and requests (Mi, 2005). Keller (1996) asserted that

> ... by developing their cultural awareness, community relations expertise and marketing skills, libraries and librarians can maintain and enhance their value in almost every aspect of library service, including access, collection development, staff development and recruitment, programmes and services, awareness, funding, and evaluation. The future role of libraries and librarians depends on their ability to connect with their communities, develop their marketing savvy, and adapt to the changing information needs of their communities. (29)

When librarians begin the process of self-awareness and self-examination, engage themselves in an ongoing process of learning about others, and understand the impact of culture on health beliefs, health practices, and health literacy, they will be in a better position to connect to and communicate with their clients and provide culturally competent information services and resources. Accordingly, there will be improved opportunities for funding, advanced and innovated information services, health literacy promotion, and professional development.

As society has become more diverse, learning about and developing an awareness of cultural and ethnic differences is becoming more and more important.

The process of professional development and cultural competence begins with self-awareness that allows an individual to analyze his or her own beliefs to avoid bias and prejudice in working with diverse cultural and ethnic customers. Becoming cultural competent is not a one-time activity but a conscious, ongoing process that develops in a variety of ways and through various cultural encounters.

CULTURAL COMPETENCE TRAINING

Librarians, working in the field of information service delivery, interact with people from diverse backgrounds. With the demographic evolution of the country and globalization of education and business, it is becoming increasingly important for librarians to respond proactively to the challenges posed by the changing environment and to develop cultural competence. However, many librarians may lack adequate training in understanding the importance of cultural competence and other issues pertaining to health literacy. With proper training, they can develop responsive and relevant approaches, services, and outreach programs to meet the needs of diverse customers.

From the key factors discussed in the literature, the author designed a cultural competency course outline that could be developed and used to educate librarians (see Appendix 4-1). The training encompasses eight modules, each of which may be expanded to fit the needs of a specific audience. The course content includes examining one's own culture through self-refection and self-critique, learning concepts related to culture and the importance of cultural competence, the influence of social and cultural factors on health and illness, and cross-cultural communication skills. The course also covers health information access and strategies for providing and adapting library services and programs relevant to the needs of customers from diverse cultural backgrounds (see Appendix 4-2). The purpose of the training is to develop librarians' awareness and understanding of culture, enhance their cultural competence, and improve their ability to interact appropriately and effectively with a broad array of individuals from diverse cultural, ethnic, and linguistic backgrounds.

IMPORTANCE OF CULTURE IN UNDERSTANDING
HEALTH LITERACY

Health literacy is increasingly recognized as a crucial factor related to healthcare delivery and health outcomes. It is defined as the degree to which individuals have the capacity to obtain, process, and understand basic health information and services needed to make appropriate health decisions (Selden et al., 2000). Health literacy involves cultural and conceptual knowledge, as well as functional skills such as listening, speaking, arithmetic, writing, and reading (Nielsen-Bohlman,

Panzer, and Kindig, 2004). A more complete and in-depth understanding of many issues surrounding health literacy can only be achieved in the context of culture.

Individuals' health literacy is mediated by their educational level, culture, and language background and is based on the interaction of their skills with health contexts, the healthcare system, the education system, and broad social and cultural factors at home, at work, and in the community (Nielsen-Bohlman, Panzer, and Kindig, 2004). The Institute of Medicine report suggests that different ways of learning, beliefs about health and illness, and patterns of communications contribute to health literacy through their effect on communication, comprehension, understanding, and decision-making (Smedley, Stith, and Nelson, 2002). The report stresses the importance of understanding and addressing health literacy within the context of culture and language. Clearly, culture and health literacy are two related concepts. For healthcare providers to deliver quality healthcare, they must be culturally competent and aware of the health literacy levels of their patients (McCabe, 2006). With cultural competence and awareness of health literacy, librarians can better serve and educate healthcare providers and health consumers about these important issues.

PROMOTING HEALTH LITERACY

The 2003 National Assessment of Adult Literacy reports that about 1 in 20 adults in the United States lack literacy in English, that is, 11 million people do not have the skills to handle everyday tasks. The adults deemed illiterate in English include people who may be fluent in another language but cannot comprehend English at its most simple level (National Center for Education Statistics, 2005). Research suggests that, while individuals with limited health literacy skills come from many walks of life, the problem of low health literacy is often greater among older adults, minorities, and those with limited English proficiency (Weiss, 2006; Schwartzberg, VanGeest, and Wang, 2005). For individuals whose native language is not English or whose culture is different from the mainstream culture, issues of health literacy are compounded by different cultures, health beliefs and practices, communication patterns, and technical terms used to convey health information. As Baker and Gollop's (2004) study demonstrated, well-known medical materials recommended for consumer health collections are replete with these technical terms and well beyond the average person's reading ability. Inevitably, these materials can present even more challenges for those with limited English proficiency.

The healthcare system is not the only sector in control of or responsible for improving health literacy and different sectors play a role in health literacy improvement (Nielsen-Bohlman, Panzer, and Kindig, 2004). As health information professionals, librarians can take a proactive role in promoting and advocating literacy through information services, resources provision, and educational programs. They can also assess the unique information needs of culturally and ethnically diverse healthcare providers, health consumers, and communities, in order to provide culturally competent services to meet these needs.

Health sciences libraries have begun to take initiatives to form partnerships with communities and organizations to develop and implement library outreach programs and activities tailored to people from different ethnic groups or with low health literacy skills. Some community-based approaches or interventions have shown a positive impact on improvement of information technology and online access to health information among minority or underserved populations. For example, the Pacific Northwest Regional Medical Library in partnership with the National Library of Medicine's (NLM) Office of Health Information Program Development developed the Tribal Connections program to improve Internet connectivity for participating Native American reservations and Alaskan native villages. The program not only helped empower tribes to make use of the Internet for health and other purposes, but also resulted in the creation of the Tribal Connections Web site and additional funding for other tribal health-related projects. The Native American Information Internship Pilot Project was initiated to help train mid-level professionals from participating tribal communities to use electronic information resources and develop and implement health information access programs. The Tribal College Outreach was established to support tribal college library outreach projects involving tribal librarians from North and South Dakota. Another project, the Tribal Librarianship Project funded by NLM, provided an opportunity for the University of Arizona (UA) Health Sciences Library to partner with the Knowledge River (KR) program of the UA School of Information Resources and Library Science in offering internships in health sciences librarianship to Hispanic and Native American students accepted into the KR program. The program focuses on library and information issues from the perspectives of Hispanics and Native Americans who comprise large ethnic groups in Arizona, but who are currently the most underrepresented groups in the library and information profession (Wood et al., 2005). These examples of the NLM-supported or sponsored outreach programs illustrate how initiatives could be taken to reach out to communities and to make meaningful contributions to current and future efforts to reduce health disparities in minority and underserved populations.

Other health literacy activities in which librarians are involved include setting standards for patient education materials (Harwood, 2003), chairing the Health Literacy Task Force (Kars, 2006), and distributing high-quality educational videos to postoperative patients (Klein-Fedyshin et al., 2005). They have served on the patient education materials review committee (Mi and Eames, 2004) and partnered with hospitals and ethnic communities to create patient education materials in languages spoken by ethnic groups in local communities (HICUP;

South Cove Community Health Center and Tufts University Hirsh Health Sciences Library, 2006). Librarians have also contributed to the construction of Web sites to increase health literacy for populations whose native language is not English. For example, HICUP (Health Information in Chinese Uniting Patients Physicians and the Public) is a Web site creation of New York University (NYU) Ehrman Medical Library, Chinese Community Partnership for Health, and NYU Downtown Hospital Patient educator. The site provides access to quality patient education materials and consumer health information written in Chinese. It also serves as a venue for English-speaking clinicians to communicate with their Chinese-speaking patients through online access to medical literature in the patient's language. Another Web site, resulting from the joint initiative of the South Cove Community Health Center and Tufts University Hirsh Health Sciences Library, contains a collection of patient information resources available in seven Asian languages. The creation of these Web sites demonstrates how librarians can help reduce health disparities through active involvement in health literacy projects and collaboration with local communities and organizations.

CHALLENGES AND OPPORTUNITIES FOR IMPROVING HEALTH LITERACY

There are numerous barriers to improving health literacy in vulnerable and underserved populations. These barriers present challenges as well as opportunities for librarians and libraries.

Quality Control of Health Information

The media, which are increasingly becoming a key source of health information for many people, are reshaping and influencing the cultures of both developed and developing countries. Institutions, organizations, and individuals that form mass media are producing and disseminating health messages to Americans. The quality and quantity of these messages have exploded in the past decade (Kickbusch, 2001). The competing sources of health information from the national media, the Internet, product marketing, health education, and consumer protection intensify the need for improving health literacy (Nielsen-Bohlman, Panzer, and Kindig, 2004) and, at the same time, present challenges as well as opportunities for librarians in disseminating and promoting health information. Librarians can contribute to the quality control process and outcomes of health information targeted to healthcare providers, administrators, and health consumers in various ways. For example, librarians can assess the reading level of medical textbooks to better tailor medical and health information to the specific needs of their communities (Baker and Gollop, 2004); help create criteria for evaluating health information resources on the Internet; verify sources of health information for healthcare professionals and health consumers; provide instruction on how to locate authentic and reliable health information on the Internet; create a consumer health information column in local newspapers; serve as invited speakers for local radio and TV channels; or create a health information blog or wiki for the public. It is clear that librarians' knowledge and understanding of their target audience can enhance their ability to provide quality and culturally-appropriate health information and to facilitate and evaluate information provision and accessibility for maximum effectiveness in different media outlets. Whether the information is delivered via print, digital media, news media, or interpersonal communication, librarians can make full use of their skills, ability, and expertise to help break barriers to health literacy by improving health information quality and making it more accessible.

Health Literacy Assessment

Many assessment tools measure reading skills to determine health literacy levels. Tools to measure other important literacy skills such as listening and speaking seem to be nonexistent. Low health literacy resulting from poor listening and speaking skills may affect patient-physician communication during a medical visit, which can result in an unsatisfactory patient-physician relationship leading to the patient's poor health status. Effective interaction is a reciprocal process in which both the patient and physician play important roles and the quality of interaction can influence one another as well as the nature of their medical exchange (Roter, 2005). Low health literate patients may have very limited descriptive and organizational skills related to oral expression. For patients whose native language is not English, they may have inadequate expressive or spoken language needed to participate fully in a dialogue with their healthcare providers. Some patients who were treated as passive learners in their traditional educational experience or social-cultural context may not be used to the process of question asking, negotiating, and joint-problem solving necessary for a medical dialogue or reference interview process. Therefore, these patients face special challenges participating in the interaction and in giving adequate descriptions of their symptoms, illness, medical history, and information needs. Clearly, it is critical for health education professionals to create and administer literacy assessment tools to assess patients' literacy levels. The necessity of designing appropriate assessment tools points to the implication for librarians to take initiatives or partner with healthcare providers and educators to create health literacy measures of different language skills.

Health Information Prescription

With increasing pressures, healthcare providers spend less and less time with patients during a medical visit and therefore, have far less time to instruct them. Because patients with communication difficulties face more challenges, they have a greater need for clear, simple, and understandable patient education information. The situation opens up a unique opportunity for librarians to present themselves as part of the healthcare team for the patients. Librarians can initiate a collaborative project with healthcare providers by introducing the "Health Information Prescription" (The National Institutes of Health and the National Library of Medicine, 2004) service to them. Healthcare providers can use the service by steering their patients to librarians for quality health information in various formats such as educational videos or easy-to-understand materials. The prescribed information can work to complement healthcare providers' oral instruction and help patients better understand and act on the health information.

Translation of Health Information

Among all cultural manifestations, language is central to social life (Nielsen-Bohlman, Panzer, and Kindig, 2004) and serves as a mechanism for communication (Porter and Samovar, 1991). It is one of the most important differences between many cultures (Argyle, 1991) and the primary means by which a culture transmits its beliefs, values, norms, and worldviews (Porter and Samovar, 1991). Language is also one of the greatest barriers in a cross-cultural situation and "differences in languages and underlying concepts may lead to problems with health-related communication" (Nielsen-Bohlman, Panzer, and Kindig, 2004: 110). To a certain extent then, language barriers account for the low level of health literacy that challenges millions of people in this country.

Education level cannot accurately predict a person's reading level or functional health literacy, especially for immigrants who graduated from high school or college in their native countries. Their English reading comprehension level may be lower than their reported number of years of completed education. Since language is important for both access to and quality of care, health information in other languages can help non-English speakers understand their health problems and access healthcare services. Librarians can take the opportunity to address and overcome health literacy by collaborating with healthcare providers and local community organizations to find and translate health information resources into other languages and make them readily available.

Building Partnerships

Another way to address the health literacy challenge is to get involved in building "interdisciplinary partnerships" (Parker and Kreps, 2005: 84) to develop educational programs and provide resources to increase the health literacy of health consumers and to teach healthcare providers about health literacy issues and how to address them in their practice. Librarians can also play a role as a cultural broker by introducing healthcare providers to culturally specific information about diverse cultural, ethnic, and racial groups which they can use to provide cultural competent care to people from diverse backgrounds.

Librarians often build their consumer health collections or provide information outreach services or programs based on their assumptions about their customers' needs. It is important to recognize that what librarians do or implement may not represent a cause or issue in the absence of cultural competence. Elturk (2003), an outreach librarian, suggests that the first step in cultural competence is to acknowledge that we do not know enough about other cultures. The next step is to seek knowledge from authentic sources and from people in the communities to learn about their cultures, hear them express their needs and issues, and find out what projects or programs interest them. Librarians can play a role by assisting the communities to implement the project and by helping them to empower themselves by providing information that can help to improve their health literacy levels and health communications. That role will provide an opportunity for librarians to become community partners and health literacy advocates.

SUMMARY

The chapter briefly discusses the influence of culture on health beliefs and health-seeking behaviors. It focuses on important issues related to cultural competence for healthcare providers as well as librarians who are involved in providing health information to healthcare providers and health consumers. In light of the important role of cultural competence in improving health literacy, the author maintains that it is critical for librarians to develop cultural competence. To help librarians develop cultural competence, a training course is proposed that outlines key content areas that can be delivered in a sequence of eight modules. The purpose of the training is to enhance and equip librarians with necessary cultural awareness, knowledge, and skills to promote and improve health literacy. Also included is a discussion of some challenges and opportunities that librarians face in their efforts to tackle low health literacy.

No matter whether librarians strive to support healthcare professionals in delivering quality healthcare to people from culturally and ethnically diverse backgrounds or disseminate health information in dealing with health literacy, there are different ways of integrating cultural competence into their practice, provision of services and programs, outreach efforts, and professional development. It goes without saying that librarians play an important role in helping America achieve its goal of being a healthier nation.

REFERENCES

American Medical Association. 1999. *Cultural Competence Compendium.* Chicago: American Medical Association.

Amodeo, Maryann, and L. Kay Jones. 1997. "Viewing Alcohol and Other Drug Use Cross Culturally: A Cultural Framework for Clinical Practice." *Families in Society* 78, no.3 (May–June): 240–254.

Anderson, Laurie M., Susan C. Scrimshaw, Mindy T. Fullilove, Jonathan E. Fielding, and Jacques Normand. 2003. "Culturally Competent Healthcare Systems: A Systematic Review." *American Journal of Preventive Medicine* 24, no.3S (April): 68–79.

Aplin, Greg. 2007. "Once Is Sometimes Too Much. Cultural Competence Can Reduce Medical Errors, Increase Patient Satisfaction." *MGMA Connex* 7, no.1 (January): 21–22.

Argyle, Michael. 1991. "Intercultural Communication." In *Intercultural Communication: A Reader*, edited by Larry A. Samovar and Richard E. Porter. Belmont, CA: Wadsworth.

Baker, Lynda M, and Claudia J. Gollop. 2004. "Medical Textbooks: Can Lay People Read and Understand Them?" *Library Trends* 53, no.2 (Fall): 336–346.

Betancourt, Joseph R., Alexander R. Green, J. Emilio Carrillo, and Owusu Ananeh Firempong. 2003. "Defining Cultural Competence: A Practical Framework for Addressing Racial/Ethnic Disparities in Health and Health Care." *Public Health Reports* 118, no.4 (July–August): 293–302.

Bryant, Susan. 2001. "The Five Habits: Building Cross-cultural Competence in Lawyers." *Clinical Law Review* 8, no.1: 33–107.

Campinha-Bacote, Josepha. 2002. "The Process of Cultural Competence in the Delivery of Healthcare Services: A Model of Care." *Journal of Transcultural Nursing* 13, no.3 (July): 181–184.

Carrillo, J. Emilio, Alexander R. Green, and Joseph R. Betancourt. 1999. "Cross-cultural Primary Care: A Patient-based Approach." *Annals of Internal Medicine* 130, no.10 (May): 829–34.

Culture and Society. 2004. In *Health Literacy: A Prescription to End Confusion*, edited by Lynn Nielsen-Bohlman, Allison Panzer, and David A. Kindig. Washington, DC: National Academies Press.

Eisenberg, John M. 1979. "Sociologic Influences on Decision-making by Clinicians." *Annals of Internal Medicine* 90, no.6 (June): 957–964.

Elturk, Ghada. 2003. "Diversity and Cultural Competency." *Colorado Libraries* 29, Pt. 4(Winter): 5–7.

Flores, Glenn, Murillo Abreu, M. A. Olivar, and Bettina Kastner. 1998. "Access Barriers to Health Care for Latino Children." *Archives of Pediatrics and Adolescent Medicine* 152, no.11 (November): 1119–1125.

Foster, Eloise C., and Gail L. Warden. 2000. "The Health Care Environment." In *The Medical Library Association Guide to Managing Health Care Libraries*, edited by Ruth Holst, Sharon A. Phillips, and Karen McNally Bensing. New York: Neal-Schuman.

Gluck, Jeannine Cyr, Robin Ackley Hassig, Leeni Balogh, Margaret Bandy, Jacqueline Donaldson Doyle, Michael R. Kronenfeld, Katherine Lois Lindner, Kathleen Murray, JoAn Petersen, and Debra C. Rand. 2002. "Standards for Hospital Libraries 2002." *Journal of the Medical Library Association* 90, no.4 (October): 465–472.

Gomez, Martin J. 2000. "Who Is Most Qualified to Serve Our Ethnic-Minority Communities?" *American Libraries* 31, no.11 (December): 39–41.

Goode, Tawara D., and Suganya Sockalingam. 2000. "Cultural Competence: Developing Policies to Address the Health Care Needs of Culturally Diverse Clientele." *Home Health Care Management and Practice* 12, no.5 (August): 49–57.

Hahn, Robert A. 1995. *Sickness and Healing: An Anthropological Perspective.* New Haven, CT: Yale University Press.

Harwood, Kerry. 2003. "Setting Standards for Written Patient Education Materials." In *Reading between the Lines: Focusing on Health Information Literacy.* September 10, 2003: The Medical Library Association Satellite Teleconference.

HICUP. "Health Information in Chinese Uniting Patients Physicians and the Public." New York: New York University Ehrman Medical Library, Chinese Community Partnership for Health (CCHP), and New York University Downtown Hospital. (December 2005) Available: http:// library.med.nyu.edu/patient/hicup/index .html

Holst, Ruth. 2000. "Libraries in Health Care Settings: An Introduction." In *The Medical Library Association Guide to Managing Health Care Libraries*, edited by Ruth Holst, Sharon A. Phillips, and Karen McNally Bensing. New York: Neal-Schuman.

Imber-Black, Evan. 1997. "Developing Cultural Competence: Contributions from Recent Family Therapy Literature." *American Journal of Psychotherapy* 51, no.4 (Fall): 607–610.

Institute of Medicine. 2002. *Speaking of Health: Assessing Health Communication Strategies for Diverse Populations.* Washington, DC: National Academies Press.

Kars, Marge. 2006. E-mail message to Betsy Humphreys, October 2.

Keller, Shelly G. 1996. "The Secret Power of Community Connections." *Reference Librarian* 54, no2: 29–44.

Kickbusch, Ilona S. 2001. "Health Literacy: Addressing the Health and Education Divide." *Health Promotion International* 16, no.3 (September): 289–297.

Klein-Fedyshin, Michele, Michelle L. Burda, Barbara A. Epstein, and Barbara Lawrence. 2005. "Collaborating to Enhance Patient Education and Recovery." *Journal of the Medical Library Association* 93, no.4 (October): 440–445.

Kleinman, Authur, Leon Eisenberg, and Beth Good. 1978. "Culture, Illness, and Care: Clinical Lessons from Anthropologic and Cross-cultural Research." *Annals of Internal Medicine* 88, no.2 (February): 251–258.

McCabe, Jennifer A. 2006. "An Assignment for Building an Awareness of the Intersection of Health Literacy and Cultural Competence Skills." *Journal of the Medical Library Association* 94, no.4 (October): 458–461.

Mi, Misa. 2005. "Cultural Competence for Libraries and Librarians in Health Care Institutions." *Journal of Hospital Librarianship* 5, no.2: 15–31.

Mi, Misa, and Cathy Eames. 2004. "Patient Parent Education and Hospital Librarians." *National Network* 29, no.2 (October): 14–15.

National Center for Education Statistics. 2005. "The 2003 National Assessment of Adult Literacy (NAAL)." Washington, DC: U.S. Department of Education and the Institute of Education Sciences. (January 2006) Available: http://nces.ed.gov/naal/

National Conference of State Legislatures, Resources for Cross Cultural Health Care, and Henry J. Kaiser Family Foundation. 2005. "Diversity Rx." (December 2006) Available: www.diversityrx.org

National Institutes of Health and the National Library of Medicine. "The Health Information Prescription." Bethesda, MD. (June 2007) Available: www.nlm.nih.gov/news/press_releases/GAhealthRX03.html

Ngo-Metzger, Quyen, Michael P. Massagli, Brian R. Clarridge, Michael Manocchia, Roger B. Davis, Lisa I. Iezzoni, and Russell S. Phillips. 2003. "Linguistic and Cultural Barriers to Care." *Journal of General Internal Medicine* 18, no.1 (January): 44–52.

Nielsen-Bohlman, Lynn, Allison Panzer, and David A. Kindig. 2004. *Health Literacy: A Prescription to End Confusion.* Washington, DC: National Academies Press.

Office of Minority Health. 2005. "What Is Cultural Competency?" Rockville, MD: The Office of Minority Health. (May 2007) Available: www.omhrc.gov

Parker, Ruth, and Gary L. Kreps. 2005. "Library Outreach: Overcoming Health Literacy Challenges." *Journal of the Medical Library Association* 93, no.4 Suppl. (October): S81–85.

Pennachio, Dorothy L. 2005. "Caring for Your Muslim Patients: Stereotypes and Misunderstandings Affect the Care of Patients from the Middle East and Other Parts of the Islamic World." *Medical Economics* 82, no.9 (May): 46–50.

Porter, Richard E., and Larry A. Samovar. 1991. "Basic Principles of Intercultural Communication." In *Intercultural Communication: A Reader,* edited by Larry A. Samovar and Richard E. Porter. Belmont, CA: Wadsworth.

Purnell, Larry D., and Betty J. Paulanka. 2003. *Transcultural Health Care: A Culturally Competent Approach.* 2nd ed. Philadelphia, PA: F.A. Davis.

Roter, Debra L. 2005. "Health Literacy and the Patient-provider Relationship." In *Understanding Health Literacy: Implications for Medicine and Public Health,* edited by Joanne G. Schwartzberg, Jonathan VanGeest, and Claire C. Wang. Chicago: American Medical Association.

Salzmann, Zdenek. 1993. *Language, Culture, & Society: An Introduction to Linguistic Anthropology.* Boulder, CO: Westview Press.

Schwartzberg, Joanne G., Jonathan VanGeest, and Claire Wang (Eds.). 2005. *Understanding Health Literacy: Implications for Medicine and Public Health.* Chicago: American Medical Association.

Selden, Catherine R., Marcia Zorn, Scott C. Ratzan, and Ruth M. Parker (compilers). 2000. "Current Bibliographies in Medicine 2000-1: Health Literacy." Bethesda, MD: U.S. Department of Health and Human Services. (May 2006) Available: www.nlm.nih.gov/archive//20061214/ pubs/cbm/hliteracy.html

Smedley, Brian D., Adrienne Y. Stith, and Alan R. Nelson. 2002. *Unequal Treatment: Confronting Racial and Ethnic Disparities in Health Care.* (Prepublication copy). Washington, DC: National Academies Press.

South Cove Community Health Center and Tufts University Hirsh Health Sciences Library. (2006). "Selected Patient Information Resources in Asian Languages." (January 2006) Available: www.library.tufts.edu/hsl/spiral

Suh, Eunyoung Eunice. 2004. "The Model of Cultural Competence through an Evolutionary Concept Analysis." *Journal of Transcultural Nursing* 15, no.2 (April): 93–102.

Taylor, Rosemarie. 2005. "Addressing Barriers to Cultural Competence." *Journal for Nurses in Staff Development* 21, no.4 (July–August): 135–144.

van Ryn, Michelle, and Jane Burke. 2000. "The Effect of Patient Race and Socio Economic Status on Physicians' Perceptions of Patients." *Social Science & Medicine* 50, no.6
(March): 813–828.

Weiss, Barry D. 2006. "Health Literacy: A Manual for Clinicians." Chicago: American Medical Association Foundation, American Medical Association. (June 2007) Available:
www.ama-assn.org/ama1/pub/upload/ mm/367/healthlitclinicians.pdf

Wells, Marcia I. 2000. "Beyond Cultural Competence: A Model for Individual and Institutional Cultural Development." *Journal of Community Health Nursing* 17, no.4 (Winter):
189–199.

Wolf, Michael S., Julie A. Gazmararian, and David W. Baker. 2005. "Health Literacy and
Functional Health Status Among Older Adults." *Archives of Internal Medicine* 165, no.17
(September): 1946–1952.

Wood, Frederick B., Elliot R. Siegel, Gale A. Dutcher, Angela Ruffin, Robert A. Logan,
and John C. Scott. 2005. "The National Library of Medicine's Native American Outreach Portfolio: A Descriptive Overview." *Journal of the Medical Library Association* 93,
no.4 Suppl. (October): S21–34.

Yan, Miu Chung, and Yuk-Lin Renita Wong. 2005. "Rethinking Self-awareness in Cultural
Competence: Toward a Dialogic Self in Cross-cultural Social Work." *Families in Society*
86, no.2 (April–June): 181–188.

Appendix 4-1. Cultural Competence Course

Course Outline

Course Title	Cultural Competence for Health Information Professionals
Course Description	Librarians, working in the field of information service delivery, interact with people from diverse backgrounds. With the demographic evolution of the country and globalization of education and business, it is becoming increasingly important for librarians to respond proactively to the challenges posed by the changing environment and to develop cultural competence. The course is designed in an attempt to help health information professionals and library personnel develop cultural competence and improve their ability to interact appropriately and effectively with a broad array of individuals from diverse cultural, ethnic, and linguistic backgrounds. Upon completion of the course, participants will develop awareness and understanding of culture and develop skills in communicating, servicing, and partnering with those from diverse backgrounds.
Target Audience	Librarians, administrators, library support staff
Length	The course includes a series of 8 modules that last 8 hours. Depending on the needs of the target audience and contextual factors, each module can be expanded and taught weekly or monthly as a series of courses.
Objectives	Upon completion of this course participants will: · Understand the importance of developing cultural competence · Develop cultural awareness and sensitivity in a cross-cultural environment. · Develop knowledge of how culture affects perceptions of health and illness · Develop abilities to interact appropriately and effectively with customers from diverse cultural backgrounds · Develop strategies for providing and adapting library services and programs responsive and relevant to the needs of customers from diverse cultural backgrounds.
Prerequisites	No prerequisites are required for participating in the training.
Delivery Strategies	To create an effective and engaging learning experience, each module can be taught in an interactive approach with the use of combined instructional methods including lecture, class and small group discussion, pair work, case study, personal reflection, individual and group exercises. Instructional media such as PowerPoint slides, videos, reading handouts, and worksheets can be used to deliver the training content.
Materials	· Instructor guide · Worksheets · Reading handouts

Appendix 4-2. Course Module Sequence

Module One—Introduction and General Concepts of Culture
· Definition of culture
· Influence of culture on thoughts and behaviors
· Examination and reflection of one's own culture and cultural bias/prejudices
· Impact of culture on interactions with people
· Definition of cultural competence and benefits of becoming culturally competent

---

Module Two—Culture and Health
· Disparities in health
· Specific diseases or illnesses associated with unique ethnic groups
· Influence of cultural beliefs, practices, values, and rituals on health and illness
· Western model of healthcare
· Family healing traditions and home remedies

Module Three—Stereotypes vs. Generalizations
· Stereotyping/racial profiling
· Difference between a stereotype and a generalization
· Difference between a stereotype and an assumption
· Influence of stereotypes on one's own thoughts, feelings, behaviors, and attitudes toward others
  different from us

Module Four—Special Cultural Factors
· Role of the family
· Perception/view of time
· Spirituality/religion
· Gender roles and sexuality

Module Five—Cross-cultural Communication
· Meaning of words
· Nonverbal communication (gesture, body position, eye contact, silence, etc.)
· Cultural communication etiquette
· Barriers to effective cross-cultural communication
· Strategies or techniques on improving cross-cultural communication

---

Module Six—Socioeconomic Status
· Low literacy
· Level of education
· Social stress and support network
· Change of environment

Module Seven—Health Information Access
· Barriers to health information access
· Working efficiently with limited English proficiency or low health literacy customers
· Approaches to reducing or breaking access barriers

Module Eight—Culturally Responsive Library Services
· Assessing health literacy of the commonly encountered groups of customers
· Reference interview strategies and techniques during cross-cultural encounters
· Library instruction incorporating unique instructional strategies in teaching culturally
  diverse library customers
· Ways to integrate cultural competence into library services, resources, and activities/programs

Chapter 5

Impact of Patient Low Literacy on the Individual and Family

Feleta L. Wilson

This chapter presents information on some of the populations most affected by low literacy, as well as the impact of low literacy on the patient and the family. In addition, the association between low literacy and health disparities is briefly addressed, as well as the need for developing partnerships between nurses and librarians to meet the complex needs of consumers who have difficulty reading and understanding health information.

Nearly two decades ago, Garcia (1988) described illiteracy as an epidemic that presents no symptoms and can result in serious consequences. The broad complexities of low health literacy are manifested in a variety of situations. For example, literacy level is not only a determinant of success in our society, but the lack of adequate literacy skills is highly correlated with a host of negative outcomes for the individual (Wilson and Williams, 2003), family (Weiss and Palmer, 2004), and the healthcare delivery system (Weiss et al., 1994).

Health literacy is a relatively new phenomenon in healthcare education, delivery, and research. Only within the last decade have researchers identified the problems associated with health literacy, the role it plays in an individual's ability to comprehend health and self-care information, and its relationship to health outcomes. Clarifying the concept is essential so that nurses and librarians can engage in developing an awareness of the phenomenon and its relationship to the outcomes of communication and health education efforts.

The nation's healthcare system is becoming more population-based—that is, people are paying more attention to risk factors in both their physical and social environments. This vision is made tangible in the U.S. Department of Health and Human Service's (USDHHS) *Healthy People 2010* (USDHHS, 2000a), a government sponsored national health promotion and disease prevention initiative that has two overarching goals including increasing "the quality and years of healthy life" and "eliminating disparities" (para. 1). One of the new objectives, in the 2010 version, specifically focuses on health literacy. Objective 11-2 (USDHHS, 2000b) states:

- "(Developmental) Improve the health literacy of persons with inadequate or marginal literacy skills."

The new objective emphasizes two key areas to attain measurable improvements. One is to develop appropriate written materials for audiences with limited literacy, while the other is to improve the reading skills of persons with limited literacy. To address these issues, health professionals can use existing resources to create plain language health communication targeted to this population. Professional publications and federal documents already provide the necessary criteria. Health literacy programs can be tailored to target skill improvement and could be offered through a variety of organizations, such as libraries, schools, and community groups.

THE IMPACT OF LOW LITERACY ON THE PATIENT

The term "health literacy" continues to evolve as nurses, physicians, health educators, and library practitioners attempt to identify a multitude of barriers facing low-literacy patients. General health literacy means knowing how to read, comprehend, and act on health-related printed or written materials (Doak, Doak, and Root, 1993). However, being able to take the health information and utilize those skills in the workplace, at home with the family, and in the community completes the health literacy continuum. While professionals are struggling to meet the information and learning needs of patients with low literacy, our patients continue to be challenged by labels on medication bottles, appointment slips, HIPAA guidelines, and informed consent forms. Completing required health forms; following recommended regimens; interacting with healthcare providers; and reading appointment slips and discharge instruction sheets, insurance applications, and basic health education documents have been identified by Baker and colleagues (1996) as major barriers patients with low literacy skills face in their attempts to navigate the healthcare system. Studies have addressed the difficulty of patients disclosing their limited reading skills because of the shame and embarrassment that further complicates the relationship and communication between the patient and provider (Parikh et al., 1996).

INDIVIDUALS WITH LOW LITERACY SKILLS: WHO ARE THEY?

It is difficult to identify a person with poor reading skills. In addition, self-reports of highest grade completed in school should not be the gold standard for determining literacy levels. Health professionals cannot assume that they can recognize patients with this deficit, because many patients are able to hide their limitation.

Many people with low literacy skills can be found among high school dropouts, immigrants, minorities, and prison inmates. The National Center for Education Statistics (2001) cites alarming statistics for high school dropouts. "Five out of every 100 young adults enrolled in high school in October 1999 left school before October 2000 without successfully completing a high school program" (para. 3). The percentage of students who eventually dropped out decreased from 1972 through 1987. With minimal changes from year to year, the dropout rate has remained relatively flat since 1987. From 1990 through 2001, between 347,000 and 544,000 students in grades 10 through 12 left school each year without successfully completing a high school program (para. 6). Further results showed that in 2001, students living in low-income families were six times more likely than their peers in high-income families to drop out of high school over the one-year period from October 2000 to 2001. About three-fourths (77.3 percent) of the dropouts in 2001 were ages 15 through 18 and about two-fifths (42.5 percent) were ages 15 through 17 (para. 4–5). This group encounters problems when they enter the healthcare system as adults, because health professionals rely heavily on written documents, pamphlets, and brochures as tools to educate patients. These tools, which health professionals view as helpful, are barriers for poor readers.

Other groups in the population likely to have low literacy skills are immigrants and incarcerated individuals. According to Comings (2001), Kirsch and his colleagues (1993) in the National Adult Literacy Survey, and the more recent National Assessment of Adult Literacy (NAAL) (Kutner et al., 2006), immigrants comprise a disproportionate total of the dropouts. Immigrants who have limited English language skills and may have been poorly educated in their native lands are now faced with trying to understand a different language as well as unfamiliar medical jargon, which adds to their confusion.

Haigler, Harlow, O'Connor, and Campbell (1994) conducted literacy level proficiency tests in several prisons across the country. Their scale ranged from the lowest reading skill (Level 1) to highest reading skill (Level 5). They found that one-third of the prison population demonstrated lower literacy skills than did the general public. Thirty-one percent scored at Level 1 on the prose scale, 33 percent at Level 1 for document literacy, and 40 percent at the lowest level on the quantitative scale.

A third population included in the NAAL study was the elderly (Kutner et al., 2006). They were assessed using measurements of "Below Basic skills, Basic skills, Intermediate skills, and Proficient literacy skills" on document, prose, and quantitative literacy. A higher percentage of adults 65 years and older had Below Basic skills and Basic skills. In addition, the NAAL reported that those 65 years and older had lower literacy levels than did their younger counterparts. Age-associated cognitive deficits and poor literacy skills make it difficult for this group to understand basic health instructions and fundamental information. Thus, they present a significant challenge for those involved in health education or the provision of health information.

Minorities, the elderly, and those individuals who live in poverty and have no insurance or are on Medicare/Medicaid, as well as those in urban settings are most likely to have low literacy skills (Kutner et al., 2006). These individuals tend to seek healthcare when they are very ill, usually do not engage in health promotion activities, and frequently use the emergency room as a resource and entry point for primary care (Wilson, Brown, and Stephen-Ferris, 2006). Unfortunately, this population often carries the burden of poor health outcomes and is more susceptible to healthcare disparities.

FAMILY HEALTH LITERACY

"Family literacy" can be defined in several ways. Literacy involves the communication process of reading, writing, speaking, and listening, but the first element, reading, is primary (Handel, 1999). Family literacy generally relates to parents engaged in their children's learning and development with the assistance of community systems, such as the schools. However, low-literacy parents try to avoid getting involved with community organizations or schools because of their reading deficit.

Today, many other social factors also influence the family and its structure. For example, the two-parent family may not be the norm in many communities. The single-parent factor changes several social dynamics and often the availability of resources, since many single mothers are young, unmarried, and tend to be poor (Handel, 1999). The role structure, communication patterns, and support networks may be different in the single parent family. Handel mentions four major categories that promote children's development and literacy: *opportunities* for learning, *recognition* of the parental role in the learning process, the level of *interaction* between the parent and child, and *modeling*, which refers to the parent's behavior. All of these categories may suffer as a result of a parent's low literacy skills.

Family literacy benefits the children, parents, families, and society. One of the strengths of a society is the status of the family and its responsibility toward obtaining healthcare for each of its members. A stable and well-structured family also encourages growth, development, freedom, and autonomy among its members. Self-reliance, self-management, intellectual growth, and the development of social skills all help determine the family's health status. According to Yin, Forbis, and Dreyer (2007), within the healthcare community there is a growing interest in the impact of the health literacy levels on the family.

Although there are a limited number of studies in the literature that specifically address "family health literacy" as a phenomenon, healthcare professionals who work with families understand the importance of having both patients and families who are knowledgeable about their health conditions, illnesses, and treatments. From a nursing standpoint, educating the child and parents about the importance of adhering to the recommended diet when the child has been diagnosed with diabetes, or teaching the parents how to properly medicate a child who has asthma, or even having parents who are knowledgeable about their child's immunizations is a critical step toward self-care and well-being.

Nurse practitioners and other clinicians have difficulty identifying parents and children with limited reading skills (Doak, Doak, and Root, 1996). To assist with the assessment of literacy, several strategies and evaluation tools are available. In 2006, Morris and colleagues developed a questionnaire called the Single-Item Literacy Screener (SILS). This instrument uses a question: "How often do you need to have someone help you when you read instructions?" As a simple single-item questionnaire, this tool is time-efficient and can be used in the clinical setting. Another instrument, the Rapid Estimate of Adolescent Literacy in Medicine— TEEN (Davis et al., 2006) can be used to assess the pediatric population. Similar to the original REALM for adults, the TEEN version contains 66 words arranged in increasing order of difficulty. The words used in the instrument were taken from a list of 116 terms found in the American Academy of Pediatrics' adolescent patient education materials.

Nurses working in the community and making home visits can observe for the presence of books in the home. Sanders, Zacur, Haecker, and Kloss (2004) conducted a cross-sectional study of parents in six-inner city clinics and reported that the presence of ten or more children's or adult books in the home was a positive indicator of adequate parental health literacy.

Screening the literacy level of parents and children should be an integral part of the initial health assessment. Other methods can be used to ensure that families leaving the clinic or the clinician's office understand what they have been taught. Parents and children often have difficulty understanding both verbal and written instructions. Therefore, visual and oral reinforcements, including the teach-back method, should be used. The teach-back method has been recommended by experts in health literacy to ensure that the patient or the family comprehends health-related instructions (Schillinger et al., 2003). This method allows for immediate feedback from the patient so that the healthcare provider can restate instructions that were incorrectly understood.

HEALTH DISPARITIES ASSOCIATED WITH
LOW LITERACY PATIENTS

The official definition of health disparities, developed in September 1999, states that "health disparities are differences in the incidence, prevalence, mortality, and burden of diseases and other adverse health conditions that exist among specific populations groups in the United States" (National Cancer Institute, n.d., para. 2). Literacy and health disparities are not two separate issues. In fact, low literacy may be a precursor to and condition of health disparities. Interventions to increase communications, improve access to health information, promote the understanding of meaning from facts, and engage transitions from knowledge to actions are likely to reduce the negative impact of low literacy on patients' access and use of health services (Nielsen-Bohlman, Panzer, and Kindig, 2004).

A summary of *Literacy and Health Outcomes*, which was prepared by the Agency for Health Research and Quality's Evidence-based Practice Center (RTI International, 2004), clearly pinpoints the influences of low literacy on the patient as well as the healthcare environment. Dr. Carolyn Clancy, director of the Agency, believes that low literacy plays a primary role in health disparities and may be viewed as a barrier to accessing basic healthcare services.

The Department of Health and Human Services (DHHS) has identified six focus areas in which racial and ethnic minorities experience serious disparities: infant mortality, cancer screening, cancer management, cardiovascular disease, HIV infections/AIDS, and immunizations. To address these disparities, the National Institute of Nursing Research (2007) has created a five-year program that establishes eight centers across the nation. The centers will develop partnerships with nursing schools that are developing research programs investigating disparities and have a significant number of minority students enrolled. These partnerships are aimed at aggressively studying health imbalances.

Baker et al. (2007) examined the cause-specific mortality disparity with the elderly. Patients with low literacy have limited knowledge about healthcare and are often poor managers of their chronic conditions. According to the authors, people with low levels of health literacy use health preventive services less often and have poor health status. The authors found that 2,094 elderly patients had adequate reading skills, 366 had marginal reading levels, and 800 participants had inadequate levels. Participants with inadequate health literacy had higher risk-adjusted rates of cardiovascular death but not of death due to cancer. Inadequate health literacy, as measured by reading skills, independently predicts all-cause mortality and cardiovascular death among community-dwelling elderly persons.

Reading skills are a more powerful variable than education for examining the association between socioeconomic status and health.

PARTNERSHIPS BETWEEN NURSES AND LIBRARIANS

The transition from a paternalistic model of healthcare delivery to a more individual and personal responsibility mode places greater emphasis on the need to understand the impact of low literacy on healthcare and healthcare delivery. New strategies are being developed to meet the needs of low-literacy patients. The strategies include:

- exploring new methods of patient instructions and health teaching (i.e., DVDs, tape recordings, video);
- creating partnerships with a variety of disciplines to address the complex need of low-literacy patients;
- assessing patient learning using such methods as the "teach-back" or show me procedure;
- using plain language when communicating with patients;
- changing healthcare policies; and
- making an effort to contain healthcare costs.

More and more, nurses and librarians are forming a natural partnership that focuses on meeting the needs of patients (Barnard, Nash, and O'Brien, 2005). Nurses are expected to keep abreast of current health information for the purposes of patient teaching and education. Yet given their work environment and time constraints, seeking out the right information at the right time may be difficult. Partnering with librarians can improve access to information tailored to the needs of patients with low literacy. The librarian, who is the gatekeeper to vital information, serves as an invaluable resource and can provide nurses with additional tools such as videos or audio recordings to supplement patient teaching.

Ideally, public or community health nurses, clinic or community health center nurses, and parish nurses can readily partner with public librarians. With the help of librarians, they can plan and implement appropriate health education programs to meet the health information needs of people living in the neighborhoods. These programs can be offered in the library, which is often seen as a neutral environment. In addition, libraries contain easy-to-read health information that can be used to teach people attending these sessions. Furthermore, the nurse and the librarian can visit churches, public housing units, senior citizen complexes, and youth community centers with easy-to-read health-related books, videos, or DVDs from the library, and lead discussions on general topics of health promotion and disease prevention.

To attain healthy communities, a theme of *Healthy People 2010*, a multidisciplinary approach is needed to minimize health disparities, promote health, prevent diseases, and improve access to healthcare, particularly among this nation's most vulnerable populations-those with low literacy skills. Access to reader-appropriate health information empowers the patient to make decisions about his or her healthcare, enables the patient and family to better communicate with the provider, and reduces barriers to care. These factors are vital in creating healthy people in healthy communities.

REFERENCES

Baker, David W., Ruth M. Parker, Mark V. Williams, Kathryn Pitkin, Nina S. Parikh, Wendy Coates, and M. Imara. 1996. "The Health Care Experience of Patients with Low Literacy." *Archives of Family Medicine* 5, no.6 (June): 329–334.

Baker, David, Michael S. Wolf, Joseph Feinglass, Jason A. Thompson, Julie A. Gazmarian, and Jenny Huang. 2007. "Health Literacy and Mortality among Elderly Persons." *Archives of Internal Medicine*, 167, no.114 (July): 1503–1509.

Barnard, Alan, Robyn Nash, and Michael O'Brien. 2005. "Information Literacy: Developing Lifelong through Nursing Education." *Journal of Nursing Education* 44, no.11 (November): 505–510.

Comings, John, Stephen Reder, and Andrew Sum. 2001. *Building a Level Playing Field: The Need to Expand and Improve the National and State Adult Education and Literacy Systems*. NCSALL Occasional Report. Cambridge, MA: National Center for the Study of Adult Learning and Literacy, Harvard Graduate School of Education. Available: www.ncsall .net/file admin/resources/research/op_comings2 .pdf

Davis, Terry C., Michael S. Wolf, Connie L. Arnold, Robert S. Byrd, Sandra W. Long, Thomas Springer, Estela Kennen, and Joseph A. Bocchini. 2006. "Development and Validation of the Rapid Estimate of Adolescent Literacy in Medicine (REALM-TEEN): A Tool to Screen Adolescents for Below-Grade Reading in Health Care Settings." *Pediatrics* 118, no.6 (December): e1707-e1714. Available: www.pediatrics.appublications .org/cgi/content/full/118/6/e1707

Doak, Cecilia C., Leonard G. Doak, and Jane H. Root. 1996. *Teaching Patients with Low-literacy Skills*. 2nd ed. Philadelphia: J.B. Lippincott.

Garcia, D. 1988. "Illiteracy and its Effect on Medical Care." *California Physician* 5, (November): 50–53.

Haigler, Karl, Caroline W. Harlow, Patricia E. O'Connor, and Anne Campbell. 1994. *Literacy Behind Prison Walls: Profiles of the Prison Population from the National Adult Literacy Survey*. (NCES 94102). Washington, DC: U.S. Department of Education.

Handel, Ruth D. 1999. *Building Family Literacy in Urban Community*. New York: Teachers College Press.

Kirsch, Irvine, S., Ann Jungebltu, Lynn Jekins, and Andrew Kolstad. 1993. *Adult Literacy in America: A First Look at the Results of the National Adult Literacy Survey*. Washington, DC: National Center for Education Statistics.

Kutner, Mark, Elizabeth Greenburg, Yin Jin, Christine Paulsen, and Sheida White. 2006. *The Health Literacy of America's Adults: Results from the 2003 National Assessment of Adult Literacy*. Washington, DC: U.S. Department of Education, National Center for Education Statistics.

Morris, Nancy S., Charles D. MacLean, Lisa D. Chew, and Benjamin Littenberg. 2006. "The Single Item Literacy Screener: Evaluation of a Brief Instrument to Identify Limited Reading Ability." *BMC Family Practice* 7 (March): 21. Available: www.biomedical-central.com/1471-2296 /7/21

National Cancer Institute. n.d. "Health Disparities Defined." Center to Reduce Cancer Health Disparities, National Institutes of Health. (September 2007) Available: http://crchd.cancer.gov/definitions/ define.html

National Center for Education Statistics. 2001. "Dropout Rates in the United States: 2000. Executive Summary." (September 2007) Available: http://nces.ed.gov/pubs2002/droppub_2001/

National Institute of Nursing Research. 2007. "Nursing Partnership Centers on Health Disparities (P20)." (September 2007) Available: www.ninr.gov/ResearchAndFunding/FundedNinrGrantsCollaborative Activities

Nielsen-Bohlman, Lynn, Allison M. Panzer, and David A. Kindig (eds.). 2004. *Health Literacy: A Prescription to End Confusion*. Committee on Health Literacy, Institute of Medicine. Washington, DC: National Academies Press.

Parikh, Nina S., Ruth M. Parker, Joanne R. Nurss, David W. Baker, and Mark V. Williams. 1996. "Shame and Health Literacy: The Unspoken Connection." *Patient Education and Counseling* 27, no.1 (January): 33–39.

RTI International—University of North Carolina Evidence-based Practice Center. 2004. *Literacy and Health Care Outcomes*. Prepared for the Agency for Healthcare Research and Quality (AHRQ) under Contract No. 290-02-0016. (August 2007) Available: www.ahrq .gov/clinic/epcsums/litsum.htm

Sanders, Lee M., G. Zacur, Trude Haecker, and Perry Kloss. 2004. "The Number of Children's Books in the Home: An Indicator of General Health Literacy." *Ambulatory Pediatrics* 4, no.5 (September): 424–428.

Schillinger, Dean, John Piette, Kevin Grumbach, Frances Wang, Clifford Wilson, Carolyn Daher, Krishelle Leong-Grotz, Cesar Castro, and Andrew B. Bindman. 2003. "Closing the Loop: Physician Communication with Diabetic Patients Who Have Low Health Literacy." *Archives of Internal Medicine* 163, no.1 (January): 83–90.

U.S. Department of Health and Human Services (USDHHS) 2000a. *Healthy People 2010*. 2nd ed. *With Understanding and Improving Health*. 2 vols. Washington, DC: U.S. Government Printing Office. Available: www.healthypeople .gov/About/goals.htm

U.S. Department of Health and Human Services (USDHHS) 2000b. *Healthy People 2010*. 2nd ed. *With Understanding and Improving Health*. 2 vols. Washington, DC: U.S. Government Printing Office. Available: www.healthypeople.gov/Document/pdf/Volume1/ 11/HealthCom.pdf

Weiss, Barry D., Jay S. Blanchard, Daniel McGee, Gregory Hart, Barbara Warren, Michael Burgoon, and Kenneth J. Smith. 1994. "Illiteracy Among Medicaid Recipients and Its Relationship to Health Care Costs." *Journal of Health Care Poor Underserved* 5, no.2: 99–111.

Weiss, Barry D., and Raymond Palmer. 2004. "Relationship Between Health Care Costs and Very Low Literacy Skills in a Medically Needy and Indigent Medicaid Population." *Journal of American Board of Family Medicine* 17, no.1 (January–February): 44–47.

Wilson, Feleta. L., and Barbara N. Williams. 2003. "Meeting the Health Education and Information Needs of Patients with Low Literacy Skills." *Journal of Wound, Ostomy, & Continence Nursing* 30, no.4 (July): 224–230.

Wilson, Feleta L., Dora Brown, and Mary Stephens-Ferris. 2006. "Can Easy-to-Read Immunization Information Increase Knowledge in Urban Low-income Mothers." *Journal of Pediatric Nursing* 21, no.1 (February): 4–12.

Yin, H Shanna, Shalini G. Forbis, and Bernard P. Dreyer. 2007. "Health Literacy and Pediatric Health." *Current Problems in Pediatric and Adolescent Health Care* 37, no.7 (August): 258–286.

Chapter 6

The Association Between Literacy and Health: Providing Health Information to Adults with Low Literacy

Heather J. Martin and C. Nadine Wathen

INTRODUCTION

"Health literacy is the degree to which individuals have the capacity to obtain, process, and understand basic information and services needed to make appropriate decisions regarding their health" (Nielsen-Bohlman, Panzer, and Kindig, 2004, para. 1). Based on this definition from *Healthy People 2010* (U.S. Department of Health and Human Services, 2000), a national health promotion and disease prevention initiative, health literacy encompasses much more than reading and numeracy skills; it is also a measure of conceptual knowledge. While even literate, educated adults can have low health literacy, the problem is even more significant for those millions of adults who cannot read.

According to a joint 2005 report by Statistics Canada and the Organisation for Economic Co-operation and Development, 41.9 percent of Canadian adults are considered to have literacy skills that are below the minimum required for "coping with the demands of modern life and work" (ABC Canada 2005, para. 10). Studies on the adult literacy situation in the United States show similar statistics, with 22 percent of adults having only basic literacy skills and an additional 14 percent who are functionally illiterate with below basic literacy skills (Kutner et al., 2006). In both the Canadian and U.S. studies, the levels of seniors with low literacy are much higher than in the general population; these are individuals who are also more likely to have chronic and complex health concerns, making low health literacy especially problematic.

A wide cross-section of the general population lives with below adequate literacy; it is not a problem solely of the immigrant and low-income communities or those without formal education. In fact, many surveys show that on average U.S. adults read three to five grade levels below their actual years of education (Blackwell, 2005) and that the largest segment of the U.S. low-literate population is white and native-born. The 2003 National Assessment of Adult Literacy included a health literacy component in their analysis (Kutner et al., 2006). The health literacy tasks were developed by the Committee on Performance Levels for Adult Literacy to fit into the existing NAAL prose, document, and quantitative scales. Distinguished by their health content, these tasks were analyzed to create a health literacy scale, which then gave a picture of the overall health literacy of America's adults.

While the survey demonstrated that 53 percent of American adults have intermediate health literacy, 22 percent have only basic health literacy and 14 percent are considered to have below basic health literacy (Kutner et al., 2006). It should be noted that the percentage of individuals with below basic health literacy levels does not include adults who could not communicate in either English or Spanish or who had a mental disability that prevented them from taking part in the assessment. NAAL defines *basic* literacy, as having the skills necessary to perform simple and everyday literacy activities. Adults who fell into the *below basic* level ranged from being completely illiterate in English to having only the most simple literacy skills. An example of a task completed successfully by someone with below basic literacy levels would be finding the date on a short medical appointment slip.

Significant health literacy disparities were seen across many of the isolated demographics studied. Higher percentages of black and Hispanic adults than white, Asian/Pacific Islander, or multiracial adults had below basic health literacy as did adults living below the poverty line. Adults 65 years of age and older had the lowest average prose, document, and quantitative scores among all age groups. In fact, this group had the same percentage of below basic literacy as did adults who did not graduate from high school. On average, women had higher levels of health literacy and fewer women than men fell into the category of having below basic health literacy (Kutner et al., 2006).

Because of the stigma of low literacy and the assumption that it primarily affects people with low incomes, many of the individuals who cannot read have kept their problem a secret, resulting in a hidden epidemic (Parikh et al., 1996; Safeer and Keenan, 2005). In fact, several studies show that physicians are often unable to identify even those patients with only marginal literacy (Bass et al., 2002; National Work Group on Literacy and Health 1998; Rogers, Wallace, and Weiss, 2006), making reaching this population even more difficult.

This chapter will explore a selection of the literature on the relationship between low literacy levels and patient care and health outcomes, and, subsequently, the role that information professionals—in particular librarians—can take in helping to narrow health literacy gaps in ways that are relevant and successful for low-literate individuals.

WHAT IS HEALTH LITERACY AND WHY IS IT IMPORTANT?

A Medical Library Association (MLA) Task Force developed a working definition of health information literacy. Stemming from the definition of health literacy proposed in *Healthy People 2010* (U.S. Department of Health and Human Services, 2000), the MLA (2003) definition combines this understanding with the concept of information literacy to propose a more comprehensive approach to the notion of health literacy:

> Health Information Literacy is the set of abilities needed to: recognize a health information need; identify likely information sources and use them to retrieve relevant information; assess the quality of the information and its applicability to a specific situation; and analyze, understand, and use the information to make good health decisions. (para. 5)

In a white paper on health literacy prepared for the 2003 Information Literacy Meeting of Experts, Grant (2002) describes some of the behaviors that can be influenced by health literacy. At the most basic level this can include the ability to understand a health practitioner's instructions or to take medication as prescribed. At a more advanced level, low health literacy can contribute to difficulty in managing chronic illness, such as diabetes, an inability to understand health interventions or to analyze the risks and benefits of such interventions, or to provide truly informed consent.

While a significant number of studies focus on the concept of health literacy and the relationship of that concept to various health indicators and outcomes, much of what is actually being measured is the ability to read (DeWalt et al., 2004). As adequate health literacy requires the ability to perform basic reading and numerical tasks (Virginia Adult Learning Resource Center, 2003) it is obvious that the presence of low literacy would equate to the presence of low health literacy. Furthermore, the current measurement tools that are used to assess health literacy do so through the assessment of basic reading comprehension. According to a systematic review of the literature dealing with literacy and health outcomes by DeWalt et al. (2004), the most common tools are the Wide Range Achievement Test (WRAT) and the Rapid Estimate of Adult Literacy in Medicine (REALM), both of which assess word recognition and pronunciation, and the Test of Functional Health Literacy in Adults (TOFHLA), which uses a fill-in-the-blank test to measure reading ability and comprehension. A related tool, eHEALS (Norman and Skinner, 2006), was developed to determine users' perceived knowledge, comfort, and skill at finding and evaluating electronic health information, as opposed to testing basic reading skills. One limitation to this tool is that it only measures users' perceptions of their e-health literacy skills and not the skills themselves.

LOW LITERACY AND POOR HEALTH

While unable to determine cause and effect, the 2003 NAAL Health Literacy component demonstrated that adults with self-reported poor health had much lower average health literacy scores than those with average, good, or excellent health (Kutner et al., 2006). It may be easy to conclude that the connection between low literacy and health lies in the fact that low literacy is often an indicator for other factors that can lead to poor health outcomes, such as poverty and lack of adequate healthcare. However, research has shown that the effect may be much more direct.

Several studies have been conducted which demonstrate that low literacy has a direct negative effect on health outcomes and the success of health interventions (DeWalt et al., 2004; Pignone et al., 2005). A recent systematic review (DeWalt et al., 2004) showed that despite a few poor studies and some inconclusive evidence, the majority of research done on the topic of reading ability and its relation to health outcomes demonstrates that adults with low literacy are 1.5 to 3 times more likely to experience adverse health outcomes than those who read at higher levels. These authors concluded that, even when accounting for age, gender, race, and income, there are relationships between reading ability and hospitalization, global measures of health, knowledge of healthcare services, and some chronic diseases.

Two studies identified by DeWalt et al. (2004) as being of good quality examined inadequate literacy as a risk factor for hospital admission (Baker et al., 1998; Baker et al., 2002). Both studies adjusted for age, gender, race, self-reported health, socioeconomic and health insurance status, and concluded that patients with lower literacy levels had an increased risk of hospital admission and that low functional literacy could be seen as an independent risk factor. One partial explanation for these findings may be that patients with limited literacy are less likely to understand emergency room discharge instructions and therefore more likely to be readmitted (Baker, 1999).

Other studies have shown that patient low literacy levels can impact healthcare costs (Weiss and Palmer, 2004; Howard, Gazmararian, and Parker, 2005). Weiss and Palmer (2004) showed that the medical costs of patients with literacy skills below a 3rd grade level were on average over $10,000 per year, while those patients with higher literacy levels were less than $3,000 per year. This statistically significant difference remained even after accounting for other confounding socioeconomic variables. The American Medical Association Foundation (2003) stated that patients with low health literacy in the United States incur an estimated annual cost of $73 billion in extra doctor visits, unnecessary or repeated tests, and extended hospitalization.

One significant way in which low literacy levels impact health outcomes is through the consequent failure of preventive health programs. One study (Scott et al., 2002) showed that even after accounting for other variables, Medicare enrollees were more likely to have lower usage of preventive health services, such as Pap smears and mammograms, if they tested as having low literacy. A study on screening mammography among low-income, low-literate women showed that of the women studied, those with lower reading abilities were significantly less likely to utilize screening mammograms (Davis et al., 1996). Both studies indicated that the lack of use of preventive health services among adults with low literacy could be related to the fact that these same individuals often have inadequate knowledge or understanding of these services. A multiethnic cohort study on the association of health literacy with cervical cancer knowledge and prevention behaviors showed that low literacy was the only factor that was independently associated with knowledge related to cervical cancer screening services (Lindau et al., 2002).

Two different studies (Bennett et al., 1998; Wolf et al., 2006) have looked at the relationship between race, literacy, and prostate cancer staging at time of diagnosis in low-income men. Both studies indicated a statistically significant difference between how advanced the cancer was at time of diagnosis and patient reading level. The study by Wolf et al. (2006) demonstrated that men with lower literacy levels were twice as likely to have their prostate cancer diagnosed at a more advanced stage. These studies provide further indication that individuals with low literacy may not be taking advantage of preventive cancer screening even when they have equal access to these services.

Errors in prescription drug use and adherence among low-literate individuals are one common area of study regarding literacy and health outcomes. Studies show that low and marginal literacy is directly associated with misunderstanding of prescription drug labels and warnings (Baker, 1999; Blackwell, 2005; Davis et al., 2006a, 2006b; DeWalt et al., 2004; Gazmararian et al., 1999; Kripalani et al., 2006; Muir et al., 2006; Kalichman, Ramachandran, and Catz, 1999). In a study of Medicare enrollees in managed care, Gazmararian et al. (1999) found that inadequate literacy skills had a significant impact on the ability of patients to take medication as prescribed; 47.5 percent of adults with low literacy skills incorrectly described the timing of medication doses when reading a prescription label compared to 11.5 percent of those with adequate literacy skills. Kripalani et al. (2006) showed that patients with inadequate literacy had 10 to 18 times the odds of being unable to identify all of their medications, compared with those with adequate literacy skills. While these studies did not address specific health outcomes of these errors, most authors postulate that these misunderstandings, which are linked to taking significantly too much (or too little) prescription medications, can have significant health impacts. When coupled with similar findings that the number of prescription medications being taken at any given time will also influence these types of errors (e.g., Davis et al., 2006b), and the fact that both low literacy and polypharmacy are more prevalent in older adults with chronic illness, the potential health risks, especially in this population, are significant.

A related area of study is the effect of low literacy on patient self-managed care. Individuals with chronic illnesses, such as diabetes or asthma, are responsible for an increasing amount of self-care, including following a medication regimen but often extending beyond that. A number of studies have found that low literacy can be a barrier to prescription drug adherence, following physician instructions, knowledge of chronic illness and care, all of which can lead to poor health outcomes in individuals with chronic illness (DeWalt et al., 2004; Mancuso and Rincon, 2006; Schillinger et al., 2002). However, the evidence is far from definitive, with other studies indicating that when certain confounding factors are accounted for, literacy may play a lesser role in disease self-management (Morris, MacLean, and Littenberg, 2006). Clearly, additional research that directly examines various kinds of literacies as causal factors (i.e., as entry criteria into the study) and measures health outcomes for an appropriate length of time, are urgently required (Pignone et al., 2005).

Low literacy not only has the potential to adversely impact health outcomes, but also affects whether patients can participate in truly informed decision-making about their own care. In Canada and the United States, informed consent forms are required for surgery or invasive procedures as well as participation in research studies and clinical trials. As standard institutional consent forms are often written at a level that requires university-level reading comprehension, far above the ability of the average individual (National Work Group on Literacy and Health, 1998), the question regarding whether most patients are fully informed as to what they consent to is murky at best. There are ethical and legal ramifications to current practice, and written consent forms should be seen as inadequate as the sole means of informed consent.

METHODS OF DELIVERING HEALTH INFORMATION TO INDIVIDUALS WITH LOW LITERACY

The discrepancy between the readability of patient education materials and patients' actual reading abilities has been well documented in a number of studies (Baker, Wilson, and Kars, 1997; Jubelirer, 1991; Davis et al., 1990; Michieulutte, Bahnson, and Beal 1990). Results of the Davis et al. study demonstrated that while the average reading comprehension of patients in five public hospitals was at a 6th grade level, the majority of patient education materials provided at those hospitals was written at an 11th–14th grade level, with standard consent forms, as mentioned above, requiring university level reading comprehension. The majority of widely available patient education materials are written at a 10th grade level or above, while the average American reads at an 8th grade level (National Work Group on Literacy and Health, 1998). As a result, not only are patient education materials and written communications provided by physicians and other health-care professionals not readable by the nearly half of the population with limited literacy, but many are difficult to understand even by the portion of the population with average reading abilities.

Several U.S. national agencies, such as the Joint Commission on Accreditation of Healthcare Organizations and the National Committee for Quality Assurance, now require healthcare providers to ensure that patients can understand the health information that is given to them. The National Work Group on Literacy and Health (1998) recommends that when written communication is necessary, materials should be written at a 5th grade level or lower and should be complemented by nonwritten—especially visual—communication for patients with limited literacy.

People at all literacy levels prefer health information that is written in clear and simple language (National Work Group on Literacy and Health, 1998). Plain language initiatives in patient education strive to create written materials that will be understandable by the greatest number of people. Plain language techniques do not simply "dumb down" health information, but rather use a conversational writing style utilizing common words and phrases organized in an easy to understand manner to best meet patient needs (Wizowski, Harper, and Hutchings, 2002).

While a great deal of low-literacy health information material does currently exist, many of these resources are created at a local level by individual practitioners and organizations (Nielsen-Bohlman, Panzer, and Kindig, 2004; Wizowski, Harper, and Hutchings, 2002)—a benefit for the local community, but limiting general-izability to other contexts. Despite increasing attention by national agencies in creating materials written at a lower reading comprehension level, and while some bibliographies and listings of health literacy-oriented resources exist (e.g., the Health and Literacy Compendium developed by World Education [1999] in collaboration with the National Institute of Literacy), our search revealed no current national (United States or Canada) databases or catalogs of these materials and their sources available to health practitioners or librarians. While fairly large scale, creating such a clearinghouse would be an excellent area in health literacy promotion in which public and consumer health librarians could be involved.

However, even patient education materials that are written in plain language at the recommended grade level will be unreadable by the portion of the population with functional illiteracy. Because of this fact it is essential that patients also have access to nonprint materials. Providing both oral and written information has proven to be the most effective way to increase understanding of medical information and tends to be preferred by patients (Mayeaux et al., 1996), and increasingly research is showing that incorporating visual aids may also provide additional benefit (Schillinger et al., 2006; Houts et al., 2006).

Nonwritten instructions for self-care and medication regimens, as well as disease information, can and should be provided by healthcare providers. However, for presumed legal and ethical reasons, there has been reluctance among librarians to take a lead role in providing this type of information (Harris, Wathen, and Chan, 2005). Nonetheless, there are other nonwritten sources of health information that can be useful for both low- and high-literate individuals that can be provided in consumer health information resource centers. These can include: picture books, three-dimensional models, slide presentations, audio- and videotapes, DVDs, and CD-ROMs, as well as computer-based multimedia and online resources.

One study on the role of pictures in improving health communication (Houts et al., 2006) showed that when pictures were linked to written or spoken content, patient comprehension of medical information markedly improved. While improvement was seen in all individuals, those with low literacy were particularly likely to benefit from this method. The National Work Group on Literacy and Health (1998) reports that the overall results of numerous studies on the benefits of CD-ROM, television, and video information sources for use with low-literacy audiences have been positive; as with plain language and picture resources, this type of information is useful and preferred by individuals at all reading levels (National Work Group on Literacy and Health, 1998).

A ROLE FOR LIBRARIANS

As the literature demonstrates, low health literacy may be linked to poorer health outcomes and higher healthcare costs. With a few exceptions (e.g., Baker, Wilson, and Kars, 1997; Baker and Gollop, 2004), much of the research performed and the literature available on this topic is found within journals of medicine and nursing. While it is essential that healthcare practitioners are actively involved in identifying at risk individuals and designing services and materials to help overcome barriers to healthcare information for adults with low literacy, librarians are in a unique position to participate in the challenge of improving health literacy. There is a distinct information gap in the literature of library and information science, and, as mentioned above, a seeming resistance among some librarians and libraries to take a leadership role in providing high quality health information. One exception is in the work of the Medical Library Association, which is making great strides in advocating the partnership between librarians and healthcare professionals and allies to promote health literacy. The key message of the communication plan of the MLA's Task Force on Information Literacy (2005) is as follows: "Health information literacy is a critical life skill that helps patients and caregivers in making medical and healthcare decisions. Medical librarians should be involved in all levels of program development" (para. 1).

Parker and Kreps (2005) point out the importance of library outreach in meeting national health literacy goals: "[L]ibrary professionals have a unique opportunity to help overcome health literacy challenges by developing new and effective communication strategies for disseminating relevant health information to audiences with differing levels of literacy" (S86). Consumer health librarians have experience and training in meeting the health information needs of the public and in identifying the potential barriers that prevent those individuals from meeting their needs. The central role for librarians is to provide accessible and understandable health material, whether this is in a public library, consumer health resource center, or clinical setting. In addition, librarians can be active in developing health literacy programs and in promoting health literacy awareness among health professionals and adult literacy education specialists.

Whenever possible, working with healthcare providers can ensure that patients are given health information that they can understand. Physicians are often unable to recognize low literacy (Pignone et al., 2005; McRay, 2005) and may provide information that is inappropriate and inaccessible to their patients (Pignone et al., 2005); therefore involving librarians with an understanding of the barriers and facilitators to providing health information to users with low literacy is a logical alliance. According to Parker and Kreps (2005), "[c]ollaborative efforts . . . between librarians and practicing physicians offer opportunities to link 'information giving' with 'information seeking'" (S86), thus emphasizing the role that librarians can play in closing the gap between healthcare providers and healthcare consumers.

The above illustrates one example of partnerships that consumer health librarians can make in order to better reach the community, however there are many others. Other state- or provincial-level exemplar initiatives include the following:

- The Access Colorado Library and Information Network (ACLIN) (www.aclin .org) and the Colorado State Library have created the Colorado Virtual Library for the residents of Colorado, including a Best Web sites service that covers several subject areas, one of which is health and medicine. "Librarians from public, academic and special libraries in Colorado have worked together to evaluate and select these sites to assist consumers in finding reliable online health information" (Chobot, 2002: 12).
- Ohio's NetWellness program (www.netwellness.org) is a partnership of health sciences faculty members from three Ohio universities who came together to "create and evaluate consumer health content for the site and staff its Ask an Expert service, where consumers can ask questions and view responses directly on the Web" (Guard et al., 2000: 375). Unlike in other jurisdictions in which librarians appear to be only bit players in CHI, Ohio's

librarians play an integral role in this program, likely because of the state's history of supporting shared information services such as OCLC (the well-known acronym for the Online Computer Library Center).

- In Canada, the Nova Scotia Health Network (NSHN) (www.nshealthnetwork.ca) is an example of a "grass-roots" service developed by librarians in response to the needs of their users and the limitations of their existing resources. The initiative is based on the idea that "the public library delivers consumer health information through its branch libraries and its public Internet access computers while the health center library provides backup for inquiries beyond the capability of public librarians and assures the quality control of the information being offered" (NSHN, 2006). The project operates province-wide to provide a Web-based consumer health information service through a collaboration between public libraries, health sciences libraries, the provincial library, several related organizations, and a University.
- From the perspective of library education, the Eskind Medical Library at Vanderbilt University (www.mc.vanderbilt.edu/biolib) is a model program where library services and "informationists" educated about health information user needs and competencies, seeking behavior and retrieval strategies are highly integrated—using an internship mode—into patient care.

At the local level, many initiatives have been developed by schools, literacy groups, public libraries, community-based organizations, senior-citizen facilities, healthcare associations and organizations, and research groups. The National Network of Libraries of Medicine (2006), in their page on health literacy, provide suggestions of collaborative initiatives such as working with Adult Basic Education and ESL initiatives to incorporate health related information into the program or partnering with community-based organizations to develop outreach programs to senior-citizen facilities to discuss health topics. Finally, there is emerging evidence regarding the use of paraprofessionals within community-based consumer health information outreach programs, to improve access to and use of health information among those with low literacy (Olney et al., 2007).

CONCLUSION

When it comes to healthcare, the right information delivered in the right way at the right time can, literally, be a lifesaver. Even when accounting for potentially confounding socioeconomic variables, the direct effect of low literacy on health outcomes is emerging as a significant one. The millions of individuals in Canada and the United States that have only basic or below basic reading and number skills are at an increased risk of hospitalization, high medical costs, and overall poor health outcomes. Many, but by no means all, of these individuals are low-income, minorities, or older adults: individuals who already have factors working against their overall health, and for whom accessing and understanding relevant health information may be particularly critical.

With their skills and training, librarians are in an excellent position to promote health literacy and to help mitigate the negative effects of low literacy on health and the healthcare experience. This is best done through provision of materials that are relevant and understandable by patients with limited reading and number skills. Providing information in plain language as well as in multiple and culturally appropriate illustrative and audiovisual formats allows accessibility to a wider audience.

Working in partnership with healthcare practitioners, community organizations, and adult literacy groups will allow a greater number of people to be served, and for specialists in various sectors to contribute their knowledge to the initiative. The Medical Library Association (2005) is vocal in advocating the importance of librarians becoming closely involved in promoting health literacy:

> Taking an active role in Health Information Literacy helps provide new opportunities for medical and consumer health librarians, increasing their visibility in their organizations, and helping to improve the overall health of the community. (3)

REFERENCES

ABC Canada. 2005. "Report Summary: Learning a Living: First Results of the Adult Literacy and Life Skills (ALL) Survey." (October 2006) Available: www.abc-canada.org/media_room/news/all_survey_summary.shtml

American Medical Association Foundation. 2003. "Health Literacy Update: Issue." (December 2006) Available: www.amaassn.org/ama1/pub/upload/mm/367/spring 2003 issue 2.pdf

Baker, David W. 1999. "Reading Between the Lines: Deciphering the Connections Between Literacy and Health." *Journal of General Internal Medicine*, 14, no.5 (May): 313–317.

Baker, David W., Julie A. Gazmararian, Mark V. Williams, Tracy Scott, Ruth M. Parker, Diane Green, Junling Ren, and Jennifer Peel. 2002. "Functional Health Literacy and the Risk of Hospital Admission among Medicare Managed Care Enrollees." *American Journal of Public Health*, 92, no.8 (August): 1278–1283.

Baker, David W., Ruth M. Parker, Mark V. Williams, and W. Scott Clark. 1998. "Health Literacy and the Risk of Hospital Admission." *Journal of General Internal Medicine* 13, no.12 (December): 791–798.

Baker, Lynda M., Feleta L. Wilson, and Marge Kars. 1997. "The Readability of Medical Information on InfoTrac: Does It Meet the Needs of People with Low Literacy Skills?" *Reference and User Service Quarterly* 37, no.2 (Winter): 155–160.

Baker, Lynda M., and Claudia J. Gollop. 2004. "Medical Textbooks: Can Lay People Read and Understand Them?" *Library Trends* 53, no.2 (Fall): 336–347.

Bass, Pat F., III, John F. Wilson, Charles H. Griffith, and Don R. Barnett. 2002. "Residents' Ability to Identify Patients with Poor Literacy Skills." *Academic Medicine* 77, no.10 (October): 1039–1041.

Bennett, Charles L., M, Rosario Ferreira, Terry C. Davis, J. Kaplan, M. Weinberger, Timothy Kuzel, M. A. Seday, and Oliver Sartor. 1998. "Relation Between Literacy, Race, and Stage of Presentation Among Low-income Patients with Prostate Cancer." *Journal of Clinical Oncology* 16, no.9 (September): 3101–3104.

Blackwell, Jean. 2005. "Low Health Literacy: How It Impacts Your Patients." In *MLA Health Information Literacy* (December). Available: www.mlanet .org/resources/healthlit/

Chobot, Mary C. 2002. *The Challenge of Providing Consumer Health Information Services in Public Libraries.* American Association for the Advancement of Science. Available: http:// ehrweb.aaas.org/PDF/ChallengePubLibraries.pdf

Davis, Terry C., Michael A. Crouch, Georgia Wills, Sarah Miller and David M. Abdehou. 1990. "The Gap Between Patient Reading Comprehension and the Readability of Patient Education Materials." *Journal of Family Practice* 31, no.5 (November): 533–538.

Davis, Terry C., Connie Arnold, Hans (J.) Berkel, Indrani Nandy, Robert H. Jackson, and Jonathan Glass. 1996. "Knowledge and Attitude on Screening Mammography Among Low-literate, Low-income Women." *Cancer* 78, no.9 (November): 1912–1920.

Davis, Terry C., Michael S. Wolf, Pat F. Bass III, Mark Middlebrooks, Estela Kennen, David W. Baker, Charles Bennett, Ramon Durazo-Arvizu, Anna Bocchine, Stephanie Savory, and Ruth M. Parker. 2006a. "Low Literacy Impairs Comprehension of Prescription Drug Warning Labels." *Journal of General Internal Medicine* 21, no.8 (August): 847–851.

Davis Terry C., Michael S. Wolf, Pat F. Bass III, Jason A. Thompson, Hugh H. Tilson, Marolee Neuberger and Ruth Parker. 2006b. "Literacy and Misunderstanding Prescription Drug Labels." *Annals of Internal Medicine* 145, no.12 (December): 887–894.

DeWalt, Darren A., Nancy Berkman, Stacey Sheridan, Kathleen Lohr, and Michael P. Pignone. 2004. "Literacy and Health Outcomes." *Journal of General Internal Medicine* 19, no.12 (December): 1228–1239.

Gazmararian Julie A., David W. Baker, Mark V. Williams, Ruth M. Parker, Tracy L. Scott, Diane C. Green, S. N. Fehrenback, Junling Ren and J. P. Koplan. 1999. "Health Literacy Among Medicare Enrollees in a Managed Care Organization." *JAMA* 281, no.6 (February): 545–551.

Grant, Sharon. 2002. "White Paper Prepared for UNESCO, the U.S. National Commission on Libraries and Information Science, and the National Forum on Information Literacy, for Use at the Information Literacy Meeting of Experts, Prague, The Czech Republic." Available: www.nclis.gov/libinter/infolitconf&meeting/papers/grant-fullpaper.pdf

Guard, Roger, Theresa M. Fredericka, Susan Knoll, Stephen Marine, Carol Roddy, Tim Steiner, and Susan Wentz. 2000. "Health Care, Information Needs, and Outreach: Reaching Ohio's Rural Citizens." *Bulletin of the Medical Library Association* 88, no.4 (October): 374–381.

Harris, Roma M., C. Nadine Wathen, and Donna Chan. 2005. "Public Library Responses to a Consumer Health Inquiry in a Public Health Crisis: The SARS Experience in Ontario." *Reference and User Services Quarterly* 45, no.2 (Winter): 147–154.

Houts, Peter S., Cecilia C. Doak, Leonard G. Doak, and Matthew J. Loscalzo. 2006. "The Role of Pictures in Improving Health Communication: A Review of Research on Attention, Comprehension, Recall, and Adherence." *Patient Education and Counseling* 61, no.2 (May): 173–190.

Howard, David H., Julie Gazmararian, and Ruth M. Parker. 2005. "The Impact of Low Health Literacy on the Medical Costs of Medicare Managed Care Enrollees." *American Journal of Medicine* 118, no.4 (April): 371–377.

Jubelirer, Steven J. 1991. "Level of Reading Difficulty in Educational Pamphlets and Informed Consent Documents for Cancer Patients." *West Virginia Medical Journal* 87 (December): 554–557.

Kalichman, Seth C., Bineetha Ramachandran, and Sheryl Catz. 1999. "Adherence to Combination Antiretroviral Therapies in HIV Patients of Low Health Literacy." *Journal of General Internal Medicine* 14, no.5 (May): 267–273.

Kripalani, Sunil, Laura E. Henderson, Ellen Y. Chiu, Rashanda Robertson, Paul Kolm, and Terry A. Jacobson. 2006. "Predictors of Medication Self-management Skill in a Low-literacy Population." *Journal of General Internal Medicine* 21, no.8 (August): 852-856.

Kutner, Mark, Elizabeth Greenberg, Ying Jin, and Christine Paulsen. 2006. *The Health Literacy of America's Adults: Results from the 2003 National Assessment of Adult Literacy* (NCES 2006-483). U.S. Department of Education. Washington, DC: National Center for Education Statistics. Available: http://nces.ed.gov/pubs2006/2006483.pdf

Lindau, Stacy T., Cecilia Tomori, Tom Lyons, Lizbet Langseth, Charles L. Bennett, and Patricia Garcia. 2002. "The Association of Health Literacy with Cervical Cancer Prevention Knowledge and Health Behaviors in a Multiethnic Cohort of Women." *American Journal of Obstetrics and Gynecology* 186, no.5 (May): 938–943.

Mancuso, Carol A., and Melina Rincon. 2006. "Impact of Health Literacy on Longitudinal Asthma Outcomes." *Journal of General Internal Medicine* 21, no.8 (August): 813–817.

Mayeaux J., Peggy W. Murphy, Connie Arnold, Terry C. Davis, Robert H. Jackson, and Tetine Sentell. 1996. "Improving Patient Education for Patients with Low Literacy Skills." *American Family Physician* 53, no.1 (January): 205–207.

McRay, Alexa T. 2005. "Promoting Health Literacy." *Journal of the American Medical Informatics Association* 12, no.2 (March): 152–163.

Medical Library Association. 2003. "Health Information Literacy: Definitions." In *MLANET*. Available: www.malnet.org/index/html

Medical Library Association. 2005. "Communicating Health Information Literacy." In *Health Information Literacy*. Available: www.mlanet.org/resources/healthlit

Michielutte, Robert, Judy Bahnson, and Pheon Beal. 1990. "Readability of the Public Education Literature on Cancer Prevention and Detection." *Journal of Cancer Education* 5, no.1: 55–61.

Morris, Nancy S., Charles D. MacLean, and Benjamin Littenberg. 2006. "Literacy and Health Outcomes: A Cross-sectional Study in 1002 Adults with Diabetes." *BMC Family Practice* 7, no.49 (August). Available: www.biomedcentral.com/1471-2296/7/49

Muir, Kelly W., Cecile Santiago-Turla, Sandra S. Stinnett, Leon W. Herndon, R. Rand Allingham, Pratap Challa, and Paul P. Lee. 2006. "Health Literacy and Adherence to Glaucoma Therapy." *American Journal of Ophthalmology* 142, no.2 (August): 223–226.

National Network of Libraries of Medicine. 2006. "Health Literacy." Available: http://nnlm.gov/outreach/consumer/hlthlit.html

National Work Group on Literacy and Health. 1998. "Communicating with Patients Who Have Limited Literacy Skills: Report of the National Work Group on Literacy and Health." *Journal of Family Practice* 46, no.2 (February): 168–176.

Nielsen-Bohlman, Lynn, Allison M. Panzer, and David A. Kindig, Eds. 2004. *Health Literacy: A Prescription to End Confusion*. Washington, DC: Institute of Medicine. Available: www.nap.edu/catalog/10883.html#toc

Norman, Cameron D., and Harvey A. Skinner. 2006. "eHEALS: The ehealth Literacy Scale." *Journal of Medical Internet Research*, 8, no.4 (November): article e27.

Nova Scotia Health Network. 2006. "Reliable Online Health Information for Nova Scotians. Nova Scotia Health Network Background Information." Available: www.nshealthnetwork .ca/background.cfm

Olney, Cynthia A., Debra G. Warner, Greysi Reyna, Fred B. Wood, and Elliot R. Siegal. 2007. "MedlinePlus and the Challenge of Low Health Literacy: Findings from the *Colonias* Project." *Journal of the Medical Library Association* 95, no.1 (January): 31–39.

Parikh, Nina S., Ruth M. Parker, Joanne R. Nurss, David W. Baker, and Mark V. Williams. 1996. "Shame and Health Literacy: The Unspoken Connection." *Patient Education and Counseling* 27, no.1 (January): 33–39.

Parker, Ruth, and Gary L. Kreps. 2005. "Library Outreach: Overcoming Health Literacy Challenges." *Journal of the Medical Library Association* 93, no.4 (October): S81–S86.

Pignone, Michael, Darren A. DeWalt, Stacey Sheridan, Nancy Berkman, and Kathleen Lohr. 2005. "Interventions to Improve Health Outcomes for Patients with Low Literacy. A Systematic Review." *Journal of General Internal Medicine* 20, no.2 (February): 185–192.

Rogers, Edwin S., Lorraine S. Wallace, and Barry D. Weiss. 2006. "Misperceptions of Medical Understanding in Low-literacy Patients: Implications for Cancer Prevention." *Cancer Control* 13, no.3 (July): 225–229.

Safeer, Richard S., and Jann Keenan. 2005. "Health Literacy: the Gap Between Physicians and Patients." *American Family Physician* 72, no.3 (August). Available: www.aafp.org/afp/ 20050801/463.html

Schillinger, Dean, Kevin Grumbach, John Piette, Frances Wang, Dennis Osmond, Carolyn Daher, Jorge Palacios, Gabriela Diaz Sullivan, and Andrew B. Bindman. 2002. "Association of Health Literacy with Diabetes Outcomes." *JAMA* 288, no.4 (July): 475–482.

Schillinger Dean, Edward L. Machtinger, Frances Wang, Lay-Leng Chen, Karen Win, Jorge Palacios, Maytrella Rodriguez, and Andrew Bindman. 2006. "Language, Literacy, and Communication Regarding Medication in an Anticoagulation Clinic: A Comparison of Verbal vs. Visual Assessment." *Journal of Health Communication* 11, no.7 (August): 651–664.

Scott, Tracy, Julie A. Gazmararian, Mark V. Williams, and David W. Baker. 2002. "Health Literacy and Preventive Health Care Use Among Medicare Enrollees in a Managed Care Organization." *Medical Care* 40, no.5 (May): 395–404.

U.S. Department of Health and Human Services. 2000. "Healthy People 2010: Volume I." Available: www.healthpeople.gov/document/HTML/ Volume1/titlepg.htm

Virginia Adult Learning Resource Center. 2003. "Virginia Adult Education Health Literacy Toolkit." Available: www.aelweb.vcu.edu/publications/healthlit/

Weiss, Barry D., and Raymond Palmer. 2004. "Relationship Between Health Care Costs and Very Low Literacy Skills in a Medically Needy and Indigent Medicaid Population." *Journal of the American Board of Family Practice* 17, no.1 (January): 44–47.

Wizowski, L., T. Harper, and T. Hutchings. 2002. *Writing Health information for Patients and Families: A Guide to Creating Patient Education Materials that are Easy to Read, Understand and Use.* Hamilton, ON: Hamilton Health Sciences Patient Education.

Wolf, Michael S., Sara J. Knight, E. Allison Lyons, Ramon Durazo-Arvizu, Simon A. Pickard, Adnan Arseven, Ahsan Arozyllah, Kathleen Colella, Paul Ray, and Charles L. Bennett. 2006. "Literacy, Race, and PSA Level Among Low-income Men Newly Diagnosed with Prostate Cancer." *Urology* 68, no.1 (July): 89–93.

World Education. 1999. "Health and Literacy Compendium." (December 2006) Available: http://healthliteracy.worlded.org/docs/comp

Chapter 7

Health Literacy for People with Disabilities

Shelley Hourston

IMPORTANCE OF HEALTH LITERACY SKILLS FOR PEOPLE WITH DISABILITIES

My work in the area of health literacy for people with disabilities began in 1998, when I became librarian and program director for the AIDS & Disability Action Program at the British Columbia (BC) Coalition of People with Disabilities. The mandate of my program is HIV prevention education for people with all types of disabilities throughout the province. We continue to publish HIV prevention and sexual health materials in plain language, as well as in audio and Braille formats.

The challenges presented by low health literacy skills soon became clear from my work with consumers, service providers, and caregivers. In 1999, we broadened the program to incorporate HIV prevention as a component of wellness, introducing the Wellness & Disability Initiative. Enveloping HIV prevention in overall health and wellness was successful in reducing the fear associated with the topic of HIV/AIDS and sexual health. The sensitivity of the latter stems from high levels of sexual abuse among people with disabilities and the long held misconception that people with disabilities are not sexual beings and not sexually active (Groce, 2004).

In providing consumer health information as well as publishing and distributing our HIV prevention materials, we saw on a daily basis the impact of low health literacy skills on health, self-esteem, and self-empowerment. In 2000, we launched the Health Literacy Network to help raise awareness among service providers (including librarians) of the critical importance of health literacy and accessible health information and services.

Definition of Health Literacy

The Medical Library Association (2003) provides a working definition of health information literacy:

> Health Information Literacy is the set of abilities needed to: recognize a health information need; identify likely information sources and use them to retrieve relevant information; assess the quality of the information and its applicability to a specific situation; and analyze, understand, and use the information to make good health decisions.

Our working definition of health literacy at the BC Coalition of People with Disabilities is similar but also includes the ability to access *health services.* Many individuals with disabilities obtain their health information from healthcare providers and when this access is limited, so is access to health information.

Health and Well-being of People with Disabilities

That health literacy is particularly important for people with disabilities is clear. According to the Canadian Council on Social Development (CCSD), people with disabilities are far less likely to be "in good health" than their nondisabled counterparts. Self-rated health reports indicated that 36.3 percent of people without disabilities felt they were in excellent health compared with only 8.1 percent of people with disabilities (CCSD, 2003). Although people with disabilities are likely to be older, a significant gap still exists when the data are examined by age group. Not only are people with disabilities less healthy, requiring more healthcare, but also they have more difficulty accessing health-care. CCSD also reports that 14.6 percent of people with disabilities said that they were unable to get the care they needed compared to only 3.9 percent of nondisabled individuals. The reasons cited included long wait-times and cost factors.

People with disabilities also report lower levels of support, which is an important element of overall well-being (CCSD, 2003). Levels of social and emotional or informational support (defined as someone to talk to about your problems or to give you advice or information in a crisis) were lower and in some cases absent. Both men and women with disabilities reported having small circles of close friends or relatives (usually five or fewer) and were less likely to experience positive social interaction.

Reasons for Poor Health Among People with Disabilities

People with disabilities are more likely than nondisabled peers to face challenges in relation to most of the determinants of health: income and social status; social support networks; education and literacy; employment and working conditions;

social environments; physical environments; personal health practices and coping skills; healthy child development; biology and genetic endowment; health services; gender; and culture (Public Health Agency of Canada, 2003). The links between these determinants and the life circumstances for most people with disabilities can be complex and interrelated. For example, depending on the age of disability onset, opportunities in education and employment vary with far-reaching consequences. Personal health practices and coping skills are influenced by factors such as support and perception of well-being described earlier. Unemployment and under-employment, poverty, poor nutrition, physical or social isolation, and marginalization contribute to poor physical and mental health.

Common Health Issues Across Disability Types

People with disabilities are more likely than those without disabilities to have a variety of chronic health conditions (CCSD, 2004a). High blood pressure, heart disease, asthma, arthritis and rheumatism, diabetes, migraines, and cataracts affect people with disabilities more often than their nondisabled peers. Although many of these conditions are common among seniors, the incidence is highest among people with disabilities across all age ranges.

Increased Contact with Healthcare Providers

Most people with disabilities require more contact with healthcare providers and they are more likely to have a regular medical doctor than nondisabled individuals. In addition, people with disabilities are one and a half times more likely than nondisabled peers to seek treatment from alternative healthcare providers (CCSD, 2004b).

Increased Use of Medication

Research indicates that regular use (at least once a week) of prescription and nonprescription medication increases with the severity of the disability (CCSD, 2004c). Among those with severe or very severe disabilities, aged 15 to 64 years, 83.4 percent of men and 90.4 percent of women regularly used medication. Increased use of medication increases the opportunity for error and drug interactions. Cost can be a barrier to getting medication, especially for those with severe disabilities, and can precipitate unsafe practices. Borrowing prescription medications from friends or relatives or sharing insulin syringes, for example, can result in even greater health risks.

Barriers to Healthcare

A number of barriers to healthcare exist for people with disabilities. Geographic isolation, inadequate or inaccessible transportation, and inaccessible healthcare provider offices and examination tables are just a few of the physical ones. Attitudinal barriers, including lack of awareness or sensitivity, are also common. For example, healthcare providers and office staff may be insensitive to disability challenges and care providers commonly make assumptions about lifestyle and healthcare needs. Ignoring sexual health concerns is common when healthcare professionals assume that a person with a disability is not sexually active.

Policies or procedures that do not accommodate the needs of people with disabilities can be challenging. Inflexible appointment times or refusing to provide home visits can make access to healthcare more difficult. Some healthcare professionals will decline a patient because of lack of expertise with their disability. This can be especially difficult in smaller centers or rural areas with fewer healthcare options.

People with disabilities may require more time to explain health concerns, ask questions, or prepare for examinations. Inadequate time and the sense of being rushed are not conducive to information exchange for people with low health literacy skills. Many report that they receive care only in the area directly relating to their disability. Exploration of preventive healthcare measures often does not occur (Kroll et al., 2006; Lewis et al., 2002; Veltman et al., 2001).

According to a Canadian government fact sheet, the incidence of violence and sexual abuse is high among people with disabilities (Canada, 2006) and is frequently perpetrated by caregivers, including physicians, nurses, therapists, and attendants. As a result, many disabled people will avoid healthcare providers. An estimated 83 percent of women with disabilities will be sexually abused during their lifetimes, and 80 percent of patients in mental health institutions have experienced physical or sexual abuse in their lifetimes. Children with disabilities are five times more likely to experience abuse than nondisabled children. In addition, research indicates that women with disabilities who have experienced physical assault and other types of violence suffer related negative health effects (Marge, 2003), but are less inclined to seek care.

People with disabilities causing paralysis or reduced sensation may not recognize medical issues as they develop. For others, lack of health insurance precludes access to care or extended medical treatments.

Incidence of Multiple Disabilities

Comorbidity increases interaction with the healthcare system and the need for medication and other treatment. Research confirms that individuals with one chronic health condition or disability are likely to have others (Broemeling, Watson and Black, 2005). Multiple health conditions and related medication use can lead to drug interactions and, therefore, the need for more complex instructions for the individual. Increased contact with healthcare providers and use of medication increases the opportunity for health literacy challenges.

Age of Disability Onset and Effect on Coping Skills

People with disabilities from a young age may have limited education and employment skills. However, they have had time to build adaptive skills and techniques to compensate for limitations. Those who have become disabled later in life may have difficulty adapting and accepting new limitations. They may feel less comfortable using assistive technology. Depending on the degree of disability or illness, older individuals may be less willing to develop coping strategies and to be proactive in their own healthcare and rehabilitation. Many suffer from depression, anxiety, or other mental health challenges that compound their health literacy difficulties.

MAJOR ISSUES AFFECTING HEALTH LITERACY SKILLS FOR PEOPLE WITH DISABILITIES

Low Literacy Skills

Among people aged 16 to 55 years, 48 percent of people with physical disabilities have literacy skills below Level 3, the commonly accepted benchmark for adequate literacy. Seventy-seven percent of people with learning disabilities are below Level 3. Among individuals without a disability, 36 percent have literacy skills below Level 3 (Kapsalis, 1999). Twenty percent of adults with disabilities have less than a 9th grade education. Half of Canadian adults with disabilities have an annual income of less than $15,000, and only 56 percent are employed, with most working in low-paying jobs (Movement for Canadian Literacy, 2004).

Low literacy skills may be directly linked to the disability as in the case of learning disabilities or to a lack of physical access to educational opportunities. In many cases, disability is a barrier to higher education and higher literacy skills when schools do not provide the necessary financial and staff resources. Individuals with disabilities may have had physical access to schools but lacked the necessary instruction and support to allow them to learn. Literacy skills are also limited by lack of integration into the workplace and society as a whole. Without use and development, literacy skills atrophy (Kapsalis, 1999). Participation in employment and broader society is also impacted by the high incidence of multiple disabilities or chronic health conditions.

Societal Barriers

Historically, people with disabilities have lacked the supports to live independently in their communities. This has contributed to institutionalization and reliance on their families, and ultimately led to an environment of paternalism. During the 1970s and 1980s, the Independent Living movement began in the United States and later in Canada. The Independent Living philosophy is based on an assumption of basic human rights for people with disabilities and an opportunity to participate fully in their communities and society at large. Like many human rights movements, success has been gradual.

Seventy percent of adults with disabilities require support for daily living, and one third of these people report that they have unmet support needs (CCSD, 2005). Caregivers, family members, friends and neighbors, and the broader community often misinterpret support needs. The so-called *medical model* of disability continues to perpetuate a notion that people with disabilities must be "cared for" and are unable to make their own decisions (The Open University, 2006). For this reason, it is often thought that people with disabilities do not need health information and, further, that they would most likely not be able to understand it. Some people also feel that people with disabilities should also be protected from unpleasant news or frightening facts.

A situation that I encounter frequently in my HIV prevention education work is the common belief that people with disabilities are not sexually active or otherwise involved in risk activities. Thus, they have no need for HIV prevention information. Some see sexual health information as "dangerous," since it can precipitate disclosure of sexual abuse or, ostensibly, may encourage people to become sexually active or promiscuous.

Whether they live in institutions or in the community, people with disabilities frequently experience social isolation and must struggle with the stereotypes and misconceptions still common in our society. The social interaction, which facilitates information exchange and conversations about health, may be absent.

Personal Barriers

Based on my experience working with people with all types of disabilities, personal barriers may be overwhelming and are usually related to the disability and the impact it has had on the person's life. For many, the notion that information can provide value or power is unfamiliar. For those who have been socially excluded by disability and poverty, exercising power or using information to leverage their rights does not occur to them. In cases where people do recognize that information would be helpful, they are frequently inexperienced in how to approach an information search or even how to articulate their interest or need to others who can help. Many do not realize that information can be converted to formats that are more accessible or easier to understand. Many experience additional challenges such as anger, resentment, low self-esteem, or lack of experience in navigating complex or bureaucratic service organizations. In addition, most disabilities are accompanied by low energy caused by pain, strain, or medication. The energy required for tending to normal daily living activities leaves little left over for an information search.

I once gave a workshop to a group of volunteers at a community organization. Many of the participants had disabilities, and most had low levels of education and literacy. All were passionate about their organization and their cause, making them motivated to learn about ways that they could use information to help themselves and others served by their organization. I soon discovered that my carefully prepared handouts on basic directories and search strategies were useless to these participants. Instead, we spent the time discussing ways of thinking about information needs and sources and ways of navigating the idiosyncrasies of readily available tools such as the telephone book or Yellow Pages Directory. We talked about terminology and how information and community resources might be described. We also discussed ways of brainstorming related information in order to find a community organization where they might find a helpful like-minded individual.

I explained the role of the public library and the wealth of resources that they could access there—free of charge. Unfortunately, some of the more assertive individuals had tried using the public library and had had unpleasant experiences. I was asked what they should do when the reference librarian did not give them the help they needed—most likely, one person said, because their clothes were dirty and they "might not have smelled very clean." A man who stuttered asked me what he should do because he was unable to communicate clearly or in a timely manner. He explained that he was often too embarrassed to witness the reactions in person, and so sometimes tried to use the telephone. He said that phone interaction was even worse as people would simply hang up.

I felt unprepared to answer these questions but offered suggestions based on my experience with human nature rather than my expertise as an information professional. I emphasized that they had a right to respectful service. I said that based on my experience as an information seeker and an information provider, service providers are human beings and sometimes have harried moments or stressful days. I suggested that when this happens they should remain patient but persistent and try a different staff person or come back another day. We talked about very basic issues such as how to cope with assumptions and biases that block communication and information. I suggested that the man who stuttered borrow a technique that a client with cerebral palsy had used with me. He could try preparing and practicing a one- or two-sentence introductory statement such as "I have a speech disability, please be patient with me." Often poor service is a result of unsuccessful communication and one or both participants not knowing what to do to improve the information flow.

REFLECTIONS FROM CONSUMERS

Health Literacy Challenges Occurring Across All Disability Types

In my work, I have observed common health literacy challenges across all types of disabilities. Low literacy skills, lack of experience seeking and using health information, difficulty understanding or communicating concepts, low energy, perception of health information as a low priority, inability or unwillingness to by-pass information gatekeepers, and lack of persistence and confidence to challenge assumptions of service providers can impede people with disabilities of all types. Unfortunately, even for those who are able to identify their information needs, retrieve relevant information, assess the quality and apply it to a specific situation, chances are high that they may not be able to implement good health decisions based on the information. When good health decisions involve a diet or therapy not covered by health insurance, seeking an alternate medical opinion, purchasing over-the-counter medications or supplements not covered by health insurance or disability benefits, or sometimes even simply securing safe, accessible housing, people with disabilities may recognize a good health decision but soon discover that it is beyond their grasp. In situations like these, one has to question just how much *power* information provides.

Physical Disabilities/Chronic Health Conditions

ACCESS TO INFORMATION THROUGH PUBLIC LIBRARIES

When discussing "access to health information," many of the people I have encountered describe public library experiences. For a variety of reasons these experiences are often less than satisfactory. In addition, people with disabilities have consistently noted that they do not believe that their public library has enough information about their specific illness or disability. It should also be noted that most of these individuals were unable to use the computer, or felt uncomfortable doing so, and hence had limited access to resources. Pseudonyms have been used in all personal stories that follow.

Physical access continues to be a significant barrier for people with physical disabilities. For those who live in rural areas, transportation may be the first barrier, and lack of accessible sidewalks, walkways, and buildings too often await those who make the effort. In urban environments, physical accessibility is also inconsistent. In my organization, we often hear of individuals being dropped off by accessible transit only to find that there are no curb dips to enable them to get off the sidewalk, leaving them stranded until they can get assistance. Accessible washrooms are also variable and sometimes placed in isolated locations that feel unsafe. One library user needed the accessible washroom but felt like an imposter—that he did not really qualify as a person with a disability because his chronic pain from arthritis and spinal stenosis did not require the use of a walker or wheelchair. Some with physical disabilities have described "learned dependence" as a problem when people give up and become passive recipients of whatever information or services others will provide for them.

Physical disabilities may be invisible and are often combined with other types of disabilities. Balance, strength, and energy are commonly affected and individuals may struggle with depression or other mental health conditions. Christine, who is physically disabled, commented that the only elevator available for her to enter the library required that she obtain a key from a staff person. She chose not to use the library rather than draw attention to herself. What may seem like small issues to an able-bodied individual can feel overwhelming to someone who must strategize each task and activity in advance and may feel *different* or *a burden* to others.

Access to materials, computers, and other equipment may be limited for people with physical disabilities. While library outreach services may meet the needs of many, others have expressed frustration with their inability to browse the library shelves as they used to. Waiting in line for accessible computer stations for catalog, database or Internet searching can seem like too much effort.

In a telephone conversation with me on February 21, 2007, Iris, a woman whose stroke had affected her left arm and leg, said that she also had a mental illness. She told me that she was too embarrassed to ask for information about stroke and mental illness and that "in the beginning, my doctor gave me information to take home but now he doesn't have time." Iris said that she repeatedly tried to use her public library but was frustrated because "they keep telling me to look in the computer." She is embarrassed to say that she is not able to use the computer and she "feels too stupid" to take a workshop offered at the library. When asked what she wants from library staff, she said, "Treat us like other people . . . with respect . . . but take time with us." She said, "I feel like I'm wasting their time, that I'm not important."

Karen has myalgic encephalomyelitis (ME) and in an e-mail to me on February 19, 2007, she described herself as "80–90 percent housebound, using a scooter and cane/knee braces to go out about twice a week for errands and appointments. I also have memory and cognitive difficulties." She added, "I have always been an enthusiastic reader and library user since early childhood. Now, I am having difficulty finding books I can read. I live rurally and so do not have access to support groups or a full range of medical care. I have cognitive issues—with the density of information in a medical research article, for instance. I have trouble reading and am comprehending at a far lower level than I'm used to. It's frustrating." Karen suggested that an online tutorial (accessible from home) to help her learn to use the online catalog would be helpful as would "book 'density' ratings for people with cognitive impairments and concentration issues."

Sharon, a library user with fibromyalgia, arthritis, and chronic fatigue, suggested to me in an e-mail February 23, 2007, that library staff who could work with people with disabilities one-on-one to help them learn to use the online catalog and other resources would be very useful. "In addition, several computers should be allocated just for persons with a disability, like a parking space. Also, when I need several books from the shelves, assistance to carry items to a desk" would be very appreciated.

Carol, a survivor of several motor vehicle accidents, lives with chronic pain and physical challenges. In a telephone conversation with me on March 16, 2007, she told me she does not have a phone, computer, or television. She said that she loves books and the library is her "only connection." Regarding access and asking for assistance, she said, "My disabilities are invisible. People don't realize and I don't like letting people know."

ACCESS TO INFORMATION THROUGH OTHER SOURCES

People with physical disabilities and chronic health conditions who are able to access the Internet, obtain health information from a variety of online support groups, disability-specific listservs, and Web sites. Christine noted that she gets health information from "her specialist, the Internet, especially in the beginning when I was first diagnosed, and from friends with the same disease." Shirley explained in an e-mail to me on March 6, 2007, that she gets her health information "mostly from the Internet, from family and friends," and from disability-specific magazines.

Other sources accessed include occupational therapists, pharmacists, and a university library while taking courses. Jeff wrote in an e-mail to me February 17, 2007, that he uses the Crane Resource Centre and Library, which provides "course-support materials in four media: recorded "talking books," Braille, large type, and ordinary print" at the University of British Columbia. For health information, he relies on people he knows and the Vancouver Resource Society, a community organization providing support to people with physical disabilities (Jeff also has MS).

In an e-mail to me on March 19, 2007, Cameron wrote that he contracted hepatitis C from intravenous drug use in the early 1980s. He learned about the disease by collecting information from "established drug user self-help organizations around the world," and from healthcare providers who treated drug users and people infected with hepatitis C. He later became active in a hepatitis C support group and began doing education workshops. I asked Cameron how information service providers could help. "[By] providing and offering a place to sit down when it is obvious that somebody is physically challenged. I am often embarrassed or ashamed of aspects of my disability and how it affects my ability to just manage some of the very basic stuff, and asking for help can be really hard. When at the library, I like to be provided with a seat at the counter where I am dealing with the librarian, and I like it when they are willing and able to take the time to bring some items to me rather than leave me struggling for fifteen minutes to get to the other end of the room, often too exhausted to bother looking for books at the end of it all anyway. Service providers can do a lot to help us feel less shame and embarrassment."

Alex is living with chronic HIV and hepatitis B. In a telephone conversation with me on February 28, 2007, he described his illnesses as affecting his mobility because of numbness in his hands and feet (peripheral neuropathy), gastro-intestinal disorders, recurrent yeast infections, and recurrent shingles. He facilitates an HIV/AIDS support group and used to be a public library user until the local AIDS service organization's library was developed. He is a strong supporter of community organizations as sources of health information and said that public libraries should refer people to community organizations for information more often. He feels that anecdotal information obtained from support groups is very useful. Alex also takes advantage of events featuring local HIV/AIDS experts as well as a national organization called the Canadian AIDS Treatment Information Exchange (CATIE). He also uses the Treatment Information Project at the BC Persons with AIDS Society, which offers an information hotline and peer counseling.

Developmental Disabilities

Individuals with developmental disabilities have a broad range of literacy and communication skills. In my work, people with developmental disabilities consistently ask for materials that are reader-friendly, including large print and materials with illustrations. Robert Melrose, librarian at the Down Syndrome Research Foundation in Burnaby, BC, co-developed a literacy program with speech-language pathologist, Susan Fawcett. In an e-mail to me, he confirmed the need for adapted materials that interest and motivate the student in reading. He noted that often students who are delayed in reading perform at higher levels in expressive language, reasoning, and comprehension of images (Robert Melrose, e-mail communication, February 9, 2007).

Roger, a middle-aged man with a developmental disability who lives with a roommate in the community, has a special interest in music and birds. He explained in a telephone conversation with me on March 12, 2007, that he knows he has a disability but "I don't like explaining it to people." He acknowledged that this sometimes makes it difficult to get information. He said that it's helpful to have a good memory. Roger is an avid public library user and said that the staff are "very, very good. They all know me . . . if they're busy, I just wait." He does get health information from the library and usually asks the staff to help him find it. When asked about advice for service providers to make access easier for people with disabilities, he said that "computers are tricky to work on" and staff "should help people more." Roger's relationship with the staff at his branch library is key to his access to information.

In 1999–2000, I conducted interviews with 20 adults with developmental disabilities living independently in the community to assess their barriers to health information. The most common challenge was low self-esteem and lack of confidence to ask for help. They felt that asking for help identified them as different and in some way lacking. Their preferred source of health information was their family doctor. The reliability of this information source was variable, depending on their communication skills and confidence and the receptivity of their physician. Health information picked up from TV or radio was typically too brief and not useful to them.

Individuals frequently obtain information from community living health nurses or support workers they know. When plain language information is not available, people with developmental disabilities need to be able to ask for clarification from someone they trust without embarrassment or shame. The service provider's lack of respect or impatience with the question is quickly communicated through body language and will affect the information flow and willingness of the client to seek information in future. Increased vulnerability to sexual abuse for people with developmental disabilities makes accessible sexual health information essential.

Brain Injuries

Brain injuries are surprisingly common. Researchers estimate that the incidence is 600/100,000 population (Cassidy et al., 2004) An invisible disability, the symptoms may be multiple and are often intermittent and unpredictable.

Access to Information Through Public Libraries

Ken suffered a brain injury in a motor vehicle accident 25 years ago. In a telephone conversation with me on February 21, 2007, he explained that he has recovered most of his speech but has difficulty writing and cannot use a computer because of the "logic and sequential steps required." He cannot remember numbers and is dyslexic—something he finds extremely difficult to accept after being a straight-A student when he was young. He has intermittent amnesia, memory loss, a poor sense of time and he loses things constantly. Ken says he has "a trail of missing things in life," including longtime friends. While living in an urban center, Ken tried to use his public library without success. Referring to computers in the library, he said "you're supposed to know how to do those things." He felt that asking for help would make the library staff think he was stupid. He felt ashamed, perceiving a "demeaning tone" and a "look of pity" from library staff. "I've walked away countless times . . . it's very frustrating." Recently, Ken and his partner, who also has a brain injury, moved to a small community where he has become friendly with the librarian. Knowing about his brain injury, she helps him find whatever he needs.

Jason has had his brain injury for 12 years following a multicar collision. In a conversation with me on March 1, 2007, he described the difficulty he has with memory, learning, and comprehension. He reads voraciously though and "jots down expressions" from the newspaper to improve his English skills. Jason rarely asks for help at the public library after a series of unsatisfactory experiences. Several years ago he went to three different public libraries (in two separate municipalities and systems) to try to find newspaper articles about his car accident. Each time, he was told that he would have to use the microfilm readers. No one accompanied him to show him how to use them. An outwardly optimistic man, Jason's perspective on the library is jarring. He says, "I rarely ask for help at the library—they don't care that I have memory problems or a brain injury. Once I showed my brain injury card . . . and they just didn't care." Asked for his advice for library staff serving people with disabilities, Jason said, "I expect librarians to give help . . . step-by-step help . . . for people who come. As far as I recall, they have never gone with me to the computer. Sometimes I feel embarrassed. I don't like to ask more of them . . . but if I understand this time, maybe next time I won't know and will need to ask the same question." I asked him if he would be interested in attending a workshop on using the library and he was immediately enthusiastic but then said that he would be worried that the instructor would not have enough time for him. Fortunately, Jason's health information needs are met elsewhere as his wife is a nurse and his friend is a physiotherapist.

ACCESS TO INFORMATION THROUGH OTHER SOURCES

In a phone conversation on February 14, 2007, Brad told me that he was a chef until his car accident seven years ago left him with a brain injury. He can no longer work, has significant short-term memory problems, vertigo and accompanying nausea and blurred vision and is unable to retain what he reads. He also has tinnitus, fatigue and "terrible depression." Brad does not use the public library because "I get lost, forget why I'm there, and can't get the point across—I lose the conversation." He also feels embarrassed about slurring his words and feels obliged to explain that his medication is the cause. Fortunately, Brad is able to obtain information about his medications from his psychiatrist and uses the Internet with the help of his wife to get other health information. He notes that he prefers to learn visually and likes videos. Information transferred aurally becomes "paisley in my head."

Low Vision or Blindness

Most of the people I have talked to who have low vision or are blind use their public library to borrow large print, audio books, descriptive videos, or DVDs, etc. Ashley tends to get her health information from her family and recommends that service providers offer more information in large print and Braille formats. She adds that high quality and accessible Web sites are a way to meet the needs of many people with disabilities. Ashley also believes that library staff should receive more training about disabilities of all types and the ways that they affect people's lives.

Andrea explained in an e-mail to me March 14, 2007, that she is blind but this is not a barrier to information. "It may take me a little bit longer to obtain specific information, but I was never in a situation where I was not able to get health

information because of my disability." As a graduate student, Andrea uses different types of libraries depending on her need. She gets health information from
electronic newsletters, Web sites, the university health services nurse, and by following up media stories with her own research. Her recommendation for library
staff: they should be trained in accessibility—both for Web sites and for assisting
people with disabilities. "Many times, staff have no idea how to help, or what to
do, and it takes time to explain exactly how they can be of help."

Low Hearing or Deafness

David has been profoundly hard of hearing for 20 years and lives with carcinoid
cancer (requiring treatment in hospital every three weeks) and post-polio syndrome. In an e-mail to me February 18, 2007, he said that for the past 12 years
he has had a hearing dog to alert him to sirens, alarms, doorbells—and his TTY
phone. Fatigue and pain contribute to his hearing challenge, as it is more difficult
to make the effort required. David describes being deaf or hard of hearing as a
"very low position on the barometer of disabilities . . . we look fine, there is no
visual disability, so often people think we should just turn up our hearing aids and
listen." He points out that hearing aids only amplify the sounds that the person
can hear and cannot replace the tones that they are unable to hear. "So our lives
are filled with guessing . . . " and filling in the gaps by speech reading. David says
that filling in the blanks to piece together conversations all day is exhausting.

   David is an avid library user and notes that his local library's fax machine is a
valuable communication tool for serving people who are hard of hearing or deaf.
He provides training sessions for new library staff on communication with people
who are deaf or hard of hearing. He says that service providers working with computers typically face the computer and not the person with the hearing disability,
making speech reading difficult or impossible. Common recommendations for
communicating with people with hearing disabilities include the following:

- Get the individual's attention before you begin to speak.
- Minimize background noises.
- Face the person with your mouth unobstructed by hands and do not chew
  gum.
- Speak clearly—do not shout.
- Be concise and avoid long convoluted sentences.
- Rephrase if necessary.
- Write messages to help communication.
- Remember that background noise or an unfamiliar accent may create gaps
  in verbal communication for someone who is hard of hearing.
- When communicating through an interpreter, face the individual requesting
  information.

As with other disabilities, people who are hard of hearing or deaf may have other issues affecting their ability to communicate and absorb information. Fatigue, medication, anxiety, and level of comfort with the person they are communicating with will impact the information flow.

Mental Health Disabilities

For mental health consumers, stigma is a major barrier to information. Sandra wrote in an e-mail to me March 5, 2007, that her disabilities include post-traumatic stress disorder, self-injury, borderline personality disorder, irritable bowel syndrome (IBS), asthma, and gastroesophageal reflux disease. She notes that due to her mental illness, it can be difficult to approach service providers by telephone or in person. She prefers to be able to find information independently. She finds it embarrassing to ask for help finding information about IBS, and "self-injury tends to be a taboo subject with not very much information available."

Janet's disabilities include depression, bipolar disorder, attention deficit disorder, and low vision. She "can't read signs, addresses, even large numbers at the library." She is "afraid to get labeled so won't ask people about health concerns." In an e-mail to me February 13, 2007, Janet said that she doesn't always understand terminology and doesn't want to "look stupid" so doesn't ask for more information.

In an e-mail on February 14, 2007, Kristy described living with chronic mental illness and pointed out that "people can get lost and very confused trying to find their way through the library maze. The disabled may need help . . . to think through the library process." She suggested that library Web sites list disability supports available and library staff have "*disability days* devoted to showing disabled people the facilities available and how to access them." Kristy and others I've talked to who live with mental illness say that they think it would be useful for service providers to receive training about disabilities and emphasized the importance of treating library users with empathy and respect. Mary, who also has bipolar disorder, said in an e-mail to me on February 13, 2007, that it would be very useful for public libraries to be more connected to community organizations to share information in both directions.

According to mental health consumers, depression and anxiety disorders are frequently undiagnosed and or untreated, adding to health literacy challenges. For those who do receive treatment, ability to access and understand health information may be affected by their medication.

Learning Disabilities

Learning disabilities are estimated to affect 8–10 percent of the population (Nielsen, 2006) and include dyslexia (affecting reading, writing, and spelling), dyscalculia (affecting arithmetic skills), dysgraphia (affecting handwriting, spelling, and composition), and dyspraxia (affecting fine motor skills) (National Center for Learning Disabilities, 2006). People with one or more learning disabilities may also have information processing disorder or attention deficit hyperactivity disorder (ADHD). Learning disabilities are invisible, may coexist with other disabilities or chronic health conditions, and make following medication or treatment regimens extremely difficult.

Carson is a middle-aged man, highly intelligent, who nearly finished his bachelor's degree. He suffered encephalitis as an infant. He has "severe learning disabilities," including dyslexia and dyspraxia, and he believes he has attention deficit disorder. Carson is morbidly obese and suffers from clinical depression and anxiety. Although he can read without difficulty, he says that his spelling is so poor that even his computer spellchecker does not help. Although keyboarding is difficult because of his poor hand-eye coordination, the computer enables him to write letters and do his coursework. When asked where he goes for health information, he says that he has a very good family doctor who is willing to spend time answering his questions. He also gets health information from a librarian at a community organization. Although an avid public library user, Carson does have some concern about asking for help from the librarians for fear of "looking stupid." He has encountered judgmental attitudes in the past.

Nielsen (2006) notes that people with dyslexia often suffer from low self-esteem, and that providing good library service to people with this disability may mean, "changing the attitude of library staff and teaching them the appropriate way to interact with and assist dyslexic library patrons." Learning disabilities are challenging for service providers because they are invisible and may cause an unpredictable array of difficulties for the client. Learning disabilities may make it difficult to formulate a question in order to ask for help, and the stigma and shame may prevent the individual from disclosing their disability.

THE ROLE OF LIBRARIANS IN HEALTH LITERACY FOR PEOPLE WITH DISABILITIES

Why Librarians?

Librarians are ideally positioned to bridge health information and the needs of people with disabilities. Our training provides us with a unique and valuable toolkit, a blend of expertise in the areas of information science and human relations. On a daily basis, librarians practice excellent communication techniques in the provision of reference services by:

- clarifying questions,
- avoiding assumptions,
- checking the client's level of understanding and current knowledge,

- remaining open and questioning how best to help,
- being respectful,
- being creative, and
- being persistent.

Our professional philosophy is particularly suited to solving the health literacy challenge because librarians:

- are steeped in an *information sharing ethic*;
- have an awareness of the impact of barriers to information access: *information have/have nots* and the *digital divide*, etc.;
- are aware of the implications of low literacy skills;
- have training in and an understanding of language and the role it plays in information access:
  - subject terminology: understanding the many ways a concept can be expressed or understood
  - the range of client skill levels in terms of expressing information needs or understanding information provided
  - the need to analyze the client's question/information need—asking questions, paraphrasing, confirming understanding and level of information required
- have experience working with people with different levels of expertise;
- have experience working with diverse audiences: seniors, youth, ESL, different cultures, people with disabilities, etc.;
- are accustomed to tapping networks and outside expertise when required to find the information (content, level, format) needed by the client; and
- enjoy the challenge of finding the *right* information for their client—the thrill of the chase—making us especially suited to ferreting out health information in a specific format or at a low reading level to meet the need of individuals with health literacy challenges.

Sphere of Influence

The diversity of environments in which we work also makes librarians well prepared to address the health literacy challenges for people with disabilities. Librarians working in all types of libraries are in a position to help. For example:

- Public libraries—available to serve people with disabilities in most communities
- Academic libraries—librarians can influence awareness of health literacy in the training of health and allied professionals as well as students with disabilities
- Special libraries, such as:
  - health research and professional associations where professionals can be educated about the information challenges and needs of their patients,

- ○ pharmaceutical and health product manufacturers where health product packaging and instructions can be created using appropriate language to address health literacy issues,
- ○ health or hospital libraries serving healthcare professionals and/or the public, and
- ○ community agencies serving people with specific disabilities or specific interests, including seniors, youth, people with English as a second language, recent immigrants, etc.

Tips from and for Librarians

Through my experience working with people with disabilities I have assembled a toolkit of communication strategies. Incorporating these recommendations will address many of the service issues and criticisms described by people with disabilities in the stories above. These suggestions were documented for workshop participants who primarily provide telephone service, but typically these apply to face-to-face communication as well. Many are obvious but the key for effectiveness is to maintain awareness.

- Listening and empathy are the best tools for interaction and are effective regardless of ability or disability. In telephone communication, listening may provide your only clue to special needs.
- Tone of voice conveys much more about your attitude than you may realize. Warmth and interest facilitate communication.
- Ask questions to clarify and assess information needed.
- Choose words carefully. Are there other words you can use to convey the information or question?
- Speaking quickly eliminates the division between the words, causing confusion or misunderstanding. If you have an accent that is unfamiliar to the listener, speaking quickly can make it even more difficult to understand.
- Pauses in your speech are especially important for people with disabilities. It separates sentences and ideas and gives the listener time to absorb the information. It also allows time for them to compose a question or to take notes.
- Allow the listener to pause. People may need longer to process what you have said and to develop a response. If they use a ventilator, for example, they may pause regularly. Avoid the urge to fill the silences.
- If possible, avoid multitasking while speaking on the telephone. Keyboarding is usually audible to the listener and can be perceived as lack of attention. If you must keyboard while talking to the person, explain why.
- If you are providing directions, names, or telephone numbers which must be written down, be aware that the listener may be slow or may have to relay the information to another person to record. In addition, the person may

not wish to disclose that he or she cannot write down the information. If appropriate, offer to mail information.

- Tell the client that they can call you back if they need to. It offers some comfort to know that they can reach a friendly voice if necessary. I have never had anyone abuse this offer.
- Never assume that the client should get a friend or family member to call for them. Making this call may have been a small step toward the client's independence—an essential element in a fulfilling and healthy life.
- Never doubt the importance of your information and understanding.

The following are suggestions offered by workshop participants. Most were information and referral staff, many of them librarians.

- Be aware of noise, light, etc., and how the surrounding stimuli can affect willingness and ability to concentrate, think and communicate.
- Be sure to give people enough time to think, formulate their response or questions and communicate with you.
- Ask questions to confirm, clarify, and explore issues but always be cautious about tone and appearing to interrogate.
- Beware of assumptions about the client's tone of voice and body language. Our interpretations are not always correct.
- Consider your own body language and tone of voice. Are you eliciting an unintended reaction from your client by glancing at your watch (in face-to-face meetings) or because you are feeling impatient or exhausted?

Cheryl Stenstrom, an independent library consultant based in Lunenburg, Nova Scotia, leads workshops on library services to people with disabilities. Discussing the challenges of providing quality library services to people with invisible disabilities, Cheryl points out the value of partnerships between libraries and relevant disability-related agencies to offer disability awareness and sensitivity training to staff. In an e-mail to me March 22, 2007, Cheryl shared recommendations and best practices discussed during her workshops:

- Review library policies for accessibility.
- Develop a disabilities advisory committee made up of people with disabilities.
- Provide space on general registration forms for disability disclosure and request for information about accessibility support.
- Use large print signage that includes symbols or images.
- Provide staff training in the use of plain language.
- Ensure that physical space and Web site are accessible.
- Offer workshops on use of adaptive technology and readers.
- Be disability-friendly—offer magnifying glasses; produce a "Start Here" guide for alternate formats; add extra signage; place a bench near the

library entrance and at the transit stop; ask a wheelchair user to review your accessible washroom for improvements; add adjustable-height tables; ensure that pay phones, photocopiers, and change machines are accessible.

- Promote your disability-friendly library in the community.

DIRECTION FOR THE FUTURE

Clearly, access to health information and services for people with disabilities is a challenge. That people with disabilities are at increased risk due to frequent interaction with the healthcare system, including increased use of medication is well documented. Low literacy, societal barriers, and personal barriers combine to create walls that are perceived as insurmountable by many.

Partnerships between libraries of all types and community agencies are an important step in improving health literacy for people with disabilities. Libraries need the expertise and experience of community agency staff and volunteers to help develop the best practices described above. Libraries can also gain access to and build credibility with people with disabilities through the gateway provided by community agencies. Community agencies should also consider the benefits of partnering with libraries. Opportunities to improve access to information and to training for their clients who "find it all on the Internet," for example, are valuable steps for increasing independence and self-empowerment.

The emergence of *community development librarianship* will help to reduce barriers to libraries and health information for people with disabilities. New librarians will be exposed to the notion of community partnerships and libraries as a key element in community development. I believe that even more could be achieved on the health literacy front if greater partnerships could be developed between academic, special, public and school libraries.

Librarians have the expertise, service philosophy, and the opportunity to be a strong force in the health literacy movement. As professionals who understand both the world of information and diverse user needs, we are ideal for this leadership role. Historically, librarians have always advocated for those without power or voice. Barriers to information are greater than ever. In the arena of health information, the consequences can be deadly. Serving people with low health literacy skills is our responsibility and at the core of our professional values—serving those who need it most. Ensuring that information is available, accessible, and usable is what we do.

REFERENCES

Broemeling, Anne-Marie, Diane Watson, and Charlyn Black. 2005. *Chronic Conditions and Co-morbidity among Residents of British Columbia.* Vancouver, BC: University of British Columbia. Centre for Health Services and Policy Research. Available: www .chspr.ubc.ca/research/patterna/chronic

Canada. 2006. Government of Newfoundland and Labrador. Violence Prevention Initiative. "Facts on Violence: Violence Against Persons with Disabilities." Available: www.gov.nf.ca/vpi/facts/disabilities.html

Canadian Council on Social Development. 2003. Disability Research Information Page. "The Health and Well-being of Persons with Disabilities." (Disability Information Sheet No. 9). Available: www.ccsd.ca/drip/research/dis9/dis9.pdf

Canadian Council on Social Development. 2004a. Disability Research Information Page. "Persons with Disabilities and Health." (Disability Information Sheet No. 14). Available: www.ccsd.ca/drip/research/ dis14/dis14.pdf

Canadian Council on Social Development. 2004b. Disability Research Information Page. "Persons with Disabilities and Their Contact with Medical Professionals and Alternative Health Care Providers." (Disability Information Sheet No. 13). Available: www.ccsd.ca/drip/research/ drip13/drip13.pdf

Canadian Council on Social Development. 2004c. Disability Research Information Page. "Persons with Disabilities and Medication Use." (Disability Information Sheet No. 11). Available: www.ccsd.ca/drip/research/ dis11/dis11.pdf

Canadian Council on Social Development. 2005. Disability Research Information Page. "Supports and Services for Persons with Disabilities in Canada: Requirements and Gaps." (Disability Information Sheet No. 17). Available: www.ccsd.ca/drip/research/ drip17/drip17/pdf

Cassidy, J. David, Linda Carroll, Paul Peloso, Jörgen Borg, Hans von Holst, Lena Holm, Jess Kraus, and Victor Coronado. 2004. "Incidence, Risk Factors and Prevention of Mild Traumatic Brain Injury: Results of the WHO Collaborating Centre Task Force on Mild Traumatic Brain Injury." [Abstract]. *Journal of Rehabilitation Medicine* 36, Suppl 43 (February). Available: www.ingentaconnect.com/content/tandf/sreh/2004/ 00000036/ A043s043/art00007

Groce, Nora E. 2004. "HIV/AIDS and Disability: Capturing Hidden Voices." *The Yale University/World Bank Global Survey on HIV/AIDS and Disability.* New Haven, CT: Yale University. Available: http://globalsurvey .med.yale.edu/capturing_hidden_voices_1 .pdf

Kapsalis, Costa. 1999. *The Effect of Disabilities on Literacy Skills.* Napean, ON: Data Probe Economic Consulting. Available: www.nald.ca/lil/english/litinfo/printdoc/effect/ effect.pdf

Kroll, Thilo, Gwyn C. Jones, Matthew Kehn, and Melinda T. Neri. 2006. "Barriers and Strategies Affecting the Utilisation of Primary Preventive Services for People with Physical Disabilities: A Qualitative Inquiry," *Health & Social Care in the Community* 14, no.4 (July): 284–293.

Lewis, Mary Ann, Charles E. Lewis, Barbara Leake, Bryan H. King, Robert Lindemann. 2002. "The Quality of Health Care for Adults with Developmental Disabilities." *Public Health Reports* 117, no.2 (March): 174–184. Available: www.journals.elsevierhealth .com/periodicals/phr/article/ PIIS0033354904501243/fulltext

Marge, Dorothy K., ed. 2003. *A Call to Action: Ending Crimes of Violence Against Children and Adults with Disabilities: A Report to the Nation.* Syracuse, NY: SUNY Upstate Medical University. Department of Physical Medicine and Rehabilitation. Available: www.upsate.edu/ pmr/marge.pdf

Medical Library Association. 2003. MLANET. "Health Information Literacy." Available: www.mlanet.org/resources/healthlit/define.html

Movement for Canadian Literacy. 2004. "Factsheet: Literacy and Disabilities." Available: www.literacy.ca/litand/3.htm

National Center for Learning Disabilities. 2006. "LD at a Glance: A Quick Look." Available: www.ncld.org/index.php?option=content&task=view &id=452

Nielsen, Gyda Skat. 2006. "Library Services to Persons with Dyslexia." (Paper presented at the World Library and Information Congress: 72nd IFLA General Conference and Council, Seoul, Korea, August 20–24). Available: www.ifla.org/IV/ifla72/papers/101-Nielsen-en.pdf

The Open University. 2006. Higher Education Funding Council for England. "Making Your Teaching Inclusive." Available: www.open.ac.uk/ inclusiveteaching/pages/under-standing-and-awareness/medical-model.php

Public Health Agency of Canada. 2003. Population Health. "What Determines Health?" Available: www.phac-aspc.gc.ca/ph-sp/phdd/determinants/ index.html#determinants

Veltman, Albina, Donna E. Stewart, Gaetan S. Tardif, and Monica Branigan. 2001. "Perceptions of Primary Healthcare Services Among People with Physical Disabilities. Part 1: Access Issues," *Medscape General Medicine* 3, no.2. Available: www.medscape.com/viewarticle/408122

Chapter 8

Health Literacy and America's Senior Citizens

Marcy Brown

In September 2006, the U.S. Department of Education published results from the 2003 National Assessment of Adult Literacy (NAAL). Using written and printed health information and three literacy scales—prose literacy, document literacy, and quantitative literacy—survey results showed that adults over the age of 65 had lower average health literacy than adults in all younger age groups (Kutner et al., 2006: v). Thirty-eight percent of seniors had *intermediate* health literacy (5), defined as "skills necessary to perform moderately challenging literacy activities" (12). Only 3 percent were considered *proficient*, while 59 percent had *basic* or *below basic* health literacy skills (12–13). The research data from NAAL leaves little doubt that many senior citizens have trouble understanding health information.

Outcomes associated with low health literacy include poor health self-management skills, lower use of preventive health services, and higher hospitalization rates (Gazmararian et al., 2003, Scott et al., 2002, Baker et al., 2002). Since senior citizens are more likely to experience a decline in health status, these poor outcomes can represent a significant expense, as well as a significant decrease in their quality of life.

While a serious problem, this relationship between seniors and health literacy is not really news. For years, studies have shown that health literacy is limited in the aged and that it leads to a whole host of health problems. This chapter provides an overview of studies concerning health literacy issues in America's aging population. The chapter is divided into the following sections:

- A review of existing research summarizing the relationship between age and health literacy, and possible reasons for the poor outcomes
- An overview of a newly defined, multidimensional health literacy model that could revolutionize interventions for older adults
- Descriptions of health literacy interventions for seniors that operate outside of any library involvement
- Summaries of interventions for seniors that are managed or comanaged by librarians
- A brief review of adult learning preferences and activities designed to meet those preferences
- Recommendations for librarians, health educators, and program planners incorporating what we know about health literacy, adult learning, and relevance to seniors

REVIEW OF EXISTING RESEARCH

Much of our existing knowledge about health literacy in the aged comes from research published by physicians from Emory University and from Case Western Reserve University. In 1999, Gazmararian et al. published their first major findings in an article in the *Journal of the American Medical Association.* The researchers interviewed more than 3,000 Medicare enrollees in Cleveland, Houston, south Florida, and Tampa. To test literacy levels, they used the Short Test of Functional Health Literacy in Adults (S-TOFHLA), wherein scores range from 0 to 100 (0–53 = inadequate health literacy, 54–66 = marginal health literacy, and 67–100 = adequate health literacy). The authors found that 34 percent of English-speaking participants had either inadequate or marginal health literacy, while 54 percent of Spanish-speaking seniors had inadequate or marginal health literacy (547). Results were also analyzed and compared across the four cities. Even after adjusting for variables such as language or income level, the participants in Cleveland were more likely to have lower health literacy (548). The authors used this result to stress that program planners should evaluate data on a local or regional level, rather than rely on national surveys and studies.

Health Literacy and Age

Using the data collected from the above group of Medicare-enrolled seniors, Baker et al. (2000) found that health literacy scores on S-TOFHLA declined 1.4 points for every year over the age of 65. This relationship between age and health literacy did not change even after investigators adjusted results for the presence of chronic disease, physical function, mental health, and visual acuity. The authors theorized that declining health literacy may be less related to lower reading ability than to an individual's working memory. Working memory includes the ability to store and manage information in the short term for complex cognitive tasks.

Health Literacy and Preventive Care

Scott et al. (2002) also used the data from the Medicare-enrolled study population to examine whether seniors with low health literacy were less likely to obtain preventive healthcare. They looked at the rates of influenza and pneumococcal vaccinations, mammograms, and Pap smears. Participation in these preventive care services was self reported rather than taken from claims data. Since Pap smears aren't recommended for most women over 65, seniors were asked whether or not they ever received a Pap smear. There was a significant association between inadequate health literacy, as measured by S-TOFHLA, and failure to receive any of the vaccinations or screening tests in question. Interestingly, years of formal education were not independently associated with any of the preventive services, a finding which surprised the researchers.

Health Literacy and Hospital Admission

Another study examined whether low health literacy was an independent risk factor for hospital admission (Baker et al., 2002). Results were based on Medicare claims for the two years following the initial interviews described above. Seniors with inadequate health literacy had a 34.9 percent hospitalization rate, those with marginal health literacy were at 33.9 percent, and participants with adequate literacy had a 26.7 percent hospitalization rate (1280). The authors adjusted for differences in age, sex, race, language, income, and years of formal education, and still determined that the risk of being hospitalized was higher for elderly persons with lower health literacy.

Health Literacy and Chronic Disease

As people age, their likelihood of contracting a chronic disease increases. Unsuccessfully managing chronic disease leads to higher healthcare costs, more hospital admissions, and lower quality of life for disease sufferers. It is plausible to suggest that to manage a chronic illness requires at least a moderate level of health literacy, so documenting the health literacy of seniors with chronic disease becomes an important factor in the development of disease management services and interpretation of outcomes.

Gazmararian et al. (2003) used their previous Medicare claims data to interview seniors who had one of four chronic conditions: asthma, diabetes, congestive heart failure, and hypertension. Fifteen-minute telephone interviews were conducted to evaluate the patient's knowledge of his or her chronic disease, using questions "designed to measure the essential concepts that are typically communicated to patients with these diseases" (268). Health literacy was again measured using S-TOFHLA. Knowledge of each chronic disease was poor, even among those participants who had adequate health literacy scores. For individuals with three of the conditions—asthma, diabetes, and congestive heart failure—disease knowledge was significantly lower for those with inadequate health literacy (271). Overall, the authors noted that "older age was associated with worse knowledge," whereas length of time with a disease and attendance at a prior class or workshop was "associated with greater knowledge" (273). Interestingly, level of formal education was again not a factor. Education did not affect how much a person knew about his or her chronic disease.

Health Literacy and Physical and Mental Health

Another study of this group of Medicare enrollees published in the *Archives of Internal Medicine* in 2005 found that low health literacy was independently associated with poorer physical and mental health. One-third of the more than 3,000 participants had marginal or inadequate health literacy. Those with inadequate skills had significantly higher rates of hypertension, diabetes, heart failure, and arthritis. They reported lower physical function, mental health, and more limitations on daily activities (Wolf, Gazmararian, and Baker, 2005).

Health Literacy and Mortality

In 2006, Sudore et al. found that men and women over age 70 with limited health literacy were more than twice as likely to have died during the study period as those with higher literacy. The investigators tested a group of community-dwelling seniors with REALM, the Rapid Estimate of Adult Literacy in Medicine (Davis et al., 1993), and then collected mortality data over the next five years. Participants with literacy scores lower than a 9th grade reading level had a 19.7 percentage of deaths, compared to the 10.6 percent in the adequate literacy group. The only characteristics that had a stronger association with mortality than health literacy were smoking and self-rated poor health.

Implications for Practice

From a practical standpoint, how can healthcare providers use all of this research on health literacy in the elderly? What do the results mean in terms of designing better interventions and improving health outcomes for seniors?

- First, acknowledge that a person's general literacy level, or years of formal education, may have no effect on his or her ability to read and understand health information and documentation. Many of the studies cited above found no association between education and health literacy level. Health literacy seems to require a complex mix of skills beyond the simple ability to read. This means that a healthcare provider or educator should never assume that a senior understands directions about a test, medication, or procedure, even if he is well educated.

- Second, redesign messages about preventive care and services which may be too complex for an aging population to understand. Print or television media campaigns that encourage regular use of preventive care should have all messages tested with seniors before final implementation.
- Third, explore alternative means of communicating chronic disease information to the elderly. Many educational materials for people with chronic diseases are printed forms, booklets, and brochures. Even seniors with adequate functional literacy may not either understand or remember the disease knowledge presented in these materials. Health educators should try new methods of educating the aged about diseases like diabetes, heart failure, or high blood pressure. Seniors who enjoy listening to music or talk radio shows may enjoy having information on audio CD. Those who are more social and mobile might benefit from an on-site support group.

A NEW MODEL OF HEALTH LITERACY

Functional literacy or formal education may not determine a person's health literacy level. General functional literacy is obviously a *component* of health literacy, but more factors come into play than an individual's ability to read. Many interventions developed over the last ten years have focused on the functional literacy component and on efforts to simplify the language used in print health materials.

In their book *Advancing Health Literacy*, Zarcadoolas, Pleasant, and Greer (2006) outline a new definition and multifaceted model for understanding health literacy that provides a framework for planning interventions to improve health literacy. Because the model contains so many dimensions relevant to the needs of seniors, it is helpful to spend some time breaking down the model and its components.

Critical to understanding the model is accepting the fact that a person can be highly literate, but have inadequate health literacy—as well as the reverse. The example the authors use is that of a single mother with a grade-school education who has learned to manage her preschool son's chemotherapy regimens. Yet someone with a degree in physics may not understand that taking multiple nonprescription drugs at one time can cause harmful interactions (46). Reading abilities alone do not make up health literacy skills.

Zarcadoolas and her colleagues point out that health literacy is "generative" (48). Being health literate means that a person is able to generalize facts and has problem-solving abilities when faced with brand-new situations. This ability to generalize and adapt on the fly is what has been missing from many preceding definitions and models of health literacy (49). A health-literate person cannot only understand the vocabulary, medication needs, and management skills for a current illness or condition, but will know what to do when a new illness arises.

The book defines health literacy as "the wide range of skills and competencies that people develop over their lifetimes to seek out, comprehend, evaluate, and use health information and concepts to make informed choices, reduce health risks, and increase quality of life" (55). The health literacy model is comprised of four overlapping areas:

1. Fundamental literacy
2. Scientific literacy
3. Civic literacy
4. Cultural literacy

▶ *Fundamental literacy* includes what we think of as basic literacy: reading, writing, and performing basic arithmetic. Because written and spoken health information can be complex, fundamental literacy is critical to health literacy. Adult basic education classes are an example of an attempt to address a low level of fundamental literacy. "Plain language" campaigns, which encourage simplifying health materials, are interventions that fall into this fundamental literacy category.

The other dimensions of the model are equally important, but more difficult to address with an educational intervention since they revolve around higher-level critical thinking skills.

▶ *Scientific literacy* includes knowledge of basic medical concepts, such as the disease process, and an understanding of technology. It also includes accepting the concept of scientific uncertainty. Scientific literacy helps an individual decide whether or not to act on a specific health message (56).
▶ *Civic literacy* allows people to evaluate and participate in public issues, and make decisions based on these evaluations and discussions. Media savvy, knowledge of governmental process, and knowledge of community relationships are included in civic literacy. In the context of health literacy, civic literacy might mean the ability to access needed health information, knowing how to judge the quality of a source, and being able to advocate for one's health needs (56–57).
▶ *Cultural literacy*, the final leg of the model, includes the skills needed to recognize and understand the beliefs and customs of individuals and groups with whom we interact. Within health literacy, cultural literacy is bi-directional: health professionals should understand the cultural aspects of the patient or consumer, while healthcare consumers need some understanding of the professional culture surrounding their doctors and other providers (57).

This four-pronged model of health literacy offers some food for thought when developing interventions that affect the health literacy of seniors. Instead of focusing on one of the above literacies, programs that address multiple types of literacy may have the greatest likelihood of success. Since this is a relatively new model, effectiveness has yet to be demonstrated. Here are some suggestions for using the model when designing health literacy interventions for older adults.

Implications for Practice

- Some senior citizens of all races and education levels share a culture that is highly relevant to health literacy—the culture of "doctor knows best." Providers and educators must acknowledge that culture and decide how best to incorporate it into health literacy programs and interventions. Elderly patients may be hesitant to question their physicians about prescribed medications, or the necessity of a certain test or procedure. They may not want to ask any questions at all, for fear of seeming disrespectful and questioning a doctor's professional judgment. Program planners must decide whether to work within this specific culture or to encourage seniors to move beyond it. Either approach may be appropriate as long as it is thoughtfully included in the planning process.
- Civic literacy implies that an individual understands the healthcare system and how specific services fit into that system. Even well-educated and highly literate adults may have trouble understanding healthcare reimbursements, supplemental insurance, and the maze that Medicare has become. Since making personal health decisions is never done in a vacuum, interventions that try to simplify the healthcare *system* could be highly effective.
- Current health literacy assessment tools, such as REALM and S-TOFHLA, focus primarily on fundamental literacy. The multi-dimensional model points to the need for new assessment tools that present a more fully developed picture of an adult's health literacy status.

HEALTH LITERACY INTERVENTIONS OUTSIDE THE LIBRARY

Few large-scale research studies evaluating the effectiveness of health literacy interventions for seniors were found in the literature. However, many health and public service organizations are currently developing or implementing small or pilot projects that seem to exist in isolation and have very little funding. Finding anecdotal information on health literacy programming takes a scattershot approach to information gathering, emphasizing the need for a centralized information source for program and project data.

The "plain language" approach appears to have been the standard way of doing a health literacy project or curriculum (Parker and Kreps, 2005). While health promotion and health education materials are admittedly often written at a very high reading level, a problem as multidimensional as poor health literacy cannot be solved by merely rewriting all health education offerings.

The projects described below, coordinated by a variety of health agencies and community groups, attempt to address more than just an individual's ability to read and understand printed information. Although they were not designed specifically with Zarcadoolas, Pleasant, and Greer's (2006) multidimensional model in mind, in many cases the programs clearly address one or more of the literacies defined above. Information on these programs was taken directly from the organization's publications or their Web sites.

What is interesting is that none of these projects mention library representation or coordination. While it is possible that a librarian participated on the project teams, this was not publicized in any promotional material. Many of them represent wonderful opportunities for library partnerships on similar initiatives in other communities.

Health Literacy Programs for Nova Scotia Seniors

In early 2007, the Seniors' Secretariat in Nova Scotia, Canada, awarded more than $20,000 to various community groups throughout the province in an effort to increase the health literacy of Canada's older adults. The Secretariat developed a guide, *A Health Literacy Manual for Older Adults*, which will serve as the roadmap for programming. The community groups selected will offer classes and workshops that include information on talking to your doctor; understanding medication instructions or nutritional labels; staying fit and active; and the importance of dental care. Each program is expected to run from 9 to 12 weeks, and many will bring in guest speakers such as nutritionists, pharmacists, and exercise specialists (Nova Scotia Seniors' Secretariat, 2007).

These multiple-week programs have the potential to address scientific, civic, *and* cultural literacy in the pursuit of health literacy. A broader approach is possible because of the recurring nature of the workshops.

Partners in Health

The American Academy of Family Physicians (AAFP) Foundation (2006) awarded the Missouri AAFP chapter a 2006 Health Literacy State Grant to expand the Partners in Health program to Farmington, Missouri. The Partners in Health program, originally developed by the American Board of Family Medicine, is designed to encourage and maximize senior involvement in the healthcare process. Workshops teach older adults how to get the most from their doctor visits by improving communication, and by providing education on patient rights and responsibilities. In Farmington, physicians W. Jack Stelmach and Rusty Ryan are recruiting retired healthcare professionals to conduct eight-week sessions for older residents. Partners in Health appears to address both civic and cultural literacy.

Talk to Me: Improving Health Literacy Through Communication

In Columbus, Ohio, public broadcasting organization WOSU collaborated with other state agencies to organize a health literacy project for older Ohio residents. For several years the radio station produced a show called *Caregivers*, focusing on aging and eldercare issues. Realizing that health literacy was essential to aging well, WOSU teamed with the Central Ohio Area Agency on Aging and a former director of the Ohio Department of Aging to create a series of broadcasts and print materials. The resulting Web site contains audio interviews with physicians, tips for both healthcare consumers and healthcare professionals, and archived news stories. An assistant professor of theater at Ohio State University got involved with her over-60 theater group; Howling at the Moon has written several health-related skits and monologues and performed at area retirement centers (WOSU Radio Health Literacy Project, n.d.).

This health literacy initiative is unique in that it uses only minimal textual information to educate and convey information. Its focus is on cultural literacy, and uses communication as a tool for patients and providers to improve health together.

SPEAK

With a Health Literacy Grant from Pfizer, a group of physicians is addressing senior health literacy from the other side of the table—the side of the clinician serving a geriatric population. Doctors Kobylarz, Pomidor, and Heath (2006) developed a tool for use by healthcare providers who work with older adults. This tool, published in 2006 and known by the mnemonic SPEAK, serves to remind clinicians of several ways to assess and address the health literacy of their patients. SPEAK, which stands for Speech, Perception, Education, Access, and Knowledge, is designed to foster clear and open communication between patient and provider. The authors assert that physician awareness of health literacy and its components is essential to improving health literacy and, eventually, health outcomes.

Health Enhancement of Rural Elderly (HERE)

A project funded in part by the national Office of Rural Health Policy, Department of Health and Human Services, HERE was designed to maximize effective use of the healthcare system by rural senior citizens in two Kentucky counties. This multiyear interdisciplinary approach began with the development of health resource guides for each county, as well as educational modules and media. Guides were coordinated by undergraduate and graduate students in public health, nursing, and social work, and were reviewed by an advisory board comprised of various healthcare professionals. The educational modules addressed basic anatomy, advanced directives, medical terminology, and pharmacology, as well as learning objectives, lesson plans, written handouts, audiovisuals, and interactive games. Workshops were scheduled for those seniors who could attend onsite events, and brochures and videos were created for those who could not. They were distributed to churches, libraries, veterans' organizations, medical clinics, physician offices, assisted living facilities, and senior centers (Western Kentucky University, College of Health and Human Services, n.d.).

This program attempts to address all four literacy types: fundamental, scientific, civic, and cultural. Offering well-written education about health and medicine addresses both functional and scientific literacy. Compiling and providing access to regional healthcare resources is an aspect of civic literacy. And having multiple distribution channels acknowledges and tries to compensate for the cultural differences in the aging population.

Promoting Adherence Through Computing and Information (PATCAI)

Dr. Raymond Ownby (n.d.) at the University of Miami Miller School of Medicine received a grant from the National Institute on Aging to develop and assess the effectiveness of a technology-based health literacy intervention. He developed an electronic system that would offer health behavior change messages and education tailored to an individual's specific language needs and health literacy level. Targeted to older patients with memory impairment, the system promoted medication adherence for prescribed cholinesterase inhibitors. Using Visual Basic, a simple interface was designed at two reading levels in English and Spanish. Messages were personalized, and included the patient's name and photo in a special printed guide. Each intervention took only 20 minutes, and cost between 13 and 25 dollars. Preliminary data showed a 10 percent increase in medication adherence among those patients enrolled in the study and tested by Dr. Ownby at the study site.

This intervention focuses primarily on fundamental literacy, but in finding simpler ways to express pharmacology concepts it also attempts to improve scientific literacy among the elderly.

LIBRARIANS AND HEALTH LITERACY INTERVENTIONS

As is the case with the health literacy interventions above, little if any evaluation data has been published for programs developed and managed by librarians. As outlined below, many public, medical, and consumer health libraries now offer outreach programs designed specifically for senior citizens. A brief review of library and information science literature reveals that the majority of these health-related programs are variations on a theme: teaching seniors to use MedlinePlus or a similar Web-based resource for health information. Many of these published case studies indicate some degree of success. The various MedlinePlus programs have been written about frequently, so below you will find only brief descriptions of a few of these. More detailed information is provided about other innovative health literacy programs that librarians have developed and implemented.

Kootenai Medical Center, Coeur d'Alene, Idaho

This comprehensive project was funded from 2003 to 2004 by a National Network of Libraries of Medicine "Access to Electronic Health Information" outreach grant. It sought to improve access to electronic health information resources for senior citizens in northern Idaho. According to primary investigator Elizabeth Hill (personal communication, 2007), the project consisted of the following components:

- Partnerships were formed with several area senior centers and agencies, as well as one consumer health library.
- Baseline computer skills and health literacy were assessed.
- Seniors were taught to use PCs and then MedlinePlus in one of more than 120 training sessions.
- The Kootenai Medical Center Web site was evaluated by four senior focus groups, and a senior-friendly Web page was designed based on resulting input.
- Hospital discharge instructions for six diagnoses were revised based on assessed community literacy levels.
- Exhibits and demonstrations were held at several health fairs.
- A computer with Internet access was placed in each of four senior centers.

Perhaps the most interesting result of this project is the finding that "literacy, health literacy, and health information literacy are three different things, requiring different skills and tool sets" (Horner, 2005: 3). Over 95 percent of the seniors tested with the REALM (Davis et al., 1993) scored at or above the 10th grade reading level, yet most of them struggled with discharge instructions written at a 7th grade reading level. This reinforces the concept that plain language initiatives alone, and those that deal primarily with fundamental literacy, are not enough to overcome a health literacy deficit.

The Kootenai Medical Center developed an infrastructure that could easily support interventions addressing scientific and civic literacy, as well as fundamental. Providing Internet access where none had been before offers a great opportunity to teach seniors how to understand and connect with healthcare resources within their own communities.

Partnering for Patient Empowerment through Community Awareness (PPECA)

Designed to raise awareness of patient safety issues among healthcare consumers, PPECA is a coalition between health science librarians, public libraries, patient safety advocates, and healthcare institutions. Funded primarily by the National Library of Medicine, in 2005 PPECA presented a series of informational workshops in public libraries throughout Northern Illinois. Programming included sessions on enhancing communication with your healthcare provider, the problems of human error in acute care or ambulatory settings, and using information to ensure safe and appropriate care. In 2006, the coalition extended its programming to "train the trainer" sessions to enable larger numbers of medical and public libraries to partner (PPECA, n.d.).

No evaluation data has yet been published from this program. However, variable programming with such a broad base of support has great potential to positively impact scientific, civic, and cultural literacy.

Stem Cell Science and Policy

In the spring of 2006, members of the National Institutes of Health (NIH) Stem Cell Task Force developed and presented a class for senior citizens on stem cell policy and research. The Task Force included Anne White-Olson, a biomedical librarian from the NIH Library (White-Olson, personal communication, 2007). The stem cell program was one of a series of lectures on science and health policy at the Johns Hopkins Evergreen Society, an organization whose mission is to provide lifelong learning for older adults. In addition to Anne, presenters included a developmental biologist and a microbiologist. Approximately 25 seniors listened to presentations and asked questions about the science behind stem cells, the administration's policy on human embryonic stem cell research, and details about federal funding for research. Participants were very engaged and asked many questions. While members of the Evergreen Society may be more educated and have a higher income level than the average person over 65, a highly targeted intervention such as this indicates a good knowledge of the audience and the type of programming appropriate to that audience.

Health Literacy at Munson

The Library Services Manager at Munson Healthcare has taken a unique approach to library-based health literacy initiatives. To improve health literacy in Traverse City, Michigan—where Munson is located—she targets health practitioners instead of the healthcare consumer. While not specific to senior citizens, this initiative is uniquely positioned to positively affect the health literacy of *all* populations, including older adults. For several years, she has supplied AMA *Health Literacy Toolkits* for physician practices and has also lectured on the importance of health literacy to doctors, nurses, clinical support staff, and any other group expressing an interest. Her most recent effort involves the creation and implementation of an online course on health literacy for all hospital staff with direct patient contact. She has recommended that this course be made mandatory and added to the annual competency education plan (Barbara Platts, personal communication, 2006).

MedlinePlus Programs

The following programs have one thing in common: they focus on providing seniors with *access* to quality health information rather than on the ability to comprehend or use such information. At this writing, most library-sponsored health literacy interventions emphasize access over fundamental literacy training or communications-based programming. In a sense, this can be seen as a civic literacy intervention. Knowing how to access needed information, as well as how to judge its quality and relevance, are issues of media and community knowledge.

WebHealth for Seniors. In Memphis, Tennessee, librarians partnered with three city-sponsored senior citizen centers to create computer labs and perform subsequent MedlinePlus training (Stephenson et al., 2004).

Pacific College of Oriental Medicine (PCOM). In 2004, PCOM worked with five San Diego organizations—a charitable clinic, two senior centers, and two public libraries—to teach free health information classes featuring MedlinePlus and other NIH databases. The program also developed instructional materials and provided some technical infrastructure. Over 3,300 older adults attended health information literacy workshops, and more 400 participated in hands-on computer training (NCLIS, 2006).

Health-e Learning. The Coordinator of Library Services at Jersey Shore University Medical Center received NLM outreach funding to manage a train-the-trainer program. Volunteer instructors were taught to use MedlinePlus and facilitate similar training sessions. Those instructors then went to senior and community centers to teach older adults how to find diabetes-related information. A single condition was chosen in order to focus and structure the learning experience (Cathy Boss, personal communication, 2007).

Utahealthnet. The Outreach Team at Utah's Eccles Health Sciences Library does consumer health training as part of the NLM project Utahealthnet. These training sessions are held at either senior centers or public libraries, in an attempt to develop relationships between older adults and their community libraries. In addition to MedlinePlus, trainers offer hands-on instruction with health-related databases on EBSCOHost (Sally Patrick, personal communication, 2006).

Healthy Choices. Led by Stamford (Connecticut) Hospital and funded by NN/LM, this program uses a train-the-trainer model to eventually educate seniors about finding reliable health information on the Internet. Public librarians are trained to guide patrons through MedlinePlus and NIH SeniorHealth, with future modules planned on Spanish resources, PubMed, and complementary and alternative medicine resources (Guillaume Van-Moorsel, listserv communication, 2007).

Searching the archives of various e-mail lists related to medical librarianship reveals that most librarians involved in health literacy are primarily offering MedlinePlus programs. Research on Internet use among the aging therefore becomes very important. In 2006, Flynn, Smith, and Freese sought to determine when and how older adults use the Internet for health information. They felt that the timing of health-related searches could provide an interesting perspective on the doctor-patient relationship. Looking for information *before* a doctor's appointment might indicate a willingness to participate in health decision making; looking for information *after* a visit might signify that not enough information was obtained from the physician. The study used data from the Wisconsin Longitudinal Study, a survey of more than 6,000 adults aged 63 to 66 years old. Among the more than 4,500 participants with Internet access, 47 percent had searched for health information online. Over half of these were unrelated to a specific health appointment, 30 percent were after a doctor's visit, and about 15 percent of the searches were done prior to an appointment (1298). In this particular sample, seeking Internet health information was associated with the presence of chronic or acute disease and with regularly taking prescription medication. Perhaps the most interesting finding was that a preference for multiple treatment choices and options was a predictor of health information seeking, but that a preference for *who* makes the decision was not.

Implications for Librarians' Practice

- Searching for health information is not absent of any context. When teaching about MedlinePlus, take time to discover the *reasons* why participants are interested in finding health information. If they want to learn more about a condition after being diagnosed, you have an opportunity to encourage greater physician-patient communication. If they are searching for health information before a health appointment, you can stress the importance of being prepared with good questions for a doctor or other healthcare practitioner.
- Familiarity with the research on how seniors use the Internet will help you structure your MedlinePlus and other database workshops to be more practical and useful. For instance, the Flynn, Smith, and Freese (2006) study

above showed that being recently diagnosed with cancer corresponded to an almost 50 percent increase in health information seeking. This finding points to the need to design cancer-specific health information workshops and market them appropriately.

LEARNING STRATEGIES FOR OLDER ADULTS

Program planners who use the Zarcadoolas, Pleasant, and Greer (2006) framework for conceptualizing health literacy may have a better understanding of how interventions might boost the health literacy of various populations. What are still required are practical suggestions for designing interventions related to those specific populations. Do senior citizens learn differently than people not in this age group? Educators should not assume that adults will not continue to learn throughout the aging process. Offering health literacy interventions for seniors requires knowledge of adult learning styles and literacy, as well as the ability to structure activities that appeal to all types of adult learners.

Print materials continue to be the primary way to educate patients about diseases, tests, and treatments. Research over the last decade provides many clues about ways to make print materials more engaging and understandable for older adults. Here are several tips to keep in mind when developing printed, text-based education (Billek-Sawhney and Reicherter, 2005: 279):

- Use a font size between 14 and 18 points.
- Use one- or two-syllable words.
- Use the active voice.
- Provide headings and subheadings.
- Use bullet points.
- Use sans serif fonts.
- Avoid yellow, orange, green, light blue, and red.
- Don't use shiny or glossy paper.
- Focus on key concepts.
- Avoid right justification of text.
- Add illustrations and diagrams.

Problems with vision increase with age, so illustrations and diagrams may be preferable to text-heavy, printed educational materials. Seniors may also appreciate audiotapes, videos, or other multimedia material. When providing print education, always take the time to verify that the person can read and understand the information. Patient educators have long advocated using the teach-back method, that is, the educator asks patients to paraphrase or demonstrate what was just taught (American Medical Association, 2003). This mechanism is important in *any* patient population, but is crucial when teaching seniors. Older persons may claim that they understand information even when they do not because of their discomfort in questioning a healthcare provider.

Seniors who are members of an ethnic minority may require additional "cultural literacy" on the part of the health educator or provider. Even immigrant or minority seniors who appear to be completely acculturated may carry underlying health beliefs that affect how they learn, understand, and use health information. As Wilson and Dorne (2005) write, Asian cultures traditionally defined illness as the result of the body's disharmony with the environment or other external factors. Hispanic populations once viewed illness as punishment for some sort of wrongdoing, or the result of a supernatural intervention. Taking the time to talk to an older patient about his or her health beliefs will allowed tailored interventions that are still respectful and culturally sensitive.

Over the past several decades, many educators and educational psychologists have created adult learning models as a simple way to think about and categorize learning styles and preferences. Assessing the Learning Strategies of Adults (ATLAS) is an assessment tool created by Professor Gary Conti (n.d.). The tool defines learners as *navigators, engagers,* or *problem solvers. Navigators* are focused learners who develop a learning plan, and then follow it. *Engagers* are passionate about learning, and learn best when actively engaged in something they find meaningful. *Problem solvers* use critical thinking strategies when approaching any new learning task.

Little research was found on whether preferred learning styles and strategies change as people age. Chesbro, Conti, and Williams (2005) found that learning styles among a sample of 210 adults over age 65 were consistent with that of the general population. Participants in this study, which used the ATLAS tool, were evenly divided among navigators, engagers, and problem solvers. Since librarians and health educators are unlikely to know the specific learning styles of intervention participants, planning at least one activity for each type of learner is critical. The following instructional suggestions are adapted from the 2005 article by Chesbro, Conti, and Williams.

Navigators often like to have both a written and verbal list of steps involved in performing a task. They appreciate a demonstration of the steps in a process, and then prefer guided and supervised practice opportunities. Feedback is important not just for navigators, but for learners of all styles and preferences.

Engagers prefer explicit information about how a new skill or activity will be immediately relevant in their lives. Hypothetical situations don't motivate this group of learners; it is best to offer them an opportunity to address a personal situation or problem. Offer engagers maximum independent learning time, providing feedback when required but not at regular intervals. Encourage reflection, and some supervised practice time is acceptable.

Problem solvers will likely want alternative solutions to each task or problem, and will need room for creativity. These learners require small amounts of time to independently formulate a plan for approaching the task. They also appreciate time to generate alternative solutions if the original idea is unsuccessful, and supervised practice and reflection are appropriate for this group as well.

Here is an example of a single classroom activity that might be designed to appeal to all three types of learners.

You are a pulmonary rehabilitation specialist teaching a class for older adults who have been diagnosed with chronic obstructive pulmonary disease (COPD). In this one-hour session, you plan to review how the participants can and should check their oxygen saturation levels in order to determine if they should use their supplemental oxygen delivery systems. To appeal to all three types of learners in a single class setting, you realize that you must offer the following:

1. Ordered steps, for the navigators in the group
2. Alternative processes or steps, for the problem solvers
3. Opportunity for self exploration, for the engagers and problem solvers
4. Plenty of practice time, for all groups
5. Feedback, for all groups

For the first item, you will create a printed handout containing step-by-step instructions for using the recommended finger oximeter to check blood oxygen saturation and heart rate. Illustrations and diagrams should be included. These steps will be provided to all participants. Read the list aloud once, and offer to clarify any confusing information and answer questions. This will satisfy the navigators in the group who prefer structured learning activities.

Problem solvers like having alternatives. They may generate those alternatives themselves, or have them offered by an educator, but they like alternative means of reaching the same end. They may ask, "What should I do if my oximeter isn't working?" It may satisfy the learning preferences of problem solvers if you facilitate a discussion about various things that may go wrong or keep the oximeter from functioning properly.

Engagers want real-life examples of why learning a new skill is important, so you are prepared with anecdotes and case studies. You might emphasize a situation in which the patient felt fine, but discovered a low oxygenation rate upon checking. Using the finger oximeter likely saved the patient's life.

Everyone needs to practice their new skills, and the engagers and problem solvers prefer unstructured, exploratory practice. Satisfy the desires of all learners by offering independent practice time while you circulate around the group, offering feedback and encouragement when needed. Navigators will use their printed steps to practice in an orderly manner, while the other two groups may experiment with how their levels change in different positions, or under different conditions.

At the conclusion of class, you realize that you have successfully responded to three very different learning styles while achieving your intended outcome—all participants know how, and why, to check their blood oxygenation.

Understanding how adults learn—and learn differently—becomes critical when designing health literacy interventions for seniors. Keep in mind the tips discussed in this section and your intervention has a greater likelihood of succeeding.

Implications for Practice

- Design and edit printed documents with senior reading abilities and lack of visual acuity in mind. Use large fonts, dark colors on light paper, plenty of white space, and clear illustrations and diagrams.
- Vision difficulties may also affect driving, particularly night driving. Many seniors do not like to attend evening workshops because of their discomfort with driving at night, so morning or afternoon classes will likely have greater participation.
- Remember that seniors may be hesitant to ask questions for fear of seeming disrespectful, so encourage older patients to use the teach-back method as a way of verifying that they understand information.
- Talk to older adults about any long-held cultural beliefs about the nature of health and illness. Tailor teaching and interventions appropriately to respect these cultural beliefs.
- In a formal class setting, offer various activities to appeal to various learning styles and preferences. Be prepared to address learners who prefer structure as well as those who want open and independent exploration. Regardless of learning style, offer plenty of practice and lots of feedback.

FUTURE DIRECTIONS FOR LIBRARIES AND LIBRARIANS

As noted earlier, a few librarians have made great strides addressing all facets of literacy that play into health literacy: fundamental, scientific, civic, and cultural. There are a number of ways in which other interested librarians can extend their skills and services into senior health literacy initiatives. While many of these programs are not designed *specifically* for an aging population, most can be easily adapted to the needs of older patients and healthcare consumers.

- For those librarians working within a provider organization, initiate a plain writing campaign for all forms and discharge instructions distributed primarily to seniors. Plain writing campaigns deal primarily with fundamental literacy, but their importance in health literacy should not be underestimated. Assemble a team of librarians, patient educators, patient advocates, healthcare professionals, and community representatives to review all print documentation to ensure lack of jargon and appropriate reading level. Most important, have seniors from a variety of educational and economic backgrounds serve as reviewers. Plan and implement a regular review schedule to guarantee that the material does not become dated and that it stays accessible.

- Present the American Medical Association's *Health Literacy* curriculum to clinicians at your institution or within your community. Barbara Platts at Munson Healthcare received grant funding to make these *Toolkits* available to physicians affiliated with Munson. While such funding may not be available to you, obtaining one copy and offering the workshop to clinicians may be a viable option. The video included with the *Toolkit* showcases actual patients for whom low health literacy created health problems. Kripalani and Weiss (2006) recommend inviting actual patients, patient advocates, or adult basic literacy students when possible to present a first-hand look at the problems of low health literacy.

- Develop partnerships between local public and health science libraries and present the PPECA workshops. Project leaders at PPECA make their facilitator's manual freely available on the Web site, as well as copies of each of the five modules in both PowerPoint and PDF formats. Three of the modules also offer streaming video from when they were originally presented in Illinois. Free access to these materials makes it easier for you to develop and customize a series of related programs in your own community.

- Use the free Be MedWise tool kit to conduct a campaign for area seniors about the proper use of non-prescription medicines. Seniors are often prone to overprescribing and polypharmacy resulting from the increased incidence of chronic disease in the aged and the number and variety of specialist physicians consulted. First launched in 2002, Be MedWise is an educational initiative spearheaded by the National Council on Patient Information and Education (NCPIE). The initiative hopes to increase awareness that over-the-counter medications are just that—medications—and should be taken with care and seriousness. The tool kit found on the Be MedWise Web site contains fact sheets, logos, brochures, press releases, and tips for using the materials (NCPIE, 2007).

These are just a few of the many programs that can be easily adapted for almost any community organization or healthcare institution. The wonderful thing is that most of them encourage partnerships between cultural and educational institutions—such as libraries—and other community-based grass roots initiatives promoting the health and welfare of a region's population. Even developers of customized health literacy programs can use existing program descriptions for brainstorming and idea generation.

There are two other specific areas in which the skills and abilities of librarians can play a key role in health literacy research and programming. As mentioned earlier, there is no single repository of information for program descriptions and accompanying evaluation data. A coalition of librarians could do much to rectify this situation. Second, librarians who plan or implement health literacy programming should make every effort to include an evaluation component into each program. Only when we know which interventions truly improve health literacy—and conversely, which do not—can we state that health literacy research and programming has improved the health of our seniors and of our nation.

REFERENCES

American Academy of Family Physicians Foundation. 2006. "Summary of Proposals Selected for 2006 Awards." AAFP Foundation. (June 2007) Available: www/aafpfoundation .org/PreBuilt/missouriafp.pdf

American Medical Association. 2003. *Help Your Patients Understand.* Video. Chicago: Author.

Baker, David W., Julie A. Gazmararian, Joseph Sudano, and Marian Patterson. 2000. "The Association Between Age and Health Literacy Among Elderly Persons." *Journal of Gerontology* 55, no.6 (November): S368–S374.

Baker, David W., Julie A. Gazmararian, Mark V. Williams, Tracy Scott, Ruth M. Parker, Diane Green, Junling Ren, and Jennifer Peel. 2002. "Functional Health Literacy and the Risk of Hospital Admission Among Medicare Managed Care Enrollees." *American Journal of Public Health* 92, no.8 (August): 1278–1283.

Billek-Sawhney, Barbara, and Anne E. Reicherter. 2005. "Literacy and the Older Adult: Educational Considerations for Health Professionals." *Topics in Geriatric Rehabilitation* 21, no.4 (October–December): 275–281.

Chesbro, Steven B., Gary J. Conti, and Bernadette R. Williams. 2005. "Using the Assessing The Learning Strategies of Adults Tool with Older Adults." *Topics in Geriatric Rehabilitation* 21, no.4 (October–December): 323–331.

Conti, Gary J. "ATLAS: Learning Strategies (learning style)." (March 2007) Available: www.conti-creations.com/atlas.htm

Davis, Terry C., Sandy Long, Robert H. Jackson, E. J. Mayeaux, R. B. George, Peggy W. Murphy, and Michael A. Crouch. 1993. "Rapid Estimate of Adult Literacy in Medicine: A Shortened Screening Instrument." *Family Medicine* 25, no.6 (June): 391–395.

Flynn, Kathryn E., Maureen A. Smith, and Jeremy Freese. 2006. "When Do Older Adults Turn to the Internet for Health Information? Findings from the Wisconsin Longitudinal Study." *Journal of General Internal Medicine* 21, no.12 (December): 1295–1301.

Gazmararian, Julie A., David W. Baker, Mark V. Williams, Ruth M. Parker, Tracy L. Scott, Diane C. Green, Nicole S. Fehrenbach, Junling Ren, and J. P. Koplan. 1999. "Health Literacy Among Medicare Enrollees in a Managed Care Organization." *JAMA* 281, no.6 (February 10): 545–551.

Gazmararian, Julie A., Mark V. Williams, Jennifer Peel, and David W. Baker. 2003. "Health Literacy and Knowledge of Chronic Disease." *Patient Education and Counseling* 51, no.3 (November): 267–275.

Horner, Marcia. 2005. "Computer Health Literacy for Seniors in Northern Idaho." Pacific Northwest Region, National Network of Libraries of Medicine. (March 2007) Available: http://nnlm.gov/pnr/funding/reports/ComputerHealthFinalReport.pdf

Kobylarz, Fred A., Alice Pomidor, and John H. Heath. 2006. "SPEAK: A Mnemonic Tool for Addressing Health Literacy Concerns in Geriatric Clinical Encounters." *Geriatrics* 61, no.7 (July): 20–27.

Kripalani, Sunil, and Barry D. Weiss. 2006. "Teaching About Health Literacy and Clear Communication." *Journal of General Internal Medicine* 21, no.8 (August): 888–890.

Kutner, Mark, Elizabeth Greenberg, Ying Jin, Christine Paulsen, and Sheida White. 2006. *The Health Literacy of America's Adults: Results from the 2003 National Assessment of Adult Literacy.* National Center for Education Statistics, U.S. Department of Education. NCES 2006-483.

National Commission on Libraries and Information Science (NCLIS). 2006. "NCLIS Health Awards for Libraries Finalists." (June 2007) Available: www/nclis.gov/award/HealthAwardsFinalistProgramDescriptions.pdf

National Council on Patient Information and Education (NCPIE). 2007. "Be MedWise: Promoting the Wise Use of OTC Medications." National Council on Patient Information and Education. (June 2007) Available: www.bemedwise.org

Nova Scotia Seniors' Secretariat. 2007. "Health Literacy Funding for Nova Scotia Seniors." Province of Nova Scotia, Canada. (March 2007) Available: www.gov.ns.ca/news/details .asp?id=20070212002

Ownby, Raymond L. "Promoting Adherence Through Computing and Information. PATCAI." (March 2007) Available: www.patcai.org

Parker, Ruth, and Gary L. Kreps. 2005. "Library Outreach: Overcoming Health Literacy Challenges." *Journal of the Medical Library Association* 93, no.4 (October): S81–S85.

"Partnering for Patient Empowerment through Community Awareness. About PPECA." (March 2007) Available: www.galter.northwestern.edu/ppecca/index.htm

Scott, Tracy L., Julie A. Gazmararian, Mark V. Williams, and David W. Baker. 2002. "Health Literacy and Preventive Health Care Use Among Medicare Enrollees in a Managed Care Organization." *Medical Care* 40, no.5 (May): 395–404.

Stephenson, Priscilla L., Brenda F. Green, Richard L. Wallace, Martha F. Earl, Jan T. Orick, and Mary Virginia Taylor. 2004. "Community Partnerships for Health Information Training: Medical Librarians Working with Health-care Professionals and Consumers in Tennessee." *Health Information and Libraries Journal* 21, Suppl.1 (June): 20–26.

Sudore, Rebecca L., Kristine Yaffe, Suzanne Satterfield, Tamara B. Harris, Kala M. Mehta, Eleanor M. Simonsick, Anne B. Newman, Caterina Rosano, Ronica Rooks, Susan M. Rubin, Hilsa N. Ayonayon, and Dean Schillinger. 2006. "Limited Literacy and Mortality in the Elderly: The Health, Aging, and Body Composition Study." *Journal of General Internal Medicine* 21, no.8 (August): 806–812.

Wilson, Stanley H. and Rachelle Dorne. 2005. "Impact of Culture on the Education of the Geriatric Patient." *Topics in Geriatric Rehabilitation* 21, no.4 (October–December): 282–294.

Western Kentucky University College of Health and Human Services. "Health Enhancement of Rural Elderly." (March 2007) Available: www.wku.edu/Dept/Academic/chhs/here

Wolf, Michael S., Julie A. Gazmararian, and David W. Baker. 2005. "Health Literacy and Functional Health Status Among Older Adults." *Archives of Internal Medicine* 165, no.17 (September): 1946–1952.

WOSU Radio Health Literacy Project. "Talk to Me: Improving Health Literacy Through Communication." (March 2007) Available: www.wosu.org/archivehealth_literacy/index/php

Zarcadoolas, Christina, Andrew F. Pleasant, and David S. Greer. 2006. *Advancing Health Literacy: A Framework for Understanding and Action.* San Francisco: Jossey-Bass.

Chapter 9

A New Digital Divide: Teens and Internet Literacy

Ellen Freda, Jonathan Hayes Goff,
and Andrea L. Kenyon

INTRODUCTION

In an effort to build a foundation of health literacy among the young people of Philadelphia and to augment teen health information on Philly Health Info.org, its consumer health information Web portal, The College of Physicians of Philadelphia piloted a teen outreach program in two urban community locations during the summer of 2005. This chapter describes The Teen Editor Program, its successes, and the lessons that we learned.

BACKGROUND

The College of Physicians of Philadelphia is a cultural and educational institution, founded as a medical society in 1787 by the city's leading physicians, including Dr. Benjamin Rush, a signer of the Declaration of Independence, and Dr. John Morgan, the founder of the nation's first medical school. The College serves the professional health community and the general public through a mission that is dedicated to advancing the cause of health, while upholding the ideals and heritage of medicine. It has an honorary Fellowship of more than 1,500 physicians, health-related professionals and distinguished members of the community. The College is home to one of the foremost historical medical libraries in the world and to the renowned Mütter Museum, an anatomy and pathology museum. Public health outreach programs such as Philly Health Info.org address the College's goal to enable individuals, families and communities to take greater responsibility for their health. Each program of the College utilizes its assets and supports objectives that fulfill the goals of education and community service.

The College's Katherine A. Shaw Public Services Division has been deeply involved in facilitating improved access to consumer health information since the early 1980s, including the creation of a Pennsylvania statewide consumer health information delivery system in collaboration with public libraries and the development of the C. Everett Koop Community Health Information Center. These programs identified an increasing need for quality health information written for the consumer. In 2003, the College launched Philly Health Info (www.phillyhealthinfo.org), a virtual and community-based regional health information service, with a goal of empowering citizens of the Philadelphia region to make better informed health decisions by raising awareness of the health issues most affecting them. Philly Health Info provides access, via the Web, to relevant health resources and events within the Greater Philadelphia region, as well as authoritative heath information culled from national Web sites. This information includes non-English and low literacy materials and affinity pages providing information tailored for specific populations.

There can be a host of problems using information located on the unregulated Internet. According to a Pew Internet and American Life report (Fox, 2006), online demand for health information has increased significantly and the need for high-quality accessible consumer medical information continues to grow. Of the 113 million adults who use the Internet to search for health information, approximately 75 percent do not consistently check the quality indicators (e.g., the date and source of the information) of the health Web sites they visit.

In their report on teens and technology, Lenhart, Madden, and Hitlin (2005) noted that 87 percent of teens in the United States, aged 12 to 17, were online. That amounts to around 21 million wired youth, 11 million of whom were online daily. Not only has usage grown, but teenagers are now using the Internet more often and in a greater variety of ways than they did in 2000. In 2005, 17 million teens played games online, 16 million looked for news, 9 million made a purchase, but only 6 million searched for health information.

The Division of Adolescent Medicine at the University of Rochester studied adolescents' familiarity and ability to spell words and phrases associated with health and disease issues (Gray et al., 2002). They examined the impact of entering commonly misspelled terms into popular search engines and the results retrieved for the user. They concluded that retrieving useful health information on the Internet is dependent on the ability to spell relevant terms. They reported that adolescents are generally not exposed to written medical terms within daily life, although they may hear them frequently from family, friends, and the media. The fear of a digital divide has resulted in measures ensuring physical access to computers and Internet connections but has done nothing to address teens' health literacy.

During the initial pilot phase of the Philly Health Info program, adults in culturally diverse and underserved sections of Northeast Philadelphia and North Philadelphia had been the target audience. Upon the conclusion of the pilot phase, we decided that we would expand our outreach to include teens. We wanted to learn more about teen health information needs and determine the feasibility of training techno-savvy teens to serve as computer health information intermediaries for their less computer savvy parents and grandparents. To learn more about teens and their health information needs we created The Summer Teen Editor Program.

SUMMER TEEN EDITOR PROGRAM GOALS

This program provided an opportunity for the College to reach out to young people to help them become arbiters of health literacy in their homes, schools, and communities as well as to acquire knowledge about teen needs and preferences for health information. The program was developed to:

- Determine the health information needs and Internet usage habits of teenagers
- Lead a serious discussion on the subjects of health information and the landscape of online information
- Examine current health information Web sites targeted toward teen populations with an emphasis on developing a critical eye to evaluating that information
- Enhance the Philly Health Info.org Teens page with the recommendations of the participants
- Determine teens' affinity for serving as health information intermediaries.

PROGRAM METHODS

Selection criteria included the availability of Internet-connected computer laboratories, as well as the ability to recruit teenage participants and support the program all summer. Based on previous community outreach experience with neighborhood organizations, we selected two North Philadelphia locations that we felt were capable of hosting this program. Both locations are in lower-income sections of Philadelphia and draw teens from all parts of the city.

The Ruffin Nichols Memorial A.M.E. Church is a longstanding member of the lower North Philadelphia community. Ruffin Nichols installed a completely wired computer lab in 2005, thus making access to information possible in a previously underserved community. Through an already established partnership between Ruffin Nichols and Neighborhood Youth Achievement Program, an organization serving the youth of West Philadelphia, we were able to work with teens from two parts of the city at a single location.

The Honickman Center, located in the North Central neighborhood of Philadelphia, offers programs tailored to help residents of the community— children, youth, adults and families—move toward greater prosperity by increasing their educational and employment opportunities through comprehensive technology and literacy instruction. The Center—equipped with 255 computers and Smart Boards in every classroom to promote interactive learning—offers a cutting-edge educational technology environment through after-school programs, technology/computer classes, adult education, workforce development, G.E.D. classes, employment skills training, and art and music programs.

Prior to beginning the program, we met with staff members from both locations to determine their interest and presented them with an outline of the program, a letter to the parents of potential participants describing the program, and flyers to recruit the teen participants. We recruited teens between the ages of 14 and 16 because we were looking for mature adolescents with good evaluation skills, as well as computer and Internet experience. We restricted participation to 10 students per location.

PROGRAM MATERIALS AND EXPENSES

All sessions took place one afternoon per week over an eight-week period, in rooms with Internet-connected computers. We provided a $20 weekly stipend to our participants in addition to other modest rewards (giveaways, food). We supplied handouts with pens at each session. The final session merged the two groups at the College of Physicians for food, final comments, and a tour of the medical museum. The teens were asked to submit their final evaluation of the Web sites we reviewed, as well as the program overall (including the instructors). After making copies for our own data keeping, we returned each teen's weekly work in a binder with other materials, including a final list of Web sites reviewed, Internet searching tips, and a personal note thanking them for their help on the program. The teens' names were listed on the Web site.[1]

OVERVIEW OF PROGRAM SESSIONS

Sixteen teens, between the ages of 13.5 and 17, participated in approximately eight weekly two-hour sessions. The first hour was spent learning and reviewing with the Philly Health Info.org staff. During the second hour, students spent time on the computer answering questions and evaluating Web sites. The challenges for each group varied—one group needed more practice time, the other needed more specific task assignments. Each week we brought handouts for that session's work, and we revised the curricula each week in response to the challenges we encountered. The program generally followed this outline described below and we included our comments about each session.

First Session

Introductory session to describe the program parameters, expectations of conduct, and goals to potential participants. Teens completed a survey on health information needs and Internet usage habits (see Appendix 9-1.). No stipend was provided, but free pens were distributed. Results of the survey can be found in Appendix 9-2.

COMMENTS

This session went according to our expectations and is recommended for any organization hoping to conduct a similar outreach to teens. It helps to establish the rules and goals for participation in the program as well as how the program may differ from what the teens are used to at school or a job.

Sessions Two Through Six

Brief lessons on evaluating Web sites and finding health information online. Lesson topics included Internet basics (including search engines and how they work), and Web site authority, currency, and bias. The majority of the time was planned for "lab" work consisting of evaluating existing health information on Web sites geared toward teens. Weekly stipends and giveaways were provided.

COMMENTS

It was immediately apparent to us that students did not make the full connection with "authority" of Web sites. They would read directly from the page about who was the "owner" but not make the next connection on how that might affect the information (are they experts on the topic? are they selling something?). Bias was another issue. Initially, they did not seem terribly concerned about questionable objectives behind Web sites. Finding an answer, often as quickly as possible, seemed more important than making a value judgment about the information on a Web page, its motivations, or its author.

Perhaps due to their own short lifespans, teens had no problem with the concept of currency and why the date of health material is relevant. They quickly rejected health information on Web sites that were older than five years by claiming "that's old."

Teens are big users of search engines (not portals) but do not know much about how they work. Many had difficulty distinguishing advertising content and did not know about other methods that can taint search engine results (paid inclusions, Google "bombing"). In addition, some students seemed unfamiliar with the concepts of creating a search statement using keywords or Boolean logic.

Sessions Seven and Eight

Teen participants compiled their findings and recommendations for Philly Health Info.org's "Just for Teens" page. The final session, held at the College of Physicians of Philadelphia, merged both groups. We provided lunch and we had a final review session to gather their thoughts. We then gave out another survey for their health and information preferences (and included some feedback we received from them) as well as an anonymous evaluation for the program overall (see Appendix 9-3). Weekly stipend, giveaways, food, and a tour of the College's historical medical museum were provided. Results of the final program evaluations are available in Appendixes 9-4 and 9-5.

COMMENTS

Perhaps due to the other adolescents and the presence of adults, as well as being in a foreign location, the teens were intimidated and did not speak much. Fortunately, we were prepared in advance and had already collected their comments, and we read them off to elicit a little more feedback. We also went around the room and called on kids, taking "yea" or "nay" votes to stimulate discussion.

SUMMARY OF PROGRAM FINDINGS

Over the course of the approximately eight summer sessions (the two groups had a different amount of sessions), 16 teens were given ample time to discover and tell us what they look for in a health information Web site. The first hour of the weekly sessions were spent discussing and reviewing Web sites with an eye toward authority, bias, and currency. During the second hour, we asked the teen participants to review health Web sites to determine whether they should be listed on Philly Health Info's "Just for Teens" Web page. They worked alone at the computer and answered both short-answer and open-ended questions concerning their likes and dislikes. Early on, we recognized some teens work and learn differently, so we complemented independent written work with group discussion and one-on-one interviews.

At both the beginning and end of the program, the teens were asked to fill out surveys to rank their Web site preferences on an importance scale, as well as through short-answer questions. In addition, during a roundtable discussion, students were asked, not only to give "yea" or "nay" votes on individual Web sites, but also to further describe the attributes that appeal to them during a Web experience.

Our findings are based not only on the data from the surveys, but also from the classwork and discussions. We have summarized the results in three categories: (1) health literacy concerns for teens, (2) what's important to them, and (3) best practices for working with teens.

Health Literacy Concerns for Teens

One of the goals for this program was to encourage teens to think critically about information on the Internet. Concepts like authority, bias, and currency were foreign to them, and, by the time the program was over, these concepts registered only a little higher. Understanding who authored a Web page and being able to easily find the "About Us" section rated low to medium in importance at summer's end. The teens also gave low marks to learning about health issues from doctors and the importance of the organization behind a Web site.

But some of the concepts we introduced made an impression: all of the teens, by the end of the program, seemed to recognize bias in Web sites. They ranked advertisements as the least important feature on a Web site, and they put a lot of stock in making sure information on a health Web site is up-to-date. These findings could suggest that locating a date and identifying an advertisement are easier concepts to grasp than questioning an author's expertise on a topic.

What Features Are Important to Teens?

All of the teenagers reported that bright color schemes, pictures, graphics, animation, and interactive features, such as games, quizzes, polls, and Q&As, were important features they look for in a Web site. How critical? Most of them would not explore a Web site any further if the front page turned them off, regardless of how useful the information could be, including providing help for school assignments.

Games were a compelling feature for many of the teens. They seemed to hold their interest almost against their wills. When prompted, the teens would admit the games were "corny" and didn't advance the educational mission of a Web site, but if left alone too long, many would spend the majority of their time exploring the "games" section of the health Web sites we looked at this summer.

The teens told us there must be well-organized informational content if you plan on holding their interest. Our teens preferred information on multiple topics as opposed to single-issue Web sites. They liked information written at a level they could relate to and understand. They liked stories written by their peers. They liked reading about celebrities. They liked advice columns. They wanted to ask their own questions and write their own stories.

Despite the importance placed on colors, graphics, and games, in the end it was informational sites like Teens Health from the Nemours Foundation (http://teenshealth.org) and 4Girls Health from U.S. Department of Health and Human Services (http://www.girlshealth.gov) that our participants would turn to answer their health questions. Both of these sites are light on fancy animation, graphics, and games, but heavy on teen-relevant content.

The lesson here is that a Web site must strike a balance between content and flair to make a lasting impression and get teens to explore other parts of the page. Games and animation might catch their attention, but only for a short period of time. Even among our most visually obsessed teens, content rated high. But they made it clear that a Web site with low graphic design, heavy amounts of white space and text on the front page will not get many teenage visitors to explore past the front page, regardless of ease of use and content.

On their final evaluation forms, the teens claimed they would have participated in the editor program for free. Our experience "in the field" suggested otherwise. Without the financial incentive, we believe we would have had less cooperation, poorer attendance, and teens leaving the sessions early.

Best Practices When Working with Teens

For fellow nonteachers who find themselves implementing an educational program or product aimed at teenagers, we found working with teens presents unique challenges. In both class discussion and anonymous survey feedback, they told us "don't treat us like kids," yet most were not mature enough to work independently. It was a delicate balance to encourage and stimulate maturity and independent thought while making sure they completed their work.

WHAT WORKED

The two groups presented different challenges. There were, however, some parallels between both groups, particularly when it came to style of instruction. While there was a range of maturity and cognitive expression, the following methods proved most effective:

- **Controlling access to computers and Web sites:** When working with teens in a computer lab or on an Internet program, it is critical to hold lectures without distractions. In other words: restrict computer use. One instructor gathered the teens at a large table for the lesson session; the other had them put down their laptop screens. Also, we had to walk around and monitor them to ensure they were on the correct page (not video or music sites). Not only did controlling access improve attentiveness, it also divided up the sessions nicely. We also had to control the number of Web sites to review; otherwise, they would quickly move through the Web sites to "get done" quicker.
- **Simultaneously collect data and feedback using different methods**—written, in-class discussion, and one-on-one: Some teens are shy, and others

only say something interesting when others are paying attention or in response to what another teen says. We found that a tripartite approach (written; group discussion; one-on-one) yielded the most complete data, and that not many kids gave enough information through one method alone.

- **Challenge the kids—even with a bit of an attitude:** For example, when one teen reported not liking a Web site because of "too much clicking," the instructor replied, "So? Is it going to kill you to have to click a few times?" This prompted the teen to defend what he viewed as unnecessary and excessive clicking; other students who had been previously silent, also chimed in and "ganged up" on the teacher. Similarly, when we had difficulty getting responses beyond "I didn't like it" or "yeah," sometimes a little confrontation or debate (playing devil's advocate) helped to spur interest and group discussion. Teens like to argue; we found that capitalizing on that proclivity stimulated useful dialogue.

- **Use humor:** They're bright, sometimes sarcastic, and always aware they are teenagers and the reputation that carries. Use some humor—even at your own expense—to get them talking. We found class discussion and overall participation increased when they were enjoying themselves.

- **Listen and repeat:** Repeat back to them what they say and point out why their feedback is important. This verbal exchange demonstrates you value their opinion and are paying attention to them, and also models how we hoped they would express themselves ("So what you're saying is, the Web site doesn't need to have a lot of pictures if the information is laid out well").

- **Review, review, review:** Many of the concepts take a while to "sink in" and it helps to keep reminding the the teens with examples and a new context each week—continuing to build upon previous lessons.

WHAT DID NOT WORK

It is important to have optimal circumstances in place to ensure the best outcome. For us, these included the computer facility and additional program support, such as promotion. In one group, several adults came each week (including a parent), which contributed to high attendance and cooperation. The other group had minimal participation from the host facility beyond supplying the classroom, and often the kids did not receive messages about the sessions.

- **Time:** The session length of two hours proved suitable because we combined lecture, class discussion, and individual lab work. Eight weeks, however, was *too long* for the goal of receiving unique feedback on different teen Web sites. The teens had less and less to say as the weeks progressed, and we were getting the same responses. While we could have *taught* a full year of weekly sessions on health informatics, our goals for this program were to gain their insights on health information and Web site preferences. In hindsight, a more concise approach would have served us well, since the teens struggled with finding new things to say. Bottom line: Extra sessions did not lead to more or richer data.

- **Critical thinking:** We were confronted with teens who were not used to constructive dialogue. We had to work hard, continuously prodding them to get information beyond the superficial level ("why didn't you like it? what about the colors didn't you like?"). They provided the briefest of answers and had difficulty supporting their responses with examples. In group discussion, the teens seemed to look for clues as to what we were looking for—the "right" answer. Even when we emphasized, "there is no right answer," they seemed programmed to want to give an answer they thought we were seeking. Case in point: after explaining who we were (including our health information Web site) at the first session, we surveyed the teens and asked what health information Web sites they use. Several listed "PhillyHealthInfo.org" although they had never visited it before.

- **Search engines:** When using search engines, they went for the quickest—often the first, not the best—result. We had to push them to explore the Web sites *thoroughly* (go to different sections, look up different topics). They would take information directly from a Web site without fully synthesizing the material and understanding what it meant. This was particularly evident with commercial Web sites that were underwritten by law firms or advertisers. There was a lack of concern or understanding about the implications.

- **Initiative:** Our expectations for this program assumed the teens would proactively identify teen health Web sites and be active partners in this program. In fact, we did not have any teen submit a site to us or do anything beyond classroom participation. The stipend had little effect other than ensuring attendance and basic participation. In final evaluation surveys, the majority of the teens said they would have done this without the stipend, but we got asked about the money and if we could give it out earlier in the session so they could leave. We found ourselves using the stipend to ensure they would stay until the end and to make them feel guilty enough to make an honest attempt at evaluation ("this is your job"). In the end, however, the stipends and other giveaways did not provide us more eager participants and proved to have little impact on the quality of responses or approach the teens had to the program.

LESSONS LEARNED

Overall, we found the students to be respectful, funny, bright, and quite savvy. Perhaps as a result of an educational history emphasizing standardized testing, many have learned to direct those talents to accomplishing a task, rather than exploring a more thoughtful and comprehensive approach to problem-solving and research. As with any group, working with teens can be both frustrating and fulfilling. Today's teenagers have a unique challenge of superb technical abilities that may mask underdevelopment of their cognitive and research skills. Educators and other outreach workers should heed this discrepancy when developing curricula and programs aimed at teenagers.

We had to be flexible and responsive to the needs of each group. We had to teach more than we had originally planned. For instance, we had not planned on spending so much time on search engines and searching techniques, or on needing to be persistent in order to obtain constructive responses, but we found the teens' skills in these areas to be lacking.

We found teens consistently responded when we used interactive Web site examples or involved them in a class discussion. Some had trouble working independently or submitting answers in writing. Others simply needed the eyes and ears of their peers to get excited about their own opinions.

We also learned to be careful with the structure of our questions and survey instruments. Most teens will provide the minimum response required. If you ask a yes or no question, you won't get more. Open-ended questions work better when trying to establish concrete ideas and preferences, but even open-ended questions may not go far enough. Follow-up questions and group discourse are often necessary to get to the heart of the matter.

Finally, the old adage, "you cannot judge a book by its cover" is a perfect metaphor for teaching teenagers. We often looked at surly faces and crossed arms, but would later be surprised by thoughtful comments that demonstrated keen interest. The quietest teen in one group (who had little to say in class, and who was frequently asked to remove headphones while rolling her eyes) mentioned at the end how much she "really enjoyed the class" and wished it had met more frequently.

OUR CAUTIONARY TALE: A NEW "DIGITAL DIVIDE"

While a digital divide among seniors has been recognized (Fox, 2005), we certainly did not find any technological barriers with the teens. They were able to manipulate multiple open windows and interact with different software programs on Web sites with ease. When we taught a shortcut, they picked it up immediately. However, we did find a barrier between online information and teen comprehension of and appreciation for the context of that information. The teens skimmed the materials and accepted information at face value. When asked who is the author of a page or how the information is substantiated, they read off the page but could not take it a step further and address how the authorship affects the information or if the information is credible. The teens would report on the colors of a Web page and say they "liked it," but the fact that it was selling something questionable (a purported "cure" for cancer) did not seem to affect their perception of the Web site. They could play an interactive game on a health Web site without ever connecting its relevance to the topic behind it.

The challenge for educating teens is to put them in circumstances that promote a more holistic approach to learning. Educators should be cognizant of teens cutting and pasting directly from Web sites into Word documents, not going beyond one page of search results or the first page of a Web site when developing assignments. We created assignments that we knew had bad first-page results.

Despite spending time explaining the problems with search engines (e.g., their commercial orientation can influence results), in the final surveys our teens reported they will continue to rely almost exclusively on search engines. While search engines produce an astounding list of results in seconds, those Web sites are not vetted for quality or accuracy. Unfortunately, teens don't see the need of using secondary resources, such as books, specialized portals and other databases that require extra time, when they have quick access to such a large quantity of information. Educators have to introduce authority, bias, and currency, and present them on the same pedestal as accuracy (the "right" answer) before young people will begin to see these issues as equally important. This can only be accomplished if emphasis and rewards are placed on the process of finding an answer as well as in the "answer" itself. We attempted to do this by creating exercises where search engines were of little use, or by asking questions that were not readily apparent without synthesizing more material.

CONCLUSION

While the opinions of the teen groups varied, the experiences of the teachers were largely the same. Ultimately, we received less editing help from the teens than we had anticipated and spent more time teaching them about Web site evaluation and research skills. We had originally anticipated the teens would "take charge" and search for Web sites and submit them to us. In fact, we found they had limited experience searching for the kind of Web sites we use (government, university and other nonprofit) and, more important, lacked the skills to determine authority, bias, and currency of information. Using PhillyHealthInfo.org and other health Web sites, the College had an opportunity to show students about the ways they can navigate the vast, sometimes misleading world of Internet resources and achieve good results. Since all participants had to demonstrate computer and Internet searching capabilities before becoming involved, we incorrectly assumed the editors would have research and Web site evaluation skills as well. While we did gain insight into teen health information and Web site preferences, we also learned about the challenges working with teenagers.

The Summer Teen Editor Program offered us an opportunity to work directly with the community through faith-based organizations. We were able to obtain valuable insights into the information needs of urban teens, which we used to improve the PhillyHealthInfo.org Web site. We were able to offer life-long skills to empower participating teenagers to access credible information for themselves, their friends, and family. The program assisted us in identifying and documenting the need for additional health literacy education for teens. Our experience showed that while teens are often thought to be techno-savvy, they are not utilizing critical thinking and evaluation skills when surfing the Internet. We hope by sharing our best practices with other information and education specialists who work with teens, we can work to improve teen health literacy and empower them to better health. The teen editor's program is currently being used as a template for teaching teens health literacy as part of the college's school education program directed at area middle and high school students.

ACKNOWLEDGMENTS

We are indebted to The Jacob & Valeria Langeloth Foundation and the Philadelphia Health Care Trust for funding the Teen Editor Program. Also thanks to the Philly Health Info.org "team," including Information Specialist Eric Darley, M.S., and Administrative Assistant Sofie Sereda. We are also indebted for the help and support of the host locations, particularly Brother Willie Davis from Ruffin Nichols Memorial A.M.E. Church, the staff from the Neighborhood Youth Achievement Program, and Project H.O.M.E.'s Honickman Learning Center & Comcast Technology Labs. Finally, we are grateful to our teen participants for teaching us so much about teenagers and their health information needs.

We dedicate this chapter to the memory of Thomas W. Langfitt, MD, Past President of the College of Physicians of Philadelphia. Under his leadership, the College moved its consumer health program and resources online with Philly Health Info.org. Dr. Langfitt was a friend, mentor, and tireless advocate for improving the health of the public through education and increased access to health information.

NOTE

1. The PhillyHealthInfo.org Web site has subsequently been changed, including the original "Just for Teens" page. The teens are no longer listed on this page, as the content has changed substantially.

REFERENCES

Fox, Susannah. 2005. "Digital Divisions." Washington, DC: Pew Internet & American Life Project. Available: www.pewinternet.org/pdfs/PIP_Digital_Divisions_Oct_5_2005.pdf

Fox, Susannah. 2006. "Online Health Search 2006." Washington, DC: Pew Internet & American Life Project. Available: www.pewinternet.org/pdgs/PIP_Online_Health _2006.pdf

Gray, Nicola, Jonathan Klein, Judith Cantrill, and Peter Noyce. 2002. "How Do You Spell Gonorrhea? Adolescents' Health Literacy and the Internet." *Abstracts of the Academy of Health Services Research's Health Policy Meeting* 19: 21.

Lenhart, Amanda, Mary Madden, and Paul Hitlin. 2005. "Teens and Technology." Washington, DC: Pew Internet & American Life Project. Available: www.pewinternet.org/ pdgs/PIP_Teens_Tech_July2005web.pdf

Curricula Development

National Network of Libraries of Medicine Middle Atlantic Region. "From Snake Oil to Penicillin: Evaluating Consumer Health Information on the Internet." Available: http://nnlm.gov/training/consumer/snakeoil/

Springfield Township High School Virtual Library's Online Activities Promoting Information Literacy. Available: http://mciu.org/~spjvweb/ifolitles.html

University Libraries, University at Albany SUNY's Internet Tutorials. Available: http:// library.albany.edu/usered/wwwdex/index.html

Appendix 9-1. Initial Survey Form

You and Your Health

For each question below, circle the number to the right
that best fits your opinion on the importance of the issue.

Question	How important is this topic to you?				
	Don't Care at All	Not Very Important	No Opinion	Kind of Important	Very Important
Pregnancy	1	2	3	4	5
AIDS and sexually transmitted disease	1	2	3	4	5
Stress and anxiety	1	2	3	4	5
Eating disorders (anorexia, bulimia)	1	2	3	4	5
Birth control	1	2	3	4	5
Alcohol and drinking	1	2	3	4	5
Steroids and sports	1	2	3	4	5
Suicide	1	2	3	4	5
Weight control and nutrition	1	2	3	4	5
Smoking	1	2	3	4	5
Sexual assault	1	2	3	4	5
Personal safety and protecting yourself from attack	1	2	3	4	5
Losing a loved one	1	2	3	4	5
Drug use	1	2	3	4	5
Popularity and self-esteem	1	2	3	4	5
Communicating with adults (school and parents)	1	2	3	4	5
Family problems (brothers, sisters, other family, money)	1	2	3	4	5
Depression and anger	1	2	3	4	5
Abortion	1	2	3	4	5
Physical fitness and exercise	1	2	3	4	5
Skin and hair care	1	2	3	4	5
Body image	1	2	3	4	5
Violence in families	1	2	3	4	5
Violence in community	1	2	3	4	5

Appendix 9-2. Initial Survey Results

Before we began our sessions we asked students to rank order a list of health topics in terms of importance to their lives. The following topics scored a "very important" from more than half of the students surveyed:

Pregnancy	Alcohol and Drinking	Personal Safety	Abortion
AIDS and STDs	Suicide	Losing a Loved One	Violence in Families
Eating Disorders	Smoking	Drug Use	Violence in Communities
Birth Control	Sexual Assault	Family Problems	Communication with Adults

Appendix 9-3. Final Evaluation Form

Your Web Site Preferences

For each question below, circle the number to the right
that best fits your opinion on the importance of the issue.

Question—Most important Web site features	How important are these features to you?				
	Don't Care at All	Not Very Important	No Opinion	Kind of Important	Very Important
Bright, eye-catching colors	1	2	3	4	5
An "About Us" page	1	2	3	4	5
Quizzes or polls	1	2	3	4	5
Information for parents or teachers	1	2	3	4	5
Games	1	2	3	4	5
A "Question & Answer" section	1	2	3	4	5
Information you can understand and relate to	1	2	3	4	5
Real stories from real teens	1	2	3	4	5
Author—Who is behind the Web site	1	2	3	4	5
Online chat	1	2	3	4	5
Search box	1	2	3	4	5
Information from nonprofit organization	1	2	3	4	5
Sad or scary topics	1	2	3	4	5
Lots of facts	1	2	3	4	5
Uses characters to tell a story	1	2	3	4	5
Animation	1	2	3	4	5
Gives advice	1	2	3	4	5
It lets you tell your own story	1	2	3	4	5

(Continued)

Appendix 9-3. Final Evaluation Form *(Continued)*

Question—Most important Web site features	How important are these features to you?				
	Don't Care at All	Not Very Important	No Opinion	Kind of Important	Very Important
It lets you ask your own question	1	2	3	4	5
Advertisements	1	2	3	4	5
Lots of pictures	1	2	3	4	5
Recent information	1	2	3	4	5
Lots of topics	1	2	3	4	5
Fast downloading	1	2	3	4	5
Topic (A-Z) Index	1	2	3	4	5

Question—When I visit a health Web site I want to . . .	How true are these statements about you?				
	Not True at All	Not Very True	No Opinion	Kind of True	Very True
Look at pictures	1	2	3	4	5
Learn a lot	1	2	3	4	5
Get my questions answered	1	2	3	4	5
Take a quiz	1	2	3	4	5
Write my own story	1	2	3	4	5
Learn from doctors	1	2	3	4	5
Know that I'm getting the best information	1	2	3	4	5
Read articles	1	2	3	4	5
Watch a video	1	2	3	4	5
Have fun	1	2	3	4	5
Know that no one is trying to sell me anything	1	2	3	4	5
Read other people's personal stories	1	2	3	4	5
Get advice	1	2	3	4	5
Ask a question	1	2	3	4	5
Learn from other teens	1	2	3	4	5
Play a game	1	2	3	4	5
Know that the information I'm getting is up-to-date	1	2	3	4	5

Appendix 9-4. Final Evaluation Results—Web Site Features

At the final session, 14 students were asked to rank Web site features according to importance on a scale of 1–5, with 5 being "very important" and 1 being "don't care at all." The following are the results with a numerical score listed in parentheses.

Information you can understand and relate to (66)	Lots of facts (55)
Lots of topics (65)	Recent information (55)
Fast downloading (64)	Quizzes or polls (54)
Bright, eye-catching colors (63)	Information for parents or teachers (54)
Games (63)	Gives advice (54)
Search box (62)	A "Question & Answer" section (52)
Animation (62)	Information from nonprofit organization (51)
Real stories from real teens (61)	It lets you ask your own question (50)
Author—Who is behind the Web site (60)	Sad or scary topics (47)
An "About Us" page (59)	It lets you tell your own story (47)
Topic (A-Z) Index (58)	Online chat (45)
Lots of pictures (56)	Uses characters to tell a story (45)
	Advertisements (45)

Appendix 9-5. Final Evaluation Results—Internet Experience Preferences

The 14 students surveyed were also asked to answer the following question: When I visit a health Web site I want to. . . . The answers provided to this question were to be ranked on a scale of 1–5 with 5 being "very true" and 1 being "not true at all." The following are the results with a numerical score listed in parentheses.

Have fun (69)	Read articles (57)
Play a game (64)	Ask a question (57)
Know that the information I'm getting is up-to-date (63)	Watch a video (55)
Get my questions answered (62)	Look at pictures (54)
Learn a lot (60)	Know that no one is trying to sell me anything (54)
Know that I'm getting the best information (59)	Take a quiz (48)
Get advice (59)	Read other people's personal stories (46)
Learn from other teens (58)	Learn from doctors (43)
	Write my own story (41)

Part III

Health Literacy Issues in Public and Hospital Libraries: Providing Programs and Services to Help Consumers Understand Their Healthcare

Chapter 10

The Health Reference Interview: Getting to the Heart of the Question While Assessing Your Customer's Literacy Skills

Karyn Prechtel

Health literacy has been defined in several ways. Some experts describe it as the ability to comprehend health-related texts (Muro, 2006). Others think of it as having a level of reading and numerical skills that allow the individual to function in the world of healthcare (Safeer and Keenan, 2005). *Healthy People 2010* defines health literacy as "the degree to which individuals have the capacity to obtain, process and understand basic health information and services needed to make appropriate health decisions" (U.S. Department of Health and Human Services, 2000:11–20). The common thread through all of these definitions is the apparent relationship between health literacy and good health. Those with higher levels of health literacy are better able to manage their health and are more likely to be healthier than those with low health literacy (Kutner et al., 2006). This chapter focuses on an individual's ability to obtain or access health information, one step in the health literacy process.

Where do consumers get health information? Some people may receive health information from traditional sources, such as newspapers, television, magazines, books, or brochures. "Adults may also get information about health issues from conversations with family, friends, or co-workers, or conversations with health care professionals" (Kutner et al., 2006:18). Another commonly used source of health information is the Internet. According to Pew Internet and

American Life Project "seventy-nine percent of internet users have searched online for information on at least one major health topic" (Fox, 2005: ii). Even so, a significant portion of people are not Internet users because they do not have the means to own or access a computer or the skills necessary to search for health information on their own. For example, "senior citizens are among the least likely people in America to have Internet access. Just 15 percent of Americans aged 65 and older go online, compared to 51 percent of their closest peers, those aged 50–64, and 56 percent of all Americans" (Fox, 2001: 4).

Many people turn to the public library to access newspapers, magazines and books related to health. Those without home Internet access may visit the public library to get online. In 2004, visits to public libraries in the United States totaled 1.3 billion, or 4.7 per capita (Chute et al., 2006: 6). At any given moment, the public library is used by the very young to the elderly, the recent immigrant to the longtime citizen, and the functionally illiterate to the scholar. Public libraries and librarians face the challenge of providing current, relevant, reliable health information to people whose language skills, literacy levels, and learning styles vary greatly.

One of the most practical tools for public librarians is the reference interview. As most librarians know, customers often have difficulty articulating their true question, and when health information is the topic at hand, it may be a struggle to ask someone for help. The two basic challenges to the health reference interview are figuring out what the customer *really* wants and finding information the customer can understand (Dewdney and Michell, 1997). If done properly, the health reference interview will assist the librarian in getting to the heart of their customer's question and may aid in the assessment of the customer's literacy skills and content needs as they relate to health information.

Determining what the customer *really* wants has always been a challenge for public librarians. Many people don't know how to phrase their questions in such a way that truly articulates what they are looking for. When asking questions related to health, this challenge is exacerbated by the following unique considerations.

- Health information can be intimidating or scary. If someone is dealing with a serious health issue, or researching a health topic for someone she loves, emotions can play a role in the formation of her question. For example, she may be frightened or confused by information that a medical professional gave her in a brief consult.
- She may not know the exact spelling of a medical term, let alone how to pronounce it, and spelling may be critical to the success of her research.
- She may have been raised in an environment that places a high value on privacy, particularly as it relates to personal or family matters.

- She may not have the language skills necessary to phrase her question well. This could be due to lack of educational opportunities, low-level English skills, or language differences between customer and librarian.

Your customer may be able speak conversational English, but may not be able to read it although he is fluent in another language. Or, your customer may have little or no education or poor comprehension skills that limit his ability to read. Finding health information that the average person can comprehend can present a challenge for public librarians, particularly because most adults read between the 8th and 9th grade level, and most written health information at a 10th grade level or higher (Safeer and Keenan, 2005). In recent years, however, the amount of print and electronic lay health information written in English and other languages, as well as for those with low literacy skills, has grown exponentially, making the task of finding relevant information a little easier.

THE HEALTH REFERENCE INTERVIEW

The reference interview involves a back-and-forth exchange between the librarian and customer, and can be considered a negotiation of sorts. It can be used to "elicit information about what the user wants to know; how the user plans to use the information; what level of detail, technical specialization, or reading ability would be useful; [and] what format of information is preferred" (Ross, Nilsen, and Dewdney, 2002: 4). Unfortunately, "reference interviews are conducted only half the time, a figure that has scarcely varied over twenty-five years of reported research" (Ross, 2003: 40). Why is this a problem? As a public librarian, my experience corresponds with reports in the literature that the original question is very often not the *real* question and the reference interview is the means by which I can determine the real question.

On paper it sounds simple, but "one of the most difficult lessons to teach a beginning reference student or librarian is to conduct the interview without thinking about what sources might answer the question" (Jennerich and Jennerich, 1997: 10). It is essential that librarians concentrate on the question and the interview process. It is "more efficient and effective than trying to answer a request before it is fully understood" (10).

Another challenge of the reference interview is querying the customer in such a way as to not appear nosey or pushy. While some people have a tendency to tell public librarians more information than is necessary or desired, there are many who, for various reasons, do not want to give much detail at all. It is very common for a customer to approach a librarian with the question: "Where are the medical books?" The librarian may follow up with, "What kind of medical information are you looking for?" and the customer is likely to add, "I just want to look around."

Conducting a proper reference interview will ensure that you avoid the "without-speaking-she-began-to-type maneuver" (Ross, 2003: 39). We've all seen this in action. The customer approaches the librarian and asks his question. Then the librarian proceeds to perform her catalog or database search without saying a word. Unfortunately, it is much too easy to assume that the customer's question is as straightforward as it is presented.

BE AWARE OF THE PERSON ASKING THE QUESTION

Gender, age and race may not play a role in determining the nature of the information needed. For example, if a middle-aged man is asking for information about breast cancer, he may have a wife, sister, or mother who has recently been diagnosed with the disease. Or, *he* may have been diagnosed recently with breast cancer and may be seeking information for himself. If a teenage girl is asking the question, she may be writing a report for school or gathering information about breast cancer prevention because of the high prevalence of the disease in her family. It is best not to prejudge or presume anything. Instead, listening to what people say will help you to narrow the possibilities and phrase your follow-up questions in order to get to the heart of the matter.

GET AS MUCH INFORMATION AS POSSIBLE

Basically, you must get as much information as you can from the customer. Your questions are meant to focus their queries. In their very informative book on conducting effective reference interviews, Ross, Nilsen, and Dewdney (2002) state that the "form in which you ask the question determines the sort of answer you are likely to get" (83). An open-ended question, which "allows people to respond on their own terms," is more useful, especially at the beginning of the interview (85). For example, if someone asks where the medical books are located, it would be appropriate to ask her "What in particular are you looking for?" If she hesitates to answer, you might say, "We have hundreds of different books related to medical information and I want to help you find exactly what you are looking for to save you time and frustration." Or, "Although we have lots of books on health information, often the most current information is available on the Internet and I can show you exactly where it is if you tell me more." According to Ross (2003), librarians should avoid asking their customer: "Have you checked the catalog?" or "Have you checked the computer?" because these questions "feed into users' anxiety about asking for help" (41).

Pretend that your customer has narrowed down the possibilities for you by asking for books related to diabetes. Should you simply give her a call number and point to the shelves, or give her the URL to a Web site? No, this is considered an "unmonitored referral," a term Ross uses "when the reference librarian gives the user a call number or refers the user to a source within the library but does not follow up or check to make sure that the source is not only found but also actually answers the question" (2003: 40).* Unless your customer insists on being left alone at this point, you should continue to help her locate relevant information. Some appropriate interview questions at this point might be: "What type of diabetes are you interested in?" "Can you tell me a little more about what you are looking for?"

ASK IF THEY HAVE A DEADLINE

Imagine that your customer has helped you narrow down the question to information about heart disease for an older man, in this case his grandfather. He may have been sent to the library by his grandfather to gather background information before his next doctor's appointment. Or perhaps his grandfather is scheduled for bypass surgery in two weeks and needs to understand what is involved in the surgery and recovery process. I recommend asking a question such as "When would you like this information?" to determine if there is a deadline. This will help you get the most relevant information into their hands in a timely manner.

IS THE QUESTION STILL NOT CLEAR?

Perhaps after all of this back and forth, your customer has been either evasive, or unable to articulate what she is looking for. Her privacy concerns may outweigh her understanding that you are merely trying to help. If you sense that privacy may be the issue, I recommend that you respect her privacy, yet not give up on the interview. Tell her that you are going to walk with her to the health books, and once you are away from the desk and in the stacks, lower your voice considerably and ask her a few more questions. She may be willing to open up to you if she believes that no one else is in earshot or that you understand her concern for privacy. You can tell her that you understand that it is difficult to talk about health topics, but that you really want to get her the best and most current information. Discretion is valued highly in our profession. You may wish to explain to your customer how important privacy is to librarians and to give her an example she will understand. For example, library customers are invariably impressed when they learn that librarians will not divulge customer information to law enforcement without a warrant or to each other without the customer's permission.

---

* From: Ross, Catherine Sheldrick. 2003. "The Reference Interview: Why It Needs to Be Used in Every (Well Almost Every) Reference Transaction." *Reference and User Services Quarterly* 43, no.1. Reprinted by permission from Reference and User Services Association, American Library Association.

Another tool you may wish to use if you are struggling to get to the real question is paraphrasing. This technique can be particularly helpful when language comprehension or cultural differences may be getting in the way. For example, if your customer has asked you for information about lung cancer, but after some questioning you are not sure if he is looking for lung cancer treatment information or information on the prevention of lung cancer, you should restate what you believe he has asked to see if it is correct. For example, based on what you've heard, you might say, "Your aunt has lung cancer and you want to know more about her options for treatment?" Or, "You are interested in learning about preventing lung cancer?"

Listen carefully to what your customer says and look at her body language when she responds to you. It is possible that she doesn't understand your questions any more than you understand her answers. If she simply nods her head in affirmation, this may be an indication of a language barrier and you may want to ask her if she is more comfortable speaking a different language. If you are unable to speak her language, find a library staff person who can and ask the customer to wait one moment for that person.

My Experience with a Vague Question

As I mentioned earlier, it has been my experience that the original question is very often not the real question. Typically, customers often ask very broad and general questions when they really want very specific information (Ross, Nilsen, and Dewdney, 2002). In her article on e-mail reference interviews, Abels (1996) indicates that "for complex information needs, a reference interview is usually required to avoid the syndrome of providing the right answer to the wrong question" (351). The following example (with details altered to protect the privacy of the customer) will help illustrate this.

I was working at an information desk one evening when someone approached me with what appeared to be a very straightforward question. This customer asked me if we had any books on the brain. He was a professionally dressed adult who appeared to be on his way to or from work. I hesitated to ask him any questions, assuming that he knew what he was looking for. I actually started to walk around the desk, intending to lead him to the books in our reference collection related to the brain, when I realized what I was NOT doing. I hadn't asked him a single question! I immediately backtracked and asked, "What aspect of the brain are you interested in?" He replied, "I would like to look at cross-sections of a brain." *Interesting, I thought.* "*We aren't going to be able to help him, however. I'll have to tell him about the Health Sciences Library at the University.* Nevertheless, I was in the reference interview mode, and I continued asking questions. "When you say cross-sections, what do you mean?"

He replied, "I would like to see the cross-sections of a brain of someone who has Asperger's syndrome."

Having narrowed down his question to something specific, I turned my monitor so that he could see what I was doing, and I started my search, first with the library catalog. I quickly switched to the Internet and went directly to the National Library of Medicine's MedlinePlus pages on Asperger's Syndrome. *Perhaps MedlinePlus will point me in the right direction, I thought.* When I reached the page with links to Asperger's syndrome information, I asked him if he had ever seen this information. His eyes lit up. It was at that point that he volunteered that he had just been diagnosed with the syndrome, and that he really didn't know anything about it.

I immediately walked him over to an available computer, logged him in, and helped him navigate to the page I had just shown him. Remarkably, there happened to be a link to the article "Adults with Asperger's Syndrome" a few lines from the top. It was like taking a child to a candy store. He thanked me, and I told him that we also had books on the subject that he could take home and read, and that they were located on a different floor. I went back to the reference desk to gather that information for him.

My customer probably thought that he would be able to understand the disease that he had just been diagnosed with by looking at the cross-sections of a brain. And perhaps he could have. But, clearly, he needed more basic information, and I had opened up a world of information to him by asking a few simple questions.

FOLLOW-UP

You have avoided the "unmonitored referral" (Ross, 2003: 40) and taken your customer to the resource on the shelf or shown him a Web site that will help answer his questions, but your job is not finished. Did he truly find the information he was looking for in that book? Does he understand the Web site? Is he able to check out the material, or will he be able to find the online information again on his own? If you think the answer to any of these questions could be no, then you have some more work to do. Remember, your customer may use the information he finds (or lack thereof) to make important decisions related to his health or the health of someone he loves. This is important stuff, not to be taken lightly.

"Research has shown that asking follow-up questions is one of the most important skills you can use in the reference interview" (Ross, Nilsen, and Dewdney, 2002: 118). You must follow up with the customer to be sure he is finding what he needs. It has been my experience that very few people come back to the service point asking for more help. It was probably difficult to approach the librarian in the first place, and to admit defeat can be embarrassing. As these authors noted, follow-up questions "can make the difference between a satisfactory experience for the user and a frustrating series of events" (118).

So how do you follow up with your customer, especially if you are busy or have other responsibilities? You have to treat the follow-up as an integral part of the reference transaction and make an effort to track the customer down or catch him on the way out of the building. This is not always an easy thing to do. I recommend making a note to yourself mentally (or physically, if that works best for you) that you have directed a customer to health material. Then in a moment between customers, leave the service point and look for him. Most people are very appreciative if you ask them if they have found the right information and they will take the opportunity to tell you whether they have.

If the answer is no, offer to find him another source. If you have exhausted your resources, ask him if you can take his name and number, research the topic further, and get back to him. If you strongly believe that you will be unable to help him further, don't stop there. Offer to refer him to another library or organization. Many hospital and academic health sciences libraries have substantial consumer health collections and are open to the public. Health-related associations (e.g., American Diabetes Association) may have small libraries or support groups that could be of assistance to your customer. You can also check their Web sites for the most current information. For example, research findings related to HIV/AIDS seem to occur almost daily, as do treatment options. Odds are that the average public library does not have the most current information available on AIDS treatments, but amfAR, the American Foundation for AIDS Research, does (www.amfar.org/cgi-bin/iowa/ index.html).

Individuals with rare disorders have been known to join forces to create organizations or associations in order to share information and support. Information on Addison's disease, Paget's disease, or Marfan syndrome may be found through MedlinePlus with a link to the National Institutes of Health Office of Rare Diseases (http://rarediseases.info.nih.gov), which in turn has links to local and national organizations concerned with these diseases.

Keep contact information on hand so that you can easily refer your customer to health sciences libraries or associations. You may also want to have maps or driving directions available to give to your customer. The best thing to remember is that the information may be out there, even though you are unable to get your hands on it. Advise your customer to be persistent.

WHAT NOT TO DO

During a health-related interview, there are several behaviors in which a librarian should not engage.

Do not interpret the health information that you help locate for your customer. "How can the staff member interpret medical information? Simply by suggesting what she/he thinks the information means" (Baker and Manbeck, 2002: 146). You may find the language easier to understand than does your customer. Nevertheless, avoid responding to the question "What does this mean?" or "Does this say...?'" Your customer has unique circumstances that bring her to you. You know nothing about her exact diagnosis. You don't know what her health professional has told her, nor do you know how the information can be applied to her unique situation. Most important, you have no specialized knowledge, education, or skills that put you in a position to interpret health information for someone else.

Never give medical advice to your customer. The only advice you should be dispensing is for the customer to take what she has found back to her healthcare professional so that she can decide if it has any bearing on her situation. Rarely is a librarian trained in one or more health fields. Most librarians, even medical and health sciences librarians, have master's degrees in Library and Information Science, not degrees in medicine. Nevertheless, some customers may place an incredible amount of trust in our ability to help them make life-changing decisions. We have all had our own health concerns or have loved ones with health issues. They may even be similar to the ones that your customer is dealing with. Nevertheless, your opinions are of no consequence to the customer and should never be given.

Many library customers will ask "What is the best...?" or "Do you think I should...?" Answers to these types of questions should be avoided at all costs. I recommend that you tell the customer that you are not in a position to answer that question. In fact, you should be prepared to tell a customer something along the lines of *"I am not a medical professional and cannot answer that question; however, I'll be happy to point you to more information to help you make that decision."*

You should never appear to make recommendations about treatments, medication, or anything else related to health information. To recommend one over-the-counter or prescription medication over the other would be considered practicing medicine without a license. This may seem obvious; however, most librarians who work with the public have chosen the profession because they want to help others. Making recommendations on material for, say, school assignments or recreational reading is second nature to us. When it comes to health information, we have to remind ourselves where to draw the line.

Never provide a recommendation for a dentist, doctor, clinic, or hospital. You may have personally had a good experience with your podiatrist, but you are in no position to refer customers to her. In fact, to recommend one doctor over another would be unethical and unprofessional. Most insurance companies and most state medical boards have referral services. You can direct your customers to these organizations. You can also refer your customer to national databases, such as the American Medical Association's DoctorFinder (http://webapps.ama-assn .org/doctorfinder/home.html) or one of many directories available through the MedlinePlus directories page (www.nlm.nih.gov/medlineplus/directories.html).

Finally, librarians should never provide a diagnosis. Your customer may tell you in explicit detail what his symptoms are. In fact, he may have come to the library or telephoned your reference department to avoid going to the doctor. Don't be tempted to help him self-diagnose. Remember, if you are not a medical professional, you are in no position to provide a diagnosis to your customer.

WHAT YOU SHOULD DO

- Help locate books, articles, or Internet information on the subject.
- Show customers how to use the material (e.g., an index or database).
- Provide quick instruction on how to navigate a Web site.
- Instruct customers on how to determine quality of the material or Web site.
- Provide referrals for other sources of information.
- Always encourage customers to discuss what they find with a medical professional.
- Be discreet.

Discretion should always be maintained during and after interactions with customers, but is particularly important when helping customers find answers to health-related questions. This involves lowering your voice at the desk or public service point, whether your customer is in front of you or on the phone. In addition, librarians often talk to one another when they have problems answering difficult questions. "When dealing with medical queries, however, librarians should not discuss a patron's question with another librarian without asking the patron's permission. To do so is a breach of confidentiality" (Baker and Manbeck, 2002: 147). This can be especially challenging if you work in a team environment. If you are in a situation where you work on reference questions as a team, you should ask your customer's permission to share her question with your teammates.

REFERENCE INTERVIEW AND LITERACY LEVELS

An important aspect of the health reference interview is the assessment of your customer's literacy levels. Giving a customer access to health information that he is unable to read or understand is a waste of his time and energy, as well as your time and resources. However, it is very difficult to detect someone's literacy skills. "For many, illiteracy is a great source of shame. It is seldom advisable to ask people directly if they can read" (Osborne, 2005: 133). Following are a few hints that may help you determine someone's literacy levels and language skills.

- Ask open-ended questions—for example, "How do you like to learn?" Customers "with limited literacy skills are apt to select non-reading options," such as videos or television programs (Osborne, 2005: 133).
- Customers with low-level reading skills may tell you that they will take the information home to read instead of scanning it immediately.
- Customers with limited reading skills may "'forget' their eyeglasses or complain of headaches" (Osborne, 2005: 134).
- If you detect that your customer is struggling with English, you may want to ask if he would prefer the information in a language other than English.

Always provide your customers with consumer-friendly material. Medical jargon may create barriers for many people. The results of a study published in 2004 by Baker and Gollop revealed that "the information found in medical textbooks on [ten] diseases under examination would be difficult for the average lay person to read" (345). The study also revealed that medical terminology would be beyond the understanding of many well-educated people. If your customer finds consumer information too basic or simple, she will not be embarrassed to ask you for something more complex. It is also much easier to tell someone that you can help find her more in-depth and professional information if needed than to tell her that you would be happy to find her something that is easier to read or understand. Avoid letting your customer think that you have exhausted your resources unless you truly have. Always conclude your interaction and give her your business card so that the customer understands that you welcome her return should she need additional information, different information, or referrals to other sources of information.

CHALLENGES OF TELEPHONE AND E-MAIL QUERIES

Telephone and e-mail inquiries for health information have their own distinct challenges. Both telephone and e-mail interactions can be misinterpreted due, in part, to the lack of nonverbal communication. In telephone inquiries, the librarian is able to hear the customer and possibly gauge his or her stress level, but other nonverbal communication cues, such as eye contact, gestures, facial expression, and posture, are missing (Jennerich and Jennerich, 1997).

Another challenge during telephone inquiries occurs when the librarian has located the information and is ready to deliver it to the customer. It is not practical or wise to read lengthy health information over the telephone. Answers must be brief and read without interpretation (Jennerich and Jennerich, 1997). This limits the amount and type of information one can give over the phone. For a thorough delivery of health information beyond simple definitions or short descriptions, you will most likely have to follow up with your customer via e-mail or regular mail. The telephone interview should include asking permission to leave brief messages on answering machines. Your customer may not want another member of his household to know why he called the library. If permission is not granted in advance, the librarian should leave a message simply asking the customer to return the call.

As librarians know, customers have been known to call with queries that seem more appropriate for medical professionals. It is imperative that as a librarian, you make it clear that you are not a medical professional. For example, if a customer calls and ask for a list of flu symptoms because they believe they may have the flu, before you attempt to find the answer, you should recommend that the customer call their doctor or another medical professional. Should you refuse to look up the answer to their question if they insist? Certainly not, but you must be careful to not interpret what you read or make any recommendation beyond seeing a medical professional. This applies to any inquiry related to health information including telephone and in-person interactions. If you sense urgency in the request or if the customer tells you that their information need is urgent or emergent, you must advise them to call 911.

Regarding e-mails, Abels notes that "in an e-mail interview, as opposed to a real-time interview, a different set of communication skills is required. Since the inability to watch for nonverbal communication cues or to listen for voice tones is inherent, e-mail communication requires careful interpretation and reading between the lines" (Abels, 1996: 348). Customers also "need to fully understand that e-mail is not to be used for medical emergencies" (Osborne, 2005: 46).

Privacy and security can be a particular concern for e-mail inquiries. Individuals who share computers may be able to intercept others' e-mail communications. Also, many people use their employer's computers or e-mail accounts for communications unrelated to work, and these are generally not guaranteed to be private (Osborne, 2005).

The exchange of health information over e-mail has benefits as well as disadvantages. The benefits of e-mail inquiries include the customer's ability to query and respond at their convenience, to print and save electronic information, and the ability for the librarian to provide hyperlinks to online information sources. E-mail also creates a written transcript of the information exchanged for both the customer and the librarian.

Experience has shown me that it is best to receive e-mail requests for information via a form on your Web site rather than simply providing your e-mail address to potential customers. The e-mail form enables you to gather information from customers that they might not realize is important or of value, such as the customer's name, e-mail address, phone number, fax number (if available), and mailing address. If you are part of a larger library system, you might benefit from knowing the customer's preferred branch library. The phone number, fax number, mailing address and preferred branch will help you deliver health information that is not easily delivered online or via the phone. Figure 10-1 is an example of an online form for e-mail queries, used by the Pima County Public Library in Tucson, Arizona.

Contact Us

Ask a Librarian: Email Reference Service

Send us your question:

The following information is required.

Name:

Email:

City:

State (or province):

Country:

Type your question

Additional Information

Deliver to library for pickup:

Some questions require a response that cannot be sent via email. Please provide one or more of the following alternatives.

Select a library location

Street Address:

Phone:

Fax:

Submit

Return to top

Ways to Ask a Librarian your Question

• Use this form.
• Call Infoline at 791-4010.
• Visit any of our library locations.

What you should know before you send us a question:

• **It may take up to three days for you to receive a response to your question.** It may take longer over holidays. If you need immediate assistance, call Infoline at 791-4010 or visit your local branch library.

• **If you do not live in Tucson or Pima County, please contact your local library first.** Research assistance to those outside Pima County (Arizona) is limited to local information and referrals specific to the Tucson/Pima County geographical area.

• **Questions should be brief and specific.** We are not able to undertake complex, lengthy research. Generally, answers will be referrals to appropriate Internet sites or will direct you to resources available within the Pima County Public Library system.

• **We are unable to provide obituaries from local Tucson newspapers through Ask A Librarian.** We are always happy to assist you in person at the Main Library. You can also search Newsbank online for local obituaries. All you need is your library card. If you do not live in Tucson or Pima County, please contact your local library for assistance.

• **Questions will remain confidential.** As with all Internet transactions, it may be possible for others to intercept information that you have sent via the web.

Other ways to contact the Library:

• **Contact Us**: use Contact Us for suggestions, feedback or questions about library services or programs.
• **Technical support**: use Ask Technical Support.
• **Suggestions**: use Suggest a Title to send us suggestions for items to purchase.

Figure 10-1. Online form for e-mail queries, used with permission of the Pima County Public Library, Tucson, Arizona, 2007.

In addition to the logistical information just mentioned, you will want to ascertain the subject of the customer's query. You may want to give guidelines about format, and helpful hints such as "Be as specific as you can." You may also want the customers to tell you if or how they have previously searched for information on the topic. Knowing that they have already searched your library's catalog is helpful. If they have exhausted the resources at their university library, you may want to be aware of this. However, customers may believe that they have searched the catalog or Internet thoroughly, but have not. Do not assume that everyone has the searching skills necessary to find the information they are looking for.

In his article on the reference interview in the digital age, Straw believes that "despite the speed of electronic messages over networks, it is a mistake for reference librarians to conclude that electronic encounters are inherently faster or more efficient. Clearly, reference librarians have to realize that many situations are better handled in a direct face-to-face encounter" (Straw, 2000: 377).* There are limits to e-mail health reference interactions. "A medium such as e-mail is ideal for handling short transactions that might require few sources or limited follow-up. When short factual questions start to drift into detailed research questions, electronic reference negotiations can bog down" (377). According to Abels, if the inquiry is broad in nature and requires a back- and-forth interaction between the librarian and the customer, it is probably better suited to a real-time in-person or telephone interaction. In her study, she compared e-mail inquiries to face-to-face interaction and noted that the reference interview process can complicate the e-mail interaction. "The passage of time [due to the e-mail exchange process] affected the information need itself, which, in turn, affected the reference interview. In some cases, an actual information need changed from one message to the next, reflecting a change in the client's knowledge base" (Abels, 1996: 348).

Is it possible to ascertain your customer's literacy level through the e-mail interaction? The experts do not agree on this matter. As Abels points out, what is "especially difficult to garner in an e-mail reference interview is information about the internal constraints of the client, such as intelligence, reading ability and level of motivation" (Abels, 1996: 354).** She believes that poor spelling is neither an indication of intelligence nor literacy levels. Poor spelling may simply be the result of typing errors, and customers should not be judged by it.

---

* From: Straw, Joseph E. 2000. "A Virtual Understanding: The Reference Interview and Question Negotiation in the Digital Age." *Reference and User Services Quarterly* 39, no.4. Reprinted by permission from Reference and User Services Association, American Library Association.
** From: Abels, Eileen G. 1996. "The E-mail Reference Interview." *Reference and User Services Quarterly* 35, no.3. Reprinted by permission from Reference and User Services Association, American Library Association.

On the other hand, in her book on health literacy, Osborne believes that punctuation and grammar errors as well as incorrect use of vocabulary can be an indication of literacy problems. When responding to a customer via e-mail, she advises, "make sure your e-mail messages are easy to read. This means using plain language principles such as common one-and two-syllable words, short sentences with no more than fifteen words, and short paragraphs with only two or three sentences" (Osborne, 2005: 47). One more thing Osborne suggests is that, although your customers may use e-mail to request information, you do not have to reply to them by e-mail. You should use your professional judgment and consider if a telephone call may be the most appropriate way to respond.

CONCLUSION

A thorough health reference interview must be conducted to connect your customers to appropriate health information for three very important reasons. First, the health reference interview allows you the back-and-forth exchange of information that will help you understand your customer's true question. Second, if done properly, you also may be able to gauge your customer's literacy levels. Giving your customer the right answer to the wrong question or giving her something that is beyond her comprehension is as inappropriate as giving her no information at all. Third, helping a customer gain access to health information she can understand and use to make important health-related decisions is the first step in helping her to become health-literate.

REFERENCES

Abels, Eileen G. 1996. "The E-mail Reference Interview." *Reference and User Services Quarterly* 35, no.3 (Spring): 345–359.

Baker, Lynda M., and Virginia Manbeck. 2002. *Consumer Health Information for Public Librarians.* Lanham, MD: Scarecrow Press.

Baker, Lynda M., and Claudia J. Gollop. 2004. "Medical Textbooks: Can Lay People Read and Understand Them?" *Library Trends* 53, no.2 (Fall): 336–337.

Chute, Adrienne, Patricia Kroe, Patricia O'Shea, Terri Craig, Michael Freeman, Laura Hardesty, Joanna Fane McLaughlin, and Cynthia Jo Ramsey. 2006. *Public Libraries in the United States: Fiscal Year 2004.* U. S. Department of Education: National Center for Education Statistics. (May 2007) Available: http://nces.ed.gov/pubs2006/2006349.pdf

Dewdney, Patricia, and Gillian Michell. 1997. "Asking "Why" Questions in the Reference Interview: A Theoretical Justification." *Library Quarterly* 67, no.1 (January): 50–71.

Fox, Susannah. 2001. Wired Seniors. Pew Internet and American Life Project. (February 2007) Available: www.pewinternet.org

Fox, Susannah. 2005. *Health Information Online.* Pew Internet and American Life Project. (February 2007) Available: www.pewinternet.org

Jennerich, Elaine Z., and Edward J. Jennerich. 1997. *The Reference Interview as a Creative Art.* Westport, CT: Libraries Unlimited.

Muro, Andres. 2006. "What is Health Literacy?" Boston, MA: World Education. (May 2007) Available: www.lincs.worlded.org/muro.htm

Kutner, Mark, Elizabeth Greenberg, Ying Jin, and Christine Paulsen. 2006. *The Health Literacy of America's Adults: Results from the 2003 National Assessment of Adult Literacy.* U. S. Department of Education: National Center for Education Statistics. (May 2007) Available: http://nces.ed.gov/pubs2006/2006483.pdf

Osborne, Helen. 2005. *Health Literacy from A to Z: Practical Ways to Communicate your Health Message.* Boston, MA: Jones and Bartlett.

Ross, Catherine Sheldrick. 2003. "The Reference Interview: Why It Needs to Be Used in Every (Well Almost Every) Reference Transaction." *Reference and User Services Quarterly* 43, no.1 (Fall): 38–43.

Ross, Catherine Sheldrick, Kirsti Nilsen, and Patricia Dewdney. 2002. *Conducting the Reference Interview: A How-To-Do-It Manual for Librarians.* New York: Neal-Schuman.

Safeer, Richard S., and Jann Keenan. 2005. "Health Literacy: The Gap Between Physicians and Patients." *American Family Physician* 72, no.3 (August): 463–468.

Straw, Joseph E. 2000. "A Virtual Understanding: The Reference Interview and Question Negotiation in the Digital Age." Reference and User Services Quarterly 39, no.4 (Summer): 376–379.

U.S. Department of Health and Human Services. 2000. *Healthy People 2010 Volume I.* (May 2007) Available: www.healthypeople.gov/document/tableofcontents.htm#volume1

Chapter 11

Public Libraries and Health Literacy

Barbara Bibel

As early as 1977, Knowles wrote an editorial in *Science* stating that individuals were responsible for their own health. He also pointed out that lack of knowledge is an obstacle to assuming that responsibility. Finally, he stated that the obligation to maintain health implies a "right to expect help with information" (Knowles, 1977: 1103). Today, the Internet is a tool that many people seem to use to learn more about health. According to the Pew Internet and American Life Project, eight out of ten Internet users sought health information. Seven million people said that the Internet played an important role when they were coping with a major illness. One out of five said that the Internet greatly improved they way that they got information about healthcare (Madden and Fox, 2006). In the *New England Journal of Medicine*, Marcus (2006) discussed the health effects of illiteracy, noting that patients who cannot read have problems complying with treatment regimens. Librarians in public libraries have responded to the health literacy challenge in different ways. This chapter focuses on collection development, community awareness, and collaboration and partnership.

Where do people go for help when they need health information? Public libraries can be one of the foremost resources for consumer health information. In many communities, people are familiar with the library and use it meet their information needs in a wide variety of subject areas (Deering and Harris, 1996). Furthermore, because they often go there for public programs, recreational reading, or to use the public access computers, some people will turn to the public library for health information (Tyckoson, 2002).

As the managed-care system gives healthcare providers little time to educate patients (Pifalo et al., 1997), people may need to find information about their conditions on their own. As a result, these authors noted that librarians are answering questions about health and medicine on a regular basis. The patrons may be students with assignments, patients newly diagnosed with a disease, or friends and family members involved in the care and support of someone who is ill. They want to learn more about a disease or condition, evaluate treatment options, find out more about prescribed drugs, or find resources and support groups. Since health information is often complex, patrons need assistance in locating and understanding it. According to Yellott and Barrier (as cited in Pifalo et al., 1997), "public librarians are quite successful as providers of health-related information. They do not overstep the boundary between information giving and providing advice; the information that they provide is generally considered by physicians to be current; and they are able to respond to a wide variety of highly technical medical questions without endangering the health of anyone" (17). Because people turn to librarians for help, librarians must be ready to provide it.

Librarians in public libraries can play a vital role in promoting health literacy by providing access to reliable, health-related resources on topics such as anatomy and physiology, diseases and conditions, nutrition, fitness, and drugs. Tyckoson (2002) noted that librarians can teach patrons how to use these sources to find the materials that they need and to evaluate what they find in print and online. In my experience as a consumer health public librarian, it is not uncommon for a patron to ask whether a particular treatment is the correct one or the best one for a given condition. When this happens, the librarian can provide objective health information and encourage the patron to discuss it with his or her healthcare provider. Informed patients who actively participate in their care have better outcomes (Ullrich and Vaccaro, 2002).

COMMUNITY ASSESSMENT

To provide quality health information service, public librarians need to do several things. First, they must assess their communities and gather demographic information about the age, ethnicity, education, and literacy levels of the population. This data is important for collection development and programming and can be found in a variety of sources, including the U.S. Bureau of the Census, state agencies, and school districts. American Fact Finder tools allow librarians to obtain a community profile at either a city, county, or census tract level that is specific to the smaller community served by a branch (see Appendix 11-1).

The U.S. Census contains a great deal of useful information and librarians can learn much about their communities by looking at the numbers. The DP-2 profile of selected social characteristics includes place of birth and citizenship, ability to speak English, and language spoken at home. A detailed community profile includes school enrollment, educational attainment, fertility and age of mother, disability, employment, and grandparents raising grandchildren as well as the gender and marital status of the grandparents. School districts and community organizations also collect relevant data. Librarians should check with local health departments to learn about prevalent health issues. All this data will help them plan programs, select materials, conduct outreach, and design classes relevant to people in the community. It will also help them market their services effectively.

COLLECTION DEVELOPMENT

A strong collection of health and medical information is the foundation for providing good reference service. Ideally, a librarian with knowledge and interest in the subject should be in charge of the collection that should include materials in the languages spoken in the community, as well as materials at a variety of reading levels. The Institute for Healthcare Advancement (www.iha4health.org) publishes the *What to Do for Health* series that contains reasonably priced books on basic healthcare for adults, infants, teens, and seniors in English, Spanish, Chinese, Vietnamese, and Korean. Since many public libraries in the United States and Canada have adult literacy programs, these books offer an opportunity for the librarians to work with the literacy staff to integrate health literacy into the curriculum.

Consumer health librarians should also collect medical and allied health dictionaries, general medical encyclopedias, and reference books about drugs. Both reference and circulating materials about basic anatomy and physiology, common diseases and conditions, prescription, over-the-counter, and recreational drugs, complementary and alternative medicine, health insurance, and caregiving should be available. Directories of local health practitioners and community organizations are also useful. Subscriptions to lay health magazines and newsletters, such as *Health*, the *Mayo Clinic Health Letter*, and *MedlinePlus Magazine*, as well as a few major medical journals such as *JAMA*, *New England Journal of Medicine*, and *Lancet* will provide good advice as well as access to major medical studies that find their way into headline news however, librarians need to be aware that these journals have high readability levels (Baker and Wilson, 1996). Medical dictionaries and sources that explain how to interpret clinical studies (for example, Greenhalgh's [2006] *How to Read a Paper*) will help both patrons and librarians who use these journals. Videos may also be popular because they provide information about common health topics as well as exercise programs, and could be useful for patrons who have low literacy skills. Computers for searching subscription databases are necessary for both staff and patrons. Some examples include the *Gale Health Reference Center* and *EBSCO Consumer Health Complete*, both of which offer comprehensive coverage of health information at the lay level. Libraries belonging to consortia can negotiate a good price for subscriptions. There is also a large amount of high-quality online information available free from government agencies and nonprofit organizations. The National Library of Medicine's *PubMed* and *MedlinePlus*, the Centers for Disease Control and Prevention (CDC), and the American Diabetes Association are examples of free resources. The *Librarians' Internet Index* (www.lii.org) is a gateway to free resources that have been screened for accuracy and currency by librarians and includes links to a wide variety of health resources.

Medical and health information changes rapidly, making it important for public librarians to maintain a current collection. In the Oakland Public library, books on anatomy and medical history have a longer shelf life, but those about diseases and drug therapy are weeded every three to five years. To find good current books librarians can refer to *Library Journal, Booklist*, and *Consumer Connection* (see Appendix 11-2 for a list of distributors of foreign-language material). *Library Journal* has an annual article about the best consumer health books of the year. *Consumer Connection*, the online newsletter of the Consumer and Patient Health Information Section (CAPHIS) of the Medical Library Association (MLA), contains reviews written by consumer health librarians. It is published quarterly at www.caphis.mlanet.org. *Críticas* reviews Spanish-language materials. It is difficult to find reviews of materials in other languages. Librarians should also pay attention to the type of questions that patrons ask since they provide clues to community information needs. For example, many questions about hypertension or diabetes may indicate the prevalence of these conditions in a given area and a need for more material on these subjects.

TRAINING

Training is the key to providing good health information service. In 1998, the National Library of Medicine (NLM) began a pilot project "to learn about the role of public libraries in providing health information" (Wood et al., 2000: 314). The Public Library Association began developing plans to promote collaboration between public libraries and both community organizations and medical libraries (Calvano and Needham, 1996). Both of these projects involve training. The two initiatives came together at the midwinter conference of the American Library Association in Washington, DC, in 2001, when NLM presented at a preconference session a paper on consumer health information that included basic tools for public librarians. Later that year, MLA unveiled its Consumer Health Credential Program for librarians. To become certified as a Consumer Health

Information Specialist, a librarian must take 12 hours of MLA-approved continuing education classes to be certified at the basic level and 24 hours for certification at Level II. Certification must be renewed every three years by taking eight hours of continuing education. Information about this program is available on the MLA Web site at www.mlanet.org/education/chc/index.html#3.

The National Library of Medicine offers free training through the National Network of Libraries of Medicine (NN/LM). Through its Regional Medical Libraries (RMLs), NN/LM makes a variety of NLM resources available to public libraries, including courses and tutorials; training materials; document delivery; items such as bookmarks, pens, and pamphlets for patrons; a directory of consumer health libraries; grant support; and staff available for consultation. The staff of the RMLs will also provide training at sites within their regions. Their Web site (http://nnlm.gov) has links to these resources. Public libraries may join NN/LM as affiliate members. Public librarians may also attend training courses offered by MLA, either at its annual meetings or at the meetings of regional sections.

Another important role for public or consumer health librarians is to provide training for people who are or will be searching the Internet to find health information. Since 92 percent of public libraries offer computer access for the community and 56 percent offer basic Internet training, adding a class about finding and evaluating health information makes sense (National Center for Education Statistics, 2003a). Librarians can also educate patrons who contact them via e-mail or chat, since 12.8 percent of public libraries now offer some form of digital reference service (Janes and McClure, 1999). By providing links to current and reliable Web sites and explaining what to look for when searching, librarians can help patrons improve their health literacy skills.

COLLABORATION AND PARTNERSHIP

The need for training is a good reason for public libraries to collaborate with local medical libraries. Medical librarians can educate public librarians about various health topics and suggest resources to fill gaps in their collections. Public librarians can educate medical librarians about the information needs of the community and about working with a wide range of patrons. When public libraries partner with local hospital or academic medical libraries, both parties gain. For example, the Oakland Public Library (OPL) in California has a long-standing partnership with both the Health Education Center and the Health Sciences Library at Kaiser Permanente Medical Center, Oakland, California. The author, a consumer health information specialist certified by MLA, and the health sciences librarian at Kaiser share resources and refer patrons to one another. They also teach quarterly classes about health information to both the OPL staff and the public. This joint training and outreach increases the visibility of both institutions and provides the public with valuable health information. Recently, the California Healthcare Foundation and its librarian joined the partnership, thereby adding the resources of a nonprofit organization that provides unbiased information on healthcare quality. These three librarians teach classes for local library staff on searching MedlinePlus and PubMed and about health sources on specific topics, such as nutrition, and on women's, children's, teens', and seniors' health. The classes have been well received, and librarians from the greater Bay Area send staff to them. In my experience, classes for the public about finding and evaluating health information online and health information for travelers are also popular. Kaiser's Health Education coordinator partners with OPL staff to present classes on health topics. Kaiser has also donated to the library a collection of videos that they produced on common health topics in English, Spanish, and Chinese. The author has assisted the Health Education Center with collection development since they do not have a librarian. These efforts increase the competency of the staff and foster respect for both institutions in the community.

Working with other staff members within the library to promote health information is equally effective. OPL has a very popular series of programs about travel, featuring the authors of the Lonely Planet Guides. Lonely Planet is based in Oakland, so the publisher is happy to supply speakers and sell books in the library. Working with her colleague who developed the program, the author was able to add a session about health information for travelers to the series. People who attended learned about the resources available from the CDC, the Department of State, and *Librarians' Internet Index* to help them plan their trips and stay healthy on the road. Evaluation forms indicated that they enjoyed the classes and wanted more training on health topics.

Another example of a successful collaboration is NOAH, New York Access to Health Online. The City University of New York, the New York Academy of Medicine, the Metropolitan New York Library Council, and the New York Public Library all worked together to create a bilingual English-Spanish database for the public that provides full-text "quality health information . . . that is accurate, timely, relevant, and unbiased" (Voge, 1998: 326). This work, involving librarians from academic, public, and medical society libraries, as well as voluntary health agencies, use the latest technologies to reach a diverse public. NOAH began as a local resource but it is now accessible worldwide through its Web site (www.noah-health.org).

OUTREACH

Outreach activities increase the visibility of the public library and highlight its role as a provider of health information. A table or booth at a local health fair, a presentation at a community meeting, or a class will lead to new collaborations and new library patrons. Oakland Public Library has a table at the annual Healthy Living Festival, a fair for seniors. A selection of relevant books, library card applications, and materials such as bookmarks advertising MedlinePlus, NIH Senior Health, and health record cards attract seniors. A health information page on a library's Web site that tells patrons how to evaluate what they find when surfing the Web and offers links to reliable Web sites is another way to reach out. OPL's Web site www.oaklandlibrary.org/links/sbssmedical.html is a good example. Here, too, partnership works well. When Kaiser Permanente in Oakland has its annual library open house during Medical Librarians' Month (October), OPL is there with library card applications and information so that Kaiser's medical staff will know that patients can get health information at the public library. When Kaiser staff teaches classes at OPL, they tell the library staff and patrons that they can use the resources at the Health Education Center and Health Sciences Library even if they are not Kaiser members.

Seventeen percent of the public libraries in the United States have adult literacy programs, thereby providing an excellent opportunity to teach health literacy skills (National Center for Education Statistics, 2003a). With 11,000,000 nonliterate adults in the United States, there is great need for these programs. The National Assessment of Adult Literacy conducted by the U.S. Department of Education in 2003 found that there were 30 million adults with no more than rudimentary literacy skills and another 63 million with skill for only simple everyday tasks (National Center for Education Statistics, 2003b). Four million of them are not native English speakers. These people cannot read prescription labels or other printed instructions that they may receive from their healthcare providers. Public librarians at libraries with literacy programs can work with instructors to include health literacy skills in their classes and create appropriate instructional materials.

Working with community organizations is an effective way to reach out because their staff members know the best way to approach specific groups. This is very important for successful outreach. If librarians do not build community trust, programs may fail. When planning classes about diabetes in Oakland, the librarian asked Kaiser to provide bilingual health educators for classes in Chinese (Cantonese) and Spanish. The librarian at the Asian branch noted that most of the people who would attend were seniors who knew little English and would need all course materials in Chinese. On the other hand, the librarian at the Cesar Chavez branch in the heart of the Latino community felt that the younger people who might be interested would prefer a class in English. Knowing this is important for preparing classes that will attract the community.

Another area where community members can help is with publicity. Word of mouth is very effective. Articles in local newspapers, newsletters, and the alternative press reach many people. Flyers in the library and posters placed in local businesses, as well as announcements in the calendar of events and on the library

Web site, will also help to attract an audience. Having attendees fill in simple evaluation forms that ask where they learned about the program in addition to the usual questions about program content will help to determine the best places to advertise.

CONCLUSION

Public libraries play an important role in providing health information and promoting health literacy. Since 80 percent of the public library systems in the United States are in rural areas, they may be the only resource available for many people (Gillaspy, 2005). By providing print resources, Internet access, and training for the public, the librarians working in these libraries promote and increase the level of health literacy in their population areas. This is very important for seniors, since those with poor health literacy have more hospitalizations, longer hospital stays, more doctor visits, and more medication and treatment errors; they lack the needed skills to navigate the healthcare system (National Academy on an Aging Society, 1999). When medical libraries join them in this effort, the result will be better health for the members of their communities. Informed patients have better outcomes because they understand their conditions and participate in their care (Donohue, 2001). Librarians can facilitate this process by providing the necessary tools.

REFERENCES

Baker, Lynda M., and Feleta L. Wilson. 1996. "Consumer Health Materials Recommended for Public Libraries? Too Tough to Read?" *Public Libraries* 35, no.2 (March/April): 124–130.

Calvano, Margaret, and George Needham. 1996. "Public Empowerment Through Accessible Health Information." *Bulletin of the Medical Library Association* 84, no.2 (April): 253–256.

Deering, Mary Jo, and John Harris. 1996. "Consumer Health Information Demand and Delivery: Implications for Libraries." *Bulletin of the Medical Library Association* 84, no.2 (April): 209–216.

Donohue, Maureen. 2001, February 15. "Patient Education Holds the Key to Better Compliance, Outcomes." *Family Practice News*. Available: http://findarticles.com/p/articles/mi_m0BJI/is_4_31?pnum=2&opg=71900964

Gillaspy, Mary L. 2005. "Factors Affecting the Provision of Consumer Health Information in Public Libraries: The Last Five Years." *Library Trends* 53, no.3 (Winter): 480–495.

Greenhalgh, Trisha. 2006. *How to Read a Paper: The Basics of Evidence-Based Medicine.* 3rd ed. London: BMJ.

Janes, Joe, and Charles L. McClure. 1999. "The Web as a Reference Tool: Comparisons with Traditional Sources." *Public Libraries* 38, no.1 (January–February): 30–39.

Knowles, John H. 1977. "Responsibility for Health." *Science* 198 (December): 1103.

Madden, Mary, and Susannah Fox. 2006, May 2. "Finding Answers Online in Sickness and in Health." Pew Internet & American Life Project. Available: www.pewinternet.org/topics.asp?c=5

Marcus, Erin N. 2006. "The Silent Epidemic—The Health Effects of Illiteracy." *New England Journal of Medicine* 355, no.4 (July): 339–341.

National Academy on an Aging Society. 1999. Fact Sheet. "Low Health Literacy Skills Increase Health Care Expenditures by $73Billion." Available: www.agingsociety.org/agingsociety/publications/fact/fact_low.html

National Center for Education Statistics. 2003a. "Programs for Adults in Public Library Outlets." Available: www.nces.ed.gov/surveys/frss/publications/2003010/index.asp?sectionID=4

National Center for Education Statistics. 2003b. "National Assessment of Adult Literacy (NAAL)." Available: www.nces.ed.gov/naal/kf_demographics.asp

Pifalo, Victoria, Sue Hollander, Cynthia Henderson, Pat DiSalvo, and Gail P. Gill. 1997. "The Impact of Consumer Health Information Provided by Libraries: The Delaware Experience." *Bulletin of the Medical Library Association* 85, no.1 (January): 16–22.

Tyckoson, David. 2002. "On the Desirableness of Personal Relations between Librarians and Readers: The Past and Future of Reference Services." RUSA Forum. Available: http://findarticles.com/p/articles/mi_m0BJI/is_4_31?pnum=2&opg=71900964

Ullrich, Peter F., Jr., and Alexander R. Vaccaro. 2002. "Patient Education: Opportunities and Pitfalls." *Spine* 27, no.7 (April): 185–188,

Voge, Susan. 1998. "NOAH-New York Online Access to Health: Library Collaboration for Bilingual Consumer Health Information on the Internet." *Bulletin of the Medical Library Association* 86, no.3 (July): 326–334.

Wood, Fred B., Becky Lyon, Mary Beth Snell, Paula Kitendaugh, Victor H. Cid, and Elliot R. Siegel. 2000. "Public Library Consumer Health Information Pilot Project: Results of a National Library of Medicine Evaluation." *Bulletin of the Medical Library Association* 88, no.4 (October): 314–322.

Appendix 11-1. A Quick Guide to Searching for Census Information

Librarians need to monitor this site often because it changes constantly. To find data at the city and county levels:

1. Go to www.census.gov.
2. Click on the American Fact Finder button. Using the Fast Facts Search Box, enter a zip code to get a fact sheet.
3. For more detailed information, choose Geographic Search. Click on Search More Options.
4. Choose the state.
5. Choose the geographic region. You may look at the maps to find the location of census tracts. They may take a long time to load.
6. Choose DP2-Profile of Selected Social Characteristics. This provides the language spoken at home. Other useful tables are QT-P14 Nativity and Citizenship; QT-P17 Ability to Speak English; and QT-P16 Language Spoken.
7. You can also choose the Fact Sheet for Community Profiles from the main page. Then select Social Characteristics and Show More. You will get tables for language spoken and ancestry.
8. You can also choose address search and enter your branch address, then choose census tract. You may want to look at all of the census tracts that your branch serves.

Note what is included in the race section. It has details of the various Asian nationalities. The Hispanic/Latino information is separate because it is an ethnic identity rather than a racial group. Hispanics may be of any race. The language information here is not detailed. It covers language spoken at home by major linguistic groups. It does note the region of birth and education attainment, which provides clues for languages used and reading levels. You can also get more information about languages from state data on state Web sites and from school districts. For example, for information about California, go to www.ca.gov, then to the Department of Education, then to Dataquest. Choose a school district and then select student demographics. Go to English learners then English learners by language and English proficiency by language.

Appendix 11-2. Sources for Foreign Materials

Asian Languages		
Chinese	**Chinese** (Continued)	**Indian Languages** (Continued)
Chiao Liu Publication Trading Company P.O. Box 50324 Sai Ying Pun. Hong Kong Books, cassettes, CDs	Pan Asian Publications 29564 Union City Boulevard Union City, CA 94587 (510) 475-1185 FAX (510) 475-1489 Books in Chinese, Japanese, Korean, and Vietnamese	Star Publications Distributors (Continued) indiabooks@aol.com www.starpublic.com/index.htm Books in all Indian languages
China International Book Trading Corp. P.O. Box 399 Beijing, China	Sino-American Books & Arts Co. 751 Jackson Street San Francisco, CA 94133 (415) 421-3345	Multicultural Books and Videos 1594 Caille Avenue Belle River, ON-NOR140, Canada (800) 567-2220
Chinatown Music and Books 1021 Grant Avenue San Francisco, CA 94133 (415) 788-2826	FAX (415) 421-3345 Books, videos, ESL materials from Taiwan	www.multiculturalbooksandvideos .com Books in over 60 languages, including all Indian languages; ESL materials
Eastwind 1435A Stockton Street San Francisco, CA 94133 (415) 772-5877 FAX (415) 772-5885 Books, cassettes, CDs, videos, CD-ROMs from the Mainland, Hong Kong, and Taiwan	Wong's TV-Radio Service 59 Waverly Place San Francisco, CA 94108 (415) 781-0535 FAX (415) 781-0535 Cassettes and CDs from Hong Kong and Taiwan	**Japanese** Japan Publication Trading Corp. P.O. Box 5030 Tokyo International Tokyo 100-131 Japan FAX 81-03-3292-0410 Books
Evergreen 760 West Garvey Avenue Monterey Park, CA 91754 (626) 281-3622 Books from Hong Kong and Taiwan	World Books 824 Stockton Street San Francisco, CA 94133 (415) 397-8473 Books, cassettes, videos	Japan Video 1737 Post Street San Francisco, CA 94115 (415) 563-5220 FAX (415) 563-5454
Kingston Culture Plaza, Inc. 228 W. Valley Boulevard Alhambra, CA 91801 (626) 570-1277	World Journal Book Store, Inc. 377 E. Broadway New York, New York 10002 (212) 226-513	Kinokuniya 1581 Webster Street San Francisco, CA 94115 (415) 567-7625 FAX (415) 567-4109
Mandarin Language & Cultural Center 1630 Oakland Road San Jose, CA 95131 (408) 441-9114 Books, cassettes, and videos from Taiwan; large children's selection	World Journal 16060 S. De Anza Blvd San Jose, CA 95129 (408) 873-3230 Books and media	Books, cassettes, CDs, videos, magazine subscriptions Kinokuniya Bookstores of America, Co., Ltd.—San Jose 675 Saratoga Avenue San Jose, CA 95129 (408) 252-1300
Nan Hai Co., Inc. 510 Broadway, Suite 300 Millbrae, CA 94030 (650) 259-2100 Videos from the Mainland	**Indian Languages** Star Publications Distributors 4/5B Asaf Ali Road New Delhi 110 002 India 91-11-328 6757 FAX 91-11- 327 3335 starpub@satyam.net.in	FAX (408) 252-1300 Books and subscriptions Taiyo-Do Record Shop, Japan Center 1737 Post Street #11A San Francisco, CA 94115 (415) 885-2818
Oriental Cultural Enterprises Co. 13-17 Elizabeth Street, 2F New York, New York 10013 (212) 226-8461	In the United Kingdom: 112 Whitfield Street London WIP 5RU (020) 7380 0622 FAX (020) 7419 9167	FAX (415) 885-0727 Cassettes, CDs

(Continued)

Appendix 11-2. Sources for Foreign Materials *(Continued)*

Asian Languages *(Continued)*		
Korean	*Tagalog*	*Vietnamese*
Korean Books	**Magat Enterprises**	**Pho Dem**
1082 E. El Camino Real, #3	3139 Alum Rock Avenue	2519 S. King Road
Sunnyvale, CA 94807	San Jose, CA 95127	San Jose, CA 95122
(408) 246-2300	(408) 251-8504	(408) 238-8638
FAX (408) 246-8996	FAX (408) 251-6214	FAX (408) 238-8638
Books, videos, cassettes, CD-ROMs		CDs, cassettes, videos

Other Languages		
Continental Book Company **Western Division** 625 E. 70th Avenue Denver, CO 80229 (303) 289-1761 www.continetalbook.com French, German, Italian, Spanish **Librairie du Soleil** Place Fleur-de-Lys 425 Boulevard St-Joseph Hull, Quebec, Canada J8Y 3Y7 011 (814)595-2414 French Canadian books **Luso-Brazilian Books** Box 170286 Brooklyn, NY 11217 (800) 727-5876 www.lusobraz.com/ Portuguese	**Raha Books** 441 La Prenda Road Los Altos, CA 94024 (650) 823-3569 info@rahabooks.com Farsi/Persian **Russia House, Ltd** 253 Fifth Avenue New York, NY 10016 (212) 685-1010 Russia@rusianhouse.net Russian **Schoenhof's Foreign Books** 76A Mount Auburn Street Cambridge, MA 02138 (617) 547-8855 Adult and children's books in 30 languages	**Szwede Slavic Books** 1629 Main Street Redwood City, CA 94603 Mailing Address: P.O. Box 1214 Palo Alto, CA 94302-1214 (650) 780-0966 FAX (650) 780-09667 slavicbooks@szwedeslavicbooks.com; www.szwedeslavicbooks.com Czech, Polish, Russian, Serbo- Croatian, Ukrainian **Jean Touzot-Librairie Internationale** 38, rue Saint Sulpice 75278 Paris Cedex 06 France (33) 01 43 26 03 88 jeantouzot@worldnet.net French

Chapter 12

Health Literacy in Canada: Highlighting Library Initiatives

Susan Murray

Although librarians have been supporting health literacy initiatives for years, there have been few articles specifically discussing their roles until recently. Parker and Kreps (2005) discussed programs to address health literacy problems and the implications for library outreach, while Burnham and Peterson (2005) wrote about how libraries can participate in the dissemination of plain language and easy-to-read health information to the general public. On the Canadian scene, it has also been difficult to find information about what librarians are doing in the area of health literacy. This chapter highlights a few health literacy initiatives by Canadian librarians.

Canada, the second largest country in area, with a population of approximately 32,984,576, has a long history in supporting programs to overcome literacy and health literacy barriers (Statistics Canada, 2007). Some job descriptions for librarians have begun to list health literacy outreach as one of the responsibilities. For example, an April 2007 posting on CANMEDLIB, the Canadian Medical Libraries listserv, for a library manager position at a health region library in Red Deer, Alberta, listed one of the responsibilities as "the development of health literacy teaching programs."

Health and learning are closely connected. "Health and social factors have a profound effect on learning, while all types of education, not just health education, support good health. Health literacy and knowledge can be a pre-requisite to making healthier lifestyle choices" (Canadian Council on Learning. 2007a, para. 2).

Health literacy, a subset of information literacy, relates to the "degree to which individuals have the capacity to obtain, process, and understand basic health information and services, needed to make appropriate health decisions" (U.S. Department of Health and Human Services, 2000, Terminology). Sometimes called health information literacy, it involves "acquisition of information when needed, assessment of information with scientific facts and expert advice as the knowledge base, and utilization of the results of the combined actions to execute knowledge-based strategies leading to informed decisions, such as the choice of a healthy lifestyle" (Hsu, Johnson, and Brooks, 2003, Background). Or as the Medical Library Association (2003) defines it: "Health Information Literacy is the set of abilities needed to: recognize a health information need; identify likely information sources and use them to retrieve relevant information; assess the quality of the information and its applicability to a specific situation; and analyze, understand, and use the information to make good health decisions" (para. 4).

The Canadian Public Health Association (CPHA) (n.d.) has been a leading force in providing training and materials in the area of health literacy. It produces a range of support material, such as a directory of plain-language health resources, a training manual for healthcare and literacy professionals, a video guide on clear communication for professionals, a guide on creating plain-language patient information materials for prescription medication, and communication strategies for diverse audiences.

But as outlined in the Canadian Council on Learning's (2007b) report "State of Learning in Canada: No Time for Complacency," there is still much to be done:

- 42 percent of the adult Canadian population lack the literacy skills needed to succeed in today's economy
- 55 percent of Canadians aged 16–65 are not able to read nutrition labels, follow medication directions, understand safety instructions, or make informed healthcare choices
- 88 percent of seniors lack literacy skills to deal with health information
- other populations with low levels of health literacy include: low-income Canadians, Aboriginal people, and recent immigrants with little formal education and/or whose first language is not English (Summary Report, 8)

CPHA held a Second Canadian Conference on Literacy and Health in October 2004 that created a "wow" moment for many attendees. Presentations focused on health literacy issues most relevant to Canadians, such as working with Francophone minorities, Aboriginal Peoples, and a diverse immigrant population (Literacy and Health in Canada, 2006). Immigrants present a special issue, since "in 2001, 61% of the immigrants who came in the 1990s used a nonofficial official language (neither English nor French) as their primary home language" (Statistics Canada, 2006, Conclusion, para. 1).

CANADIAN LIBRARY SCENE

What are Canadian librarians doing to support health literacy? It is difficult to get a detailed picture of what librarians in a variety of Canadian institutions are doing because even some consumer health information (CHI) intermediaries do not recognize what they are doing as health literacy interventions. For example, a public librarian building a collection to include plain-language health materials supports health literacy efforts. Public librarians, who assist the public in finding accessible health information, also play an important role in the area of health literacy. A hospital librarian involved in developing easy-to-read patient material supports health literacy efforts. Consumer health information center staff, particularly those based in hospitals, assist in the development of plain-language materials for patients. Finally, academic librarians have long played a role in imparting information literacy theory and skills to students and faculty at their institutions (Kasowitz-Scheer and Pasqualoni, 2002). By working with faculty and staff on health literacy outreach initiatives, they are able to reach a broader group of users both outside and within their institutions.

Many librarians across the country support the work of the Canadian Health Network (CHN), a national, bilingual health promotion program (www.canadian -health-network.ca). Formally launched on November 25, 1999, CHN is a collaboration of national, provincial, and territorial nonprofit organizations, universities, hospitals, libraries, and community organizations with the goal of helping Canadians find the information they are looking for on how to stay healthy and prevent disease. "CHN is part of Health Canada's commitment to the health lane of the Canadian Government's Information Highway, created to support Canadians to make informed decisions about their own health" (Canadian Health Network, 1999, para. 1).

The following sections of the chapter focus on examples of health literacy efforts in Canada with librarian involvement.

BRITISH COLUMBIA

The Irving K. Barber Learning Centre has been working in partnership with Telus in developing tools to support health literacy. It has:

- contributed stories and links to reliable online health information to the Telus portal (www.helth.mytelus.com);
- created a CHI Web site (www.ikebarberlearningcenter.ubc.ca/health/) which includes:
  - a multimedia collection featuring information literacy tools,
  - an archive of past consumer health stories, and

    o tutorials on searching Google and Healia for CHI (Katherine Miller, personal communication, March 26, 2007).

NOVA SCOTIA

Michelle Helliwell is a librarian with Library and Knowledge Services, a shared service of South Shore Health, South West Health and Annapolis Valley Health authorities in Nova Scotia. In a personal communication with the author (March 23 and 26, 2007), she mentioned being responsible for the evaluation and management of patient education materials, as well as providing library support to the Community Health divisions of the three District Health Authorities (DHA).

She has developed a very successful health literacy curriculum aimed at health care providers. Her three-hour workshop covers:

- understanding health literacy as a determinant of health,
- aspects of giving information: the reference interview, and
- creating plain-language and clear design material.

The workshops have been customized for different groups, such as public health, addictions staff, primary health care coordinators, nurse managers, physiotherapy, occupational health, dieticians, public relations, accreditation teams, long-term care, community outreach workers, literacy practitioners and public librarians. Various forms of the workshop have also been delivered to external partners, such as Nova Scotia Hearing and Speech, local offices of the Nova Scotia Department of Community Services, Boards of Literacy Networks in western Nova Scotia, and at several conferences.

In December 2006, Helliwell conducted an audio conference "Health Literacy Skills Can Impact Anyone" for the Education Institute, a division of the Ontario Library Association that coordinates online educational courses and Web and audio conferences. She is currently expanding the workshop to a full day and focus on writing effective patient education materials.

Helliwell is also working on knowledge exchange projects to "push out" the information and leverage action on health literacy. She is involved in an initiative in western Nova Scotia entitled "Building Health and Education Links Through Literacy," or Links Through Literacy for short. The goal is to decentralize the knowledge of health literacy and create and support local champions in the community. The initiative is also beginning to address the need to bring public libraries into the fold, as they are seen as key vehicles, particularly in rural areas, for being able to provide quality health information.

A one-day symposium titled "Links Through Literacy: Building Gentle Partnerships" was held in June for an audience of Community Health Board assistants and community-based Learning Network coordinators—an audience of about 30 participants. Among the activities were an assisted reading exercise (designed to simulate reading difficulties), a short presentation about health literacy, and a presentation from one Community Health Board assistant, who also happens to be the Chair of the Literacy Network in her area, trying to demonstrate where links can be made.

In addition, Helliwell has been working with the three DHAs and representatives of community-based adult learning networks and community health boards; they have created health literacy themed material on diabetes that will be introduced as curriculum aids to all level one and two adult education classes in Nova Scotia this fall. The material will be evaluated, and one of the goals is to encourage healthcare providers to go into these classrooms to allow adult learners to be able to ask questions and learn in an environment where they feel comfortable.

According to Helliwell, evaluation from the "Links Through Literacy: Building Gentle Partnerships" symposium will be reviewed to determine priorities and next steps. The group is committed to a sustainable project where growth is measured and steady. The growth will match efforts for a revamped health literacy workshop for healthcare providers that will be available by Fall–Winter 2008.

ONTARIO

In the author's experience at the Toronto Public Library (TPL), when immigrants arrive in Toronto, they often take advantage of public library services. According to the 2001 census, over 790,000 immigrants or nearly one-half of all newcomers to Canada settled in the Toronto area during the period 1991–2000 (Toronto Public Library, 2007a). They often do not speak one of the official languages, find the healthcare system difficult to navigate, and may find it difficult to find suitable housing.

In consultation with the community and a variety of partners, the Toronto Public Library developed a range of services for newcomers, including library materials in over 100 languages; English as a Second Language classes at many locations; and a telephone interpretation service available in more than 90 languages (Toronto Public Library, 2007d). Since 2001, settlement services targeting newcomers have been offered at libraries through the Settlement and Education Partnerships in Toronto (SEPT) program. In 2007, settlement workers were available at seven locations throughout the year and based at more than 40 TPL branches during the summer to help newcomers with settlement information and interpretation (Toronto Public Library, 2007c).

TPL also has developed a range of services for adult literacy:

- Free one-on-one tutoring in basic reading, writing, and math is available for English-speaking adults at nine library branches (Toronto Public Library, 2007a).

- The Toronto Public Library's Guide to Getting Good Information: A Step-by-Step Manual for Literacy Instructors (Livingston and Robinson, 2003a) covers such topics as choosing a good book, developing a research topic, visiting a library, as well as how to access government, community and health information. The section on health information emphasizes the important connection between health and literacy:

  Health information can have a profound effect on quality of life and covers the full range of life events from the birth of children to the care of elderly relatives. This session reviews four major sources of health information and students practice using tables of content and indexes. (Livingston and Robinson, 2003b)

The Consumer Health Information Service (CHIS) (Toronto Public Library, 2007b), a provincial service funded by the Ontario Ministry of Health Promotion, is located at the downtown Toronto Reference Library. CHIS seeks to overcome the health literacy barriers commonly faced by newcomers, as well as those with limited literacy skills. To deal with health literacy, CHIS has developed a multi-faceted approach including:

- CHIS has prepared a file that brings together many of the health-related services that newcomers are seeking.
- CHIS offers hand-on courses in English and French on "Locating Reliable Health Information on the Internet" to assist consumers in building critical skills to select appropriate health resources.
- When assisting the public at the information desk, CHIS staff use plain language and simple phrases to determine what resources best meet the consumer's needs.
- The collection includes a range of print and electronic materials from easy-to-read resources to professional medical resources.
- CHIS hosts a variety of health talks which offer an opportunity for the public to listen to experts and ask questions.
- CHIS staff have taught workshops on health literacy at health sciences and information science conferences. For example, the author delivered a presentation at the 2007 Ontario Libraries Association Conference that included Toronto Public Library staff in the audience. As a result, she has been asked to present a half-day course on health literacy for TPL staff in eleven branches who work in the area of literacy outreach.

QUEBEC

Lorie Kloda is a librarian at the McGill University Life Sciences Library where she coordinates information literacy instruction in the Faculties of Medicine and

Dentistry. Kloda is involved in projects promoting health literacy for consumers. She has written and spoken about three health information literacy projects where academic librarians have collaborated with community partners:

- Collaboration with researchers to train volunteers to deliver health information to oncology patients
- Collaboration with researchers to design a depository of evidence-based stroke interventions with accompanying health materials for the public
- Collaboration with McGill University's Mini-Med School to reach members of the community and to provide health literacy support (Kloda, 2005, 2006)

CONCLUSION

This chapter has included a brief and selective review of health literacy projects involving librarians across Canada. Health literacy is a serious and multifaceted problem. There are opportunities for librarians to collaborate with other groups, such as public health departments and organizations, local literacy organizations, a range of health associations, and other types of libraries. Librarians in Canada are rising to the challenge to ensure that barriers to health care are eliminated, but more work has to be done.

REFERENCES

Burnham, Erica, and Eileen Beany Peterson. 2005. "Health Information Literacy: A Library Case Study." *Library Trends* 53, no.3 (Winter): 422–433.

Canadian Council on Learning. 2007a. Health and Learning Knowledge Centre. Available: www.ccl-cca.ca/CCL/AboutCCL/KnowledgeCentres/HealthandLearning/

Canadian Council on Learning. 2007b. "State of Learning in Canada: No Time for Complacency. Summary Report on Learning in Canada 07." Available: www.ccl-cca.ca/CCL/Reports/StateofLearning/ StateofLearning2007.htm

Canadian Health Network. 1999. "Questions and Answers." Internal Document— Background Information for Panellists Developed for the November 25, 1999 Launch.

Canadian Public Health Association. n.d. HRC Publications—Literacy. Available: www.cpha.ca/english/hrc/hrcpubs/literacy.htm

Hsu, C. Ed, Lynn F. Johnson, and Ann N. Brooks. 2003. "Promoting Health Information Literacy Collaborative Opportunities for Teaching and Academic Librarian Faculty." *Academic Exchange Quarterly* 7, no.1 (Spring): 200–206. Available: www.higher-ed.org/AEQ/mo2283fe04.htm

Kasowitz-Scheer, Abby, and Michael Pasqualoni. 2002. "Information Literacy Instruction in Higher Education: Trends and Issues." ERIC Digest. Syracuse, NY: Clearinghouse on Information and Technology. Available: www.ericdigests.org/2003-1/information .htm

Kloda, Lorie A. 2005. "Health Information and Community Outreach." In *Proceedings WILU 2005: 34th Annual Workshop on Instruction in Library Use.* Guelph, Ontario, Canada. Available: http://eprints.rclis.org/archive/00006533/

Kloda, Lorie A. 2006. "Promoting Health Information Literacy to the Wider Community: The Mini-Med School Experience." In *Proceedings of the Canadian Health Libraries Association 2006 Conference.* Vancouver, British Columbia, Canada. Available: http://eprints.rclis.org/archive/00006532/

"Literacy and Health in Canada. Perspectives from the Second Canadian Conference on Literacy and Health." 2006. *Canadian Journal of Public Health* 97, no.2 Suppl. (May–June): S1–S48.

Livingston, Brenda, and Joan Robinson. 2003a. "Introduction." In *Toronto Public Library's Guide to Getting Good Information: A Step-by-Step Manual for Literacy Instructors.* Toronto, Ontario, Canada: Toronto Public Library. Available: www.tpl.toronto.on.ca/pdfs/spe_ser_lit/intro.pdf

Livingston, Brenda, and Joan Robinson. 2003b. "Session 3." In *Toronto Public Library's Guide to Getting Good Information: A Step-by-Step Manual for Literacy Instructors.* Toronto, Ontario, Canada: Toronto Public Library. Available: www.tpl.toronto.on.ca/pdfs/spe_ser_lit/session3.pdf

Medical Library Association. 2003. "Health Information Literacy: Definitions." Available: www.mlanet.org/resources/healthlit/define.html

Parker, Ruth, and Gary L. Kreps. 2005. "Library Outreach: Overcoming Health Literacy Challenges." *Journal of the Medical Library Association* 93, no.4 Suppl. (October): S81–S85.

Statistics Canada. 2006. "Literacy Skills Among Canada's Immigrant Population." Available: www.statcan.ca/english/freeub/81-004-XIE/2005005/impop.htm

Statistics Canada. 2007. "Canada's Population Clock." Available: www.statcan.ca/english/edu/clock/population.htm

Toronto Public Library. 2007a. "Adult Literacy Services." Available: www.tpl.toronto.on.ca/pdfs/spe_ser_lit_index.jsp

Toronto Public Library. 2007b. "Consumer Health Information Service." Available: www.tpl.toronto.on.ca/uni_chi_index.jsp

Toronto Public Library. 2007c. "Multicultural Services and Programs." Available: www.tpl.toronto.on.ca/mul_ser_settlement.jsp

Toronto Public Library. 2007d. "Newcomer Information Service at the Library." Available: www.tpl.toronto.on.ca/mul_set_partnership.jsp

U.S. Department of Health and Human Services. 2000. *Healthy People 2010: Volume 1.* "Chapter 11. Health Communication." Available: www.healthypeople.gov/document/HTML/Volume1/11HealthCom.htm

Chapter 13

Consumer Health Services in Hospitals: The Front Line for Health Literacy

Julie Esparza

With the release of the 2004 Institute of Medicine report on health literacy and its impact on society, awareness has been growing of the need to counteract this problem (Nielsen-Bohlman, Panzer, and Kindig, 2004). Consumer health services (CHS) in hospital libraries have been and continue to be one way to address the problems of health literacy. According to Perryman (2006), the first hospital libraries started in the mid-1800s were for patients and provided non-fiction educational material with an emphasis on moral and religious teachings. In 1971, Helen Yast, the Library Director at the American Hospital Association, remarked, "In my opinion, health education for both patients and the public is a responsibility which medical libraries can no longer shirk..." (615). In 1996, the Consumer and Patient Health Information Section (CAPHIS) of the Medical Library Association (MLA) introduced *The Librarian's Role in the Provision of Consumer Health Information and Patient Education*, a policy approved by MLA. The document outlined what CHS were and the roles of librarians in the process. While this and other documents provide how-to guides on providing CHS, the real question is "What CHS are hospital libraries actually providing?" The purpose of this chapter is to provide an overview of CHS provided through hospital libraries to internal customers (hospital staff), external customers (consumers), and how hospital librarians are creating partnerships to bridge the gap in health illiteracy.

CONSUMER HEALTH SERVICES IN HOSPITAL LIBRARIES SURVEY (CHSHL)

In order to determine the breadth and scope of consumer health services in hospitals, the author conducted a review of the library literature addressing health literacy and hospital libraries. On January 24, 2007, a general inquiry requesting information about CHS in hospitals libraries was sent to Medlib-L (Medical Library Association [MLA] national listserv), CAPHIS (Consumer and Patient Health Information Section of the MLA listserv), and the HSL-LIST (Hospital Libraries Section of the Medical Library Association listserv). After receiving very few responses, the author created the *Hospital Consumer Health Services Library Survey* in SurveyMonkey (see Appendix 13-1). Questions were based on the programs and services highlighted in the literature review. Announcement of the survey was sent on February 20, 2007, to MEDLIB-L, CAPHIS, and HSL-LIST. Because of technical difficulties, the survey did not appear on HSL-LIST, and therefore, the responses included below are only from the other two listservs. Only library staff in libraries based in hospitals or providing services directly to the clinical setting were asked to respond to the survey. Staff in consumer education departments that are not a part of the library were asked not to participate in the study. Academic medical centers that have direct clinical consumer health services were included, but not those that did not provide specific targeted services. The survey closed on March 9, 2007.

The total number of responses was 201, of which 144 were complete. Of those survey respondents, 74 percent were associated with private not-for-profit systems, 60 percent were part of a larger health system, and 71 percent were teaching hospitals. Response rate based on bed count was as follows: over 500 beds = 27 percent; 400–499 beds = 10 percent; 300–399 beds = 18 percent; 200–299 beds = 17 percent; and 100–199 beds = 17 percent. Ninety-nine percent of the respondents had a library on site. The responses to the survey questions are outlined below. Since respondents were asked to check all that applied, only those responses with significant percentages will be discussed. Following each response category are relevant examples culled from the literature to illustrate how these CHS are being provided in the practical setting.

INTERNAL PARTNERSHIPS

The first question on the survey asked whether the library provides education to or partners with internal hospital committees. Four responses were provided, and respondents were asked to check all that applied. They are listed in Table 13-1 in descending order of frequency.

Table 13-1. Library and Internal Hospital Consumers

Question: The library provides the following education and/or partnerships
with internal hospital customers

Response categories	Percentage of Respondents
The library staff plays a role on the hospital patient education committee.	63
The library plays a role in promoting clear communication through the editing or creation of hospital education materials.	38
The library promotes to all hospital staff (including physicians) health literacy programs such as AskMe3 or the teach-back and show-me process advocated by the AMA Foundation.	24
The library plays a role in the patient safety committee in regard to health literacy.	17

Respondents were prompted to add additional comments on this question about their internal partnerships with hospital committees. Five respondents commented as follows:

The librarian is on the health literacy committee. (2 responses)

I forward any information about literacy issues to a person who is a literacy advocate and also to the chair of the Patient and Family Education Team.

My boss in the Medical Library is on the patient education committee. I am the Consumer Health Librarian (separate area), and I am not on a committee.

The library used to have a representative on the patient education committee and in the creation of hospital education materials, but cutbacks eliminated the ability to serve on this committee when the solo librarian position was cut from .88 FTE (full-time equivalent) to .5 FTE.

Evidence from the Literature

In February 2007, the Joint Commission released *"What Did the Doctor Say?":
Improving Health Literacy to Protect Patient Safety.* In this white paper, the Joint Commission discusses what healthcare organizations need to do:

1. Make Effective Communications an Organizational Priority to Protect the Safety of Patients
2. Address Patients' Communication Needs Across the Continuum of Care
3. Pursue Policy Changes that Promote Improved Practitioner-Patient Communications (6, 7 and 9)

Librarians in hospitals have a unique skill set that can be brought to participation in Patient Education Committees (PECs). The "Standards for Hospital Libraries 2002" (Standard 5) states that librarians should be on "the patient education team(s), as reflected in minutes or other documentation (preferred)." They should consult "with team concerning selection, creation, and quality filtering of sources for patient education materials." They should provide or facilitate access to "patient education materials for clinical staff" and market "library services directly to patients and families." Finally, they should teach "search skills for patient education electronic resources" (Gluck et al., 2002: 468).

A search of MEDLIB-L shows an active participation by many information professionals working in hospitals to fulfill these roles. Discussion on how to lead and/or motivate a Patient Education Committee, questions concerning education materials being evaluated, and discussion of how to teach staff to use resources dominate a search by the author on "patient education." However, few examples were found in the literature on CHS and participation on PECs.

Veteran's Administration (VA) facilities exhibit strong usage of Patient Education Committees and the librarians have excellent relationships with these programs (Renner and Schneider, 1991). The librarian on the committee at James A. Haley Veterans Hospital in Tampa, Florida, is reported to provide professional information on patient education, organizes patient education information to prevent duplication and outdated material, and provides information to the educators working with the patients. A database of educational programs prevents spending energy recreating the same services by different patient educators in different VA facilities. As liaison to the clinicians at the medical center for patient education issues, "the Library serves as a focal point for all patient education resources" (212). Schneider is still with the VA and not only continues to serve on the PEC at Haley Veterans Hospital but also serves Veterans Integrated Service Network's (VISN) Patient Education Work Group for the entire VA network (Schneider, e-mail communication, 2007).

At the University of Medicine and Dentistry of New Jersey, participation on the PEC provided the catalyst in 1999 for the Cooper Library to provide consumer health information via a computer system. Through unique partnerships with information services, patient transport (for delivery of the physical information) and nursing, they found a way to increase their role in providing CHS. Through the use of the Clinical Information System, requests for consumer information grew to an average of "200 to 267" requests per month (Calabretta and Cavanaugh, 2004: 77). A subsequent survey of 32 users of the service found that the nurses felt it saved them time and helped prepare the patient for discharge. Membership on the PEC enabled the librarians to identify how they could provide a unique information service to patients and highlight their unique skill set.

There are several other successful programs stemming from involvement in PEC. One example is from University of Pittsburgh Medical Center (UPMC). According to Klein-Fedyshin et al. (2005), librarians worked with nurse educators and other medical staff to improve discharge instructions for patients in the postoperative period after cardiac surgery. Nurses provided the names of potential patients. The library entered their names into the library's circulation system, then provided an education video and a self-addressed envelope for patients to return the video. The researchers surveyed those who had received the video. Of the 147 respondents, 96 percent of them watched the videotape and felt that it improved their self-care behaviors (442). From this educational initiative that grew out of participation in a PEC, CHS allowed for performance improvement that directly impacted patients, that is, some of them deferred making calls to their physicians because the video explained what they needed to know.

Patricia Hammond (2005), Librarian of the Community Health Education Center (CHEC) at the Virginia Commonwealth University Medical Center, has not only integrated CHS but also influences the training of medical students throughout their training. The CHEC serves as a resource when the students must create their own patient handouts. In addition, the librarian teaches a fourth-year elective in the medical school, titled "Providing Health Information to Patients."

The Neuro-Patient Resource Centre at Montreal Neurological Hospital helps collaborate on bilingual patient education materials (Burnham and Peterson, 2005). They "edit the information and, when needed, change the language to something that can be understood by people who do not have a medical vocabulary" (431). The Resource Centre brings plain language to complex medical topics. At times they use pictures to provide a point of reference for the patient. The authors reported "this, perhaps more than anything influenced the Resource Centre's acceptance as part of the patient care team" (431).

Paul and Schneider (2006), in their article "Leading a Plain Language Program," discuss their work in these initiatives at the Treadwell Library of the Massachusetts General Hospital. While trying to find appropriate consumer health material in simple and easy-to-read formats, the librarians discovered that even material provided by government agencies often falls short of plain language. After attending workshops, they brought the concept of plain language to their facility through a series of in-house workshops. They continue promotion and education to their clinical staff through printed materials for self-study, a lunchtime workgroup, and a vast amount of resources located from the Treadwell Library Web site (http://massgeneral.org/library.default.asp?page-plain language).

AVAILABILITY OF COLLECTION

The next question on the CHSHL survey focused on how collections were made available to the public. The participants were provided with seven responses and asked to check all that applied. The responses are listed in Table 13-2 in descending order of frequency.

Table 13-2. Availability of Collection to the Public

Question 2: Please denote how your library collection is made available to the public.

Response Categories	Percentage of Respondents
Library staff will assist the patron in finding relevant consumer health information.	93
Library staff will assist the patron in finding relevant medical information.	88
Library is open to the public and the public may browse all materials.	82
There is a dedicated consumer health book, audiovisual, and journal collection.	72
Consumer health information is provided in multiple languages.	56
Individuals using the library (regardless of affiliation) may obtain a library card and check out materials that circulate.	36
Consumer health library collections are available with specific services (i.e., cancer library with oncology services).	25

Fifteen respondents to the CHSHL survey also included other comments on this section of the survey. A few examples of their comments are included here:

Library staff "rounds" on the floors unit by unit, visiting every new admission we can with bookmarks and information about consumer health information services in the library.

While everybody is welcome to use the collection, only our inpatients, outpatients coming back with regular appointments, and regular staff may check items out.

Customers and state residents may obtain a card that allows them to check out materials from the consumer health information collection.

Families of inpatients (and the patients themselves) may check out circulating consumer health information on a day-by-day basis.

Individuals using the library (regardless of affiliation) may check out materials that circulate (but don't get a card).

CHI materials may be borrowed with a valid public library card.

Two librarians responded to the author's initial general inquiry on MEDLIB-L, CAPHIS, and HLS-List listservs. In her e-mail, Bayorgeon (January, 2007) at Affinity Health System in Wisconsin commented on the variety of places CHS are offered.

The Library Services Department at Affinity Health System in Wisconsin supports several innovative consumer health programs you may be interested in hearing about. We have a consumer health library that focuses on fitness, wellness, sports injuries etc. located in space Affinity leases at a YMCA in Oshkosh, WI. It is staffed by a part-time librarian. We also just opened a consumer health library at St. Elizabeth Hospital in Appleton, WI in a coffee shop in a new entrance that was recently added to the hospital. We also have a librarian staffing this popular location. In addition, we have a combined consumer health library and professional library at Mercy Medical Center in Oshkosh that is only six years old.

From Hazleton General Hospital in Hazleton, Pennsylvania, Curry (February, 2007) e-mailed and mailed the following information.

Beginning with a Commonwealth of Pennsylvania Library Services and Technology Act (LSTA) grant the creation of the Greater Hazleton Health Alliance Community Health Library was established in 1999 offering books in nontechnical language for the community. Funding to continue building the collection was obtained from the Luzerne Foundation in 2002. Moving into the community followed with a second LSTA "Establishing Consumer Health Information Website at Local Public Libraries and Hospital Library Sites" in 2004. In the last grant "Health Kiosk" machines were placed in public library spots to provide consumer health information in written and video format. The Community Health Library provides library cards to members of the community so they may utilize the consumer health collection. In addition the library will mail information directly to the home through the use of a dedicated "Info Line" and to visitors of the library. A Cancer Patient Education Cart stocked by the library contains free brochures and pamphlets that patients can take with them as needed.

Evidence from the Literature

When it comes to library collections, the literature varies on descriptions of consumer health services. Some collections concentrate on providing multicultural collections based on the population they may serve, while others concentrate on making the consumer health materials easily found through the creation of their own taxonomies. Given the limited space of this chapter, some examples of successful programs and their classification schemes will be highlighted.

One long-standing movement in addressing consumer health in hospitals is the vision of Planetree Health Resource Center (PHRC), which was founded in 1978. The philosophy of the hospital administration centers on the patient and actively promotes libraries in hospitals and encourages patients to question their care. According to Cosgrove (1991, 1994), through the patient-centered model, "information can empower people and help them face health and medical challenges" (57). The Planetree Health Resource Center, located on the San Francisco campus of California Pacific Medical Center (Pacific Presbyterian Medical Center), "combines the openness of a public library with the specialization of a medical library collection" (Cosgrove, 1994: 58). Providing a place for people to obtain consumer health information was just the start. The Planetree Classification Scheme was developed to make finding information easier. The multicultural emphasis of the collection meant they served all visitors regardless of language needs. The 1994 article has an appendix giving an overview of the classification system used in the Planetree system (see also, Cosgrove, 1991).

Pittman and Jagodynski (2005) discuss the Maxwell & Eleanor Blum Patient and Family Learning Center (PFLC) at Massachusetts General Hospital (MGH). Open since 1998 on the first floor of the hospital, the PFLC had over 32,000 visitors in 2004. With computers for Internet access and purchased consumer information from commercial vendors, MGH's own patient education material, and other typical resources found in other consumer health libraries, the librarians set up an interesting method of identifying the subject areas on which they based their collection. Using actual DRGs from the hospital and demographic data, they have developed three levels of obtaining material for their collection. Level 1 designation means they will attempt to collect as much reference and consumer material as possible for that topic, Level 2 means they will collect major reference books in that area with one or two consumer health resources, and Level 3 means it is a low priority for the collection and information will be obtained from general reference materials. The PFLC attempts to collect in a variety of languages and educational levels to match the needs of their patients and their families. The appendices in this article are an excellent resource since they outline evaluation forms used for media, as well as their own services.

Librarians at the Reuben L. Sharp Health Science Library, Cooper Hospital/University Medical Center, Camden, New Jersey, work in tandem with the hospital's Consumer Health Education Center. As well as maintaining a supply of patient handouts, the librarians also have eight basic areas in which they collect materials for the circulating collection. These areas cover drug information, family medical guides, alternative health care, disease/condition specific guides, pregnancy and related topics, infant and child care, aging and the aged, and wellness. Hospital staff notify the library staff about "hot topics" that may be of interest to patients. The consumer health materials are separated from the regular primary medical reference collection to make browsing easier for consumers. Also twice a month the library provides a Current Health Care Issues (CHCI) bibliography and reprints of selected articles. Provided to the public as well as staff, this service highlights programs within the hospital (Calabretta, 1996).

Burnham and Peterson (2005) report that the Neuro-Patient Resource Centre at the Montreal Neurological Hospital maintains a "bilingual (English and French) collection of monographs written in plain language on neurological and psychiatric disorders, as well as books on coping with chronic illness, pain, and death for adults and children" and general medical reference texts (428). Also provided are brochures that patients and/or their families and friends can take with them.

In their article, Galganski, Phillips, and Ross (2005) talked about several specific libraries. In both the pediatrics and oncology areas, the collections are small but have reference materials for browsing. In the Oncology Patient Library, there are books that circulate. Neither of the libraries is staffed but a librarian checks on the collection and the computers once a week. While the Oncology Patient Library has seen little collection loss, the Family Resource Center in the pediatrics area has seen a 37.5 percent decrease in the collection.

PACKETS OF INFORMATION

Another question on the CHSHL survey focused on what information was provided to consumers. Eight response categories were provided, and respondents were asked to check all that applied. Because only 3 percent of respondents replied that they charged fees, this category is not discussed further. The response rate is outlined below in descending order of frequency as well as the responses to "Other" category.

As was expected, a large number of respondents indicated that they provide consumer information to visitors while they wait, through their postal service, and via e-mail in the form of links to quality consumer Web sites. A surprising percentage of respondents (83 percent) also provided medical information to patients in the form of packets.

Twelve respondents provided additional information, a few examples of which are provided here:

We research consumer (customer or state-resident) questions and provide printouts and copies of both consumer-oriented and professional-level resources in response to questions.

We compile CH information and mail it to patrons' homes at no charge. We also have a separate collection for just brochures and booklets as well as a huge Web site that includes multilingual health information.

The nurse who requested the info for a specific inpatient will document the delivery of information to the patient.

Patients, families or friends can request information. They come to the library. I don't usually deliver it.

We also prepare packets of information for our outpatient areas to have on hand. We will also fax information. We also provide information to our clinicians for them to use in patient education (they document the delivery of the information).

Librarian will assist family friends and other family members who do not live in the area, but call long distance (from around the country and around the world!) . . . and I will service those calls, too.

Evidence from the Literature

Numerous examples of patient information delivery (packets prepared for an individual request) are reported in the literature. As Hammond (2005) points out, "when individuals come . . . [looking for information], they usually have an immediate, pressing need for health information. This is not the appropriate time for a librarian to offer instruction about proper research technique" (41). The following examples provide insight into the role of the library in the continuum of patient care.

Tarby and Hogan (1997) at the Crouse Hospital, in Syracuse, New York, discuss the implementation of a pilot study working with the oncology unit to provide

Table 13-3. Packets of Information for Customers

Question 3: Please check the printed information your library staff will prepare for consumers.

Response Categories	Percentage of Respondents
Library staff will provide printed information in the form of consumer health packets to patrons while they wait (no cost).	85
Library staff will prepare customized packets of medical information for patrons (no cost).	83
Library staff will provide printed information in the form of consumer health packet to patients, their families, or friends and deliver it the patients' rooms in the hospital (no cost).	76
Library staff will provide printed information in the form of consumer health packets to patrons through the United States Postal Service (no cost).	74
Library staff will provide printed information in the form of consumer health packets to patrons via e-mail in the form of links to Web sites (no cost).	73
Library staff will provide printed information in the form of consumer health packet to patients, their families, or friends after discharge from the hospital through an alerting process set up internally to notify the library of the information need (i.e., same-day surgery area has a form individuals can fill out to request information as part of their discharge process) (no cost).	13
When delivering information to patients, their families, or friends to the patients' rooms, the library staff document the delivery of information in the patients' charts under patient education (as part of JCAHO patient education).	12

patient education material. While major data were collected on the oncology unit, the overall service was offered to the entire hospital. With the implementation of the project, consumer health requests rose from 3 percent to 30 percent over an 18-month trial period (160). The authors found that a one-page education sheet or brochure was not helpful to the average patient, many of whom wanted more detailed information. Patient information requested was delivered in a variety of formats, including faxes to the patient's unit. They set high standards for delivery of information, with a completion requirement of two hours when the library was open.

Spatz at the Dalles, Oregon, Planetree Health Resource Center includes a discussion of information packets. This service instead of being initiated by a patient request to the nurse or library has a more proactive approach. Nursing staff make rounds to discover patients' information needs and then relay the information to the Resource Center staff. One interesting point is that when a nurse facilitator is on vacation or sick and the Resource Center staff take over, the service information requests go up. Spatz speculates that the nurse completing many tasks may not be able to focus on the information need of the patient whereas, for the Resource Center staff, the patient's information need is their only focus when they visit the patient. The librarians at the Dalles, Oregon, Planetree Health Resource Center have now taken over this function in order to facilitate the process (Strube et al., 2006).

In Toronto, the Consumer Health Information Service (CHIS) is a collaborative effort that includes the Toronto Hospital, "Faculty of Library and Information Science and the Centre for Health Promotion at the University of Toronto, the Ontario division of the Consumer's Association of Canada and the Metropolitan Toronto Reference Library" (Koba, 1995: 990). Consumers can access the library in person or by calling several dedicated lines. The government funds the endeavor, which allows patient education packets to be sent out. Some requests come directly from consumers but as with other services health professionals use the service to obtain information to provide to their patients.

An innovative contract among the Sharp Library at Cooper Hospital/University Medical Center in Camden, New Jersey, and other facilities created the South Jersey Regional Library Cooperative's Online Health Information Service to provide information packets to librarians, medical professionals, and consumers free of charge. Calabretta (1996) mentions that often packets are being requested by health professionals to give to patients. Different types of libraries (public, academic, hospital) may request information for patrons. In addition, direct requests may be made by individuals to the providing libraries. Delivery of information can be through fax, courier service, or the postal system.

At the Eskind Biomedical Library at Vanderbilt University Medical Center in Tennessee is an innovative program called Patient Informatics Consult Service

(PICS) (Williams et al., 2001). Using an "information prescription," a multi-disciplinary team works to provide the patient with the best consumer health information (185). Physicians view the service as a way to ensure that patients receive quality consumer information and the PICS librarians not only provide information to allow the patient to cope with their health issue but also educate the patient on how to identify quality resources on their own. The use of the written prescription allows the PICS librarians to know exactly what the patient needs without having to rely on the patient's ability to recall what information they need. Presenting all points of view on topics is important to the librarians in making sure the information is balanced. Because the packets are personalized, they can be provided at the appropriate educational level. The healthcare professionals requesting the information for the patient also receive a copy so they are aware of the information given and can discuss it with the patient. At the time of publication, no formal evaluation of the service had been done, but feedback from patients and healthcare professionals was positive (Williams et al., 2001: 188).

At the Mayo Clinic in Rochester, Minnesota, the Patient Education Center provides packets of information via the U. S. Postal Service to those who request information and "are unable to visit the library" (Raffel, Dierkhising, and Ivnik 2002: 44). On average 200 packets are mailed each month. In their study, surveys were mailed to 260 users of the service. Data were obtained on the impact of the health information given from the 130 returned surveys. According to the respondents, the benefits of receiving the health information were they learned more about their condition (85 percent), shared the information with others (58 percent), felt they understood what their physician had told them (53 percent), had a better understanding of treatment options (52 percent), and were less anxious about their condition (44 percent) (47). In a breakdown of anxiety level "having a better understanding is more strongly associated with feeling less anxious" (46).

The Patient Education Resource Center (PERC) at the University of Michigan Comprehensive Cancer Center sends around 30 to 40 information packets and evaluation forms to patients each month. Volk (2002) analyzed the data from 119 returned evaluations between April 2000 and February 2001. She found that 61 percent of the 119 respondents "felt the information had made an impact on treatment or quality of life" (61). Using a "PERCmobile" stocked with printed patient education material and a laptop for Internet searching, the librarian visits the oncology floors once a month so that patients can receive customized information. The interaction between the librarian and patient or family member can be an immediate search or a form may be filled out for an in-depth search to be done at a later time. From evaluations, the interactive searching sessions benefit the users by allowing the librarian to show them efficient search strategies. One hundred percent of the respondents felt "they gained new knowledge in the sessions" (62).

Tape (2004) talks about how many cancer centers are incorporating consumer health resources into their education plans. Using a written prescription provided by the physician, the librarian finds the information needed by the patient. When Gundersen Lutheran Cancer Center, La Crosse, Wisconsin, opened their main consumer health library they made sure a librarian was included. Later with its success and proposal of a cancer center consumer library, providing a way to supply specialized consumer health information became a necessity to help relieve the physician of having to search for information while the patient waited. The librarians already being used as part of the care team in multiple units "act as a filter or a faucet, controlling information in a way that helps patients." Tape quotes Melinda Orebaugh, Director of the Gundersen Lutheran Cancer Center, who stated that physicians "are very excited about the capabilities of a librarian to make their job easier, more efficient" (35). Patients are returning, thus increasing repeat business for the program. The goal of aiding the professionals to provide better care means the physicians in turn see the library as a necessary extension of the patient care experience.

At Englewood (New Jersey) Hospital and Medical Center, Lindner and Sabbagh (2004) provide "rounding service" in the form of patient education rounds. After 20 years of providing packets of information for those calling or walking into the library, they embarked on direct unit visits in 2002. Nurses, patients, and their family members would request information when the librarians made contact. Working with the nursing staff, patients who may need more patient education are identified. In addition the librarian visits rooms asking patients if they need information. Before leaving the room, the patient is always asked if any of their questions should not be shared with their nurse. Normally patients do not mind the nurse knowing what they have requested, but if they request that the librarian not disclose information to the nursing staff then that request is honored. A feedback form is given (when the patient has no objections) to the nurse detailing what has been given to the patient. This article has several examples of useful forms, including the feedback form to the nurse and a disclaimer. With downsizing affecting the service, there is an excellent volunteer training help sheet.

As mentioned above in the section on Patient Education Committees, Calabretta and Cavanaugh (2004) had a direct service with the units through the use of the hospital's Clinical Information System to provide patient information. Through the system, direct requests are made by clinical staff in the computer system. The library would provide information to the patient through transport personnel, and, at the request of an uneasy physician, a chart copy was also included so the doctor would know what the library gave the patient. The librarian's record in the Clinical Information System recording the completion of the information request is a critical step to the patient education for the hospital. While undertaking this service, the library identified a need for nurses to request medical or nursing information in order to enhance patient care. Infograms for the professional were added to the Clinical Information System to allow professionals to request clinical information. Using the same delivery method as for the patient allowed the health professional to have the information in a timely fashion. While the authors discussed several survey instruments, unfortunately examples were not included in the report. The authors also mentioned that additional evaluation would be done, and it is hoped that they will provide examples of their tools so they may be used by librarians in other institutions.

Though the service is not discussed in detail by Pittman and Jagodynski (2005), they "[provide] pre-operative patient education materials," take calls from patients, and provide overall patient information for before and after their visit to the Stoeckle Center for Primary Care Innovation (58). What is extremely useful in this article is their User Satisfaction Survey that could be used by other libraries to evaluate patient education provided to patients, their families, or visitors to the library.

According to Schneider (2005), the use of printed information prescription pads enhances clarification and prevents miscommunication to the librarian on what the patient needs. As she states, medical terms can often sound the same but have a very different course of treatment. Her example includes a consumer newly diagnosed with "lipoma—a benign lump of fatty tissue" in comparison to "lymphoma, a serious form of cancer" was used in her report (75). Publicity is the key to getting a service such as this off the ground. Through outreach and attending department meetings, the Patient Education Librarian was able to let physicians know about the service. The printed prescription forms appear in a variety of ways. An alert can even be sent to the library through the electronic medical record. Clinicians like the service since it reduces the time they have to spend finding information for patients. One interesting by-product of the prescription form is that patients view the "'prescription' as a mandatory rather than optional procedure, and are more likely to come to the library for the requested information" (78). Schneider reports on survey results for over two years which found that respondents using the prescriptions thought the service was "excellent or very good" (79).

Clinical Nurse Specialists, at Aurora St. Luke's Medical Center, Milwaukee, Wisconsin, identify patients who would benefit from information. This is done at the beginning of the day following nursing meetings. They identified the afternoon as the best time for librarians to make rounds since family members are often in the room at that time and tests are more likely to be finished for the day. Observing any infection control protocol, librarians enter the room and introduce themselves to the patient and other individuals present. Several forms are provided in the appendix of the article detailing how information is collected. A disclaimer form is returned with the patient information. After several months, librarians were given access to the hospital's Emtek software to document patient encounters. This relieves the nurse of the burden of entering the information and enhances the patient record for JACHO education requirements. At Aurora Medical Center, Oshkosh, instead of obtaining a list of patients, the librarian attends their Interdisciplinary Rounds Team. This allows the librarian to listen to the staff's concerns or needs for the patient. Participation in the team eliminates the necessity of the nurse repeating information needs that may have already come up in the meeting. At the Aurora Bay Care Medical Center in Green Bay, Wisconsin, the librarian visits the Medical/Surgical Units. Charge nurses are asked to provide patients who should be contacted. No evaluation of the service has been done as of yet but the authors of the article are looking to see the role their service plays in patient satisfaction in the future (Strube et al., 2006).

OUTREACH SERVICES

Outreach is important in CHS but respondents showed less response when it came to this category of questions with regard to CHS. Respondents were asked to mark all services supplied.

Four of the respondents to the CHSHL survey provided additional comments about Web site marketing. Two mentioned that their Web pages are on the hospital intranet only. One respondent stated that her/his library subscribes to ThePatientChannel.com, which provides patient care information and resources

Table 13-4. Outreach Services

Question 4: Please check all consumer health services outreach provided by your library.

Response Categories	Percentage of Respondents
On your hospital Web site the library has a Web page highlighting consumer health services provided by your library.	65
Educational programs on searching the Internet for quality health information are provided by library staff.	50
Library staff attend local health fairs to advertise the consumer health services provided by the library staff.	40
Library staff attend local health fairs to promote quality Internet resources such as MedlinePlus.gov.	39
On your hospital Web site the library has a Web page that provides an "Ask the Librarian" button.	38
Educational programs on consumer health issues are a regular part of consumer health offerings of the library.	22

to patients, friends, and family. The fourth respondent stated that the library provides subject links on their Web pages dealing with consumer health. In addition, 14 people provided general comments on the CHSHL survey about outreach services, a few of which are provided here:

Library staff promotes services through the state's public libraries and promotes services to public libraries at meetings of librarians.

The Patient Health Library (separate from the Medical Library) sponsors health fairs in-house for patients, family members, and employees.

Library staff performs free blood pressure checks—all were trained by AHA-certified instructor and passed a test before performing this service. Library director writes a monthly health column published in the local newspaper. We partner with local high school and community college to host classes and student assignments. A summer preschool Health Activity and Story Time one morning per week.

Attends local support group meetings to promote library services and useful resources.

Librarian does outreach for area schools and conducts classes on how to find health-wellness info, MedlinePlus, PUBMED, and Internet safety.

Promotion through print marketing materials distributed to the community, as well as articles in local newspaper.

Evidence from the Literature

Hospital Web site administrators are often willing to host a Web page highlighting library services offered to the public. It is not surprising that 65 percent of the respondents indicated this type of outreach. Normally for the library, this type of advertising does not require additional marketing dollars and with proper placement on a hospital's Web site, can steer consumers to the library. A large and diverse group of reports and studies have been done on Web sites and hospital libraries.

Fulda and Kwasik (2004) analyzed consumer health Web sites of libraries in the South Central Chapter Region of the MLA. Evaluating 49 Web sites, they found that hospital Web sites had a more professional appearance and provided information to consumers through purchased information resources. While this research was done in 2004, it shows that hospitals were marketing consumer health information services on their Web sites. While the authors do not state whether the hospital or the librarians were driving this outreach, the focus on consumer health services appears to be a part of the hospital marketing goals.

Galganski, Phillips, and Ross (2005) report on the creation of specific Web sites to meet the needs of two clinical areas, The Family Resource Center (pediatric patients and their families) and the Oncology Patient Services Library. The consumer health librarian created a "Checklist for Web Sites Linked from OSF [Saint Francis Hospital] Sites" that was used to assess the accuracy, authority, objectivity, quality, currency, ease of use, intended audience, spirit of mission, and scope and security of Web links (35). In their article, they provide a copy of their checklist that others can use to evaluate a particular Web site for inclusion on their Web site. The successful use of these two specifically targeted Web sites suggests that patients and their families are often looking for very specific information when searching a Web site.

Calabretta, Cavanaugh, and Swartz (2003) discuss the creation of a Web site to educate consumers about health information on the Web. Realizing that there was no way to capture everything, they decided to be very selective in what resources would be listed on the consumer health pages. "Professional organizations, government agencies (federal and state), consumer/self help groups, and super health sites as well as topical sites specializing in alternative medicine, cancer information and drug information" would be included on the Web site (18). When the Web site was up and running, the library staff was able to aid clinicians by adding subject areas and then identifying useful consumer health links in those areas to expedite patient education.

Dickenson and Fuller (2005) report on how the Web site of the Stanford Health Library has become another tool in the education of patients. Originally the Web site was a way to provide brochure information but, through the innovative action of the library staff, it became a strong marketing tool. The Web site provides links to a variety of resources loosely organized on an adaptation of the National Library of Medicine's Medical Subject Headings. Also incorporated into the design are gender- and age-specific sections, making information easier to find. Interactive videos are available online and once a library card has been obtained, e-books can be checked out through the Web site. This places the Stanford Health Library on the same progressive level as larger public libraries in the services provided through their Web sites. Also consumers may request reference assistance through the Web site and responses are in the form of links to free quality consumer information.

Charbonneau and Workman (2002) describe the experience of bringing consumer health information in 24 languages to the Internet. The Spencer S. Eccles Health Science Library at the University of Utah and the Hope Fox Eccles Clinical Library in Salt Lake City collaborated to identify quality consumer health information to be included in the 24 Languages Project. The Clinical Librarian (CL) at Hope Fox Eccles Clinical Library working with the staff scanned items and saved them to network drives. The CL was responsible for the Web site link creation and placed the documents for access on a server. All feedback to the website is evaluated by the CL and the Web site has been moved and updated to improve features for the users. The unique skills of the hospital library staff were needed to evaluate the materials and to organize how consumers can search for needed information.

Another successful project involving hospital librarians is MedInfoRus. Friedman, Dolinsky, and Perelman (2005) wanted to provide a resource for the many other hospital librarians who called them when seeking information for Russian speakers in New York City. As Russian-speaking librarians, they were considered to be a unique resource in a melting pot where over half a million Russian-speaking individuals live. The Patient Information section gathers materials from a range of quality Web consumer health resources. Broken into broad subject areas, the information provided is listed in links in English that facilitates searching by the non-Russian speakers who must provide information to a sick patient or family members. A unique resource on the Web site is a tutorial for Russian speakers on how to use PUBMED.

The CHSHL survey also revealed that 50 percent of the respondents educate consumers about finding quality information on the Internet. Helfner (2006) discusses a series of seminars to "instruct patients, family members, and care providers" (25). At Brigham and Women's Hospital, the Kessler Library staff realized that their "Reference Databases and Tools" page was not well used, based on other statistics for their Web site (27). Using monthly health observances identified by the National Health Information Center and relevant databases, the staff offered hour-long classes that were divided into equal parts of tutorial and actual search practice. Continuing education was offered to nurses who took the course. The Kessler Library staff plans additional outreach using this format in different locations and will provide the materials developed in the first series through the hospital intranet.

According to Spatz (2000), The Planetree Health Resource Center (PHRC) marketed their facility directly to the public by attending community talks, educating physicians on how they could help their patients, and starting an incentive program with the local school systems. Teachers in the local school district were required to attend an in-service program to learn about what the Resource Center could offer teachers and their students. Because students often make field trips to the PHRC, the staff makes sure students know where consumer health information is located and how they can go about educating themselves. The Resource Center's lecture series soon outgrew the confines of the Resource Center and had to move to a bigger facility. These community health presentations take place twice a year over a five- to six-week period. Each person attending received a specialized packet of information prepared by the Resource Center as a continuing education measure. The PHRC was able to convince annual planners of The Dalles' Health Fair to base the fair near the Resource Center. This led to greater outreach, which resulted in a partnership with other community organizations, such as the Tobacco Education and Prevention Coalition

(TEPCO), in order "to build a centralized collection of tobacco-related educational materials for use by both area teachers and members of the general public" (385).

The Health Sciences Center Library at the Stony Brook (New York) University Medical Center participates in a Mini Medical School promoted by the School of Medicine. Teaching consumer searching skills is the goal of the Library's component of instruction. Instructing consumers on how to find quality consumer health information is done through "Patient 101: Taking Charge of Your Health Care by Using Evidence-Based Information" (Chimato and Werner, 2006: 19). Participants are screened and broken into beginner and advanced classes based on their computer skills. Beginners start with a general search of the Internet, which is followed by a discussion on how to identify quality information on the Internet. Using the MLA's "'Top Ten' Most Useful Websites" (20), participants are shown quality resources against which they can judge other Web sites. Advanced participants are actually instructed on using PUBMED to find evidence-based medicine. Chimato and Werner reported the results of their evaluations from their two-week courses over a period of four years and noted that 86 percent of the participants felt the sessions were "just right for them" (22). The participation of the Health Sciences Center Library in Mini Medical School resulted in the award of the Presidential Award for Team Achievement.

PARTNERSHIPS AND SERVICES

Two questions on the CHSHL survey asked respondents if they partnered with public libraries or community organizations, while the last questions asked whether they were planning to increase their consumer health services in the coming fiscal year. Thirty-one percent (45 respondents) have public library partnerships and 17 percent (23 of 137 respondents) have community partnerships. Fifty-one percent of the respondents plan to increase consumer health services in the next fiscal year.

When asked to describe their experiences with these partnerships with public libraries, 44 respondents complied. Their comments, summarized here, reveal the multiple ways they collaborate with public librarians. The numbers in parentheses indicate the number of times an activity was mentioned.

- Public librarians refer questions or patrons to them. (15)
- Health sciences librarians sent print material or brochures to public librarians. (11)
- Health sciences librarians teach public librarians or consumers or recommend books to purchase. (8)
- In a consortium and shared resources. (OPAC, databases, Web sites) (6)

A few of the original comments are included here to show how the partnerships work:

> We are part of a library consortium that has partnered medical libraries with public libraries for the provision of medical and health consumer information for many years. Fewer requests are received as the public librarians become more familiar with the good sources of information that are increasingly available on the Web. We have also partnered with a library consortium to provide training sessions to public librarians (before the MLA initiative!).

> The "yes" answer to this question is with a very broad understanding of the term "partnership." I periodically visit the public library branches, introduce myself and leave my business card & MedlinePlus cards. I get four or five calls/year from public librarians, consulting on health reference. I call them about as many times for nonmedical information for the hospital staff & physicians.

> The hospital library director "moonlights" several hours a week (two evenings and all day Saturday) at the public library branch a few blocks from the hospital. She answers all medical questions posed at the reference desk (and has these questions telephoned to her at the hospital library when she is not working at the public library). She serves as a liaison between the hospital and the public library, encouraging development of mutually beneficial programs offered at the public library.

> Public library staff work in this center two days per week to provide consumer health and disability/rehabilitation information. We work closely together and share recommendations and programming ideas.

> Our collection is listed in an online public library system catalog. Patrons can borrow our material through that system; there is a driver who picks up and delivers books requested from our collection or requested from the public library by our employees. Works very well.

Evidence from the Literature

Few reports concerning partnerships between public and hospital libraries were found in the published literature. One of the earliest reported collaborations was between a hospital library and a public library and the formation of CHIPS (Consumer Health Information Program and Services/Salud y Bienestar) in the 1970s (Goodchild et al., 1978). Focusing on serving a specific geographical area with a multicultural population, the project brought a physical library on consumer health materials together by using information freely available from community organizations. Educational programs were developed to provide education for consumers. A unique aspect of the project was the rotation of public library and hospital library staff between the different facilities to provide cross-training in different environments for the professionals.

With mergers and nonprofit hospitals becoming for-profit institutions in the 1990s, many hospital libraries were reduced in size or ceased operations. A unique partnership was formed in Ohio between the Barberton Citizens Hospital and the Barberton Public Library. Faced with closing the Community Health Library, the medical librarian made a proposal to offer the 170 square foot space to the public library as a branch site. With administrative approval, negotiations took place between the director of the public library and the medical librarian. Location, funding, and operational issues were paramount to the discussions. Through a variety of funding sources, the Barberton Public Library took over the library with the hospital "providing the space, a telephone line with a direct dial number, internal data line for computers [outside their protected network]" (Greenberg, Kirbaway, and Sievert, 2002: 54). The hospital provides marketing support through the creation of print materials. As a win-win situation, the hospital did not cease a popular service but continued to provide it at minimal cost. The public library gained an additional facility but did not pay for building a new site. The Community Health Library Branch is still a valuable resource for the community after more than six years of service.

Kolakoski (2005) at the Franklin Medical Center Health Science Library in Greenfield, Massachusetts, reports on three projects to connect physicians to the community and market the Consumer Health Information Center. Working with the Greenfield Public Library, Northfield Public Library and 26 other outlying rural libraries, several programs were started. One was the "Library Connections for Health," wherein the Greenfield Public Library staff updated their health collection and clinicians from the hospital gave a number of health-related programs. Material displays were created to correspond to the topics. At some of the events, visitors could visit tables to discuss questions with the clinicians. Prizes, free food and drinks, and handouts of materials helped draw people to the sessions and enhanced their experience. The second project was the "Blood and Guts" program designed to attract younger children and encourage them to go into the health professions. Hospital staff were enthusiastic volunteers for educational sessions. Displays incorporating equipment used by clinicians and educational tools helped make the sessions interactive. Book displays were once again used to highlight discussion topics. At the last "Blood and Guts" session, over 170 people attended. The third project, also called "Library Connections for Health," was funded by a National Network of Libraries of Medicine New England Region grant to provide health information to libraries in 26 towns in Franklin County. Kolakoski conducted a survey of these public libraries. From the responses, a binder was developed to highlight reliable health resources with annotations discussing what the resource contained and how to access information from it. When the author visited every public library to deliver the binder, she discovered that some librarians did not respond to the survey because they did not receive many enquires regarding health topics. After talking with them, Kolakoski stated that "hospital library personnel were willing to customize plans based on the needs of each public librarian" (69), and offer MedlinePlus instructions "to librarians who request it" (70).

CONCLUSION

The results of the survey suggest that consumer health services in hospital libraries are ongoing. Few studies were found in the literature on the association of consumer health collections and services by librarians with length of stay, the effectiveness of educational material, and repeat visits (this means money for hospitals) for chronic health conditions. Studies involving quality measures and delivered health information may not be possible for a solo librarian with very little resources, but medical centers with libraries directly working with the care of patients may be able to move this vital research forward.

While the Joint Commission (2007) document *"What Did the Doctor Say?": Improving Health Literacy to Protect Patient Safety* is groundbreaking by stating that there is a problem, it includes no mention of programs involving libraries. As this chapter shows, librarians are using many types of programs to bridge the gap between what the doctor is telling the patient and the patient's understanding of what the doctor said. Only through concrete data will the talents of librarians be seen as vital to the patient experience. Then administrators, who may feel that consumer health services are unnecessary, will understand what a unique role librarians can play in helping clinicians educate their patients.

ACKNOWLEDGMENT

The author thanks Donna Record at Deaconess Health System for her assistance and support during the writing of this chapter.

REFERENCES

Burnham, Erica, and Eileen Beany Peterson. 2005. "Health Information Literacy: A Library Case Study." *Library Trends* 53, no.3 (Winter): 422–433.

Calabretta, Nancy. 1996. "The Hospital Library as Provider of Consumer Health Information." *Medical Reference Services Quarterly* 15, no.3 (Fall): 13–22.

Calabretta, Nancy, and Susan K. Cavanaugh. 2004. "Hospital Information Services. Education for Inpatients: Working with Nurses Through the Clinical Information System." *Medical Reference Services Quarterly* 23, no.2 (Summer): 73–79.

Calabretta, Nancy, Susan K. Cavanaugh, and Betty Jean Swartz. 2003. "Growing a Web Page: The Evolution of a Consumer Health Resource." *Journal of Consumer Health on the Internet* 7, no.3: 15–22.

Charbonneau, Deborah H., and T. Elizabeth Workman. 2002. "Providing Online Health Information in Many Languages: A Utah Hospital Library Experience." *Journal of Hospital Librarianship* 2, no.3: 39–49.

Chimato, Mary Carmen, and Susan E. Werner. 2006. "Building Community Relationships: How the Library Can Make It Happen." *Journal of Hospital Librarianship* 6, no.2: 15–25.

Consumer and Patient Health Information Section (CAPHIS/MLA), Medical Library Association. 1996. "The Librarian's Role in the Provision of Consumer Health Information and Patient Education." *Bulletin of the Medical Library Association* 84, no.2 (April): 238–239.

Cosgrove, Tracey. 1991. "The Planetree Health Resource Center." In *Managing Consumer Health Information Services*, edited by Alan M. Rees, 166–184. Phoenix, AZ: Oryx Press.

Cosgrove, Tracey L. 1994. "Planetree Health Information Services: Public Access to the Health Information People Want." *Bulletin of the Medical Library Association* 82, no.1 (January): 57–63.

Dickenson, Nancy A., and Howard J. Fuller. 2005. "Growing a Virtual Consumer Health Library: A Decade of Experience." *Journal of Consumer Health on the Internet* 9, no.1: 17–23.

Friedman, Yelena, Luda Dolinsky, and Rimma Perelman. 2005. "Providing Access to Consumer Health Information for the Russian-Speaking Population." *Journal of Consumer Health on the Internet* 9, no.1: 25–32.

Fulda, Pauline O., and Hanna Kwasik. 2004. "Consumer Health Information Provided by Library and Hospital Websites in the South Central Region." *Journal of the Medical Library Association* 92, no.3 (July): 372–375.

Galganski, Carol J., Ann Phillips, and Christine Ross. 2005. "Collaborating with Patient Care Units to Provide Consumer Health Information." *Journal of Consumer Health on the Internet* 9, no.3: 25–35.

Gluck, Jeannine Cyr, Robin Ackley Hassig, Lenni Balogh, Margaret Bandy, Jacqueline Donaldson Doyle, Michael R. Kronenfeld, Katherine Lois Lindner, Kathleen Murray, JoAn Petersen, and Debra C. Rand. 2002. "Standards for Hospital Libraries 2002." *Journal of the Medical Library Association* 90, no.4 (October): 465–472.

Goodchild, Eleanor Y., Judith A. Furman, Betty L. Addison, and Harold N. Umbarger. 1978. "The CHIPS Project: A Health Information Network to Serve the Consumer." *Bulletin of the Medical Library Association* 66, no.4 (October): 432–436.

Greenberg, Roni, Barbara Kirbaway, and Charlotte Sievert. 2002. "Community Health Public Library Branch Located in a Hospital." *Journal of Hospital Librarianship* 2, no.3: 51–56.

Hammond, Patricia A. 2005. "Consumer Health Librarian." *Reference Services Review* 33, no.1: 38–43.

Helfner, Cara. 2006. "Brigham and Women's Hospital's Consumer Health Database Searching Seminar Series: The First Year." *Journal of Consumer Health on the Internet* 10, no.2: 25–35.

Joint Commission. 2007. *"What Did the Doctor Say?": Improving Health Literacy to Protect Patient Safety*. Oakbrook Terrace, IL: The Joint Commission.

Klein-Fedyshin, Michele, Michelle L. Burda, Barbara A. Epstein, and Barbara Lawrence. 2005. "Collaborating to Enhance Patient Education and Recovery." *Journal of the Medical Library Association* 93, no.4 (October): 440–445.

Koba, Halyna. 1995. "Ontario's Health-Information Service: A Province-wide Resource for Patients." *Canadian Medical Association Journal* 153, no.7 (October): 990–991.

Kolakoski, Lauri Fennell. 2005. "Bringing Health Care Information to Rural Public Libraries: How One Hospital is Reaching Out to its Local Community." *Journal of Hospital Librarianship* 5, no.4: 65–72.

Lindner, Katherine L., and Lia Sabbagh. 2004. "In a New Element: Medical Librarians Making Patient Education Rounds." *Journal of the Medical Library Association* 92, no.1 (January): 94–97.

Nielsen-Bohlman, Lynn, Allison M. Panzer, and David A. Kindig, eds. 2004. *Health Literacy: A Prescription to End Confusion.* Washington, DC: National Academies Press.

Paul, Carolyn J., and Elizabeth Schneider. 2006. "Leading a Plain Language Program." *Journal of Hospital Librarianship* 6, no.2: 51–58.

Perryman, Carol. 2006. "Medicus Deus: A Review of Factors Affecting Hospital Library Services to Patients between 1790–1950." *Journal of the Medical Library Association,* 94, no.3 (July): 263–270.

Pittman, Taryn J., and Kristen M. Jagodynski. 2005. "Consumer Health Within an Academic Medical Center: State-of-the-Art Services and Technology." *Journal of Hospital Librarianship* 5, no.4: 51–64.

Raffel, Kathleen K., Ross Dierkhising, and Marie Ivnik. 2002. "Health Information Mailed on Request: Impact on Users, Considerations for the Provider." *Journal of Hospital Librarianship* 2, no.1: 41–56.

Renner, Iris A., and Janet M. Schneider. 1991. "Consumer Health and Patient Information Services in the U.S. Department of Veterans Affairs." In *Managing Consumer Health Information Services,* edited by Alan M. Rees, 206–217. Phoenix, AZ: Oryx Press.

Schneider, Janet M., 2005. "Information Therapy and Librarians: Quality Prescriptions for Health." *Journal of Hospital Librarianship* 5, no.4: 73–80.

Spatz, Michele A. 2000. "Providing Consumer Health Information in the Rural Setting: Planetree Health Resource Center's Approach." *Bulletin of the Medical Library Association* 88, no.4 (October): 382–388.

Strube, Kathleen, Mary Lou Hoffmann, Amy Melchiors, Holly Egebo, and Lucy Webb. 2006. "Patient Information Rounds in a Hospital System." *Journal of Hospital Librarianship* 6, no.4: 13–28.

Tape, Sean. 2004. "Adding a Librarian to the Care Team: Gundersen Lutheran Cancer Center's Innovative Program." *Hematology and Oncology News and Issues* 3, no.7 (July): 34–36.

Tarby, Wendy, and Kristine Hogan. 1997. "Hospital-based Patient Information Services: A Model for Collaboration." *Bulletin of the Medical Library Association* 85, no.2 (April): 158–166.

Volk, Ruti. 2002. "Innovative Information Services and Products for Cancer Patients and Families: The Experience of the Patient Education Resource Center (PERC) at the University of Michigan Comprehensive Cancer Center." *Journal of Hospital Librarianship* 2, no.2: 55–63.

Williams, M. Dawn, Kimbra Wilder Gish, Nunzia B. Giuse, Nila A. Sathe, and Donna L. Carrell. 2001. "The Patient Informatics Consult Service (PICS): An Approach for a Patient-centered Service." *Bulletin of the Medical Library Association* 89, no.2 (April): 185–193.

Yast, Helen. 1971. "Hospital Libraries in the 1970s." *Bulletin of the Medical Library Association* 59, no.4 (October): 615–616.

Appendix 13-1. Consumer Health Services in Hospital Libraries Survey

A. Demographic Information

Please complete this section of questions that request information about you and your hospital.

1. Ownership of Hospital

   Federal
   State/Local Government
   Private, Not for Profit
   Investor-owned or private, for-profit
   Don't Know
   Other (please specify) _____

2. Hospital part of a larger health care system?

   Yes   No   Don't Know

3. Teaching Hospital?

   Yes   No

4. Number of beds as listed in the AHA Directory

   | 6-24 | 50-99 | 200-299 | 400-499 |
   | 25-49 | 100-199 | 300-399 | 500+ |

5. Hospital has a library onsite?

   Yes   No

6. Do you receive funding through an academic institution?

   Yes   No

7. Do you provide consumer health services as a part of your library services?

   Yes   No

   If they answered "Yes," then they would go on. If they answered "No," then they were thanked for participating.

B. Consumer Health Services

Please check all the consumer health services you supply. Many hospitals provide these services but they may come out of a public education department. Please check off items only if they are out of the library budget. [Library staff refers to professional and paraprofessionals paid out of the budget of the library or volunteers.]

8. The library provides the following education and or partnerships with internal hospital customers (check all that apply).

   ___ The library promotes to all hospital staff (including physicians) health literacy programs such as AskMe3 or the teach-back and show-me process advocated by the AMA Foundation.
   ___ The library staff plays a role on the hospital patient education committee.
   ___ The library plays a role in the patient safety committee in regard to health literacy.
   ___ The library plays a role in promoting clear communication through the editing or creation of hospital education materials.
   ___ Other (please specify): _____

9. Please denote how your library collection is made available to the public (check all that apply).

   ___ Library is open to the public and the public may browse all materials.
   ___ Consumer health library collections are available with specific services (i.e., cancer library with oncology services).
   ___ Individuals using the library (regardless of affiliation) may obtain a library card and check out materials that circulate.
   ___ Consumer health information is provided in multiple languages.
   ___ There is a dedicated consumer health book, audio/visual and journal collection.
   ___ Library staff will assist the patron in finding relevant medical information.
   ___ Library staff will assist the patron in finding relevant consumer health information.
   ___ Other (please specify): _____

10. Please check the printed information your library staff will prepare for consumers.

___ Library staff will prepare customized packets of medical information for patrons (no cost).

___ Library staff will prepare customized packets of medical information for patrons (charge fees).

___ Library staff will provide printed information in the form of consumer health packets to patrons while they wait (no cost).

___ Library staff will provide printed information in the form of consumer health packets to patrons through the United States Postal Service (no cost).

___ Library staff will provide printed information in the form of consumer health packets to patrons via e-mail in the form of links to Web sites (no cost).

___ Library staff will provide printed information in the form of consumer health packet to patients, their families, or friends and deliver it the patients' rooms in the hospital (no cost).

___ Library staff will provide printed information in the form of consumer health packet to patients, their families, or friends after discharge from the hospital through an alerting process set up internally to notify the library of the information need (i.e., same-day surgery area has a form individuals can fill out to request information as part of their discharge process) (no cost).

___ When delivering information to patients, their families, or friends to the patients' rooms, the library staff documents the delivery of information in the patients' charts under patient education (as part of JCAHO patient education).

___ Other (please specify): _____

11. Please check all consumer health services outreach provided by your library.

___ On your hospital Web site the library has a Web page highlighting consumer health services provided by your library.

___ On your hospital Web site the library has a Web page that provides an "Ask the Librarian" button.

___ Educational programs on searching the Internet for quality health information are provided by library staff.

___ Educational programs on consumer health issues are a regular part of consumer health offerings of the library.

___ Library staff attend local health fairs to advertise the consumer health services provided by the library staff.

___ Library staff attend local health fairs to promote quality Internet resources such as MedlinePlus.gov.

___ Other (please specify): _____

12. Do you have a partnership with a public library to provide consumer health services?

Yes   No

13. Please describe your experience(s) in this partnership:

_____
_____
_____

14. Do you have a partnership with any community organizations (churches, local cancer society, etc.) to provide consumer health services?

Yes   No

15. Please describe your experience(s) in this partnership:

_____
_____
_____

16. Do you plan to increase consumer health services in the coming fiscal year?

Yes   No

17. Please add any information not covered above that would be interesting to share with your colleagues on Consumer Health Services supplied by your library:

_____
_____
_____

Chapter 14

Health Literacy in Action— The Bronson Experience

Marge Kars

According to Dutcher (2005), public and academic librarians have collaborated with community organizations to address health information and health disparities. Hospital librarians have also been doing their part through the development of consumer health libraries, providing information to patients and their families in reader-appropriate formats. Another role for hospital librarians in the health literacy movement is partnering with other departments within their organizations to develop health literacy programs. This chapter describes some of the successful health literacy efforts at Bronson Healthcare Group in Kalamazoo, Michigan.

LITERATURE REVIEW

Beales (2005) proposed an interesting and thought-provoking perspective on the phrase "health literacy," which she suggested is inaccurate. "Health illiteracy" is a more accurate way to describe the concept of being unable to understand medical information or use that information to make one well or stay healthy. However, she acknowledged, "Illiteracy is an ugly word. It carries a stigma" (18). She suggested that a primary role for librarians in dealing with health illiteracy is one of active participation, wherein they would "bring our literature down to a level that is appropriate for *them*" (18). Some ways for librarians to address issues of health illiteracy include the following:

- Use collection development tools to compile "easy-to-read" materials.
- Raise the awareness of physicians, nurses, and other providers to health literacy issues.

- Become involved in patient education in your institution.
- Be an advocate for the adoption of "grade-level standards for all written materials" (24).
- "Educate administrators, who are in a position to make policy, about the problem of health illiteracy" (24).

Exploring opportunities for librarians working with patients with low literacy skills, Sostack (2007) suggested that librarians are "in a unique position" because not only can they create a shame-free learning environment for people with literacy issues, but they can also offer them "a broad range of health information materials" (1). Gillaspy (2005) suggested two ways public librarians could have an impact on health literacy: "They can include easy-to-read health materials in their collections" (486), and, to address the health literacy crisis in the United States, public librarians can provide "continuing adult literacy programs" (487).

Burnham and Peterson (2005) reported their collaborative efforts in the Neuro-Patient Resource Centre at the Montreal (Canada) Neurological Hospital. "The goals of improving health literacy and health information literacy inform almost all the activities of and services provided by the Neuro-Patient Resource Center" (428). The center provides up-to-date health information, written in plain language, in both French and English, which are the official languages of Canada. Staff at the center collaborate with health professionals to produce information for patients on "diagnostic tests, clinic handbooks, caregiver guides, and fact sheets on specific disorders and procedures" (431). The authors suggest that librarians need to leave their libraries and partner with others in their community, a recommendation also endorsed by Parker and Kreps (2005).

In 2005, the Medical Library Association (MLA) published *Communicating Health Information Literacy*. This document outlines the role medical librarians can take in their organizations as hospitals develop health literacy programs. The key message is, "Health information literacy is a critical life skill that helps patients and caregivers in making medical and health care decisions. Medical librarians should be involved in all levels of program development" (1). According to MLA, by taking an active role in the health literacy movement, medical and consumer health librarians will be provided with new opportunities to increase visibility in their organizations and to improve the overall health of the community. Librarians should start or serve on a health literacy initiative in their organizations and provide the training and resources needed to deal with these issues. These activities will encourage healthcare decision makers to place librarians on program committees and involve them in the planning and implementation of health literacy initiatives. The end result will be that medical and consumer health librarians will be recognized as allies in the fight for improved health literacy.

THE BRONSON INITIATIVES

Bronson Methodist Hospital (BMH) is a 345-bed tertiary care facility in Kalamazoo, Michigan. As part of the Bronson Healthcare System, BMH is a Level 1 trauma facility and serves a nine-county area with a population of one million. The Healthcare System includes 26 physician practices, and five diagnostic centers. The Bronson Healthcare Group (2007) developed a Plan for Excellence. Their vision is, "Bronson will be a national leader in healthcare quality," and their mission is, "To provide excellent healthcare services." Included in the Plan are the Requirements for Excellence: Safe, Effective, Patient and Family Centered, Timely, Efficient, and Equitable Care.

The hospital's experience with providing patient information is not unique and reflects what happens in other institutions across the country. Information for patients is provided in writing so that it is consistent and portable. We want patients to take the information with them, read it more than once, and share it with their families or caregivers. Some of the information is purchased from commercial publishers, while other material is written by our clinical staff who speak the unique language of medicine. Therefore, consent forms, test or procedure instructions, and discharge instructions were written at or above the 12th grade reading level. Because 19 percent of the population of both the city and county of Kalamazoo read at the lowest literacy level (National Institute for Literacy, 1998), a considerable number of our clients (patients and families) would not have the literacy skills necessary to read these materials.

Bronson has a long history of providing community access to health information. In 1987, we opened a consumer health information center (HealthAnswers) in response to physicians' requests for a place to house lay material about diagnoses, tests, or surgery. The center included health information in print and video formats from national health associations, as well as popular books on health. As we worked to build this consumer health collection, it became clear that much of the published information was written at a higher reading level than was appropriate for our customers.

In 2003, the Vice President for Quality and Safety spearheaded Bronson's Health Literacy Task Force and asked the author to chair the committee. Other committee members were drawn from Education Services, Finance, Home Healthcare, Outpatient Diagnostics and one of the Bronson medical practices. Having administrative support has contributed to the viability and sustainability of the Task Force, whose goals include the following items:

- Bring the reading level of patient forms and patient education materials to the 6th grade reading level.
- Provide patients and their families with high-quality lay health information documents about specific diagnoses, consents, and health-related decisions.

- Train health professionals and nonclinical staff in the use of communication tools that support the individual health information needs of patients and families.
- Create awareness that low literacy can be a barrier to learning.

Initially, the Health Literacy Task Force reported to Bronson's Patient Safety Committee. In 2007, the reporting structure was changed. The Task Force now reports to the Continuum of Care Committee (n.d.) that focuses on "optimal care to our patients through revision of admission, plan of care and discharge processes." The Task Force formalized a process wherein all relevant staff and hospital committees review revised information forms, which are now written at the 6th grade level, before they are delivered to patients. Both the Risk Management and the Legal Affairs departments reviewed the revisions to make sure that "easy-to-read" does not take away from the intent of the document. In addition to reading level, forms are written in the active voice, using everyday language and short sentences. The easy-to-read format also includes more white space.

It is important to note that the Task Force was not an initial success. In fact, it faltered and nearly ended because we were not ready for the amount of preparation needed to help staff understand the reason for the move to easy-to-read patient information. Though we were invited to present information at meetings, we received few requests to evaluate or rewrite patient education material. We began to realize that the emphasis on an easy-to-read format was changing the culture of the organization. We lost most of our committee members within the first year because of our inactivity. It took several months before we received a request to revise discharge instructions from outpatient surgery. Things have really changed over the past few years, as more physicians and staff recognize the need to address health literacy and its inherent problems. Currently, we receive two or three requests a week to review and revise patient information material. The author and the Director of Education Services work with individual departments and the Bronson Forms Committee to create easy to read materials.

Because Bronson is patient and family centered, volunteers review all patient information and education forms. Their critiques have helped us focus on what the patient wants to know, not what we think the patient should want to know. Five to ten hospital volunteers review the forms for clarity and understanding. They look for easy-to-read, everyday language, large type font, substantial amounts of white space, and clear drawings or images. We ask the volunteers to rate the patient information using an assessment tool adapted from several assessment forms found on the Web. If the volunteers suggest a change, the form comes back to the Task Force for further revision. Once the volunteers agree to the revisions, the form is sent to the Forms Committee for approval and use in the hospital.

The process also includes an evaluation of forms every three years. Since 2003, the Task Force has reviewed and revised over 200 patient forms, including consent, patient education, and preadmission and discharge forms. The committee's initial plan called for revising a minimum of six patient information forms each year, beginning with the most frequently used forms, including Bronson's Surgical Procedure Consent Form, Consent for Inpatient or Outpatient Treatment, and the Release Assignment Form. (Examples of the Release Assignment Form in its original and revised states are included in Appendix 14-1 and Appendix 14-2.)

OTHER BRONSON HEALTH LITERACY INITIATIVES

Ready to Read

Bronson Methodist Hospital partnered with Kalamazoo Public Library and other community agencies in 1997 to create Ready to Read, an emergent literacy initiative that focuses on bringing books to children from birth to age five. The program is based on several national models, including the Reach Out and Read (ROR) model of pediatricians giving books to children at well child visits and talking with parents about the importance of reading to children at an early age. The primary goal of Ready to Read "is to assure that children in Kalamazoo County arrive at school, having been read to by parents, ready to read and learn" (Kars and Doud, 1999). The program includes:

- Volunteers reading to children at multiple community sites
- Pediatricians prescribing reading aloud to children and distributing books at well child visits
- Two local hospitals giving a book to each baby born at the hospital
- Librarians holding workshops for parents on ways to share books with young children

BMH is one of the founding members of this collaboration and took the lead by providing a book to each baby born at the hospital. The manager of the health sciences library at Bronson, author of this chapter, is cochair of the collaboration. In 2007, Ready to Read continues to be a successful community collaboration. Along with the 12 pediatric practices that give books to children at well child visits we have partnered with WIC (Women, Infants and Children), the Immunization Clinic at the Family Health Center, and Kalamazoo County Healthy Babies/Healthy Start to provide books for babies and information to parents about the importance of reading to children at an early age.

Translation Services

The Hispanic population of Kalamazoo mirrors the Hispanic population of most Michigan counties, approximately 3 percent (Michigan Population by

County, 2005). Because the Hispanic population in Bronson's nine-county service areas varies from 1.6–7.4 percent, we chose to translate the commonly used forms, such as the admission and registration forms, into Spanish. Bronson employees are required to use either certified Clinical Interpreters for Spanish or Sign Language or use Language Line over the phone interpreting when communicating with patients and families who speak a language other than English. Bronson contracts with certified Spanish and Sign Language interpreters as well as having employees who are certified interpreters available for emergency situations. When interpreters are not available, clinical staff has access to Language Line to support their communication with patients for whom English is a second language.

Educational Program

Another literacy-related initiative is SMART (Semester of Math and Reading Taught at Bronson). In 2006, Bronson Education Services, the Bronson Health Foundation, and the Kalamazoo Public School system worked together to create a free adult education class for Bronson employees. Employees may be referred to this program by their supervisors or they can self-refer. Adult education teachers from Kalamazoo Public Schools teach classes two days a week at Bronson.

Health Professionals

Patients, their families, and employees are not the only ones receiving health literacy attention. BMH has also focused on training health professionals and support staff in the use of communication tools. BMH purchased copies of the American Medical Association (2003) video *Helping Your Patients to Understand* and made them available for staff meetings in hospital departments and physician practices. Beginning in 2004, this video became part of the hospital-wide orientation, as well as specific department orientations.

In addition to the efforts described above, the Health Science Library and the nurses at BMH have started literacy projects, described in the following sections.

THE HEALTH SCIENCES LIBRARY INITIATIVE

In 2003, the Health Sciences Library collaborated with Bronson's Information Technology department on a project to provide wireless laptops to four patient units. This project had two goals:

1. Provide a means for patients to stay in contact with family, friends, school, and work during their stay as inpatients.
2. Provide access to accurate, current, and easy to read and understand health information.

Each of the four units—Pediatrics, Antepartum, General Surgical Unit, and General Medical Unit—received four wireless laptops that were attached to over-bed tables. Patients could request a laptop from their nurse for the duration of their hospital stay. Each laptop was delivered with a contract of responsibility, a list of appropriate health Web sites, and a survey for the patient or their family to complete about their experience with the computer. Patient care staff on each unit were shown MedlinePlus (www.medlineplus.gov), including the Interactive Tutorials and list of Easy to Read topics and were asked to show these resources to patients who requested a laptop computer. Completed surveys, which were sent to the health sciences library, showed that having access to a laptop made a difference in the patient's stay. Some examples of their comments follow:

- Made the time go faster.
- Gave patients something to occupy the time.
- Allowed them to stay in contact with family, friends, work or school.
- Gave them access to health information so they could better understand their illness and treatment.

Though initially considered a "patient satisfier," the project soon became a "dis-satisfier" for those patients who requested a laptop computer and were told they were all in use. To rectify the situation, four additional laptop computers were purchased for the library and delivered to patients on request. In 2007, 30 additional laptops have been purchased and are available to patients who request them. Evaluation of this service is ongoing.

THE NURSING INITIATIVE

Education Services introduced the "teach-back" method as part of the clinical assignment for all new nursing staff at Bronson in July 2007. "Teach-back is a method to ensure understanding of information being communicated, often used between a caregiver and a patient, by asking the receiver of the information to 'teach back' what was said" (Joint Commission, 2007: 53). According to a National Quality Forum (2005: 14) publication, the teach-back method has been widely recommended by experts "as an effective mechanism for communicating with patients with low literacy because it increases patient retention, gives providers a gauge of how well patients understand information, and actively involves patients in the discussion."

At BMH, nursing preceptors work on a one-to-one basis with new nursing staff to train them and ensure their competency. The preceptor teaches the competency and provides written information to support the training and reason behind it. Upon completion of the training, the preceptor signs off that the new hire is competent to use the teach-back method.

LESSONS LEARNED

Experience on the Health Literacy Task Force at Bronson Methodist Hospital has taught the author some valuable lessons that may help other librarians. First and foremost, librarians who are starting (or involved with) a health literacy committee at their hospitals should make sure that they have the support of the top administrators who can help to maintain the momentum and "put pressure" on the various department heads to ensure that all patient materials are written at the 6th grade level. Because the health literacy initiative came from the top down (i.e., BMH's Vice President for Quality and Safety), the Health Literacy Task Force has been able to sustain its original concept, meet the original goals, and add new goals, such as the teach-back procedure.

At BMH, we faltered and lost many members of the Task Force because of inactivity early in our development. In hindsight more communication would have served us better. Keeping Task Force members aware of progress by e-mail or phone would have taken a minimum amount of time but would have kept their interest in our project. Librarians can also display information about the health literacy project in the library or create a column in the hospital newsletter dedicated to this topic.

Furthermore, a health literacy task force should include at least one person from each department in the hospital that provides written patient materials. The more diverse the membership, the more information and education about health literacy will spread throughout the hospital. The increased awareness among the staff will ensure not only that all patient materials will be submitted to the task force and rewritten at the 6th grade level, but also that the task force will be able to continue, gain respect, and meet it goals.

This chapter demonstrates that librarians, using their unique skills of literature evaluation and history of providing information to all levels of readers, can play an active role in helping their organizations develop and institute a health literacy plan.

REFERENCES

American Medical Association. 2003. *Help Your Patients Understand.* Chicago: Author. Videocassette.

Beales, Donna L. 2005. "Health Literacy: The Medical Librarian's Role. *Journal of Hospital Librarianship* 5, no.3: 17–27.

Bronson Healthcare Group. 2007. Unpublished internal communication.

Burnham, Erica, and Eileen Beany Peterson. 2005. "Health Information Literacy: A Library Case Study." *Library Trends* 53, no.3 (Winter): 422–433.

Continuum of Care Committee. n.d. Unpublished internal communication.

Dutcher, Gale A. 2005. "Community-Based Organizations' Perspective on Health Information Outreach: A Panel Discussion." *Journal of the Medical Library Association* 93, no.4, Suppl. (October): S35–S42.

Gillaspy, Mary L. 2005. "Factors Affecting the Provision of Consumer Health Information in Public Libraries: The Last Five Years." *Library Trends* 53, no.3 (Winter): 480–495.

Joint Commission. 2007. *"What Did the Doctor Say?": Improving Health Literacy to Protect Patient Safety.* Oakbrook, IL: Author.

Kars, Marge, and Mary Doud. 1999. "Ready to Read: A Collaborative, Community-wide Emergent Literacy Program." *The Reference Librarian* 67/68: 85–97.

Medical Library Association. 2005. Communication Health Information Literacy. (July 2007) Available: www.mlanet.org/pdf.healthlit/heal_comm._plan.pdf

Michigan Population by County. 2005. (July 2007) Available: www.mdch.state.mi.us/pha/osr/CHI/POP/HPO5CO1.htm

National Institute for Literacy. 1998. *The State of Literacy in America.* Washington, DC: Author.

National Quality Form. 2005. *Implementing a National Voluntary Consensus Standard for Informed Consent: A User's Guide for Healthcare Professionals.* Washington, DC: Author.

Parker, Ruth, and Gary L. Kreps. 2005. "Library Outreach: Overcoming Health Literacy Challenges." *Journal of the Medical Library Association* 93, no.4, Suppl. (October): S81–S85.

Sostack, Maura. 2007. "The Hidden Shame of Adults with Low Health Literacy Issues." *MLA News* no.392 (January): 1, 12.

Appendix 14-1. Original Version of the Bronson Hospital Release Assignment Form

Side 1

CONSENT TO TREATMENT: I, the named patient, request admission to Bronson or its Outpatient Department for the purpose of receiving hospital, medical and/or emergency treatment and do hereby voluntarily consent to:

(i) routine diagnostic procedures deemed necessary (for example, but not limited to, laboratory examinations, x-ray examinations administration of drugs, and administration of intravenous fluids);

(ii) Hospital care by Hospital as is deemed necessary;

(iii) The Hospital may post, verbally announce and/or identify me by name while I am using Bronson Hospital Services
☐ Yes ☐ No

(iv) such emergency care as prescribed by the attending physician(s), his/her assistants or designees, including such Hospital personnel as he/she may deem necessary; and

(v) release of entire medical record from this Emergency Room visit to Dr. _____ . This includes information regarding treatment of drug and or alcohol dependency or abuse, mental health treatment or testing and treatment of HIV or related diseases.

(vi) to such medical treatment, therapy and therapeutics by Dr. _____ , his/her assistant(s) or designees(s) as is deemed necessary.

I am aware that the practice of medicine and surgery is not an exact science. I acknowledge that no guarantees or promises have been made to me as to the results of the medical care or treatment which I hereby authorize.

I have been given information regarding my rights and responsibilities while I receive services at Bronson Hospital.

I recognize that Bronson is not liable for any act or omission in following the instructions of my above designated physician, his/her assistant(s) or designee(s) and that all physician's assistants and other specialized personnel furnishing services to me, including radiologists, pathologists, anesthesiologist, and any others who are not actual employees of Bronson, are independent contractors and are not agents of Bronson and that Bronson has no responsibility to me for their acts of omissions.

I acknowledge that treatment and medical records may be reviewed by approved students, faculty and staff for teaching, study and research purposes. Information identifying patients will not be published without prior patient consent.

I authorize the obtaining of specimens of body fluids, tissues or products for the purpose of tests, procedures and medical research as deemed appropriate by my physician, and the appropriate disposition of same.

I understand an HIV (AIDS virus) test or other blood tests may be performed upon me without my written consent after a health care worker or anyone who transported me or otherwise assisted in my care sustains a skin cut, mucous membrane or open wound exposure to my blood or other body fluids.

I certify that I have read both sides of this document or have had it read to me, received a copy hereof, and am the patient, or am duly authorized by the patient as patient's agent to execute the above and accept its terms. I have had the opportunity to ask any questions that I may have, and my questions have been answered to my satisfaction.

Date of Signing _____   Patient Signature _____

Witness _____   Parent or Guardian Signature _____

Relationship Signature _____

RELEASE ASSIGNMENT FORM
(SEE REVERSE SIDE)

FORM 70019 (5/01)   White • Medical Records 760   Yellow • Patient

Appendix 14-1.   Original Version of the Bronson Hospital Release Assignment Form *(Continued)*

Side 2

INPATIENT /OUTPATIENT /EMERGENCY REGISTRATION
RELEASE/ASSIGNMENT FORM

1. RELEASE OF MEDICAL INFORMATION: THE HOSPITAL MAY DISCLOSE ALL OR ANY PART OF THE PATIENT'S MEDICAL RECORD TO ANY AGENCY WHICH IS OR MAY BE LIABLE UNDER CONTRACT FOR ALL OR PART OF THE HOSPITAL BILL, (including, but not limited to, hospital or medical service companies, insurance companies, physician billing services, health care service plans, worker's compensation carriers, welfare funds AND the patient's employer) or to physicians, agencies, companies or facilities involved with continuity of care.

2. MEDICARE PATIENTS RELEASE OF INFORMATION: I certify that the information given by me in applying for payment under Title XVIII of the Social Security Act is correct. I authorize any holder of medical or other information about me to release to the Social Security Administration or its intermediaries or carriers any information needed for this or a related Medicare claim. I request that payment of authorized Medicare benefits be made either to me or on my behalf for any services furnished me by or in Bronson or its outpatient department, including those physician services billed by Bronson.

3. I understand that BILLING OF INSURANCE IS A SERVICE ONLY AND IS NOT A GUARANTEE OF PAYMENT. If the insurance does not pay within 30 days of billing, I understand that I AM FINANCIALLY RESPONSIBLE FOR THE FULL AMOUNT OF THE BILL. Although Bronson Hospital may participate with your health insurance, you may also receive a bill from the Radiologist, Pathologist, Anesthesiologist or Emergency Room Physician. If you are receiving services from these physicians, please contact their office to inquire about insurance participation.

4. I hereby assign payment directly to Bronson of any medical benefits payable to me under the conditions of my policy for services given on or starting this date at a rate not to exceed Bronson's regular charges, and/or those amounts permitted by contract with the patient's insurance or health care plan. I understand that I am financially responsible to Bronson for charges not covered by this agreement. This assignment covers both basic and major medical benefits.

    ANNUAL AUTHORIZATION: I request that payments of authorized insurance benefits be paid to Bronson for all services which are a benefit of policies identified to Bronson for this purpose. This authorization shall remain in effect for one year from this date unless revoked in writing by the insured.

5. RELEASE: Bronson takes all possible precautions to safeguard your property, but disclaims any responsibility for valuables not deposited for safekeeping at the time of admission or during your medical treatment or stay at Bronson. I hereby release Bronson of all responsibility for valuables not deposited for safekeeping or for articles lost or damaged which are kept in my possession during my medical treatment or hospital stay.

(SEE REVERSE SIDE)

19-B(R-1-00)

Appendix 14-2. Revised Version of the Bronson Hospital Release Assignment Form

Side 1

⊞**BRONSON**

Name:_____Date of Birth:_____

Affix Patient Label

I _____ request admission to
Bronson Methodist Hospital, Bronson Vicksburg or Bronson Outpatient Testing for procedures
or treatments including:

Laboratory tests, x-rays, drugs, and IV fluids.

Hospital care by the hospital as necessary.

I agree to more testing and treatment if it is needed. My doctor may ask other healthcare staff
to help with treatment.

I agree to all these procedures or treatments.

Hospital staff has my permission to post or call my name unless I check the "No" box.
          ☐   No

I want my own doctor _____or others involved in my care to have a
copy of the medical record from this visit. This includes information regarding treatment of:
- drug and or alcohol dependency or abuse
- mental illness
- testing and treatment of HIV or related diseases.

I know that medicine is not an exact science. No guarantees or assurances have been made to
me about the results of the procedure or treatment.

I have been given information regarding my rights and responsibilities while I receive services
at Bronson Hospital.

Some of the physicians and their employees providing services to me, including Radiologists,
Pathologists, Anesthesiologists, and Emergency Room doctors are independent contractors.
Bronson is not responsible for their actions.

I know that approved students, faculty and staff may look at my treatment and medical records
for teaching or research. Information identifying me will not be published without my consent.

I agree that tissues, organs or body fluids taken from my body may be tested or kept for the
purpose of research or teaching. I agree the Hospital may discard these in the proper way.

I know an HIV (AIDS virus) test or other blood tests may be done without my written consent
after someone who has assisted in my care is exposed to my blood or other body fluids. An
example would be a skin cut.

9003175-E (6/07) Equivalent to 9003078-S   **Registration Release Form**   Side 1 of 2
OPTIO WH20-TU-5HT   *Adult and Peds Use*

Appendix 14-2. Revised Version of the Bronson Hospital Release Assignment Form *(Continued)*

Side 2

Affix Patient Label

Bronson Methodist Hospital or Bronson Vicksburg Hospital may share all or part of my medical record with anyone responsible for all or part of my hospital bill.

My insurance can pay "Hospital" directly for the procedures or treatment covered by insurance. "Hospital" can act in my behalf to pursue payment of claims under my health plan. I agree to work with "Hospital" in its attempt to receive payment if my health plan refuses all or part of the payment. I am responsible for charges not covered by my insurance. This authorization will be in effect unless changed in writing by me.

Release of information for Medicare: The information I gave the hospital is correct.
The hospital may release my medical information to anyone responsible for paying this or a related Medicare claim.

Payment of Medicare benefits should be made to Bronson or me for any services. I know that I am responsible for the full amount of the bill if the insurance company does not pay within 30 days. I may also receive a bill from the Radiologist, Pathologist, Anesthesiologist or Emergency Room Physician. If I received services from these physicians, I will contact their office and ask about insurance participation.

Bronson is very careful to safeguard my property. I know I can deposit any valuables I have in the safe when I am admitted. Bronson is not responsible for valuables not deposited for safekeeping.

By signing this form, I agree:
I have read this form or had it explained to me.
I fully understand what it says.
I have been given time to ask questions and I have had my questions answered.

_____
Date of Signing

_____
Patient Signature

_____
Witness

_____
Parent or Guardian Signature

_____
Relationship Signature

9003175-E (6/07) Equivalent to 9003078-S
OPTIO WH20-TU-5HT

Side 2 of 2

Part IV

The Future:
Ways to Initiate
and Become Involved
with Health Literacy
Programs

Chapter 15

Intervention Programs for Health Literacy

Cleo Pappas

Health literacy interventions presuppose knowledge of the health literacy issue. One working definition of health literacy is "the ability to read and understand health information and to make decisions based on that information" (National Institute on Deafness and Other Communication Disorders, 2003: para. 2). Another definition of health literacy is the "degree to which individuals have the capacity to obtain, process, and understand basic health information and services needed to make appropriate health decisions" (Selden et al., 2000: para. 7). Successful interventions seek to empower the individual by providing access to the tools he or she requires, whether the intervention is information in a native language, sign language, attention to cultural requirements, or a readability level that will allow self-management.

This chapter defines interventions, discusses a few representative ones, and directs the reader to tools that assist in the creation of health literacy interventions. It addresses literacy interventions from a variety of perspectives, exploring the roles of librarians, pharmacists, other healthcare professionals, the Joint Commission on Accreditation of Healthcare Organizations (JCAHO), and the Institutional Review Boards (IRBs) of universities and hospitals. It will examine the assessment of the low health literacy patient, consequences of low health literacy, and identification of local groups that can provide help.

WHAT IS AN INTERVENTION?

An intervention is an action that changes the status quo. The *Oxford English Dictionary* (1989) defines an intervention as the "action of intervening, 'stepping in,' or interfering in any affair, so as to affect its course or issue." Health literacy interventions aim to correct the misinformation or lack of information that are the result of poor reading or comprehension skills. They literally "come between" the health consumer and the provider to assist the consumer and may take many forms. For example, the Food and Drug Administration, MedlinePlus, and other consumer health products provide easy-to-read publications in a variety of languages. Other interventions target health practitioners in an effort to provide them with an understanding of health literacy issues. Busy practitioners often are not aware of signals from their patients that their instructions or explanations are not understood. The Harvard School of Public Health Health Literacy Studies (www.hsph.Harvard.edu/healthliteracy/) offers curricula for teaching low-literacy patients as well as summary reports on literacy research. Businesses, too, employ health literacy interventions. Language Line Services (www.languageline.com) is a global company that offers translation and interpreter services for 150 languages providing invaluable assistance to pharmacists, banks, insurance agencies, and the transportation industry.

Health literacy is a broader concept than consumer health education. In addition to clarifying medical information, health literacy interventions seek to match the delivery mode of the information to the patient who is receiving it. Such interventions take into account patients' reading levels, cultures, traditions, and any other potential barriers to their ability to understand and apply information to their unique situations. It can be argued that the challenges inherent in addressing health literacy issues belong to everyone because not addressing them impacts all people in terms of economics and environment. A society that cannot pay its medical bills serves no one, and the consequences spill over the boundaries of class and geography.

In a report titled "Literacy and Health Outcomes," Berkman et al. (2004) performed a literature search to examine interventions created to ameliorate the effects of health literacy on health outcomes. The authors noted that most studies on health literacy interventions have been published within the past ten years. Furthermore, the outcome most often measured was increased knowledge rather than behavioral changes, which have greater impact on health outcome than does increased information, a deficiency that the investigators acknowledged.

POOR HEALTH LITERACY

Poor health literacy may stem from age, cultural issues, and functional literacy. The Nebraska Department of Education (1999) defines functional literacy as "a level of reading and writing sufficient for everyday life but not for completely autonomous activity" (Glossary General F-J). A person whose native language is not English may function quite well without reading English-language materials until a health problem occurs. In a 1992 survey of adult literacy in the United States, two-thirds of the participants, close to ten thousand adults, functioned at the lowest levels of literacy, a level that would prevent them from reading directions on a bottle of medicine (Foulk, Carroll, and Wood, 2001).

DO READING LEVELS CORRESPOND TO CONSUMER NEEDS?

Studies seem to suggest that the readability levels of some health materials diverge significantly from the reading levels of the consumers who need them. The results of a reading ability study by Jackson et al. (1991) found that 528 adults whose reading levels were assessed read 4.6 grade levels below their last grade completed in school. Their average reading level was that of a fifth-grader. Yet, an examination of the reading level of typical health information materials showed them to require anywhere from an 11th to a 14th (college sophomore) grade reading comprehension level (Davis et al., 1990). Hospital consent forms examined in the same study presupposed a college reading level. A more recent study revealed a striking mismatch between the reading ability of stroke patients and their caregivers and the level of written materials provided them (Hoffman and McKenna, 2006). The average level of the materials required approximately an 11th grade reading ability while the patients' average Rapid Estimate of Adult Literacy in Medicine (REALM) scores approached a 7th to 8th grade level (289). Finally, Hoffman and McKenna noted that there was a disparity between reading ability and completed years of education reported.

Schillinger et al. (2003) tracked how many times primary care physicians measured diabetic patients' understanding and recall of their outpatient communications in which new concepts were introduced. The authors attributed patients' improved glycemic control to the doctors' inclination to ask them simply to restate the instructions they had been given. Schillinger et al. also theorized that physicians avoid assessing patients' recall and comprehension, fearing the time impact. "Primary care physicians caring for patients with low functional health literacy and diabetes mellitus assessed patients' recall and comprehension in only 1 of 5 visits and for fewer than 1 of 8 new concepts" (87). Interestingly, exchanges with patients that included such feedback did not take more time than those that did not.

What can professional healthcare providers do to assist in what has become a problem of major proportions? The first step is to become aware of the issue. Health professionals should not make assumptions about patients' ability to understand what they are told or given to read. Second, health professionals should be aware that interventions occur on a community as well as an individual level and that health literacy interventions may take a variety of forms. Large, global initiatives involve collaboration between institutions and professionals.

Librarians can find, make available, and promote materials that are easy to read, graphical in nature, or aural. Both librarians and clinicians can evaluate existing materials with readability assessments and rewrite them. Librarians can determine for physicians what local groups and programs are available for patient referral or locate resources for their individual institution.

It is often difficult to assess adults' functional literacy levels because it is common for them to have developed coping skills that mask their true abilities (Blackwell, 2005). It is important for the healthcare professional to be aware of such coping or masking mechanisms. Foulk, Carroll, and Wood (2001) suggest a few signs or "giveaways." They suggest clinicians note if a patient asks for assistance in filling out forms or request calls rather than mailed information. They say it is important to notice if a patient brings a friend who assumes responsibility for filling out forms. They even suggest watching the patient's eyes to see if they move as the patient reads. Additional recommendations include handing the patient material to read upside down, demonstrating, wherever possible, and never assuming that patients know how to read.

CONSEQUENCES OF POOR HEALTH LITERACY

What is the relationship between health literacy and health? What are the consequences of poor health literacy? The burden and consequences of low-literacy levels and the inability to understand health information sufficiently to make good judgments regarding personal healthcare rest not only with the individual but also with the community. The National Academy on an Aging Society (n.d.) estimated that costs attributed to low health literacy levels may well reach $73 billion annually. Individuals with low literacy tend to avoid preventive care and are less likely to comply with treatment recommendations, thereby initiating a downward spiral in their health. They are hospitalized more frequently with longer length of stays, use emergency departments more frequently, and do not comprehend the healthcare maintenance needs of chronic diseases (Nielsen-Bohlman, Panzer, and Kindig, 2004).

THE ROLE OF JCAHO

The Joint Commission on Accreditation of Healthcare Organizations plays a significant role in advocacy for health literacy. In the Joint Commission's 2005 *Comprehensive Accreditation Manual for Hospitals—Update 3*, Section 1 within "Patient-Focused Functions" is titled "Ethics, Rights, and Responsibilities." The first standard listed (RI.1) states, "The hospital follows ethical behavior in its care, treatment, and services and business practices" (RI-2). Standard RI2.1 requires medical staff to obtain informed consent, and RI.2.180 requires the hospital to "protect and respect research subjects' rights" (RI-2).

JCAHO's (2002–2003) *Comprehensive Accreditation Manual for Ambulatory Care* stipulates requirements that fall even more clearly within the scope of health literacy interventions. The section "Education of Patients and Family" (Standard RI.2.100) states, "The organization respects the patient's right to and need for effective communication" (RI-12). Performance elements of that standard include "[w]ritten information provided is appropriate to the age, understanding, and, as appropriate to the population served, the language of the patient" (RI-12).

INSTITUTIONAL REVIEW BOARDS (IRBs) AND INFORMED CONSENT

Informed consent for medical procedures, clinical trials, or any study involving human participants presents a unique perspective on health literacy. IRBs are responsible for the safety of patients and/or research participants. The Declaration of Helsinki established, in 1989, the international standard for biomedical research involving human subjects:

> Each experimental procedure involving human subjects should be clearly formulated in an experimental protocol which should be transmitted for consideration, comment and guidance to a specially appointed committee independent of the investigator and sponsor.... In the United States, federal law assigns to the committee the name institutional review board, and the authority and responsibility for approving or disapproving proposals to conduct research involving human subjects. (World Medical Association, 1989)

The mission of IRBs is "to ensure that the research is ethically acceptable and that the welfare and rights of research participants are protected" (Hulley et al., 2001: 216) One of the questions that IRB committees ask is whether informed consent has been obtained and documented (Shamoo and Resnick, 2003). There have been efforts to create informed consent forms at a readability level accessible to more people.

In May 2003, the National Quality Forum published a document entitled *Safe Practices for Better Healthcare.* Safe Practice 10 deals specifically with the problems communication barriers pose to informed consent (Wu et al., 2005). Safe Practice 10 states, "Ask each patient or legal surrogate to recount what he or she has been told during the informed consent discussion" (viii). It further specifies that informed consent forms should be written in the primary language of the patient and should use simple sentences. Provider and patient should discuss the nature and the scope of the procedure. An interpreter or reader should be provided for non-English-speaking patients, low vision or deaf patients, and low-literacy patients. An interpreter or reader must be capable of explaining high-risk procedures in depth. However, Safe Practice 10 is a voluntary consensus standard.

In their article on patients' understanding of clinical trials, Stead et al. (2005) bring several troubling issues to light. For example, they found that patients have difficulty comprehending concepts such as the random allocation process, the use of placebo, and double blinding and also believe—in spite of being given information to the contrary—that their doctors would, under no circumstances, give them anything that was not of therapeutic value. In patients' minds, the only reason to participate in a clinical trial was to receive treatment better than that to which they currently had access. Stead et al. also found that patients questioned the morality of allocating participants to a placebo group, assuming that such assignment would interrupt current treatment protocols and put them at risk, even though patient education materials explicitly stated this would not happen. Participants also interpreted the use of a computer for randomized allocation as disturbing and thought that the randomization process should be handled by someone who had the individual patient's best interests in mind during the assignment process. The notion that their personal physician might be complicit in what they saw as an impersonal, blinded assignment process violated their standards of the doctor-patient relationship in which the individual patient's good is the guiding principle. The concept of double blinding further reinforced to them the idea that their own care might be compromised. Overall, patients' confidence in the clinical trials process rested on the notion that either they or their physician could choose to which group they were assigned, an element of choice that does not exist in the clinical trials process.

Stead et al. offer several interventions that are relevant not only to the clinical trial process but may also be generalized to health information literacy. In addition to presenting clearly written materials that explain what is going to happen, they suggest it is important to explain why things will happen. What purposes do double-blinding, random allocation, and a placebo serve? Stead et al. believe that patient distress regarding randomization should be addressed and that patients should be reassured that their current care regimen will not be put at risk. Finally, the authors call for a revision of national guidelines, not only to develop an explanation of research methods and the logic behind them, but also to prepare patients to accept that a double-blind procedure prevents even their own physician from knowing which group (control or experimental) the patient is in.

How to Widen Informed Consent

The use of computers in the informed consent process was found to be helpful by patients in a study examining the needs of trial participants with potential cognitive impairment (Jimison et al., 1998) Researchers constructed an interactive tool that tested several methods including text, video, bulleted slides, pop-up definitions, graphics, icons, and audio for obtaining informed consent. Participants were comfortable with the idea of replacing a paper document with such an approach and felt it gave them more control by allowing them to move at their own speed, thereby lessening personal stress and enhancing their understanding. It was noted that such a method might save physician time as well as provide a consistent level of quality to the informed consent process. IRB members' legal obligation to keep a paper version of the consent document led to the suggestion that such a tool may be used to prepare for and enhance the physician-patient consultation.

A systematic review of informed consent published in *JAMA* concluded that the best way to help clinical trial participants understand the process in which they have enlisted is to offer one-on-one dialogue (Flory and Emanuel, 2004:1599). The authors examined trials that compared standard informed consent process with informed consent designed to enhance participants' understanding, whether using "multimedia, an enhanced form, extended discussion, test/feedback, and miscellaneous." They noted that multimedia tools may enhance retention of information, which is valuable in and of itself, but that this concept needs further examination and testing to be confirmed. In addition, Flory and Emanuel felt that the unique contribution of multimedia might be to "standardize disclosure" for trial participants. Removing some standardized content from an enhanced form did help patients, but tests of enhanced forms were skewed because the form is the only source of information for the participants. Their conclusion was that face-to-face assistance with a "qualified person" and the standard consent process is "the most reliable approach to improving understanding, based on currently available evidence."

Participation of African Americans in Clinical Trials

Corbie-Smith et al. (1999) found that low participation of African Americans in clinical trials is a matter for concern. In citing reasons for refraining from participating, focus group respondents in their study mentioned knowing of individuals participating in clinical trials for payment, not wishing to be a guinea pig, mistrust of physicians, lack of confidence that fellow African Americans would benefit due to discrimination, and fear of infection. Focus group respondents' understanding of informed consent was that its purpose was to protect physicians and hospitals from litigation. In addition, respondents expressed the view that doctors would encourage and promote participation in a study with promises they "probably would not keep" (541). Finally, focus group respondents made a distinction between "knowing" (being told about a process) and "understanding" how that process worked and what the implications of the process were for individual patients (541).

As suggestions for increasing African Americans' participation in the clinical trial process, participants listed several ideas:

- Improved information
- Adequate time to make decisions
- The need to discuss the issue with family and friends
- Performing their own research
- A video presentation
- Allowing participants access to physicians throughout the study
- Including clinical trial methodology, its purposes and importance, in elementary and secondary school education (Corbie-Smith et al, 1999: 541–542)

Clearly, these requests fall within the realm of health literacy and reveal yet another reason to promote it—to give individuals the tools whereby they may be equipped to participate in clinical trials from an informed state.

In a 2004, Practice Alert, Henley and Peters caution physicians that disparity of care is not accounted for entirely by population or system factors. Some groups, such as African Americans, are more prone to inequity in healthcare due to environmental or socioeconomic influences. However, research reveals that some disparities represent opportunities for relatively easy resolution. Henley and Peters first suggest that doctors militate for their patients through political means, either by joining organizations or by participating actively in political agendas that would remediate socioeconomic inequities and improve access to healthcare. The following list summarizes a few of their practical guidelines for ensuring that an individual practice adheres to equitable treatment patterns for all its patients:

- Consider the health literacy level of your patients when planning care and treatment, when explaining medical recommendations, and when handing out written material.
- Ensure that front desk staff is sensitive to patient backgrounds and cultures.
- Provide culturally sensitive patient education materials.
- Keep a list with the names and numbers of community health resources.
- Develop a plan for translation services. (195)

ROLE OF LIBRARIANS

Hammond (2004) has suggested that hospital librarians take the initiative to enlighten their communities regarding local health literacy. She suggested hospital librarians "consider producing a report about literacy" in the community they serve using resources such as the "National Institute for Literacy (www.nifl.gov), state departments of education, local literacy organizations, and standardized test scores from public schools" (10). (See Appendix 15-1 for a list of health literacy resources for librarians.) She proposed purchasing health literacy videos for viewing by relevant hospital committees and working with education departments to integrate health literacy issues into staff training programs. She also pointed out that librarians who know how to assess reading levels can assist their institutions by creating forms and education materials that lie within the skill range of low literacy readers.

Librarians from the Library of the Health Sciences at the University of Illinois at Chicago have spearheaded several collaborative initiatives applying university resources to area community sites. In her analysis of these endeavors, principal investigator Carol Scherrer (2006) offered tips that are applicable to a host of collaborative activities. She stressed that a needs assessment must include what the constituents perceive as their needs. In other words, they should be asked what they need to know. Healthcare professionals, including medical librarians, must be prepared for the fact that community leaders have different perceptions of what is necessary or desirable information and service. In addition, their timetables tend to be different. Training needs to be available when community groups meet which is not necessarily during the workday of the library.

Another example of librarians collaborating with several agencies to effect an improvement in healthcare literacy is the Hmong Health Information Promotion and the Hmong Health Education Net, both funded by the National Library of Medicine (NLM) Specialized Information Services Division (Allen, Matthew, and Boland, 2004). The Hmong are Laotian refugees. The Hmong Health Information Promotion and the Hmong Health Education Net, which address the needs of a special population as a collaborative effort with the Northern Wisconsin Area Health Education Center (NAHEC), worked with the NLM to research a wave of immigrants whose health needs were blocked by a lack of cultural and social support systems. The authors stated, "We need to walk in their shoes before rushing into solutions based on our personal worldview of libraries and the World Wide Web as free sources of knowledge on a wide variety of topics, including health and disease" (301). When considering low health literacy issues, cultural sensitivities must be taken into consideration in addition to linguistic issues.

The authors made a series of valuable suggestions for librarians seeking to improve health information access. Identify potential partners in the endeavors. "Successful networking extends beyond local organizations" (301). They suggested that networking with other organizations serving the target population is a good way to find opportunities for collaboration while at the same time assessing what the real needs of that population are. They remind readers that when working with a cultural group other than their own, flexibility is vital both to the success of the endeavor and to its continuation. "By working with populations instead of doing for them, the products—health education programs and information resources—will be more valuable for these groups" (303). The authors' work with the Hmong population revealed the Hmong's desire for "individualized, face-to-face health education" (307).

It is important to consider technological resources. For example, audio materials may be helpful but not if CD or DVD players are not available. The people in this study just did not have CD or DVD players. The authors also found picture stories very helpful. In addition to obstacles caused by the high-tech nature of U. S. society, the researchers found that immigrant populations do not arrive with skills that help them cope with our healthcare system. In addition to language and cultural barriers, the authors discovered a host of factors influencing their target population. Hmong immigrants came from developing countries vulnerable to many diseases. Some had lost friends and family to political strife in their homeland. Often victims of rape and torture, they had fled their homeland and traveled under horrific circumstances. Yet, their culture's tradition was to deal with mental health issues, including post-traumatic stress disorder, within the family unit by using ritual healers.

Allen, Matthew, and Boland (2004) offer several suggestions for uncovering collaborative partners. They suggest Area Health Education Centers or AHECs as a good start. There is an online resource on AHECs at www.nationalahec.org. They also propose as partners health departments, hospitals, clinics, managed care programs, and local branches of organizations, public and hospital libraries, and academic institutions. They have found that tacking health initiatives onto other events is a good way to reach people. Health fairs, health exhibits, and health education programs can occur in tandem with other community events. They cite as an example, 300 people attending an event held during a soccer tournament also received health information. Its manager credits a location close to the food stands and morning hours with the success.

ROLE OF PHARMACISTS

Cuellar and Fitzsimmons (2003) stressed the importance of patient education as the pharmacist's responsibility. They called for pharmacists to understand the cultures they serve and note that simply translating information is usually not delivering good healthcare. Finally, they emphasize the need for pharmacists to examine both print and verbal interactions and to reassess their methods of evaluating patient care.

Andrus and Roth (2002) examined the consequences of poor health literacy and its implications for pharmacists. In their review, they concluded that the first step in addressing the problem is acknowledging that it exists and they included a series of recommendations to improve patient education materials. The interventions they compiled serve as a foundation for anyone interested in beginning a health literacy intervention at any level of complexity. The quality of their recommendations serves both as a useful primer and as an introduction to health literacy interventions. A few of their proposals follow:

- Personalize the message.
- Reinforce and repeat information often.

- Use simple words with one or two syllables.
- Avoid large amounts of background information. (294)

A study by Svarstad, Bultman, and Mount (2004) demonstrated that state regulations, the age of the pharmacist, and the activity level of the pharmacy impacted whether assistance was offered as well as the quality and the amount of assistance. Their observational, cross-sectional study examined 306 community pharmacies in eight states.

The American Pharmacists Association has conducted a review of adherence interventions, which include adherence aids, refill or follow-up reminders, regimen simplification, written and oral education, and comprehensive management (Krueger, Felkey, and Berger, 2003). Their findings indicated that adherence aids tend to be product oriented rather than patient oriented. One of their conclusions is a need for leadership by the American Pharmacists Association in establishing a national adherence intervention initiative.

Bower and Taylor (2003) addressed the issue of patient compliance with pharmaceutical instructions. The authors set out to examine ways that information content can be modified to enhance patient compliance. Their study was limited to patients' intent to comply with instructions delivered in a drug's label information insert. They measured intent to comply, not actual compliance, and justified their approach by asserting that intent to comply is "not only an antecedent of actual behavior, but also a strong predictor of that behavior" (146). Participants included 260 upper-level university students. Bower and Taylor found that patient intention to comply can be influenced by several factors, including negative frame and language manipulation. Language manipulation refers to using plain language rather than medical jargon. A "negative frame" means that consequences of noncompliance are included in the drug instructions. Indeed, this is a concept that has implications for all consumer health publications. In addition to providing instructions in the consumer's native language and at his or her level of literacy, tell the patient what will happen if he or she is noncompliant. "Typically, it is up to the product user to imagine what result may stem from noncompliance and how that result may occur" (146). The authors' conclusion is that to avoid instructions that are too long, only that noncompliance that represents extreme danger should be incorporated. "Therefore, perhaps, the consequences of noncompliance should be included in those cases where particularly dangerous consequences may result if the instructions are ignored" (154).

READABILITY

Assessing readability and rewriting materials are not the only way to ensure patient understanding and adherence. The incorporation of pictograms or pictographs is another initiative that research is finding to be successful. Pictographs are "pictures that represent ideas" (Houts et al., 1998: 84). The authors tested the following hypothesis: "When information about managing cancer symptoms at home is presented orally with pictographs and the same pictographs are present during recall, memory will be greater than when the same information is presented orally without pictographs. We are also interested in the percent of the information recalled correctly—since, for the technique to be useful clinically, most, if not all, must be remembered accurately" (85). Their initial research suggested that pictographs can enhance short term recall. Their study had some limitations, however. It was small (21 subjects) and the subjects were college students, whose reading abilities may be assumed to be above average. Yet, the significance of their results merit consideration. The mean recall with pictographs was 85 percent, but the mean recall without pictographs was 14 percent. The authors justify their research from several perspectives. Because patients are leaving hospitals sooner, families are absorbing more care responsibilities for more serious situations. Also, the authors suggest that the research surrounding memory and learning can be applied to the area of health literacy.

A subsequent study by the same researchers used clients from an inner city job-training program (Houts et al., 2001). The second study examined the following questions: "Can people with low literacy skills (less than 5th grade reading level) remember large numbers of actions (236) for long periods of time (4 weeks)?" (233). Their results suggest that simpler pictographs elicited fewer errors by the participants. They also drew the conclusion that recall rates of low-literacy individuals does approach that of literate individuals when similar pictographs are used. They add that the suggestions for creating easy-to-read patient education materials contained in the book by Doak, Doak, and Root (1996), *Teaching Patients with Low Literacy Skills*, can be applied to the preparation of pictographs as well.

Yet, there exists some cautionary advice regarding the use of pictographs that needs to be considered, too. A study by Grieshop, Stiles, and Domingo (1995) that focused on the ability of farm workers of Mexican origin to interpret safety information revealed several important caveats. Finding effective visual language is especially important in safety literature, otherwise known as hazard communication. The authors point out that the designers and receivers of this highly specialized format come from different segments of the population, and they stress that several questions need consideration. "What information or knowledge is the pictorial meant to relay? Who is the sender? Who is the receiver? In what medium is the pictorial to be distributed?" (132). Their study examined to what degree workers understood the messages that the safety illustrations intended to convey. They discovered that the subjects' language, education, exposure to television and print, and training affected their interpretation of visual warnings. Furthermore, subjects rated illustrations for understandability, acceptability, and preference. Acceptability, defined as "to what degree respondents were able to identify with illustrated images and illustrated tasks" was largely determined by similarity to the respondents' cultural background or their work situations (128). The lesson to draw from this research and apply to health literacy interventions is that pictographs should resemble the culture of their intended audience lest they inadvertently create unconscious barriers.

CONCLUSION

Health literacy interventions may take place on an individual, local, or global level, and each has a variety of challenges. From the older adult who will not admit deafness to the immigrant who has survived physical and psychological trauma, individuals needing health literacy interventions represent a diverse population. Recognition of the problem by healthcare givers is the first step, followed by a willingness to deal with the issues. Clinicians can train their staff to be culturally attuned and to be on the lookout for low literacy levels. Librarians play an integral role at every phase. They can publicize the problem, research it, and develop, assess, and when necessary, modify interventions. As librarians engage in this process, they learn that it is indeed true that "Leadership and learning are indispensable to each other" (Kennedy, 1963).

REFERENCES

Allen, Margaret, Suzanne Matthew, and Mary Jo Boland. 2004. "Working with Immigrant and Refugee Populations: Issues and Hmong Case Study." *Library Trends* 53, no.2 (Fall): 301–328.

Andrus, Miranda R., and Mary T. Roth. 2002. "Health Literacy: A Review." *Pharmacotherapy* 22, no.3 (March): 282–302.

Berkman, Nancy D., Darren A DeWalt, Michael P. Pignone, Stacey L. Sheridan, Kathleen N. Lohr, Linda Lux, Sonya F. Sutton, Tammeka Swinson, and Arthur J. Bonito. 2004. *Literacy and Health Outcomes.* Evidence Report/Technology Assessment No. 87 (AHRQ Publication No. 04-E007-2). Rockville, MD: Agency for Healthcare Research and Quality.

Blackwell, Jean. 2005. "Low Health Literacy: How It Impacts Your Patients & What You Can Do About It." (August 2007) Available: www.mlanet.org/pdf/resources/low_literacy.pdf

Bower, Amanda B., and Valerie A. Taylor. 2003. "Increasing Intention to Comply with Pharmaceutical Product Instructions: An Exploratory Study Investigating the Roles of Frame and Plain Language." *Journal of Health Communication* 8, no.2 (March–April): 145–156.

Corbie-Smith, Giselle, Stephen B. Thomas, Mark V. Williams, and Sandra Moody-Ayers. 1999. "Attitudes and Beliefs of African Americans Toward Participation in Medical Research." *Journal of General Internal Medicine* 14, no.9 (September): 537–546.

Cuellar, Lourdes M., and Dana S. Fitzsimmons. 2003. "Raising Pharmacists' Cultural Awareness." *American Journal of Health-System Pharmacy* 60, no.3 (February): 285–286.

Davis, Terry C., Michael A. Crouch, Georgia Wills, Sarah Miller, and David M. Abdehou. 1990. "The Gap between Patient Reading Comprehension and the Readability of Patient Education Materials." *Journal of Family Practice* 31, no.5 (November): 533–538.

Doak, Cecilia C., Leonard G. Doak, and Jane H. Root. 1996. *Teaching Patients with Low Literacy Skills.* 2nd ed. Philadelphia: J. B. Lippincott.

Flory, James, and Ezekiel Emanuel. 2004. "Interventions to Improve Research Participants' Understanding in Informed Consent for Research: A Systematic Review." *JAMA* 292, no.13 (October): 1593–1601.

Foulk, David, Pamela Carroll, and Susan Nelson Wood. 2001. "Addressing Health Literacy: A Description of the Intersection of Functional Literacy and Health Care." *American Journal of Health Studies* 17, no.1 (Winter): 7–14.

Grieshop, James I., Martha C. Stiles, and I. V. Domingo. 1995. "Drawing on Experience: Mexican-Origin Workers' Evaluation of Farm Safety Illustrations." *Journal of Agricultural Safety and Health* 1, no.2 (April 1): 117–133.

Hammond, Patricia A. 2004. "Developing a Health Literacy Action Plan." MLA News, no.364: 1, 10. (March 2007) Available: www.mlanet.org/members/pdf/news/2004/mar_news.pdf

Henley, Eric and Karen Peters. 2004. "10 Steps for Avoiding Health Disparities in Your Practice." *Journal of Family Practice* 53, no.3 (March): 193–196.

Hoffmann, Tammy, and Kryss McKenna. 2006. "Analysis of Stroke Patients' and Carers' Reading Ability and the Content and Design of Written Materials: Recommendations for Improving Written Stroke Information." *Patient Education and Counseling* 60, no.3 (March): 286–293.

Houts, Peter S., Rebecca Bachrach, Judith T. Witmer, Carol A. Tringali, Julia A. Bucher, and Russell A. Localio. 1998. "Using pictographs to enhance recall of spoken medical instructions." *Patient Education and Counseling* 35, no.2 (October): 83–88.

Houts, Peter S., Judith T. Witmer, Howard E. Egeth, Matthew J. Loscalzo, and James R. Zabora. 2001. "Using pictographs to enhance recall of spoken medical instructions II." *Patient and Education Counseling* 43, no.3 (June): 231–242.

Hulley, Stephen B., Steven R. Cummings, Warren S. Browner, Deborah Grady, Norman Hearst, and Tomas B. Newman. 2001. *Designing Clinical Research.* Philadelphia: Liippincott Williams & Wilkins.

Jackson, Robert H., Terry C. Davis, Lee E. Bairnsfather, Ronald B. George, Michael A. Crouch, and Helena Gault. 1991. "Patient Reading Ability: An Overlooked Problem in Health Care." *Southern Medical Journal* 84, no.10 (October): 1172–1175.

Jimison, Holly B., Paul P. Sher, Richard Appleyard, and Yvonne LeVernois. 1998. "The Use of Multimedia in the Informed Consent Process." *Journal of the American Medical Informatics Association* 5, no.3 (May–June): 245–256.

Joint Commission on Accreditation of Healthcare Organizations. 2002-2003. *Comprehensive Accreditation Manual for Ambulatory Care.* Oakbrook Terrace, IL: Author.

Joint Commission on Accreditation of Healthcare Organizations. 2005. *Comprehensive Accreditation Manual for Hospitals—Update 3.* Oakbrook Terrace, IL: Author.

Kennedy, John F. 1963. "Speech Prepared for Delivery in Dallas the Day of His Assassination, November 22, 1963." (August 2007) Available: www.quotationspage.com/quote/3225.html

Krueger, Kem P., Bruce G. Felkey, and Bill A. Berger. 2003. "Improving Adherence and Persistence: A Review and Assessment of Interventions and Description of Steps Toward a National Adherence Initiative." *Journal of the American Pharmaceutical Association* 43, no.6 (November–December): 668–678; quiz 678–679.

National Academy on an Aging Society. n.d. "Low Health Literacy Skills Increase Annual Health Care Expenditures by $73 Billion." Available: www.agingsociety.org/agingsociety/publications/fact/fact_low.html

National Institute on Deafness and Other Communication Disorders. 2003. "Why Johnny Is Sick: Researcher Strengthens Health, Literacy Link." (May 2005) Available: www.nidcd.nih.gov/health/inside/spr03/pg2.asp

Nebraska Department of Education. 1999. Reading Writing Frameworks. Glossary General F-J. (June 2007) Available: www.nde.state.ne.us/READ/FRAMEWORK/glossary/general_f-j.html

Nielsen-Bohlman, Lynn, Alison M. Panzer, and David A. Kindig (eds.). 2004. *Health Literacy: A Prescription to End Confusion.* Washington, DC: National Academies Press.

Oxford English Dictionary. 1989. (July 2007) Available: http://dictionary.oed.com/cgi/entry/50119833?single=1&query_type=word&queryword=intervention&first=1&max_to_show=10

Scherrer, Carol S. 2002. "Outreach to Community Organizations: The Next Consumer Health Frontier." *Journal of the Medical Library Association* 90, no.3 (July): 285–293.

Schillinger, Dean, John Piette, Kevin Grumbach, Frances Wang, Clifford Wilson, Carolyn Daher, Krishelle Leong-Grotz, Cesar Castro, and Andrew B. Bindman. 2003. "Closing the Loop: Physician Communication with Diabetic Patients Who have Low Health Literacy." *Archives of Internal Medicine* 163, no.1 (January): 83–90.

Selden, Catherine, Marcia Zorn, Scott C. Ratzan, and Ruth M. Parker (compilers). 2000. *Health Literacy* (Current Bibliographies in Medicine; no. 2000-1). Bethesda, MD: National Library of Medicine. Available: www.nlm.nih.gov/archive/20061214/pubs/cbm/hliteracy.html

Shamoo, Adil E. and David B. Resnik. 2003. *Responsible Conduct of Research.* New York: Oxford University Press.

Stead, Martine, Douglas Eadie, David Gordon, and Kathryn Angus. 2005. "Hello, Hello—It's English I Speak!": A Qualitative Exploration of Patients' Understanding of the Science of Clinical Trials." *Journal of Medical Ethics* 31, no.11 (November): 664–669.

Svarstad, Bonnie L., Dara C. Bultman, and Jeanine K. Mount. 2004. "Patient Counseling Provided in Community Pharmacies: Effects of State Regulation, Pharmacist Age, and Busyness." *Journal of the American Pharmaceutical Association* 44, no.1 (January–February): 22–29.

World Medical Association. 1989. "Declaration of Helsinki: Recommendations Guiding Physicians in Biomedical Research Involving Subjects." Available: www1.umn.edu/humanarts/instree/Helsinki.html

Wu, Helen W., Robyn Y. Nishimi, Christine M. Page-Lopez, and Kenneth W. Kizer. 2005. *Improving Patient Safety Through Informed Consent for Patients with Limited Health Literacy.* Washington, DC: National Quality Forum.

Appendix 15-1. Resources on Health Literacy for Librarians

The following interventions are organized according to the audience most likely to need or apply the information contained therein. However, some material could reasonably be included under more than one heading. Librarians should be familiar with these resources both for their own professional responsibilities and to be able to recommend them to their respective patron bases. Furthermore, there is never a guarantee that the Web sites associated with the interventions will remain available. They are all viable as of April 2008. Sufficient information is included with each intervention so that a search of the Web should reveal a site whose Web address has changed.

For Clinicians

Only resources not available through a database search are included here.

Ask Me 3
http://www.npsf.org/askme3/
> Funded by Pfizer, Inc. and sponsored by the Partnership for Clear Health Communication. Find informational brochures, posters, fact sheets, and guidelines that are free to download as well as bulk ordering information. Encourages patients to ask their health providers three main question: What is my main problem? What do I need to do? Why is it important for me to do this?

CDC's Office of Minority Health
www.cdc.gov/omhd
> Discusses disease burdens, environmental issues, minority health issues and news, and efforts to eradicate racial and ethnic health disparities. Links to a number of Disease Fact sheets that include disparities statistics are provided.

Cross Cultural Health Care Program (CCHCP)
www.xculture.org/
> Sponsored by the W.K. Kellogg Foundation, the goal of this organization is to make their programs and publications available at the national level. Researchers publish studies aimed at uncovering culturally and linguistically successful interventions. Offers instruction in cultural competency and interpreter training, including a 40-hour interpreter-training course titled "Bridging the Gap."

Diversity Rx, Resources for Cross-Cultural Health Care
www.diversityrx.org/
> Find links to a discussion list, glossary of interpretation terms, standards for interpreters, model programs, and federal laws.

Harvard School of Public Health, Health Literacy Studies
www.hsph.harvard.edu/healthliteracy/
> Aimed at health professionals, this site includes an overview on health literacy, research reports, curricula for teaching low literacy patients, instructions for writing and evaluating print materials, and a series of related Web page links.

Health Information Translations
www.healthinfotranslations.com
> Initiated and supported by The Ohio State University Medical Center, Mount Carmel Health System , and Ohio-Health. Information is currently available in ten languages but more are planned.

Health Literacy and Patient Safety: Help Your Patients Understand
www.ama-assn.org/ama/pub/category/8035.html
> An album container with a video, manual, brochure, tabletop display and buttons. Author is Barry D. Weiss along with the American Medical Association and the American Medical Association Foundation. Designated as a Continuing Medical Education (CME) program.

Institute of Medicine Report
Unequal Treatment: Confronting Racial and Ethnic Disparities in Health Care
www.iom.edu/CMS/3740/4475.aspx
> Results of a study requested by Congress to investigate inequity in healthcare access and treatment, to determine the source of such inequity, and to recommend measures to remediate such inequity. The report found that race, even when insurance, ability to pay, and economic status were comparable, to be a determining factor in quality of care.

Mini-Conference on Health Literacy and Health Disparities. Proceedings from the Mini-Conference on Health Literacy and Health Disparities
www.ama-assn.org/ama1/pub/upload/mm/433/mini_conf.pdf
A 78-page PDF file from the July 2005 White House Conference on Aging held in Chicago.

Office of Minority Health
www.omhrc.gov/
Sponsored by the U.S. Department of Health and Human Services. Under the Cultural Competency tab, select "Training Tools for Physicians and Others." Included are "Teaching Cultural Competence in Health Care: A Review of Current Concepts, Policies and Practices," "A Family Physician's Practical Guide to Culturally Competent Care," and "Resources to Implement Cross-Cultural Clinical Practice Guidelines For Medicaid Practitioners." Of special note is a link to the CLAS national standards (Assuring Cultural Competence in Health Care, 2000). There are 14 standards organized according to three themes: Culturally Competent Care, Language Access Services, and Organizational Supports for Cultural Competence.

Quick Guide to Health Literacy
www.health.gov/communication/literacy/default.htm
U.S. Department of Health and Human Services. Includes tools and strategies to assist in the delivery of improved health information and literacy services. Sample 87 slide PowerPoint presentation for staff education. Access to entire chapter "Objective 11-2. Improvement of Health Literacy" from *Communicating Health: Priorities and Strategies for Progress*.

Reach Out and Read (ROR)
www.reachoutandread.org/
ROR promotes literacy via the waiting rooms of participating physicians and hospitals. Books of developmentally appropriate material are given to children between six months and five years when they come to the office for a wellness visit. In addition, staff instructs parents in the value of reading to their children. There are ROR programs in 2,482 hospitals and clinics in all 50 states.

Skills for Chronic Disease Management
By Rima Rudd, Lisa Soricone, Maricel Santos, Charlotte Nath, and Janet Smith is available from the National Center for Study of Adult Learning and Literacy (NCSALL). The goal of this project is to assist patients with chronic disease management. Skill interventions include: reading medicine labels, following directions, and measuring dosages correctly; using measurement tools to monitor health; monitoring symptoms and talking to healthcare professionals; and making critical decisions about healthcare. To order the Health Literacy Study Circle + Facilitator's Guide: Skills for Chronic Disease Management at $33.00/copy, go to the NCSALL Order Form: <www.ncsall.net/?id=674>

SPIRAL: Selected Patient Information Resources in Asian Languages
http://spiral.tufts.edu/topic.html
A joint initiative between the South Cove Community Health Center and Tufts University's Hirsh Health Sciences Library that is funded by a grant from the New England Region of the National Network of Libraries of Medicine under contract NLM-00-101/SMS. Find information organized according to health topic in the following languages: Cambodian/Khmer, Chinese—Simplified, Chinese—Traditional, Hmong, Korean, Lao Thai, and Vietnamese.

Discussion Lists

CLAS-talk
Sponsored by Resources for Cross-Cultural Health Care and the DiversityRx Web site (www.diverstyRX.org) for discussion by those responsible for implementing Culturally and Linguistically Appropriate Services. To join, send an e-mail to the list moderator at rcchcl@aol.com.

Health & Literacy Discussion List
www.nifl.ogv/mailman/listinfo/Healthliteracy
Sponsored by the National Institute for Literacy

A Librarian at Every Table (ALAET)
www.cas.usf.edu/lis/a-librarian-at-every-table/
Maintains alerts and information regarding community based collaborative initiatives that advocate social justice and human rights. Archives are available to nonsubscribers at http://mailman.acomp.usf.edu/pipermail/a-librarian-at-every-table/

MLA-Healthlit
http://nsl.mlahq.org/mailman/listinfo/mlhealthlit
Sponsored by the Medical Library Association

National Council on Interpreting in Health Care
www.ncihc.org/becoming.htm
Membership in the organization is required to participate in the discussion list.

National Institute for Literacy Health Literacy
www.nifl.gov
Health and Literacy mailing list.

Patient Education Network
http://uuhsc.utah.edu/pated/patednet/
Sponsored by the University of Utah Hospitals and Clinics. Discusses current patient education issues.

StaffEdNet
http://uuhsc.utah.edu/pated/staffednet
Sponsored by the University of Utah Hospitals and Clinics. Discusses current patient education issues. Intended for staff educators.

For Industry and Institutions

American Translators Association
www.atanet.org/
Find a directory of translation and interpreting services, a directory of language services companies, and a 28-page booklet entitled "Getting It Right," a series of tips for non-linguists who need to purchase translation services. There is a certification program, continuing education, practice tests, and links to necessary enrollment forms.

Health Literacy Consulting
www.healthliteracy.com
Founded by Helen Osborne, includes a free e-mail newsletter published April to October, "Countdown to Health Literacy Month." Osborne offers presentations and workshops on various topics related to Health Literacy and is available to write and edit literacy projects. Osborne may be reached at Helen@healthliteracy.com or by phone at: 508-653-1199. She is the author of three books:
1. *Health Literacy from A to Z: Practical Ways to Communicate Your Health*
2. *Message Partnering with Patients to Improve Health Outcomes*
3. *Overcoming Communication Barriers in Patient Education*

Language Line Services
www.languageline.com
1.877.886.3885
info@languageline.com
Global company that offers translation and interpreter services for 150 languages, 24 hours a day, 7 days a week. In addition, offers supportive training to staff, free e-mail newsletter, a dual handset telephone, and an on-line tutorial for clients. Currently used by Osco Pharmacies.

National Council on Interpreting in Health Care
www.ncihc.org/
An organization of healthcare interpreters committed to equal and equitable access for culturally competent healthcare.

National Literacy and Health Publications
www.nlhp.cpha.ca/
Sponsored by the Canadian Public Health Association and funded by the National Literacy Secretariat. Aim is to demonstrate to health professionals the link between literacy and health. Established the Plain Language Service in 1997 to assess, design, and revise any documents intended for the public. The Plain Language Service is fee based. Publishes a Directory of Plain Language Health Education Materials in French and English. A guide to publishing materials appropriate for low-literacy readers and a directory of 50 organizations and Web sites categorized by subject.

The Role of Corporate Giving in Adult Literacy
www.caalusa.org/corporategiving.pdf
Published in March 2006 by the Council for Advancement of Adult Literacy and funded by the Verizon Foundation, discusses the impact and funding patterns of corporate support for literacy projects. Its purpose is to

encourage companies to initiate or to expand their commitment to such philanthropies. The American Library Association assisted in the implementation of the survey. Available as a free pdf download from the site. Bound copies of the report are also available directly from CAAL at $10 each plus postage for a simple spiral-bound version, or $25 a copy plus postage for a higher-end bound version.

For Librarians

1on1Health
www.1on1health.com
> Sponsored by GlaxoSmithKline. The site offers accessible information regarding common health topics in three formats: look, listen, and learn. Spanish and some Chinese documents are available.

Area Health Education Centers
www.nationalahec.org/home/index.asp
> Developed by Congress in 1971 to mentor healthcare givers of underserved populations. Along with the HETC (Health Education Training Centers) which developed later in 1989, fosters and applies academic medical resources to local, community-based needs.

Bringing Health Information to the Community (BHIC)
http://library.med.utah.edu/blogs/BHIC/
> A blog that posts information regarding conferences, grants, environmental health, rural health, and minority health concerns and outreach. Maintained by Siobhan Champ-Blackwell, Community Outreach Liaison of the MidContinental Region, National Network of Libraries of Medicine. There is an option to receive a digest version via e-mail.

Bureau of Primary Health Care Web
http://bphc.hrsa.gov/
> Maintains a database of health professional shortage areas searchable by state, county, and discipline. Sponsored by the U.S. Department of Health and Human Services and the Health Resources and Services Administration. Offers information for clinicians, health center grantees, and those seeking low-cost healthcare.

Center for Adult English Language Acquisition
www.cal.org/caela
> Funded by U.S. Department of Education/Office of Vocational and Adult Education. Offers instructional tools, program development tools, and ESL Resources.

Chicago Environmental and Public Health Outreach Project
www/uic.edu/depts./lib/projects/resources/cephop/

Clear and Simple: Developing Effective Print Materials for Low-Literate Readers
www.cancer.gov/cancerinformation/clearandsimple
> A step-by-step guideline prepared by the National Cancer Institute.

Ethnomed
www.ethnomed.org/
> Contains medical and cultural information regarding immigrant groups. Designed to be available as a local resource in community institutions, such as clinics and libraries. Although originally designed for immigrants in the Seattle area, the site has grown so that it is appropriate for most locations. There are handouts in Asian languages and PDF files for documents written in languages that do not use the Roman alphabet. A joint project of University of Washington Health Sciences Library and the Harborview Medical Center's Community House Calls Program.

Family Health and Literacy
www.worlded.org/us/health/docs/family
Julie McKinney and Sabrina Kurtz-Rossi
> One hundred-page health education PDF document to use when working with low-literacy families. Includes philosophical foundations and theory of health literacy, activities for families to engage in together, and easy health materials for beginning readers and English speakers.

Health Information Literacy
www.mlanet.org/resources/healthlit/
> The Medical Library Association has compiled resources for both Health and Information Professionals and Health Consumers. Note especially the Adult Education Health Literacy Toolkit from the Virginia Adult Learning Resource Center for its wide-ranging but simple explanations and suggestions.

Healthy Roads Media
www.healthyroadsmedia.org/
> Provides free health education materials in a variety of formats: handouts, audio, multimedia, and Web page video. Settings are adjusted so that videos will work even with slow Internet connections. Languages available are Arabic, Bosnian, English, Hmong, Khmer, Russian, Somali, Spanish, and Vietnamese. Materials are organized according to topic, language or format. A collaboration with Creative Commons, http://creativecommons.org/, a nonprofit organization that provides flexible copyright protection and freedoms for contributing creators and offers all its creative tools free of charge.

How to Write Easy to Read Health Materials
www.nlm.nih.gov/medlineplus/etr.html
> From MedlinePlus. Step-by-step directions, evaluation tips, software, guidelines, and bibliography.

Health Literacy Resources for VA Library Network
www.mdmlg.org/Health-Literacy-Resources.pdf
> Developed by Janet Schneider, Patient Education Librarian. A comprehensive site that has compiled books, bibliographies, Web sites, online videos, instructions on how to develop low health literacy materials, readability formulas, and free graphics.

Hints to Help You Write Effective Handouts
www.u-write.com/hints-content.shtml
> Offers suggestions for the content, illustration, design, and production of patient education brochures or handouts.

Making Your Web Site Senior Friendly
www.nlm.nih.gov/pubs/checklist.pdf
> A 15-page checklist of research-based guidelines to help create an accessible Web page.

National Adult Literacy Database
www.nald.ca/index.htm
> Available in French and English, with links to resources, Web sites, and full-text documents on literacy research. Provides information free of charge. Supported by National Literacy Secretariat of Human Resources and Skills Development Canada with additional funding from the government of the Province of New Brunswick.

National Association of Community Health Centers, Inc. (NACHC)
www.nachc.com/
> Serves and supports Community, Migrant, Public Housing and Homeless Health Centers that provide medical care regardless of the ability to pay.

National Center for Farmworker Health
www.ncfh.org/
> Resource Center contains over 200 items, including slide shows, patient educational tools, and videos. Items are available for loan or purchase and may be previewed at the Web site.

National Institute for Literacy
www.nifl.gov/
> Administered by the Secretaries of Education, Labor, and Health and Human Services and organizations from academia, business, and the private and nonprofit sectors.

NCSALL National Center for the Study of Adult Learning and Literacy
www.ncsall.net/index.php?id=251
> Section on literacy and health leads to a bibliography of resources on culture and healthcare. Also, find PDF downloads of the six-volume report *Review of Adult Learning and Literacy*, A Project of the National Center for the Study of Adult Learning and Literacy.

¿No Comprende? Spanish Health Information Resources for English-Speaking Librarians
http://nnlm.gov/training/nocomprende/nocomprendedesc.html
> Sponsored by the National Network of Libraries of Medicine. Offers course materials for English-speaking librarians serving Spanish-speaking patrons. Links to vocabulary sites and online Spanish health resources.

Patient Education Materials An Author's Guide
http://uuhsc.utah.edu/pated/authors
> From the University of Utah Health Sciences Center. Includes a sample permission letter and substitute word list. Addresses copyright information, literacy facts, and readability testing.

Pfizer Principles for Clear Health Communication
www.pfizerhealthliteracy.com/media/chc-principles.html

Funded by Pfizer, Inc. and sponsored by the Partnership for Clear Health Communication. Provides guidelines for creating consumer materials.

Simply Put
http://www.cdc.gov/od/oc/simpput/pdf

A free, downloadable 48-page PDF containing guidelines for preparing brochures and fact sheets. Includes tips on translation, layout, and a checklist for easy-to-read documents. Published by the Centers for Disease Control.

Understanding Health Literacy and Its Barriers
www.nlm.nih.gov/pubs/cbm/healthliteracybarriers.html

A bibliography in the *Current Bibliographies in Medicine* (CBM) series published by NLM. Consists of 651 citations from January 1998 through November 2003, plus selected earlier and later citations.

Virginia Adult Education Health Literacy Toolkit
www.aelweb.vcu.edu/publications/healthlit/sections/

Published by the Virginia Adult Learning Resource Center. Designed for adult education instructors and administrators to encourage them to teach health literacy to their students and to understand the impact of low health literacy has on them.

For Patients

America's Literacy Directory
www.literacydirectory.org/

A database that finds programs focused on GED, math, or reading. Enter address or zip code and distance you are willing to travel.

Center for Drug Evaluation and Research
www.fda.gov/cder/index.html

Sponsored by the U.S. Food and Drug Administration. Selecting the "Specific Audiences" tab reveals links to Spanish publications and fact sheets as well as an index to drug specific information.

Easy-to-Read Documents from MedlinePlus
www.fda.gov/opacom/lowlit/7lowlit.html

A list of easy-to-read documents, some of which are also available in Spanish. In addition, there is a link to "How to Write Easy-to-Read Health Materials."

Easy-to-Read Publications from the Food & Drug Administration
www.fda.gov/opacom/lowlit.html

Material in Spanish or English on a variety of topics. May be downloaded as PDF or html files with instructions for printing as brochures.

Health Communities Online Resource Education
www.healthcoreinfo.org/

Offers resources in Spanish and links to MedlinePlus as well as other sources on a variety of health topics. Sponsored by the Medical Center of Central Georgia, a medical and public health library.

Healthfinder
www.healthfinder.gov/justforyou/

Sponsored by the National Health Information Center and U.S. Department of Health and Human Services. Section titled "Just for You" focuses on healthcare needs of specified age groups, ethnicities, and caregiving roles. Available in Spanish.

Literacy Information and Communication System (LINCS)
www/worlded.org/us/health/lincs/aboutus.htm

LINCS maintains a Health and Literacy Special Collection whose goal is both to assist in the furtherance of health education to special populations as well as to provide direct access to vetted health education for those populations.

NIH Senior Health
http://nihseniorhealth.gov

Developed by the National Institute on Aging and the National Library of Medicine. Enhancements include text size, contrast level, and some spoken text.

Partnership for Safe Medicines
www.safemedicines.org
> The Consumer Links tab offers a Spanish-language option from this organization of patients, clinicians, and health industries formed to protect consumers from counterfeit or contraband medications.

WE LEARN (Women Expanding/Literacy Education Action Resource Network)
www.litwomen.org
> WE LEARN is a national U.S. organization that directly addresses the issues of adult women's literacy and the needs of women in adult basic education. WE LEARN is an educational nonprofit 501(c)3 membership organization. There are some health related materials on the Web site, a few of which are graded for reading level.

Readability Assessments

Andrus, Miranda R., and Mary T. Roth. (2002). "Health Literacy: A Review." *Pharmacotherapy* 22, no. 3 (March): 282–302. (PMID: 11898888)
> Examines the consequences of poor health literacy. Includes tables of correlation between readability assessments, discusses word recognition tests, comprehension tests, the Test of Functional Health Literacy in Adults (TFHLA), and addresses impact of research results on pharmacy and healthcare. Also offers strategies for improving patient education.

De Santi, Roger J. 1986. *The De Santi Cloze Reading Inventory*. Needham Heights, MA: Allyn and Bacon. $19.50.
> Words in a text are eliminated. The reader then fills in the blanks. There are formulas to determine how successfully this procedure has been completed, and a good score indicates that the test reader has been able to comprehend the material content. Find instructions at Instructional Strategies Online http://olc.spsd.sk.ca/DE/PD/instr/strats/cloze/. Information on scoring is on the Reading in the Content Area page at www.alt.wcboe.kl2.md.us/manifold/technolog/instruct/msde07/module14/modl14_activity_c.htm.

Flesch, Rudolf Franz. 1951. *How to Test Readability*. New York: Harper, 1951.
> When using Microsoft Word to create a document, from Tools, select Options. Select the Spelling & Grammar tab. Put a checkmark in front of "Show Readability Statistics." This will enable the Flesh-Kincaid Readability Tool that will report the grade-school reading level of the current document.

Fry, Edward. 1977. *Elementary Reading Instruction*. New York: McGraw Hill.
> The Fry Testing Readability Formula uses a graph to plot the average number of syllables and average number of sentences per 100 words. The graph then determines the grade level of the material.

Gunning, Robert and Richard A. Kallan. 1994. *How to Take the Fog Out of Business Writing*. Chicago: Dartnell.
> Gunning Fog Index. Available: www.msu.edu/course/aee/201/Audience/tsld006.htm

Juicy Studio
http://juicystudio.com/services/readability.plp
> Enter the URL of a Web site to compute its readability level using several established algorithms.

Micro Power & Light Co.
www.readability-software.com/
8814 Sanshire Avenue, Dallas, TX 75231
phone: (214) 553-0105; fax: (214) 341-9118
E-mail: info@micropowerandlight.com
> Offers several text analysis software programs for MAC and PC.

Davis, Terry C., Michael A. Crouch, Sandra W. Long, Robert H. Jackson, P Bates, Ronald P. George, and Lee E. Bairnsfather. 1991. "Rapid Assessment of Literacy Levels of Adult Primary Care Patients." *Family Medicine* 23, no.6 (August): 433–435.
> The article describes the development of the Rapid Assessment of Adult Literacy in Medicine (REALM) tool. For English-speaking adults. Consists of words that are typically difficult for low-literacy readers. Requires less than 10 minutes to administer, fairly easy, enjoyable to administer.

McLaughlin, G. H. (1969). "SMOG grading: A new readability formula." *Journal of Reading* 12, no.8 (XXX): 639–646.
> Available: http://uuhsc.utah.edu/pated/authors/readability.html

Chapter 16

Forming and Funding Collaborations to Address Health Literacy

Kristine Alpi and Dina Sherman

Literacy has been tied to health status for many years, particularly in developing countries (Grosse and Auffrey, 1989). Of the many factors that contribute to health outcomes, the role of health literacy, defined as the ability to read, understand, and use health information, is becoming better understood (RTI International, 2004). Because it is a multifactorial issue, health literacy may be best addressed through collaborative efforts and the Internet is a rich resource for identifying potential partners. Collaborations among adult educators, health professionals, librarians, advocates, and granting agencies already exist, so those who want to get involved can look to them for inspiration and examples. These partnerships can be extended, both nationally and locally, with funding and organizational support as well as infusions of new energy and ideas. In this chapter, we provide a brief overview of some collaborations that address health literacy and provide some information on finding and working with funding agencies.

It seems that librarians may not be playing as big a collaborative role in health literacy as one might expect. For example, in April 2004, both the Agency for Healthcare Research and Quality (RTI International, 2004) and the Institute of Medicine (IOM) produced major reports on health literacy and its impact on health outcomes, with limited mention of librarians (Nielsen-Bohlman, Panzer, and Kindig, 2004). The IOM committee included a literacy expert, Dr. Victoria Purcell-Gates, a Professor of Literacy and Teacher Education at Michigan State University, but did not include any librarians.

IDENTIFYING EXISTING HEALTH LITERACY COLLABORATIONS

Collaborations form to bring together strengths of diverse groups. Many health professionals working on health literacy have substantial experience in patient education or medication adherence, but may not be familiar with the work of librarians, literacy experts, or educators. Increased interest in and funding for health literacy research have propelled organizations to join together in efforts to measure health literacy and address the disparities between the information needed and what is available. "Health literacy is bigger than any one person, program, or profession," says Helen Osborne, president of Health Literacy Consulting and founder of Health Literacy Month. "It takes all of us working together to solve the worldwide problems of health literacy communication" (Helen Osborne, personal communication, August 18, 2006).

Osborne's Health Literacy Consulting site not only lists resources for those interested in health literacy, but is also the gateway to Health Literacy Month—celebrated every October. The Health Literacy Month Web site acts as a "virtual" meeting place for health literacy advocates. Participants are encouraged to post their projects on the site, which are searchable by year, country, and key phrase. This Web site also has Health Literacy Month resources, including a free downloadable logo, as well as buttons and bookmarks for purchase. The American Medical Association (AMA) Health Literacy site (www.ama-assn.org/ama/pub/category/8115.html) also provides links to resources, such as toolkits, videos, and information from partnerships around the country.

In November 2004, the Langeloth Forum on Libraries and Health Information brought together more than 35 specialists in health information access (Zeisel, 2005). A two-day program showcased best practices in health information in public libraries, enabling librarians to exchange strategies and consider ways to replicate successful models nationwide. Many of the projects and services presented were partnerships, and most of them continue today. Examples of successful partnerships between librarians and health organizations include the Rochester, New York, CLIC-on-Health: Community & Library Information Collaboration on Health (www.cliconhealth.org/) (Miller, Phillips, and Sollenberger, 2006); the REACH 2010 project in New Orleans (www.blackwomens health.org/site/PageServer?pagename=RS_ourresearch); and the Colonias project along the Mexican border in Texas (Olney et al., 2007).

Some nationwide health programs include health literacy as one of many objectives, while others focus solely on this issue. Healthy People 2010 is a national initiative backed by a consortia of over 400 national membership organizations. They are challenging individuals, healthcare providers, communities, and professionals to take specific steps to ensure that everyone can enjoy good health and long life (U.S. Department of Health and Human Services, 2000a,b).

To see what is happening in your state in response to Healthy People 2010 goals, visit their Web site at www.healthypeople.gov/implementation/stateplans.htm.

Launched in 2002, the Partnership for Clear Health Communication (2004) was the first national coalition of organizations working together to promote awareness of low health literacy and its effect on health outcomes. The Partnership also develops and researches practical solutions to improve communication between healthcare providers and patients. The group is committed to offering free, low-cost resources and programs, as well as medical education and practice management tools, to healthcare professionals and organizations that provide information to patients. The organization's first initiative was AskMe3, a tool designed to improve communication between patients and providers. The Partnership is guided by a solution-based action agenda that is closely aligned with the IOM report identifying a number of recommendations to government agencies, private funding agencies, educational institutions, and healthcare systems and providers. The Partnership Action Agenda includes:

- educating patients and providers about health literacy;
- developing and applying practical solutions to improve patient-provider communication;
- conducting nationally coordinated research to further define the health literacy issue and evaluate solutions; and
- increasing support for health literacy policy and funding.

The complete list of Partnership for Clear Health Communication members is available online at (www.askme3.org/newpartnersA-G.asp). Although this group is easy to join (see www.p4chc.org/join-pchc.aspx) and representative of the diversity of those concerned with facilitating health communication, as of July 19, 2007, the only library members are the Fairfax County Public Library, the Palm Beach County Library System, and the Medical Library Association. There are several regional groups working together and it is easy to envision the value that local librarians could add. Librarians need to join these collaborations and share their considerable expertise by identifying appropriate materials, recruiting speakers to address important issues, and ensuring that patients and health consumers get local information that they can understand and act upon.

Extending Existing Library Collaborations

Librarians are critical partners in the effort to address low health literacy and provide quality, understandable health information, but they cannot have a broad impact on healthcare if they work alone. Library staff members often improve health literacy on an individual level by working with and helping a single patient or family member achieve better understanding of health materials. However, many other opportunities are lost when people with literacy concerns do not visit their local libraries. By bringing together partners from all areas concerned with health literacy—hospitals, clinics, educators, advocates, government and granting agencies, and community organizations—librarians can maximize the use of materials by those with health concerns, increase awareness and use of library and community resources for prevention and wellness, and promote healthy communities.

Each party brings important contributions to the table. Librarians have ways to share and provide access to information that many smaller organizations may not, yet often it is the small community-based organizations (CBOs) that can effectively reach individuals who do not know where to begin looking for help. Many libraries are a source for video and audio materials, yet we have heard from some librarians that they may not purchase many health videos for fear of the cost or concern about the currency of the medical information they contain. Organizations that produce health materials and wish to make them broadly available would do well to provide some circulating or free distribution copies to their local public or school libraries. It is our experience that school librarians are underutilized as a way to get quality health information to children and teenagers, as well as to their parents and guardians, some of whom may have low literacy skills. To address health literacy, public librarians could collaborate with school librarians in their community.

Enriching Opportunities for Librarians

Librarians have done excellent work in helping document the research and policy discussions on health literacy. Selden et al. (2000) contributed to the narrative and extensive bibliography on health literacy. Their bibliography helps define and describe the evidence base for advancing health literacy programs by examining theories, strategies, and tactics in the published literature. The 2003 update by Zorn, Allen, and Horowitz (2004) focused on barriers to health literacy. While bibliographies are valuable contributions, librarians should carve out a greater role in the health literacy partnerships, such as setting up systems to assess the readability of materials and helping healthcare professionals get the right materials to their patients. Health policy workers also need help spreading their messages to consumers. One potential example is the large health information gap related to the Medicare part D drug benefit. It is a major project being addressed within AskMe3 and the Partnership for Clear Health Communication and a great opportunity to emphasize the crucial role of health literacy for the Medicare population. This project has been taken up by pharmacies and pharmacy students as a community outreach role and a reason to seek additional funding (UCSF, 2006), but it does not seem that librarians serving seniors are leveraging this demand for information to seek additional health literacy funding or partnerships.

National conferences and local meetings are where dialogue and networking begin. The authors' review of the attendee and presenter lists from several national meetings on health literacy revealed that librarian participation has not been extensive. As librarians, it seems natural that we contribute to the health literacy discussion, but we may need to work harder to convince those from other disciplines to understand our unique and important role. Inviting literacy organizations and librarians outside of the health sciences to meetings could be a starting point. There have been sessions at the Medical Library Association (MLA) annual meetings as early as 2001 on health literacy, such as "Speaking Plainly: Meeting the Health Information Needs of Low-Literate Consumers," which included invited speakers from the Florida Library Coalition and the State Library of Florida. In the fall of 2002, MLA formed a heath literacy task force that focused on health information literacy to carve out a niche for the librarians (see www.mlanet.org/resources/healthlit/). "Health Information Literacy: rEvolution in Roles" was the title of the symposium at MLA's 2007 annual meeting.

Librarians and health professionals can provide content for literacy curriculum development and be referral partners for literacy and English as a second language (ESL) students' health concerns. Literacy professionals can provide guidance to practitioners on making materials more accessible. Relevant and truly useful health materials can be produced when health professionals and literacy educators collaborate. An example of this is the Health Education Literacy Program (HELP) developed by Lauren Schwartz (2003) of the New York City Poison Control Center in collaboration with Literacy Partners. The goal of HELP is to promote medicine safety to adults with limited literacy skills. Even more importantly, literacy educators can help health professionals learn to approach clients to talk about information handling skills in a way that reduces shame and embarrassment that act as barriers to disclosure of needs (Parikh et al., 1996) Joint event and trainings on health literacy issues allow diverse professionals to share perspectives and broaden horizons.

Identifying and Assessing Local Partnerships

While these national partnerships are an excellent start to collaborations, establishing and nourishing local groups is equally important. Asset mapping has been used to identify partners for health literacy efforts (Teens, 2005). Asset mapping involves documenting a community's tangible and intangible resources (assets) and viewing the community as a place with strengths to be preserved and enhanced, rather than deficits to be fixed. Asset mapping involves inventorying assets and capacity, "building relationships, developing a vision of the future, and leveraging internal and external resources to support actions to achieve it" (Kerka, 2003, para. 2). For a good explanation of asset mapping, see www.cete.org/acve/docgen.asp?tbl=tia&ID=170.

One health literacy-related project, "Community YouthMapping," was carried out by two teams of high school students, one from the Harlem Children's Zone based in Harlem, New York, and the other from the Pinellas County 4-H Youth As Resources program, which covers St. Petersburg and Clearwater, Florida (Teens, 2005). Staff from the Academy for Educational Development trained teens in data-entry and communication skills as well as the challenges posed by a lack of health literacy. These students then canvassed pharmacies, clinics, and other healthcare organizations; collected written materials and analyzed them for readability; and interviewed fellow citizens about their understanding of health information. Other partnership opportunities with students can come through Community Campus Partnerships for Health (www.ccph.info/) or other service learning efforts.

Asset mapping shows that New York City is rich with libraries, healthcare organizations, literacy programs, media outlets, and other potential partners. Creating a network or coalition has been a popular way to formalize the relationship between partners, thereby strengthening all involved. We have seen how organizations partner for specific grants or projects, but have difficulty maintaining active relationships and ongoing activities without the impetus of external requirements. In successful partnerships, collaboration may result in benefits beyond what outcomes have been outlined in a project proposal. Regular meetings of the coalition encourage brainstorming, joint programming, and the creation of resources for the public to meet newly discovered needs. Staff development occurs naturally in these partnerships, as participants from various organizations inform one another of their activities and their special knowledge areas. The Center for the Advancement of Collaborative Strategies in Health (2004) has created a partnership self-assessment tool that organizations can use to collect partnership members' perspectives about the collaborative process and generate a report on the strengths and weaknesses of the partnership.

LOCAL EXAMPLE: NEW YORK HEALTH LITERACY COLLABORATIONS

This section describes the expansion of local health information access projects and the creation and health literacy efforts of the New York Area Coalition for Health Information Access (NYACHIA). Libraries for the Future (LFF) and the Brooklyn Public Library's (BPL) Science and Industry Division partnered in 2000 to initiate the *Brooklyn Health Information Access Project*. Designed to demonstrate how to improve access to health information through sustainable community-library collaboration, the project evolved into the *Brooklyn Health Information Access Coalition*. This Coalition included representatives from over 30 community-based organizations, local hospitals and clinics, health advocacy groups, and libraries in Brooklyn. The Coalition's primary objectives are to coordinate the sharing and provision of health information and resources among community organizations, health providers, and the public library; to advocate for individuals' access to health information and resources, recognizing barriers such as literacy; and to improve the access to health information and resources for Brooklyn organizations. Through its focus of bringing together community members and the public library, the Coalition took an important first step toward improving the community's health—*by better facilitating access to health information and knowledge* (Sonenberg, 2005). BPL still meets with local health organizations, but the coalition does not have a Web presence.

Meanwhile all around New York City, other partnerships were taking form. The National Network of Libraries of Medicine funded a public library consumer health information pilot project that included the Brooklyn Public Library and the New York Public Library. This project provided training for library staff and consumers on National Library of Medicine resources, such as MEDLINE and MedlinePlus, as well as promotional materials and access to interlibrary loan of health materials (Wood et al., 2000). In 2000, the Queens Borough Public Library began a partnership with the Queens Health Network to bring better health-related information to library customers and better library services to hospital patients. Through the partnership, programs by medical experts on topics such as "Prostate Health" and "Over-the-Counter Medication Safety" were made available in the libraries, as were free screenings for medical conditions such as depression and childhood asthma (Queens Borough Public Library, 2001). The New York Public Library, which serves Manhattan, Staten Island, and the Bronx, joined the Bronx Health Link, Inc. (www.bronxhealthlink.org), a Bronx-wide network of diverse service providers, organizations, coalitions, agencies, community stakeholders, residents, and students that shares news and local information about health and wellness in the Bronx, which is still going strong today.

New York librarians and health organizations were already collaborating with several organizations interested in affecting health literacy by improving access to health information. The Metropolitan New York Library Council (METRO) has a Special Interest Group (SIG) on Consumer Health Information (www.metro.org/SIGs/chi.html). Several members of this SIG were volunteer editors for the Web site, New York Online Access to Health or NOAH (www.noah-health.org), a joint effort of New York City librarians as well as volunteer librarians and health professionals from around the country (Voge, 1998; Gallagher, 2005). NOAH editors are concerned with health literacy and consider the readability of English and Spanish resources when they mark some materials as easy-to-read—a tag that is appended to some material that is considered easier to read than other resources on the topic selected for NOAH. Materials need not have a measured readability at a specific reading level to be assigned this designation. Elsewhere in New York, the Westchester Public Library offered a Health category on the Web site (http://firstfind.info), which is a collection of easy-to-find, easy-to-use Web sites in plain and simple English.

In 2002, Libraries for the Future convened a group of librarians, leaders of community-based health organizations and social service agencies, and others providing health information from all five boroughs of New York City to discuss ways to address disparities in access to health information. Out of this meeting emerged the New York Area Coalition for Health Information Access (NYACHIA), which promoted dialogue and action on issues of access to health information in the New York metropolitan area. NYACHIA members believed that collaboration between librarians and community partners was essential to removing barriers to health information and to promoting healthy communities. Health literacy, and the accompanying efforts for plain-language and culturally appropriate healthcare services, was a topic on which NYACHIA could mobilize.

Providing a meeting point for librarians and healthcare professionals to share skills is a main goal of coalitions like NYACHIA. Many literacy programs are located in libraries, and many librarians and adult educators have knowledge and experience with literacy concerns (Duval and Main, 1993). However, as the first author observed while pursuing a health education degree, not all health professionals charged with creating health materials have experience using plain language, assessing reading levels, or creating culturally sensitive materials. Librarians working with individuals or families seeking health information develop their own assessment of people's needs through questions and observations during the reference interview, which is part of their professional training and experience. Generally librarians do not use standardized instruments to assess people's health literacy or familiarity with medical terminology. Librarians do evaluate materials for their suitability for a particular consumer, based on their own experience and intuition as well as quality guidelines, but, unlike patient education committees, they generally do not apply formal material review instruments such as the Suitability Assessment of Materials (Doak, Doak, and Root, 1996). Finding the right match between people who need information and the materials that are available on their topic is a skill librarians have honed and can share, especially with new healthcare providers.

Information on health literacy has been shared across disciplines in New York through conference discussions and workshops. NYACHIA has organized several programs to bring librarians and those working in all areas of the health field together. On April 30, 2002, New York area librarians joined forces with LFF and the New York Academy of Medicine/Middle Atlantic Region, National Network of Libraries of Medicine to present the first area conference on health literacy. Keynote speaker Dr. Rima Rudd of the Harvard School of Public Health headlined the all-day conference that consisted of a morning lecture open to a wide audience and an afternoon of active learning among invited participants. This meeting provided a wealth of information and networking opportunities to over 100 representatives from libraries, community organizations, and healthcare settings. The conference was sponsored by METRO's Special Interest Group on Consumer Health and was supported in part through a grant to Libraries for the Future from the Helena Rubinstein Foundation.

Prior to the actual event, NYACHIA wanted to get information from the invited participants about the materials they provided to their clients and the current state of their health information partnerships. Approximately 80 paper and e-mail pre-conference surveys were sent out a month prior to the event to those libraries and organizations invited to attend the afternoon group activities (see Appendix 16-1). Thirty-five people responded, including 22 librarians. Most of the health sciences librarian respondents were part of the METRO Consumer Health SIG and therefore already connected to local health information activities. Respondents gave multiple and sometimes conflicting responses to the question about the reading level of their materials. Eight (25 percent) of 31 pre-conference respondents reported that they did not know the reading level of the materials they produce or purchase. Collaborative activities reported in the pre-survey varied from putting out the fliers of another institution to jointly applying for grants.

Evaluations were also distributed right after the conference. These showed that only 16 percent of the respondents were unaware of the reading level of their materials. Of the 61 total respondents, 31 percent of organizations reported that the majority of their materials were above the 12th grade reading level, and an additional 44 percent said that the materials were between the 9th and 12th grade reading levels. These postconference evaluations also indicated that 87 percent of the 23 participants who responded to a question about future conferences or trainings were interested in participating in these further opportunities to improve health literacy (Libraries for the Future, 2003).

NYACHIA was not the only New York organization promoting health literacy efforts. In February 2003, the Yonkers Public Library hosted a conference titled "Communicating Health Information Conference: The Literacy Crisis in Healthcare." The interest generated by the 2002 conference and these other New York activities led to a demand for skill-building training. NYACHIA arranged a Health Literacy Workshop for local librarians and community-based health educators and information providers on August 19–20, 2003. Audrey Riffenburgh, a leading health literacy expert and part of the Clear Language Group consortium, trained participants in important skills for identifying and creating easy-to-understand health information materials. The workshop, made possible through grants to Libraries for the Future from the Pfizer Health Literacy Initiative and The Helena Rubinstein Foundation, provided librarians and healthcare professionals with the tools and hands-on experience needed to evaluate printed materials and health Web site information. Participants learned readability analysis and methods for choosing and creating reader-friendly, easy-to-understand health materials that would meet the needs of their intended audiences. They also were trained on how to direct the public to appropriate health information on the Internet.

After the conference and training, NYACHIA did not have funding to support large-scale events but wished to continue actively promoting health literacy partnerships. In September 2003, the Medical Library Association offered a satellite teleconference, "Reading Between the Lines: Focusing on Health Information Literacy." The goal of the broadcast was to enhance the knowledge of information professionals about the concepts of health information literacy and to highlight opportunities for using these principles in the provision of quality consumer health and patient education information services. The objectives for the program mirrored some of NYACHIA's previous efforts:

- To provide an overview of the broad range of topics, issues, and people involved in health information literacy
- To examine roles librarians might play in this arena
- To assist health information professionals in identifying potential partnerships in their communities for future collaboration

Since many people were unable to view the broadcast in September, NYACHIA, the New York Public Library, and the New York Academy of Medicine partnered to sponsor a free taped screening and discussion of the program on November 13, 2003. Network member libraries were able to borrow this video from their Regional Medical Library, and other organizations could request this video through interlibrary loan.

Involving public and health librarians expands the possibilities of health literacy partnerships. In New York City, several health libraries are open to the public and were active in NYACHIA. Two of these are the Library of the New York Academy of Medicine and the Public Health Library (formerly known as the HIV Resource Library) of the New York City Department of Health and Mental Hygiene. On December 9, 2003, the New York City Health Literacy Initiative, a collaboration of the Literacy Assistance Center with the Mayor's Office, was launched with over 175 literacy professionals, health professionals, policymakers, grant agencies, and librarians in attendance.

NYACHIA is no longer active, but it has been followed in New York City by the Bronx Health Literacy Collaborative that includes many people previously active in NYACHIA. The Collaborative consists of Bronx-based community health providers, hospitals, literacy education providers, and campuses of The City University of New York. Its members include: Affinity Health Plan, Bronx District Public Health Office, Bronx Community Health Network, Bronx Health Link, Hostos Community College, Lehman College Adult Learning Center/Institute for Literacy Studies/MPH Program, Literacy Assistance Center,

North Bronx Health Network, and the Urban Health Plan. Many of the participants in its events come from other areas of New York.

NYACHIA may revitalize itself to coordinate events on both health literacy in general and specific areas of health information needs. Data from the first-ever national assessment of health literacy, called the Health Literacy Component of the National Assessment of Adult Literacy, will surely bring additional opportunities to share and discuss the findings. NYACHIA members are interested in exploring additional collaborative possibilities with literacy service providers. The Literacy Assistance Center in New York has launched many new relationships; links are shown on the list of the resources (www.lacnyc.org/resources/links/health.htm). This New York City focus on health literacy has led to the creation of an Office of Adult Education under the leadership of Anthony Tassi within the Office of the Deputy Mayor for Education and Community Development in New York City. This office will expand coordination and funding for local efforts toward increasing adult health literacy.

IDENTIFYING FUNDING FOR COLLABORATIVE EFFORTS

Now that you want to collaborate, how do you find support for health literacy efforts? The library's mission and vision often drive library initiatives and participation in coalitions. If the case can be made that health literacy is part of the library's mission, there may be ways to include health literacy activities in the library's regular budget. If health literacy is a new area of programming for the library, the detail and structure required by most grantors can help to create a practical and well-thought-out project designed to lead to measurable outcomes.

Initial Identification of Funding Organizations

Developing relationships with the library's or institution's development officer or department is the first step to successfully achieving external funding. Donors who already have made an investment in your organization are likely to be interested in expanding that relationship. Be sure that the development office knows what you need (a desiderata list) and have to offer in terms of projects or opportunities and the dollar amount it will take to achieve success. If your organization is doing strategic planning or large-scale development campaigns, be sure that those involved are aware of health literacy and its potential impact for the organization.

As interest and awareness in health literacy have expanded, there are more funding agencies interested in supporting health literacy initiatives, including those who focus on health or literacy in general. While federal and state funding is available, local funding may be easier to obtain. An example of a local partnership funded locally is the "Adult Health Literacy Tool Kit," part of an ongoing health literacy program initiated by Literacy Suffolk, Inc., and the Stony Brook University

School of Medicine, made possible through a grant from the Long Island Community Foundation (www.literacysuffolk.org/healthLiteracy.cfm). Larger organizations are often more interested in the applicant's funding history. If just starting out, it is easier to seek, achieve, and perform well with a small grant than to put a lot of energy into applying for a larger, more competitive one that may not be funded. If proposal writing support is short and you are trying to hit a wide range of granting agencies, see if a common grant application is acceptable to your local funders. The common grant application format has been adopted by groups of granting agencies to allow applicants to produce a single proposal for a specific community of agencies (see http://foundationcenter. org/findfunders/cga.html). Before applying, check that your project matches the funder's stated interests and ascertain whether a letter of inquiry would be preferred in advance.

Locating funding sources begins with searching. The Foundation Center (http://foundationcenter.org/) has branches in Atlanta, Cleveland, New York, San Francisco, and Washington, DC. They also produce the print and online versions of the *Foundation Directory* which may be available at your large public or state libraries or via a subscription held by the development office. The Center's tutorials and fact sheets for nonprofit grant seekers are helpful, especially the Proposal Writing Short Course, which is available in English, Spanish, Russian, Portuguese, Chinese, and French. If you partner with culturally or linguistically focused community organizations, having this course available in these other languages may be useful. The Center also offers a free online newsletter, *Health Funding Watch* (http://fdncenter.org/hfw/), that is e-mailed to registered users.

Reviewing the literature is another way to identify funding sources. The National Library of Medicine's PubMed indexing includes only federal funding sources. For other funding agencies, search PubMed or EBSCO's CINAHL database for relevant articles and review the acknowledgments in the full-text articles to determine who funded the research. You may be able to apply to the same foundations and/or corporations for your next grant. Another source is the free Educational Resources Information Center (ERIC) database (www.eric.ed.gov), where you can find literature about health curricula within literacy programs. Finally, Internet searching can supplement these other avenues of identifying funding sources. Here are some relevant Internet sites in addition to those already referenced:

ACP Foundation Patient-Centered Health Literacy Program
http://foundation.acponline.org/health_lit.htm

Health Literacy Foundation
www.healthliteracyfoundation.org

Pfizer Clear Health Communication
www.pfizerhealthliteracy.com

Project SHINE (MetLife Foundation) Health Literacy Initiative
www.projectshine.org/healthliteracy/geninfo.htm

Collaborative applications can be a blessing or a curse. Some agencies prefer to fund collaborative applications because they can expand the reach and scope of the project. Each organization provides its own unique strengths and audience. Librarians in particular can add a great deal to any collaboration. "Libraries are an integral part of our communities," said Scott Moyer, president of the Langeloth Foundation (www.langeloth.org). "They are highly trusted institutions and are accessible to people of all ages, backgrounds, and income levels" (Scott Moyer, personal communication, August 21, 2006). If applying for collaborative grants, be sure that each partner understands the flow of funding for the project. It is easier for the funding body to pay all the funds to one organization, which then disseminates money across the partners. However, if the partner receiving the funding is required to take a large percentage off the top for indirect costs, then the partnership may seek to funnel the funds through the organization with the lowest indirect cost rate in order to keep more of the funds available for the actual project work. In addition, collaboration can go beyond those implementing the project—to the granting agency itself. Grantors may suggest other foundations or organizations for you to approach for funding. In addition, they may be able to give your project direction, based on the experiences they have with previous grant receivers. "Sharing the cost helps to minimize the risk," explains Moyer. "You can take more chances because there is less at stake. Also, knowing that other funders are interested in a project adds to its credibility" (Scott Moyer, personal communication, August 21, 2006).

WORKING SUCCESSFULLY WITH FUNDING AGENCIES

Maintaining a positive relationship with your funding agency takes the same patience and care as any relationship. If you have not worked with them before (or even if you have), the Foundation Center offers online courses on fundraising and foundations that can be very helpful. Some are free; others are available for a small fee (http://foundationcenter.org/getstarted/learnabout/foundations.html).

Here are some things to remember when you are part of a grant-funded project:

- Stay in regular contact with your assigned program officer. If you are not sure how often you should be in touch, ask at the beginning of your project.
- Be sure to share success stories along the way—funders often use anecdotal information on successful projects when meeting with their board.

• Follow the guidelines on required reporting carefully, and include as much documentation as you can. This includes photographs, evaluations, quotes, and more.

SUSTAINING COLLABORATIONS IN HEALTH LITERACY

Sustainability of a project is important to those directly involved and those funding it. The question of "What next?" is important to consider. Will the project continue after the grant period, and if so, how will it be funded? If the project is not going to continue beyond the initial grant period, then what are the goals of the project, and how will they be evaluated and used?

CONCLUSION

Considering the challenges inherent to cooperative ventures and the time it takes to achieve measurable outcomes, partnerships need a way to determine, at an early stage, whether they are making the most of their collaboration. Weiss, Anderson, and Lasker (2002) have developed a measure, partnership synergy, which assesses the degree to which a partnership's collaborative process successfully combines its participants' perspectives, knowledge, and skills. An examination of the relationship between partnership synergy and six dimensions of partnership functioning (i.e., leadership, administration and management, partnership efficiency, nonfinancial resources, partner involvement challenges, and community-related challenges) indicated that partnership synergy was most closely related to leadership effectiveness and partnership efficiency.

Keeping that in mind, collaborations, more often than not, result in some sort of positive outcome. Collaborative projects, even if it they do not achieve all of their planned goals, often cause an evolution in the relationships between the partners. These stronger relationships can result in new opportunities for all involved. Staff development, resource sharing, a better understanding of the communities being served, and new collaborative events and projects are all positive outcomes that, while not as easily measured, can be equally rewarding.

REFERENCES

Center for the Advancement of Collaborative Strategies in Health. 2004. *Partnership Self-Assessment Tool.* New York: New York Academy of Medicine. (March 2007) Available: www.cacsh.org/psat.html

Doak, Cecilia C., Leonard G. Doak, and Jane H. Root. 1996. "Assessing Suitability of Materials" in *Teaching Patients with Low Literacy Skills.* 2nd ed. Philadelphia: J.B. Lippincott. (July 2007) Available: www.hsph.Harvard.edu/healthliteracy/doak4.pdf

Duval, Beverly K., and Linda Main. 1993. "Library Education for Literacy Librarians." *Education for Information* 11, no.2 (June): 105–121.

Gallagher, Patricia E. 2005. "The 'New' NOAH: Sleeker Look; Still the Same Quality-Filtered Bilingual Information." *Journal of Consumer Health on the Internet* 9, no. 3: 1–13.

Grosse, Robert N., and Christopher Auffrey. 1989. "Literacy and Health Status in Developing Countries." *Annual Review of Public Health* 10: 281–297.

Kerka, Sandra. 2003. "Community Asset Mapping: Trends and Issues Alert no. 47." (July 2007) Available: www.cete.org/acve/docgen.asp?tbl=tia&ID=170

Libraries for the Future. 2003. "Evaluation of Health Literacy Work among Libraries and Community Organizations in the New York City Area: Report highlights." (March 2007) Available: www.lff.org/programs/hlconfeval.pdf

Medical Library Association. 2003. "Reading Between the Lines: Focusing on Health Information Literacy." (March 2007) Available: www.mlanet.org/education/telecon/healthlit/goal.html

Miller, Kathleen M., Linda L. Phillips, and Julia F. Sollenberger. 2006. "CLIC-on-Health Reality Check: From Assumptions and Planning to the Realities of Implementation." *Journal of Consumer Health on the Internet* 10, no. 1: 1–16.

Nielsen-Bohlman, Lynn, Allison M. Panzer, and David A. Kindig (eds.). 2004. *Health Literacy: A Prescription to End Confusion.* Washington, DC: National Academies Press. (March 2007) Available: www.nap.edu/books/0309091179/html/

Olney, Cynthia A., Debra G. Warner, Greysi Reyna, Fred B. Wood, and Elliot R. Siegel. 2007. "MedlinePlus and the Challenge of Low Health Literacy: Findings from the Colonias Project." *Journal of the Medical Library Association* 95, no.1 (January): 31–39.

Parikh, Nina S., Ruth M. Parker, Joanne R. Nurss, David W. Baker, and Mark V. Williams. 1996. "Shame and Health Literacy: The Unspoken Connection." *Patient Education and Counseling* 27, no.1 (January): 33–39.

Partnership for Clear Health Communication. 2004. "IOM Report on Health Literacy: The Partnership for Clear Health Communication Working to Provide Practical Solutions to Low Health Literacy Epidemic." (March 2007) Available: www.askme3.org/iom.asp

Queens Borough Public Library. 2001. "Annual Report: Customer Service." (March 2007) Available: www.queens.lib.ny.us/index.aspx?page_nm=Annual_Report01_serv

RTI International—University of North Carolina Evidence-based Practice Center. 2004. *Literacy and Health Care Outcomes.* Prepared for the Agency for Healthcare Research and Quality (AHRQ) under Contract No. 290-02-0016. (March 2007) Available: www.ahrq.gov/clinic/epcsums/litsum.htm

Schwartz, Lauren. 2003. *Health Education Literacy Program (HELP).* New York: NYC Poison Control Center. (March 2007) Available: http://nyc.gov/html/doh/html/poison/poison2.shtml

Selden, Catherine, Marcia Zorn, Scott C. Ratzan, and Ruth M. Parker (compilers). 2000. *Health Literacy.* Bethesda (MD): National Library of Medicine. (March 2007) Available: www.nlm.nih.gov/archive//20061214/pubs/cbm/hliteracy.html

Sonenberg, Nina. 2005. "Libraries for the Future: Innovation in Action. New York: Libraries for the Future." (July 2007) Available: www.lff.org/documents/LFFInnovationinAction.pdf

"Teens Battle Low Health Literacy in their Communities." 2005. *In Focus* 5(3). (March 2007) Available: http://infocusmagazine.org/5.3/spotlight.html

University of California, San Francisco. "UCSF Pharmacy School receives major grant from Amgen Foundation for Medicare Part D outreach." (December 8, 2006) Available: http://pub.ucsf.edu/newsservices/releases/200612081/

U.S. Department of Health and Human Services. 2000a. *Healthy People 2010: Understanding and Improving Health.* 2nd ed. Washington, DC: U.S. Government Printing Office. (July 2007) Available: www.healthypeople.gov/Document/pdf/uih/2010uih.pdf

U.S. Department of Health and Human Services. 2000b. Health Communication (Chapter 11) in *Healthy People 2010: Understanding and Improving Health.* 2nd ed. Washington, DC: U.S. Government Printing Office. (July 2007) Available: www.healthypeople.gov/ Document/pdf/Volume1/11HealthCom.pdf

U.S. Department of Health and Human Services. "Healthy People 2010: State Healthy People Plans." (March 2007) Available: www.healthypeople.gov/implementation/ stateplans.htm

Voge, Susan. 1998. " NOAH—New York Online Access to Health: Library Collaboration for Bilingual Consumer Health Information on the Internet." *Bulletin of the Medical Library Association* 86, no.3 (July): 326–334.

Weiss, Elisa S., Rebecca Miller Anderson, and Roz D. Lasker. 2002. "Making the Most of Collaboration: Exploring the Relationship between Partnership Synergy and Partnership Functioning." *Health Education & Behavior* 29, no.6 (December): 683–698.

Wood, Fred B., Becky Lyon, Mary Beth Schell, Paula Kitendaugh, Victor H. Cid, and Elliot R. Siegel. 2000. "Public Library Consumer Health Information Pilot Project: Results of a National Library of Medicine Evaluation. *Bulletin of the Medical Library Association* 88, no.4 (October): 314–322.

Zeisel, William. 2005. *Community Health Connections: Emerging Models of Health Information Services in Public Libraries,* based on the Langeloth Forum on Libraries and Health Information. New York: Libraries for the Future. (July 2007) Available: www.lff.org/ documents/communityHealth.pdf

Zorn, Marcia, Marin P. Allen, and Alice M. Horowitz (compilers). 2004. *Understanding Health Literacy and Its Barriers.* Bethesda, MD: National Library of Medicine. (March 2007) Available: www.nlm.nih.gov/pubs/cbm/healthliteracybarriers.html

OTHER USEFUL WEB SITES

American Medical Association Foundation. " Health Literacy: What Others Are Doing." (March 2007) Available: www.ama-assn.org/ama/pub/category/11231.html

Health Literacy Consulting. 2006. "Health Literacy Month." (August 2006) Available: www.healthliteracy.com/hl_month.asp

Libraries for the Future. "Health Access." (March 2007) Available: www.liff.org/programs/ health.html

Medical Library Association. 2003. "Health information literacy." (March 2007) Available: www.mlanet.org/resources/healthlit/define.html

Appendix 16-1. METRO Special Interest Group on Consumer Health One-Day Conference on Health Literacy Preconference Survey

We would greatly appreciate your help in evaluating the current state of health literacy work among libraries and community organizations. Please take a few minutes to fill out this short survey. This survey is not intended to be anonymous. Please give us your address so we can reach you for follow-up at a later date. Please return the survey by April 29, 2002.

Name	
Title	
Organization	
Address	
City, State, ZIP	
Phone	
Fax	
E-mail	

"*Health literacy* [is] the ability to use English to solve health-related problems at a proficiency level that enables one to achieve one's health goals, and develop health knowledge and potential."

Harvard health literacy specialist Rima Rudd (2001)

"*Literacy* [is] using printed and written information to function in society." A literate person can understand, interpret, and apply written material to accomplish daily tasks.

The 1992 National Adult Literacy Survey (NALS)
Center for Health Care Strategies, Inc.
Fact Sheet on Health Literacy

Is the general literacy level of your client community a concern for your organization? Why or why not?

Is your organization addressing the issue of health literacy in its work? Why or why not?

Do you develop or distribute health materials to your clients or community members? Yes or no?

If yes, please answer the three questions below. If no, why not?

What type of materials and on what topics if you do not cover all health issues? Pamphlets, Web sites, books, audiotapes, and videos on all health topics for all ages.

Format:
____ pamphlets   ____ audiotapes
____ books   ____ Web sites
____ videos   ____ other (please specify) _____

Do you distribute health materials in languages other than English? What languages?

At what reading level are the majority of the health materials written?
____ Don't know   ____ 9th–12th grade
____ 5th grade and under   ____ Above 12th grade
____ 6th–8th grade

Appendix 16-1. METRO Special Interest Group on Consumer Health One-Day Conference on Health Literacy Preconference Survey *(Continued)*

Describe your experience locating and distributing appropriate health materials for your clients or community members. Do you refer staff or clients elsewhere for materials that you do not have available?
Have you ever collaborated with a library/community partner? If yes, please describe your current or past collaborative program with a library/community partner.
Do you see health literacy as an area for productive collaboration with a library/community partner? Why or why not?
What benefits would you expect from partnering with a library/community partner to address health literacy?
What obstacles do you see that might hinder partnering with a library/community partner to address health literacy?

About the Editors and Contributors

Marge Kars, MSLS, is Manager of the Health Sciences Library and Bronson HealthAnswers, a consumer health information center at Bronson Methodist Hospital in Kalamazoo, Michigan. She chairs Bronson's health literacy initiative, working with other hospital departments to train staff on health literacy issues as well as rewriting patient information in an easy-to-read format. She is a literacy volunteer in Kalamazoo, co-chairing Ready to Read, an emergent literacy collaboration, and literacy programs at the Kalamazoo Juvenile Home.

Lynda M. Baker, PhD, is Associate Professor in the Library and Information Science Program at Wayne State University in Detroit and teaches courses on health sciences librarianship, consumer health, advanced reference, and research methods. She was the principal author of the book *Consumer Health Information for Public Librarians*, which was published in 2002. She has published a number of articles on readability of consumer health materials. Her main research focus concerns health information needs and seeking-behaviors, and she has conducted research with various groups of people.

Feleta L. Wilson, PhD, RN, is an Associate Professor in the College of Nursing at Wayne State University. Over the past 16 years, Dr. Wilson has developed a program of research on patient education and patient health literacy. She has authored and co-authored numerous articles published in *Western Journal of Nursing Research, Nursing Science Quarterly, Journal of Pediatric Nursing, Reference and User Services Quarterly*, and *Public Libraries*. In addition, Dr. Wilson serves as Principal Investigator on research grants from the National Institutes of Health (NIH), National Cancer Institute, National Institute on Aging, National Institute for Nursing Research (NINR), and Blue Cross Blue Shield of Michigan Foundation.

* * *

Kristine Alpi, MLS, MPH, earned her Bachelor's Degree in Spanish and her Master's Degree in Library Science from Indiana University, and a Master of Public Health in Community Health Education from Hunter College of the City University of New York. She completed a National Library of Medicine Associate Fellowship and the Northeast Regional Public Health Leadership Institute Fellowship. Ms. Alpi is Associate Library Director and Lecturer in Public Health at Weill Cornell Medical College of Cornell University. A volunteer Spanish editor of New York Online Access to Health, she also participated in the New York Area Coalition for Health Information Access.

Barbara Bibel, MA, MLS, CHIS, is a reference librarian in the Science/Business/Social Science Government Documents Department of the Oakland Public Library. She has a BA in French from UCLA, an MA in Romance Languages from Johns Hopkins University, and an MLS from the University of California, Berkeley. She is certified as a Consumer Health Information Specialist, Level II, by the Medical Library Association.

Marcy Brown, MLS, does business as Envision Research, an information consultancy providing instructional design services as well as research, planning, and project support to libraries and other information agencies. She is an adjunct professor at both Drexel University and the University of Maryland University College, and is working toward a second master's in instructional design and technology. Ms. Brown has published many peer-reviewed and contributed articles, and her poster *Using the Performance Analysis Process to Improve Patient Education Projects* won MLA's Best Hospital Research Poster in 2005. She is a senior member of the Academy of Health Information Professionals.

Julia Esparza, MLS, is Clinical Medical Librarian at Louisiana State University—Health Sciences Center at Shreveport. Previously she was Medical Librarian at Deaconess Health System in Evansville, Indiana, where she was trained as a GE Healthcare Six Sigma Green Belt. She has a Master's Degree in Library and Information Science from Indiana University and a bachelor's degree from the University of Evansville. She serves as Section Council Representative for the Cancer Librarians Section, previously served on the Murray Gottlieb Prize Jury, and is also a member of the Consumer and Patient Health Information, Hospital Libraries, and Nursing and Allied Health Resources Sections of the Medical Library Association.

Ellen Freda, EdM, has a Master's Degree in Educational Psychology and previously headed a pediatric literacy program at a hospital-based clinic. She served as Outreach Coordinator for PhillyHealthInfo.org from 2002 to 2006, and was responsible for working with community organizations to promote health literacy, developing curricula for different populations.

Jonathan Hayes Goff, MS, has a Master's Degree in Library and Information Science and over four years of experience working with electronic library collections and resource databases. He has served as the Content Manager of the PhillyHealthInfo.org project since October 2004.

Shelley Hourston, MLS, graduated in 1991 after working for four years as a library technician in a school library. She has worked as a technical/systems librarian and database editor/coordinator in special libraries, and as an information specialist in a private college. She has provided business research services as a consultant and published a current awareness newsletter for human resources professionals. For the past nine years, she has worked as a program director at the British Columbia Coalition of People with Disabilities in Vancouver; additionally, she coaches individuals in career change, work/life balance, and resilience issues. You can contact her at the BC Coalition of People with Disabilities (wdi.bccpd.bc.ca) or her Web site (www.shourstonandassociates.com).

Andrea L. Kenyon, AMLS, Program Director for Philly Health Info, has a master's degree in Library Science and has over 20 years of experience in developing consumer health information programs. She is co-author of *The Public Librarian's Guide to Providing Consumer Health Information*, published by the Public Library Association.

Heather J. Martin, MISt, is currently the Librarian at Learn and Serve: America's National Service-Learning Clearinghouse. She provides reference and referral services and literature searches to the service-learning community on a national level and ensures an up-to-date and comprehensive resource collection. Her previous experience as an intern at Princess Margaret Hospital Patient Education Library and the Canadian AIDS Treatment Information Exchange informed her research interest in the ways information professionals can best meet the health information needs of underserved and marginalized communities.

Misa Mi, MLIS, MA, is a senior information resources specialist at the Medical Library of the Children's Hospital of Michigan, Detroit Medical Center. She received her MLIS from Wayne State University and MA in teaching from Oakland University. She is completing her doctoral degree in instructional technology at the College of Education, Wayne State University. Misa has published numerous articles on topics of cultural competency, needs assessment, library instruction evaluation, and medical/health resources. Misa is currently a member of the Medical Library Association, Hospital Libraries Section/Medical Library Association, Michigan Health Science Libraries Association, Metropolitan

Detroit Medical Library Group, and Association for Educational Communication and Technology.

Susan Murray, MLS, MA, AHIP, is Manager of the Consumer Health Information Service at the Toronto Public Library. She has spoken and written extensively in the area of consumer health information, and was the author of *Developing a Consumer Health Information Service: A Practical Guide* (1995). Susan was a member of MLA's Health Information Literacy Task Force and teaches workshops on health literacy.

Cleo Pappas, MLIS, is Assistant Professor and Assistant Information Services Librarian at the University of Illinois at Chicago, Library of the Health Sciences. She combines her writing and teaching skills with her interest in evidence-based research methodology. Along with curriculum-integrated instruction, her responsibilities include serving as liaison to the College of Applied Health, Disabilities Services, and the Department of Medical Education.

Charlene Pope, PhD, MPH, CNM, is Assistant Professor at the Medical University of South Carolina (MUSC) College of Nursing (CON) and Associate Nurse Executive for Research at the Ralph H. Johnson VA Medical Center in Charleston, South Carolina. After 20 years of practice in nurse-midwifery and a Master's in Public Health, she received a PhD in education, with a concentration in sociolinguistics. Dr. Pope completed a postdoctoral fellowship in preventive cardiology to investigate the role of communication in health behavior and health service research. She studies health encounter variations by age, race, ethnicity, and language and literacy status.

Karyn Prechtel, MA IRLS, is Managing Librarian at the Joel D. Valdez Main Library of the Pima County Public Library (PCPL) system in Tucson, Arizona. She holds a Master's in Information Resources and Library Science from the University of Arizona. Prior to her present position, she served as a consumer health subject specialist, a supervising librarian where she oversaw PCPL's "Infoline" telephone reference service, and a reference librarian. She has over 17 years of experience working with customers in the public library setting.

Nancy Schaefer, MATESOL, MLIS, is Assistant Librarian and Liaison to the Public Health and Community Health Departments at the University of Florida in Gainesville. She taught biomedical information resources to county and state health department workers in North Florida on a 2001–2002 subcontract from the National Network of Libraries of Medicine and created preformulated searches in PubMed's Special Queries for two Healthy People 2010 focus areas. Prior to becoming a librarian, Nancy taught English as a Second Language for 12 years. Her current research focuses on the health information needs of students, faculty, and patients, particularly those facing special linguistic, cultural, or literacy challenges.

Dina Sherman, MLS, earned her master's degree from the University of Pittsburgh and her bachelor's degree from Vassar College. She was a librarian with the Carnegie Library of Pittsburgh and the Brooklyn Children's Museum, and a Program Officer, focusing on Health Information, for the nonprofit organization Libraries for the Future. She was also a consultant for Health Literacy Month. She is currently the Senior Manager of School and Library Marketing for HarperCollins Children's Books. Her article (co-authored with Betsy Diamant-Cohen) "Hand in Hand, Museums and Libraries Working Together" was published in *Public Libraries* in 2003.

C. Nadine Wathen, PhD, is Assistant Professor in the Faculty of Information and Media Studies, University of Western Ontario. She holds a Canadian Institutes of Health Research–Ontario Women's Health Council New Investigator Award to support her research, which examines women's health decision-making, including intervention research in the area of violence against women; projects to translate and mobilize research evidence in women's health to policy and practice; and projects on how people living in rural areas seek and use health information. Nadine has developed and published evidence-based clinical practice guidelines in preventive health care and women's health, and has extensive expertise in research methods, systematic reviews, communication, and knowledge translation.

Index

Page numbers followed by "a" indicate appendix; those followed by "t" indicate table; those followed by "f" indicate figure.